CONTEMPORARY
COSTUME FILM

Space, Place and the Past

Julianne Pidduck

bfi Publishing

'ʍʄʝʝᴊᴉᴑ

First published in 2004 by the
British Film Institute
21 Stephen Street, London W1T 1LN

The British Film Institute promotes greater understanding of,
and access to, film and moving image culture in the UK.

Cover design: Jethro Clunies-Ross
Cover image: Gillian Anderson as Lily Bart in
The House of Mirth (Terence Davies, 2000)

Set by Servis Filmsetting Limited, Manchester, UK

Printed in the UK by St Edmundsbury Press, Bury St Edmunds, Suffolk

British Library Cataloguing-in-Publication Data
A catalogue record for this book is available from the British Library

ISBN 1-84457-024-X (hbk)
ISBN 1-84457-054-1 (pbk)

Table of Contents

Acknowledgments

This book has been through several incarnations and places of writing, and I am greatly indebted to many people at every stage. In Montréal, Kim Sawchuk's irreverence and her conversation over many coffees have sustained me, and Marty Allor has been extraordinary in so many ways as a teacher and as a friend. In the UK, Richard Dyer has offered splendid insights as an astute reader and an inspiration with his work and friendship. I also gratefully acknowledge the invaluable support of Jackie Stacey and Ginette Vincendeau. Ongoing exchanges with Belén Vidal, Dimitris Eleftheriotis and John Caughie have been crucial to this book. Further, I would like to thank Lauren Berlant, whose great insights on 'intimacy' have been formative to this project; thanks also to the organisers and participants of Berlant's 2001, 2002 and 2003 visits to Lancaster.

I also gratefully acknowledge the rigorous feedback of Brenda Longfellow, Catherine Saouter and Katie Russell at the dissertation stage. My appreciation is also extended to my colleagues at different institutions, especially Imogen Tyler, Scott Wilson, Annette Kuhn, Charlotte Brunsdon, Ed Gallafent, Karen Lury and Janine Grenfell. Thank you also to Andrew Lockett and Tom Cabot at the BFI, and to the anonymous readers of the manuscript for their valuable feedback.

A special thanks goes to Robyn Diner, Kirsten McAllister, Annie Martin, Adrian Heathfield, Adrienne Scullion, Michele Aaron, Janet de Paiva, Lisa Brown, Polly Richards and Bruce Bennett for their insights and their humour. For their heroic eleventh-hour reading and feedback, cheers to Jane Mulderrig, Kirsty Stevenson, Maureen McNeil and Katrina Roen.

To my grandmother Thelma Emms, who lived to be 100 but sadly not to see this book: her love of the 'pictures' is still with me. Thanks also to Stephen, Celia, Meara and Teresa Pidduck, who have sustained me with phone calls and care packages. Jo-Anne Pickel, who didn't enjoy *Orlando*, has been a mainstay with her wry humour and patient reading. Finally, my deepest thanks to Anick Druelle, who made it possible to finish and move on to new things.

This book is dedicated to my parents Beverley and Douglas Pidduck.

Introduction
Microcosms and Miniatures

A diminutive woman's figure emerges from a wreath of smoke beside a steaming loco-motive, as an intertitle announces this is New York 1905. At first she appears only in silhouette, wearing a shapely tailored Edwardian gown and voluminous veiled hat, and carrying a parasol and a small case. Walking toward the camera with a slight swagger, she conveys a self-assured and sensual leisured femininity. This figure evokes fashion photographs of the period featuring elegant women walking in the park or street: 'the dash, the vivid, abstract shapes, a face, a body, and clothes all perceived as a mysteri-ous, not quite personally identifiable mobile unit'.[1] This first shot of Terence Davies's *The House of Mirth* (2000) bears a striking resemblance to the opening scene of Iain Softley's *The Wings of the Dove* (1997), which takes place in the London Underground in 1911.

Adapted from a novel by Edith Wharton, *Mirth* chronicles the downfall of the impoverished, aristocratic Lily Bart (Gillian Anderson). A beautiful relic from another era, she is often framed in doors and windows with painterly compositions and lavish gowns underscoring her status as aesthetic object. Meanwhile, Helena Bonham Carter's costumes and performance as Kate Croy in *Wings* exude a simmering sexual-ity, literalising the obscure erotics of Henry James's novel. From parallel beginnings, the films track their heroines' navigation of sexual innuendo and economic peril on the margins of British and American early twentieth-century societies. Like many contem-porary costume films, *Mirth* and *Wings* foreground the romantic desires and social aspirations of female protagonists against the constraints of convention, sexual repres-sion and economic disadvantage.

Kate Croy (Helena Bonham Carter) in the London tube: social climbing and simmering sexuality in *The Wings of the Dove*

A tireless social climber motivated by the fear of poverty, Kate seeks to exploit her rich aunt's patronage to find a secure position within the exclusive circles of Lancaster Gate. In this sexually charged adaptation, the otherwise mundane public space of London Transport becomes a site of fantasy, and from under the wide brim of her elaborate headgear, Kate exchanges lascivious glances with a young man who is later revealed as her fiancé, Merton Densher (Linus Roache). However, Merton, a mere journalist, is not approved as a suitor by Kate's Aunt Maud, and Kate's subsequent quest for wealth leads to the tragic death of her friend Milly and the end of her relationship with Merton.

In *Mirth*, Lily is caught between her Old New York birthright and the rise of the nouveau riche. Trained only to attract a rich husband, like Kate, Lily's quest for social position excludes her true love Lawrence Selden (Eric Stoltz) as a suitor. Cast out of society for apparent sexual misdemeanors, Lily lacks the skills to support herself and is left to die alone in a seedy Lower East Side apartment. *Mirth* and *Wings* both knowingly deploy intertextual scenic cues and melodramatic tropes, and Kevin Jackson comments that 'the image of Lily emerging from a cloud of railway steam evokes *Anna Karenina*, and hints proleptically at her sticky end'.[2] Classic settings for *Letter from an Unknown Woman* (1948) or *Brief Encounter* (1945), train stations evoke the possibility of chance encounters and the tragedy of lost love. The train station also indicates an ambivalence toward the trappings of modernity that is common in period drama. Living at the start of a new century of mass travel and urban life, Lily and Kate are set apart from the bustle of the city streets by their elaborate gowns. *Mirth* and *Wings* navigate the industrial noise and jostling crowds of twentieth-century life at the twilight of another era whose defining qualities are imagined as slowness and leisure, elaborate courtship, exquisite gowns, lavish furnishings and intricate class hierarchies.

This book develops a cultural study of contemporary costume film through the conceptual prisms of space and movement. My approach engages with, and extends, British debates about heritage cinema and feminist accounts of costume film framed through psychoanalytic theories of the gaze and narrative. In the place of conceptual frames of the nation or the spectator in a darkened cinema, this book juxtaposes the films' textual treatment of space and place with their cultural and historical contexts of production and consumption. Stylistically, temporally and spatially separate from the present, these microcosms of nineteenth- and early twentieth-century England and Europe, or Renaissance England, resonate in complex ways with contemporary experience. *Mirth* was shot in Glasgow, standing in for New York, and the film's opening shot has a kind of placelessness. The almost interchangeable quality of these films' opening shots effaces geographical specificity, giving the images a saturated, allegorical quality. Yet the films' locations – New York, London, Venice – carry specific national connotations vital to narratives of particular period milieux, travel and cross-cultural encounter. If there is an ambiguity and suggestiveness to their sense of place, temporally these scenes are poised with equal ambivalence in the early years of a new century. Trains, the metropolitan crowd, the steam ship (as in *The Portrait of a Lady* (1996), *The Golden Bowl* (2000) or *Orlando* (1993)) present interruptions – incursions of modernity into settings that are for the most part resolutely bourgeois, precolonial, pastoral and white.

Do these mannered interiors present a nostalgic flight from the social and political contradictions of the present, or do they offer a retrospective canvas for the working through of contemporary dilemmas? These films return again and again to mythical points of origin for Anglo-American culture: the Victorian era as a period of sexual and social repression (*The Piano* (1993), *Angels & Insects* (1996)), the Edwardian period of increasing sexual and social openness, the pastoral of the English novel (the Austen and Forster adaptations), and the English Renaissance as an era of foundational cultural expression and political emergence (*Shakespeare in Love* (1998), *Elizabeth* (1998)). Often charged with conservative nostalgia, costume drama's lively and multi-faceted engagement with these, and other, periods indicates a continuing dialogue between past and present. At times these films are steeped in regret for a lost cultural and social coherence (such as that of pastoral Edwardian England). But they also offer incisive critical rewritings of the past, as with *Gosford Park*'s (2001) reinvention of the upstairs/downstairs Edwardian drama.

The twinned opening shots of *Mirth* and *Wings* suggest how costume drama can be read through recurring spatio-temporal set pieces such as the woman at the window, the figure at the writing desk, the ball, the country walk, the sightseeing trip or the train station. Following Deleuze, I address these segments of cinematic space-time as 'movement-images' that operate as structuring narrative and thematic tropes. If genre functions as a patterning of repetition and difference, this topographical approach tracks structuring discourses across a wide range of films: desire and romance in a (post)modern age; middle-class aspiration and the erasure of the working class; retrospective struggles over the performance of gender and sexuality; retrotourism and the idea of Europe; creativity and authorship in an age of cultural recycling; gendered, colonial, classed and queer histories. These issues are addressed through spatial frames – both the films' intricate textual spatiality, and the cultural and critical locations through which they travel. These recursive modes of analysis highlight both costume drama's increasingly international scope, and the symbolic struggles over the meanings, affective resonances and ownership of the past that take place within its frame.

Scholarship on period drama tends to assess British heritage cinema, American popular cinema and avant-garde works separately. *Contemporary Costume Film*, in contrast, addresses these different modes of film-making as a single significant and multi-faceted cultural phenomenon. Adaptations of Austen, James, Forster, Wharton, Wilde and Marlowe are juxtaposed with historical biography (*Mrs Brown* (1997), *The Madness of King George* (1994), *Elizabeth*) and experimental works (*Orlando*, *Daughters of the Dust* (1991), *The Piano*, *Caravaggio* (1986), and *Edward II* (1991)). Differing in stylistic and political address, these subgenres share a cultural and industrial intertext. Early 90s feminist films *Orlando* or *The Piano* enter market niches and cultural spaces facilitated by the success of 80s heritage cinema. Further, Sally Potter's and Derek Jarman's anti-heritage interventions are only intelligible in relation to dominant British film and television period drama.

I analyse English-language costume dramas produced in the 90s and early 2000s set before World War I. The scope is somewhat flexible so as to include two key films set in the 30s, *The Remains of the Day* (1993) and Robert Altman's *Gosford Park*, as well as several significant films from the 80s (*Dangerous Liaisons* (1988), *Amadeus* (1984) and *Caravaggio*). Although this study is limited to English-language examples, this mode of film-making is characterised by hybrid patterns of financial backing, production credits, casts, crews and settings. This book extends the national focus of the British heritage cinema debates to examine these films as global products addressing international audiences. In fact, they are often explicitly engaged at a narrative and scenic level with international travel and tourism and cross-cultural encounter. These English, American and European settings are marked by retrospective discursive struggles over modern subjectivity, national identity, gender, sexuality, class and colonialism. My overarching emphasis is on the films' retrospective renderings of power and desire. Given the foundational status of English cultural traditions for English-speaking audiences worldwide, these concerns are both uniquely English, and more broadly British, European and international.

Costume Drama as Microcosm

Historical cinema in its many guises – historical fiction, period drama, literary adaptation, costume film, or what has more recently been called 'heritage cinema' in a British context – has been a staple in film history. As the naming of a cultural phenomenon suggests its critical framing, in this book I use the term 'costume drama' as a refusal of historical or literary authenticity. 'Costume' suggests the pleasures and possibilities of masquerade – the construction, constraint and display of the body through clothes. For Renée Baert, clothing is 'a semiotically dense and complex social form', a 'tissue that separates the self from the social'.[3] Costume is inextricable from historical discourses of the self, and costume drama's play of identity and masquerade retrospectively explores Western subjectivity through the characters of the nineteenth-century novel and historical biography. The second term, 'drama', is for Peter Brooks 'an exciting, excessive, parabolic story [distilled from] the banal stuff of reality'.[4] If drama suggests an intensification of everyday life, then costume film plays out vivid episodes within the frame of the past.

This mode of film-making has been routinely dismissed by critics, most damningly as an ideologically conservative mirror of glorious national pasts. For Robert A. Rosenstone, 'historical' fiction that engages 'directly or obliquely, the issues, ideas, data, and arguments of the ongoing discourse of history' is valued more than costume drama, which 'uses the past as an exotic setting for romance and adventure'.[5] However, cinema can never offer an unmediated window onto the past, and historical fiction and costume drama alike depict the past through the stylistic, critical and generic vocabularies of present cultural production. This book adopts a revisionist interest in the cinematic past, where the site of symbolic struggle is not some unmediated history, but rather the 'memory-images'[6] that circulate in the moment of production and consumption.

This book treats costume drama as a series of mannered and self-reflexive microcosms. As a liminal and carefully encoded generic world, costume drama facilitates the dramatisation, the ritual rehearsal of deeply felt contemporary dilemmas in a world that is known, yet apart. With their precise codes of *mise en scène*, costume and gesture, the enclosed interiors of costume drama evoke the miniature world of the doll's house. Susan Stewart describes the poetics of the miniature as essentially theatrical, spilling over with detail, suggesting a bounded completeness that is somehow representative: 'The world of things can open itself to reveal a secret life – indeed to reveal a set of actions and hence a narrativity and history outside the given field of perception.'[7] Explicit microcosms abound within costume drama: the secret garden in Agnieszka Holland's 1994 film of the same title; the plays embedded in *Shakespeare in Love*, *The Age of Innocence* (1993), *Mansfield Park* (1999), *Topsy-Turvy* (1999) and *An*

Ideal Husband (1999), and the fascinating and terrifying ant world in *Angels & Insects*. These microcosms are bristling with self-consciousness. This is especially the case from the mid-90s, where the films gesture knowingly to the complex parallels between narrative, play within the play, and social and historical intertexts.

The microcosm often provokes claims of insular nostalgia. In his influential critique of British heritage cinema, Andrew Higson describes 'intimate epics' where 'the self-conscious visual perfectionism of period details create a fascinating but self-enclosed world. They render history as spectacle, as *separate* from the viewer in the present.'[8] To some degree, all entertainment involves a flight from the everyday, and the common denigration of particular (gendered) modes of escape often rests on a narrow account of the political. Often perceived as a woman's genre, costume drama shares some of the abuse regularly levelled at soap operas and popular romance. Gendered accounts of (historical) significance, taste and quality are intertwined with the development of the historical epic, literary adaptation, British 'quality' cinema and television, melodrama and the 'woman's film'. Threaded through the critical question of the economy of scale, the following account of popular and academic discourses surrounding these modes of film-making offers a foundation for a study of contemporary costume drama.

The historical epic, with its elaborate sets and casts of thousands, was a crucial product of silent cinema from D.W. Griffith's *The Birth of a Nation* (1915) and *Intolerance* (1916), to Cecil B. DeMille's *The Ten Commandments* (1923) and *Cleopatra* (1934). The Hollywood epic of the sound era was epitomised by remakes of earlier classics, such as DeMille's 1956 *The Ten Commandments* and Joseph L. Mankiewicz's 1963 *Cleopatra*, starring Elizabeth Taylor and Richard Burton; other key films of this era were the Charlton Heston vehicles *Ben-Hur* (1959) and *El Cid* (1961). Often set in biblical or medieval times, the epic (like costume film) has often been scorned by film critics for its emphasis on spectacle, costume and the body rather than identifiable historical events. For the most part, this tradition has declined internationally since the 60s. Morris Dickstein argues that film and television period dramas of the 70s and 80s such as *Brideshead Revisited* (1981) and *Chariots of Fire* (1981) 'avoid the grand historical moments – thunderous battles, larger-than-life heroes, masses of churning humanity. They are dramas of personal conflict, anguish, or desire set in the recent past rather than the age of Samson and Delilah or the Roman centurions.'[9]

This tendency has persisted into the 90s and early 2000s with an emphasis on intimate contained spaces. The distinction between the epic and the intimate costume film corresponds with Deleuze's two aspects of the 'action-image'. While the epic addresses tragic action on the broad stage of 'antiquarian or monumental history' (large scale of the action-image), the small form of the action-image works on

> a modist or modellist conception, as though the dressmaker, the designer had taken the place of the architect and the antiquarian. In the costume film, as in the comedy of manners, the 'habitus' are inseparable from the outfits [*habits*], the actions are inseparable from the state of the costumes which constitute their form.[10]

Clearly, the large and small scales of the action-image correspond to gendered economies of scale and significance. Alongside blockbusters *Braveheart* (1995), *Gladiator* (2000) and *Titanic* (1997), art films such as Bernardo Bertolucci's *The Last*

Emperor (1987), Martin Scorsese's *Gangs of New York* (2002) and Francis Ford Coppola's *Bram Stoker's Dracula* (1992) project a larger scale and ambition of period drama. Often associated with masculine auteurist projects and bravura performances by headlining stars, these films develop a broader tableau of heroic action that contrasts with the more pervasive 'feminine' intimate sphere of literary adaptation, romance and historical biography.[11]

Contemporary Costume Film scrutinises the intimate tradition, where the past is depicted on a smaller canvas through the prisms of romance, desire and the body. This is a limited theatre of action that amplifies a nuanced boudoir politics, and an oblique narrative economy of detail often associated with femininity. 'Small scale' evokes Stewart's miniatures, where implied insignificance points to the diminished critical status of costume drama. In reading the miniature, I take this undeniably flighty subgenre of films seriously, but not as an uncritical celebration. Rather, I analyse how costume film uses specific generic and intertextual vocabularies to meaningfully address contemporary experience through the frame of the past.

Questions of cultural value and gendered significance in historical film can be traced back to debates over popular British historical biographies of the 30s; this group of films was exemplified by Alexander Korda's *The Private Life of Henry VIII* (1933), *Catherine the Great* (1934) and *Rembrandt* (1936). Marcia Landy notes that the Korda studio's influential formula, combining historical spectacle with the private life of the historical persona, serves 'the function of mythologizing monarchs (or any upper-class individual), while it also humanizes them'.[12] These films are not without their critics. For instance, Jeffrey Richards argues that Korda's 'private life' formula 'avoids concentration on real issues, social, political, economic, religious problems that might cause controversy'.[13] In response, Landy foregrounds the films' more subtle politics of gender and sexuality.[14] Evidence of the continuing appeal of the personal aspects of historical celebrity, Korda's formula persists in recent biopics *Amadeus, Elizabeth, Shakespeare, Madness, Mrs Brown, Vincent & Theo* (1990), *Immortal Beloved* (1994) and *Pandaemonium* (2000).

At issue is an epistemological and political question about how we map social and political meanings onto historical cinema – issues that arise with subsequent cycles of British costume film and literary adaptation. In the 30s and 40s, Gainsborough Studios was best known for its wartime melodramas – popular costume films including *Madonna of the Seven Moons* (1944), *The Wicked Lady* (1945) and *Jassy* (1947). In contrast with Korda's prestige productions, these films were based on popular historical novels and were marketed largely toward women and the working class. Lambasted by critics of the time as lowbrow escapist romances, these films have recently been championed by feminist scholars for their allegorical exploration of female sexuality – a point that I will return to below.

The persistent dismissal of Gainsborough films by critics of the period contrasts with their celebration of British postwar 'quality cinema'.[15] This term was coined 'in the midst of postwar cultural reconstruction which covered all the arts. For the cinema this attempt to found a British tradition of quality hinged on the distinction of the best of British cinema distinct from the mere entertainment of Hollywood.'[16] 'Quality' was commonly derived from classic adaptations including *The Importance of Being Earnest* (1952), and David Lean's *Great Expectations* (1946) and *Oliver Twist* (1948). Shakespeare as an English cultural icon figures centrally in this group, with Laurence

Olivier as director and star of *Henry V* (1944), *Hamlet* (1948) and *Richard III* (1955). Staples of British cinema, classic literary adaptations are continually remade (as with Oliver Parker's 2002 version of *The Importance of Being Earnest*). Endemic to British film-making, Shakespeare adaptations continued apace in the 80s and 90s. Given the extensive scholarship devoted to Shakespeare adaptations,[17] this book does not address them in any depth, although I do examine *Shakespeare in Love*.

Discourses of quality, national culture and gendered taste reappear in the 80s and 90s British heritage cinema debates. During the re-regulation of British public service broadcasting in the 80s, television adaptations such as *Brideshead Revisited* and *The Jewel in the Crown* (1984) exemplified renewed discourses of British 'quality'. Charlotte Brunsdon identifies four components of British quality production as being a literary source; 'the best of British acting'; money on screen or high production values; and heritage export.[18] During the same period, an associated lush group of films emerged, notably *Chariots of Fire*, Richard Attenborough's *Gandhi* (1982) and David Lean's *A Passage to India* (1985). Also released in 1985 was the Forster adaptation *A Room with a View*, a film with a US$3 million budget that garnered $24 million in North America, and $57 million worldwide.[19] From the team of producer Ismail Merchant, director James Ivory and screenwriter Ruth Prawer Jhabvala, *A Room with a View* inaugurated a profitable formula featuring Edwardian English pastoral settings, a spectacular visual style, European retrotourism, and an identifiable troupe of British character actors.

These recent films and television serials have come to stand in for a controversial aesthetic and historical vision. Many critics associated 'quality' film and television's conservative account of the national past with the politics of Thatcherite Britain. From the historical context of the Falklands/Malvinas War of 1982 and the miners' strike of 1984, Tana Wollen reads the heritage 'screen fictions' as a regressive, nostalgic mobilisation of the national past.[20] In turn, Higson argues that heritage cinema offers a seductive escape from the contradictions of the present and the past:

> By turning their backs on the industrialized, chaotic present, they nostalgically reconstruct an imperialist and upper-class Britain. . . . The films thus offer apparently more settled and visually splendid manifestations of an essentially pastoral national identity and authentic culture: "Englishness" as an ancient and natural inheritance, *Great* Britain, the *United* Kingdom.[21]

The heritage cinema debates suggestively address issues of space, place and the past. Higson claims that the heritage tourism of the 80s furnishes the iconography (costumes, furnishings, objets d'art and aristocratic character types) of heritage cinema. This 'nostalgic display' is perfectly situated in 'a recurrent image of an imposing country house seen in extreme long shot and set in a picturesque, verdant landscape'.[22] For Cairns Craig, the heritage film's monumental Edwardian interiors indicate insularity: 'We are indulged with a perfection of style designed to deny everything beyond the self-contained world the characters inhabit. . . . The issue of affording a room is never in question, only the quality of its view.'[23] Within these discourses, the tastefully furnished country house comes to stand for an ossified 'museum' vision of the national past. However, the current significance of what I call (following Henry James) the 'house of fiction'[24] is under dispute.

Alison Light responds to Craig that 'we should read the return to Edwardian England in the 80s as much as a rejection of Thatcherism and its ethics as a crude reflection of it'.[25] Claire Monk also rejects an ideological reading of heritage cinema spectatorship, claiming that these films create 'spaces in which identities (whether those of characters and nations within the film or the spectators viewing it) are shifting, fluid and heterogeneous'.[26] If these films have been widely taken up by feminist scholars, Richard Dyer also notes their widespread, frequently sympathetic attention to lesbian and gay characters and narratives.[27] For these critics, costume drama's elegant pasts do not misrepresent an 'authentic' national past, but rather offer fantasy zones for the exploration of national identity, gender and sexuality.

The British heritage cinema debates are a key a point of departure for *Contemporary Costume Film*. I draw extensively from the feminist and queer scholarship on costume and the body, but situate these bodies and their narrative trajectories within specific geographical and temporal milieux. I also take on board salient critiques of heritage cinema – particularly with reference to class and nostalgia – interrogating these claims across a wide array of films. However, given the range of films considered in this book, I neither celebrate nor demonise costume film. Instead, I explore the continuing contemporary fascination of these films, while tracing their normative qualities and their startling capacity for innovation and social critique. Centrally concerned with costume film's retrospective assemblages of power and desire, this book considers intersecting dynamics of gender, sexuality, class and colonialism within an explicitly international genre.

Inter/national Contexts of Production and Reception

The current cultural and economic context of technological convergence and global finance affects how, where and for whom films are made. Historically, an international market dominated by Hollywood has been the backdrop against which distinctive European national cinemas have sought to develop. One important aspect of the British heritage cinema debate concerns the stakes of English or British culture and history for export. John Caughie notes that from the 80s British film production increasingly catered to American markets. The films produced did not address contemporary Britain and domestic audiences, but rather offered prestige period dramas aimed at foreign consumption.[28] This account underscores the British struggle for autonomous cultural production. But at issue here is not only how the nation is reflected to itself, but also its representation abroad and the intersection of different national pasts.

The transatlantic cinematic exchange between Britain, Western Europe and the US has a long history. For instance, Korda's 1933 *The Private Life of Henry VIII*, starring Charles Laughton, 'was the British film that broke the barriers to the American market'.[29] The film 'was to prove a milestone not only for London Film Productions [Korda's company] but for the British industry itself, for it was so successful that it inspired new confidence in British production'.[30] Where many critics retain a focus on British cinema, Landy emphasises the popularity of 30s British Korda and Gainsborough films in North America, and how they intersected with Hollywood costume film production. Similarly, Helen Taylor argues that Margaret Mitchell's novel *Gone with the Wind*, and its subsequent film adaptation, profoundly affected female audiences on both sides of the Atlantic.[31] *Gone with the Wind* – 'arguably the most famous' costume drama[32] – epitomises the 'woman's picture' of the 30s and 40s; other examples include *Queen Christina* (1933), *The Scarlet Empress* (1934), *Anna Karenina* (1935), *Jezebel* (1938), *The Private Lives of Elizabeth and Essex* (1939), *Wuthering Heights* (1939), *Pride and Prejudice* (1940), *Letter from an Unknown Woman* and *The Heiress* (1949).

These films were popular in Britain and North America alike, and many of them featured British and European subject matter (Elizabeth I, Mary Queen of Scots) and British actors.[33] There were many European creative personnel on the British Korda and Gainsborough productions, from the Hungarian Korda down through the ranks. Further, Cook argues that Gainsborough Studios 'evoked a Europeanised artistic tradition in which formal adventurousness and experiment were combined with cultural prestige and, above all, visual pleasure'.[34] Although recent films still trade on 'quality' British players, production personnel and sources, contemporary costume drama is produced and marketed on an even wider international scale than its predecessors.

Within an international film industry conceived on an American industry logic, costume drama has traditionally been grouped in the minor, art film sector that accounts for between one and nine per cent of the US theatrical box office, earning around five per cent of revenues annually.[35] Building on the prestige of 1960s and 1970s European art cinema, the success of 80s British period films *A Room with a View*, *Gandhi* and *Chariots of Fire* was largely measured in their American box office earnings. Small-budget productions that made considerable profits, these films emerged in the 80s and early 90s, a period when many distributors for small prestige productions facilitated a brisk international trade. In a slightly later example, Jane Campion's French-financed, Australian-produced *The Piano* was picked up by Miramax and aggressively marketed to critics and audiences alike; showered with awards, the film's gross international box-office takings were over US$116 million, including $7 million in Australia, $16 million in France, $6.5 million in the UK and $40 million in the US.[36] *The Piano* illustrates the crossover phenomenon so vital to the boom in 90s costume drama: 'low-budget films (*The Piano*'s was $8 million), often expressing a "personal vision", that move from art-house openings to embrace much larger audiences than most art movies'.[37]

Miramax exemplifies the international resurgence of art cinema. Throughout the 90s, this small New York-based company profitably distributed independent American and European art cinema such as *Enchanted April* (1992),[38] *The Crying Game* (1992) and *Il Postino* (1994). When acquired by Disney in 1993, it gained access to the parent company's powerful video and television distribution arms.[39] It also gained increased production capacities[40] for *The English Patient* (1996), Douglas McGrath's *Emma*, starring Gwyneth Paltrow, (1996), *Shakespeare in Love*, *Mansfield Park*, *An Ideal Husband* and *The Golden Bowl* (2000). As a company, it is notorious for aggressive marketing campaigns that push controversy and explicit sexuality.[41] Miramax exemplifies a sea change in the commercial success of art cinema, where formerly such films had been considered hits with a $5 million US gross.[42] However, 90s costume dramas far surpassed this mark with *Shakespeare in Love* (US $100 million), *The English Patient* ($78 million), *Sense and Sensibility* ($43 million), *Gosford Park* ($41 million), *Elizabeth* ($30 million), *Howards End* ($25 million), *An Ideal Husband* ($18 million), *The Madness of King George* ($15 million) and *The Wings of the Dove* ($14 million).[43] These revenues are augmented by ancillary markets, especially home video and television network and cable deals.[44]

An increasingly profitable turn in costume film emerges within a global audiovisual economy of convergence. For instance, *Elizabeth* was produced by the British company Working Title (*Edward II*, *Four Weddings and a Funeral* (1994)), and distributed by the former Dutch company PolyGram Filmed Entertainment. PolyGram was subsequently bought up by the Canadian-based multimedia conglomerate MCA, which also controls Universal Pictures.[45] The MCA/PolyGram and Disney/Miramax mergers exemplify a broader 90s trend, where the Hollywood majors moved into specialised, art-house and crossover markets.[46] If these multinational companies are often US-based, the production personnel, actors, settings and subject matter are increasingly international, and the national specificity of films becomes diffuse: *Elizabeth* had an Indian director, Australian, French and American (as well as British) stars and was backed by British, American and French finance. Within this context, Higson suggests that 'Britishness' is merely a brand to distinguish the product from Hollywood; ultimately the case study of *Elizabeth* prompts him to ask: 'Does it still make sense in the global economy to describe the film as "British" or "English"?'[47]

Films like *Elizabeth*, *Shakespeare in Love*, *Orlando*, *Carrington* (1995), *Wilde* and *The Wings of the Dove* have been dubbed by Higson, following Monk, as 'post-heritage'; these films share 'a concern with the depiction of transgressive sexuality and/or sexual activity . . . against a backdrop of luxurious aristocratic or Bohemian lifestyles and living spaces'.[48] This term evokes an increasingly self-conscious, sexual and performative tendency of late 90s British costume film. I would argue, however, that these qualities are crucial to costume film's legacy and can be clearly identified in British and American works since the 80s including *A Room with a View*, *Amadeus*, *Caravaggio*, *Interview with the Vampire: The Vampire Chronicles* (1994), *Dangerous Liaisons*, *Valmont* (1989) and *Quills* (2000). In the latter part of the book, I specifically address these films' heightened corporeality and sexuality, with particular attention to 'queer' costume and the historical biopic.

Costume film's reconfiguration of gender, sexuality and the body against spectacular period settings can be seen as an international phenomenon. Clearly, Hollywood auteurist productions *Amadeus*, *Dangerous Liaisons* or *Bram Stoker's Dracula* set 80s and 90s costume film landmarks, while *The Age of Innocence*, *The Bostonians* (1984), *Daughters of the Dust*, *The Scarlet Letter* (1995) and *The Crucible* (1996) explore uniquely American period idioms. Jane Campion's distinctive feminist and Australian/New Zealand lens on costume and adaptation is also influential for the formal and thematic terrain of recent costume film. *The Piano* and *The Portrait of a Lady* emerge within a sequence of Australian period film-making dating back to the 1970s.[49]

The recent boom in costume drama extends far beyond English-language productions. Struggles over gender and sexuality set within symbolic Chinese historical periods are enacted in Zhang Yimou's *Raise the Red Lantern* (1991), and *To Live* (1994), Chen Kaige's *Farewell, My Concubine* (1993) or Ang Lee's *Crouching Tiger, Hidden Dragon* (2000). Meanwhile, an influential aesthetics of violence and erotic corporeality emerges in *Cyrano de Bergerac* (1990), *The Horseman on the Roof* (1995) and *Joan of Arc* (2000),[50] while Shekhar Kapur's *Elizabeth* borrows extensively from the bloody erotics of Patrice Chéreau's *La Reine Margot* (1994). These works often include strong allegories of specific national pasts addressed to national audiences. But they also share cross-cultural intertexts, often projecting thematic concerns (notably explorations of gender and sexuality) that are legible to international audiences within a common international art cinema distribution circuit.

This international phenomenon harks back to costume dramas from 50s and 60s European art cinema. Luchino Visconti's *Senso* (1954) and *The Leopard* (1963) exemplify a mode of Italian prestige co-production conceived on an operatic scale of set design, costume, music and emotional register. *Senso* depicts an adulterous romance between an Italian countess (Alida Valli) and an Austrian soldier (Farley Granger) against the 1860s backdrop of the Austrian occupation of Italy. *Senso*'s international storyline and cast indicate a trend toward cultural syncretism in European cinema of the period. Max Ophuls' films *Madame de . . .* (1953) and *Lola Montès* (1955) present another auteurist signpost in European costume drama.[51] Projecting cultural credentials of 'quality' on an international arena, European art cinema forms an important industrial and stylistic antecedent to contemporary costume drama. Art cinema's codes of literary and cinematic authorship have been reconfigured to market a wide range of films, from Merchant Ivory productions to Scorsese's *The Age of Innocence*, Campion's *The Portrait of a Lady*, or Greenaway's *Prospero's Books* (1991).

Issues of cultural value and trans/national cinemas point to the thorny question of audiences. For a largely interpretive project such as this one, readings of these films are guided by implied contexts of reception. The political stakes of the heritage cinema debates, for instance, rest on competing assumptions about gender and class audience formations. Monk points to the pervasive dismissal of female and older middlebrow audiences as being outside an assumed mainstream (for which, read youthful and male) demographic.[52] In contrast, feminist scholarship on Gainsborough and more recent costume cinema explores the creative possibilities of fantasy and escape for female audiences. Debates about heritage audiences are mostly confined to the British context, but Higson's analysis of *Elizabeth*'s reception indicates the film's wide appeal for British, American, European, Japanese, Australian and Brazilian audiences.[53] This book explores a wider scope of cultural meanings that extend beyond the frame of the nation, though the composition and expectations of international audiences are elusive.

In North America, for example, costume drama is perceived differently than in the UK. Colloquially, the films are seen as 'chick flicks', and for the most part costume film is reviewed by critics as a benign, even pedagogical genre in a culture industry exploding with violence, explicit sexuality and lowbrow entertainment. Seemingly, the middlebrow credentials of British quality are operative here as well, although in a rare nationalist critique Martin Hipsky claims that the popularity of 'Anglophilic' period films in the US constitutes a regressive and colonialist 'conspicuous consumption'.[54] For the most part, the assumption of costume film's core audience coming from a '25–44 age group, upscale educated with a female bias'[55] holds across these two contexts, and this assumption guides my analysis.

I explore a pervasive liberal feminist discourse that constructs an international Western, female audience through films such as *Sense and Sensibility* (1995), *Mansfield Park* or *Elizabeth*. This is not to claim that female feminists constitute the films' sole audience for these works. Rather, I suggest that part of the films' rhetorical power arises from a timely deployment of Western feminist discourses of romance, individualism and aspiration. Further, many observations in this book evoke broadly Western discourses of subjectivity, gender, desire, romance, sexuality, class, empire and tourism.

I argue that these films travel so well precisely because they deploy, rework and sometimes subvert foundational English cultural references and discourses. Drawn from
canonical traditions such as the English novel and theatre, these references are part of
a common postcolonial cultural legacy for English-speaking audiences. If this revisionist discourse analysis (like the films themselves) overlooks elements of national
and local specificity, past and present, it seeks instead to think about how cultural
forms travel.

While a fully international account exceeds the parameters of this project, this
book highlights transnational relations of gender, sexuality, class and colonialism within
recent English-language productions. For even the most resolutely English films are
shot through with implicit and explicit references to the colonies – sometimes incidental, and sometimes considered, as in *Orlando* or *Mansfield Park*. Like the
Gainsborough melodramas or the works of Ophuls and Visconti, many recent films
trade on cinematically lush accounts of European travel and cross-cultural encounter;
for instance, in the James and Forster adaptations Anglo-American protagonists experience a cultural or sensual awakening through contact with European people and settings. Travel and the coding of national and regional locations are integral to this
book's topographical analysis of space, place and the past. In the next section, I turn
to a broader theoretical consideration of these questions.

Topographical Frames: Space, Movement and Methods

Following Mikhail Bakhtin, Robert Stam insists on the *dialogic* nature of culture, the
'infinite and open-ended possibilities generated by all the discursive practices of
culture, the entire matrix of communicative utterances within which the artistic text is
situated'.[56] Bakhtin writes of 'the "deep generating series" of literature – that is, the
complex and multidimensional dialogism, rooted in social life and history'.[57] A dialogic
approach to costume drama moves beyond a monolithic 'closed' reading (heritage
spectacle as bourgeois nostalgia) to a polyphonic reading, where the bounded microcosm of costume drama becomes a site of struggle. Bakhtinian analysis insists that
historical power formations are embedded within cultural texts, whose meanings are
'reworked by boundless context. The text feeds on and is fed into an infinitely per-
mutating intertext, which is seen through ever-shifting grids of interpretation.'[58] This
mode of cultural analysis addresses multiple, intersecting and contradictory horizons
of intelligibility: nation, gender, sexual and class identities, postcolonial contexts and
subjects.

Bakhtin's concept of the 'chronotope' insists that the resonance of cultural texts is
powerfully inflected by the passage of time and their dissemination across different cultural contexts. Literally 'space-time', the chronotope provides a concrete and flexible
tool for examining cultural texts through the spatio-temporal articulation of genre: 'In
the literary artistic chronotope, spatial and temporal indicators are fused into one carefully thought-out, concrete whole. Time, as it were, thickens, takes on flesh, becomes
artistically visible; likewise, space becomes charged and responsive to the movements
of time, plot and history.'[59] More than an aesthetic concept, the chronotope is emphatically social – an open figure describing a dialogic relationship between the representational space-time of literature and social subjects living in particular historical times
and places:

The work and the world represented in it enter the real world and enrich it, and the real world enters the work and its world as part of the process of its creation, as well as part of its subsequent life, in a continual renewing of the work through the creative perception of listeners and readers. Of course this process of exchange is itself chronotopic: it occurs first and foremost in the historically developing social world, but without ever losing contact with changing historical space.[60]

Bringing into relief the spatio-temporal forms of literature, the chronotope raises the question of the adaptation of literature, a central point of reference for contemporary costume dramas. Adaptations of Austen, James, Wharton and Woolf are based on classic novels, while the Wilde adaptations, *The Madness of King George*, *Edward II* and *Shakespeare in Love* adapt theatrical works. The literary credentials of these classic, modernist and postmodernist works figure centrally in the films' commercial and cultural intertexts, as do discourses of authorship-as-brand. In postwar European art film and more recently in popular cinema, the name of the author has come to 'function as a "brand name", a means of labelling and selling a film and of orienting expectations and channelling meaning and pleasure in the absence of generic boundaries and categories'.[61] For Belén Vidal, 'the literary', like 'the author', is not a sign of authenticity, but is rather part of the intertext of what she calls 'the literary film' – a category not limited to literary adaptations, but encompassing a wide array of period dramas.[62] Stam's and Vidal's intertextual approaches refute the problematic notion of 'fidelity' that measures cinematic adaptations as mere copies of a literary original.

If the referent of costume drama is not a literary original or authentic historical event, a topographical approach points to a different articulation of text/world/subject inscribed through space and time. Bakhtin's chronotope forms a suggestive point of departure, and scholarship on melodrama and the 'woman's film' also develops helpful links between costume drama and the social horizon of meaning. This work seeks to understand how melodrama and the 'woman's film' mediate social and political experience through the exploration of affect, subjectivity and power. Psychoanalytic accounts of melodrama examine codes of space and music, emphasising expressive codes of spatial and psychological compression. Geoffrey Nowell-Smith argues that melodrama 'does not "reflect" or "describe" social and psychic determinations. Rather, it *signifies* them.'[63] A melodramatic expressive modality highlights the experience of the oppressed, particularly the situation of women; one compelling example is the spatial use of the house as a signifier of constraint and passivity.[64]

This 'structure of feeling' is often taken up in the movement-image of the woman at the window, a recurring trope in recent costume film. I argue that this trope indicates a widespread topography of interiority and compression that can be seen, for example, in *The Portrait of a Lady*, *The House of Mirth* or *The Age of Innocence*. The James and Wharton adaptations particularly evoke a repressive Victorian spatiality that links the psychodynamics of the screen with the nineteenth-century novel. Following Bakhtin's account of literature as a 'deep generating series', the conflicts and contradictions worked through in these films are not limited to a specific historical period, but are negotiated in the tension between the Victorian past as microcosm, and a contemporary self-conscious horizon from which to read it. The present-day anchorage of narration in the present day is most evident in *The Portrait of a Lady*, where the period film is prefaced by a stylistically distinct sequence. Here, through late twentieth-century Australian girls' reflections on love, Campion's present-day vantage point is juxtaposed with the narrative expectations of period romance. This doubled address is a recurring feature of contemporary costume drama. Indeed, part of the difficulty of assessing the dramatic and social stakes of many of these films arises from their knowing sensibility, and persistent post/modern strategies of quotation, irony and parody.

Many critics comment on this doubled economy of deep feeling and distance. Higson argues that this 'fascinating but self-enclosed world'[65] sets history apart from the viewer, while the knowing distance created by heritage spectacle precludes an affective engagement with characters and narrative drama. Meanwhile, for Linda Hutcheon, postmodern culture deploys irony productively, where a film like *Amadeus* offers a 'rethinking and reworking of the forms and contents of the past'.[66] Meanwhile, parody – the dramatic send-up of the conventions of realist period drama through excessive costumes, performances and *mise en scène* – is a favoured mode of critique in the Wilde adaptations, *Orlando*, *The Madness of King George* and *Angels & Insects*. But costume drama's doubled address does not always facilitate social critique, commonly lingering wistfully (if knowingly) but without critical commentary on the trappings of the past. The challenge facing the critic is to distinguish between nostalgic celebration and self-conscious critique of empire or the ascendancy of aristocratic or bourgeois values.

Costume drama's paradoxical doubled address aligns with the microcosm's concentric frames of perception and allegory. The contemporary viewer is at once inside and outside these mannered microcosms of the past, and the resulting play of surfaces and depth, witty remove and deep feeling provide some of the genre's greatest pleasures. The microcosm is one core spatial concept guiding this book's topographical analysis; and arising from this notion of costume drama as 'bounded space' is an interrogation of affective proximity and distance, the tension between identification and critique. A related concept concerns the inside/outside dialectic: both the films' lively traffic between domestic and public spheres, and a theoretical meditation on interiority and exteriority as modes of subjectivity and performance. I explore these abstract themes by reading the films' symbolic and dramatic renderings of trans/national, regional and intimate 'space' and 'place'. This array of spatial themes guide the topographical approach to film theory developed in this book: not a method per se, but a way of thinking about film through the ideas of space and movement.

Bakhtin's chronotope suggests a link between the text and the world that evokes the social subject (the focus of psychoanalytic theory), but is elaborated through social and textual renderings of space and time. This is to suggest that not only do we read films through the processes of identification, voyeurism, fetishism and desire, but also through cinematic productions of global image space, the spatio-temporal structures of genre, narrative temporality, national and cultural milieu. Grounded in a Marxist aesthetics that understands power relations as embedded in cultural forms, the chronotope explores the sedimentation of historical relations of difference. While Bakhtin writes primarily about class and urban/rural relations, this concept can be extended to consider the interlocking spatial treatments of gender, sexuality and colonialism.

If Bakhtin's thought provides an intertextual historical field for thinking about costume drama, Deleuze's philosophical exploration of cinematic movement is also fundamental to this project. The notion of 'topographical' cinematic thought is borrowed from Patricia Mellencamp's account of Deleuze:

> Deleuze's way of thinking about cinema is *cinema*tographic, not psychoanalytic; it
> focuses on topography more than narrative. Regarding Deleuze's first observation,
> movement is not limited to the cause-effect logic of narrative, or to figures 'moving'
> through space, or to cameras dollying, tracking. Action is only one kind of movement;
> the others are perception and affection.[67]

Beginning from the film still, what appears as an 'immobile section of movement', Deleuze insists that the cinematic image offers a distinctively modern image that arises in and through time and movement: 'Cinema does not give us an image to which movement is added, it immediately gives us a movement-image. It does give us a section, but a section which is mobile, not immobile.'[68]

The nuances of Deleuzian thought exceed the scope of this book, in which I pragmatically adapt the movement-image to address the spatial rather than the temporal aspects of his *Cinema* project. In general terms, Deleuze critiques the dominant structuralist theory of cinema as a language, and posits a different epistemology of the image. Rather than a representation of the real that is often perceived as false, Deleuze describes a relation of immanence between subject and film. D.N. Rodowick argues that, for Deleuze, 'cinematographic perception is not entirely false; it is part of quotidian perception. ... In other words, what counts ... is the brute empiricism of the image in movement, the immediate evidence of our eyes.'[69] Films as assemblages, fragments of space-time, can be analysed following certain recurring cinematic signs: perception-image, action-image, affection-image, and so on. Rather than focusing on specific films, narratives, genres and film-makers (although he privileges auteurist and art cinema), Deleuze reads these signs across different texts and traditions. Where Deleuze is predominantly interested in form, I adapt this approach to address thematic movement-images. In this way, I analyse costume drama through recurring movement-images that form discursive regularities: the woman at the window, the writing desk and the letter, the ball, the country walk, the trip to Europe.

To complement Bakhtin's literary articulation of space and time, Deleuze's work is powerful for film analysis in his attention to four aspects of cinematic movement:

> First is the plane of immanence or the whole aggregate of images as a universal regime
> of acentered variation (the Image). Next comes the 'perception of movement' with
> the emergence of centers of determination [Deleuze's provisional term for the
> 'subject']. . . . Third is movement in its most common sense, an elapsed spatial
> trajectory. The fourth variation completes the passage from matter to spirit, intuiting
> movement, matter, and image in their identity with time: becoming, change,
> emergence of the new, creative evolution.[70]

This last aspect of movement crystallises an interesting paradox that runs through this book. Deleuzian thought foregrounds movement, becoming, transformation, and has been most obviously deployed in relation to dynamic cinematic genres such as action cinema. In contrast, Bakhtin's Marxist legacy carries the slowness of historical, social and subjective change – the weight of oppression and struggle. This tension echoes recursively between costume drama's own intransigent stasis (and imputed conservatism), and its tremendous quiet energy, which has generated stunning formal innovation, a healthy crop of crossover popular hits, as well as spoofs and parodies.

This problem of stasis and movement intersects with core dilemmas in feminist film theory. Teresa de Lauretis has influentially laid out a gendered economy of narrative space and movement, where masculine characters are associated with dynamism and transformation and female characters are immobile.[71] Laura Mulvey and Mary Ann Doane extend this paradigm to the spatial properties of genre.[72] Following this train of thought, costume drama appears to be a quintessentially 'feminine' genre characterised by limited character mobility or physical, social and corporeal constraint. In fact, preoccupations of speed and slowness represent another theoretical dimension of this project. I have become fascinated by the characteristic slowness and digression of these films, and how this tempo contrasts with a pervasive trajectory of female *becoming* against fraught backgrounds of class and colonial struggle (*Orlando*, *The Piano*). Finally, extensive desiring movements of social aspiration and travel are bound up with intensive vectors of desire and interiority: while female characters may find ambition at odds with their romantic desires (*Elizabeth*, *The Portrait of a Lady*), male protagonists are increasingly placed within (melo)dramatic situations where deep longing and suffering produce a more sensitive and deep-feeling masculinity (*The Age of Innocence*, *The Remains of the Day*).

Deleuze's three varieties of movement-image are suggestive as analytic categories for exploring these different aspects of cinematic movement. Each variety implies a distinct critical/affective mode of analysis corresponding to the cinematic spatiality of specific shots.

> These three kinds of spatially determined shots can be made to correspond to these three kinds of varieties: the long shot would be primarily a perception-image; the medium shot an action-image; the close-up an affection-image. But, at the same time . . . each of these movement-images is a point of view on the whole of the film, a way of grasping this whole, which becomes affective in the close-up, active in the medium shot, perceptive in the long shot – each of these shots ceasing to be spatial in order to become itself a 'reading' of the whole film.[73]

Aligned with the long shot, the perception-image addresses conditions of visibility, and relates to the philosophical problem of perception. For Deleuze, perception is subtractive, and proceeds through framing that selects and organises nouns (bodies, animate and inanimate), ordering relations in time and space. I extend the notion of the perception-image to insist on *the interdependence of audiovisual elements at work within the frame*. In this way it becomes possible to read the frame not only through narrative space,[74] but also through secondary trajectories and details – the servant's hand, queer and non-normative sexuality, classed and colonial voices. For Deleuze, the perception-image situates the protagonist(s) within an allegorical or realist milieu. If the establishing shot determines a field of vision and a field or location, I address the aesthetic and social rendering of landscape (Austen's pastoral countryside or the tangled New Zealand bush of *The Piano*); historical national milieux (James's symbolic plotting of British,

European, and American locations); and the country manors or suburban 'houses of fiction' framing dramas of interiority, repression and desire.

The action-image constitutes the second category of movement-image: 'Just as perception relates movement to "bodies" (nouns), that is to rigid objects which will serve as moving bodies or as things moved, action relates movement to "acts" (verbs) which will be the design for an assumed end or result.'[75] Characterised by the medium shot, this plane addresses narrative, the frame of the human body, actions and intentions. Of particular interest here are the gendered and classed articulations of movement (agency) and stasis (passivity or constraint). As mentioned above, the large form of the action-image ('masculine' genres such as the Western, the epic, the action film) foregrounds muscular, extensive movement and dynamism, whereas the small form of the action-image ('feminine' genres) foregrounds indirect action, intensive (interior) movement and more restricted fields of action. Within costume film's miniatures, nuanced relations of desire, power and agency emerge through subtle economies of gesture, costume, *mise en scène* and performance. Throughout this book, the action-image is read through the spatio-temporal problem of genre and narrative – the subtle articulations of agency, pleasure and desire that unfold in costume drama's digressing plots.

The third aspect of movement-image is the affection-image that corresponds to the close-up. The affection-image raises subtle yet essential cinematic properties of feeling, affect and intensity. 'Affectivity' ushers in a register of intensities that are raised by psychoanalysis, but which, for Deleuze, exceed the framework of oedipalised desire. Deleuze describes the affection-image as 'a coincidence of subject and object . . . [where] the subject perceives itself, or rather experiences itself or feels itself "from the inside" (third material aspect of subjectivity). It relates movement to "quality" as lived state (adjective).'[76] For Deleuze, the affection-image is exemplified by close-ups of hands and faces that highlight emotion and expression. Costume drama read through the close-up evokes subtle registers of feeling (longing, passion, sentiment and nostalgia) that can both liberate and entrap the characters – and, by extension, the audience. The close-up is also a figure associated with subjectivity: the deep-feeling interiority evoked by adaptations of the nineteenth-century English novel, or the surface play of deception and masks in more theatrical films such as *The Madness of King George*, the Wilde adaptations or *Dangerous Liaisons*.

This book is organised into two parts. The first, 'The Spaces of Costume Drama', lays out a topographical account of conventional costume drama. With an emphasis on generic norms, I examine the spatio-temporal organisation of a dominant mode of realist costume drama with reference to the Austen, James and Wharton adaptations. Chapter One presents a topographical reading of the Austen adaptations, scrutinising the films' liberal feminism in relation to class, colonialism and the whisper of lesbian sexuality. In Chapters Two and Three, I examine the compressed spatiality of Victorian/Edwardian 'houses of fiction', investigating the complex spatiality of gender and desire in the James and Wharton adaptations. Chapter Four considers the centrality of international travel to costume film's trajectories of desire and self-discovery, with a particular emphasis on the 'idea of Europe' as the imagined site of Western socio-political and cultural origins. The films considered in this chapter encompass both the James and Forster adaptations and a series of historical biographies of artists, writers and musicians.

The second half of this book is called 'Costume Drama Reassembled'. With particular attention to formally innovative and critically engaged films, I further explore problems raised in the first part of the book: feminist revisionism, class and colonialism, costume, sexuality and the body. Chapter Five examines the problem of narrative movement in relation to the gendered and colonial spaces of *Orlando* and *Daughters of the Dust*. In Chapter Six, I address both normative and critical accounts of class with reference to *Jude* (1996), *Gosford Park*, *The Remains of the Day* and *Angels & Insects*. Chapter Seven examines a trajectory of 'queer' appearances and interventions in period film, notably the Forster and James adaptations, Derek Jarman's *Caravaggio* and *Edward II*, and the *Wilde* biography and adaptations. Finally, Chapter Eight examines several distinct discourses of sexuality and the body, with particular attention to *The Piano*, *Dangerous Liaisons*, and historical biographies *The Madness of King George*, *Elizabeth* and *Shakespeare in Love*.

Notes

1. Anne Hollander, *Seeing Through Clothes* (Berkeley: University of California Press, 1993), p. 331.
2. Kevin Jackson, 'The House of Mirth', *Sight and Sound*, November 2000, p. 54.
3. Renée Baert, 'Skirting the Issue', *Screen* vol. 35 no. 4, 1994, p. 356.
4. Peter Brooks, *The Melodramatic Imagination* (New Haven: Yale University Press, 1995), p. 2.
5. Robert A. Rosenstone, 'The Historical Film as Real History', *Film-Historia* vol. 5 no. 1, 1999, p. 18.
6. See Raphael Samuel, *Theatres of Memory* (London: Verso, 1994), p. x.
7. Susan Stewart, *On Longing* (Durham: Duke University Press, 1993), p. 54.
8. Andrew Higson, 'Re-presenting the National Past: Nostalgia and Pastiche in the Heritage Film', in Lester Friedman (ed.), *Fires Were Started* (Minneapolis: University of Minnesota Press, 1993), p. 113.
9. Morris Dickstein, 'Time Bandits', *American Film* vol. 8 no. 1, October 1982, p. 40.
10. Gilles Deleuze, *Cinema 1: The Movement-Image* (Minneapolis: University of Minnesota Press, 1986), p. 163.
11. I thank Belén Vidal for suggesting this point.
12. Marcia Landy, *British Genres* (Princeton: Princeton University Press, 1991), p. 61.
13. Cited in Landy, *British Genres*, p. 56.
14. Ibid., p. 56.
15. Debates over the cultural value of costume film find parallels with French film, where the 'Tradition of Quality' flourished in the postwar years in a tradition of historical fiction (*La Marseillaise* (1938)) and literary adaptation (*Caroline Chérie* (1951)). Popular with French audiences of the period, especially women, these films were later devalued against the aspirations of a (masculinist) auteurist national cinema of the French New Wave. See Noël Burch and Geneviève Sellier, *La Drôle de guerre des sexes du cinéma français: 1930–1956* (Paris: Nathan Université, 1996).
16. John Caughie, *Television Drama* (Oxford: Oxford University Press, 2000), p. 209.
17. See, for example, John Collick, *Shakespeare, Cinema and Society* (Manchester: Manchester University Press, 1989) and Lynda E. Boose and Richard Burt (eds), *Shakespeare, The Movie* (London: Routledge, 1997).

18. For an incisive analysis of the discourses around 'quality' television, see Charlotte Brunsdon, 'Problems with quality', *Screen* vol. 31 no. 1, Spring 1990.

19. These figures refer to net profits. See Long, cited in Martin Hipsky, 'Anglophil(m)ia: Why Does America Watch Merchant-Ivory Movies?', *Journal of Popular Film and Television* vol. 22 no. 3, Autumn 1993, p. 98.

20. Tana Wollen, 'Over our shoulders: nostalgic screen fictions for the 1980s', in John Corner and Sylvia Harvey (eds), *Enterprise and Heritage* (London: Routledge, 1991), p. 180.

21. Higson, 'Re-presenting the National Past', p. 110.

22. Ibid., p. 115.

23. Cairns Craig, 'Rooms without a view', *Sight and Sound*, June 1991, p. 10.

24. Henry James, 'Preface', *The Portrait of a Lady* (Ware, Hertfordshire: Wordsworth Editions, 1996), p. 7.

25. Cited in Ginette Vincendeau, 'Introduction', in Ginette Vincendeau (ed.), *Film/ Literature/ Heritage* (London, BFI, 2001), p. xix.

26. Claire Monk, 'The British "Heritage Film" and its Critics', *Critical Survey* vol. 7 no. 2, 1995, p. 122.

27. See Richard Dyer, *The Culture of Queers* (London: Routledge, 2002), pp. 204–6.

28. See Caughie, *Television Drama*, pp. 208–9.

29. Landy, *British Genres*, p. 61.

30. Low, cited in *British Genres*, p. 61.

31. See Helen Taylor, *Scarlett's Women* (New Brunswick, NJ: Rutgers University Press, 1989).

32. Susan Hayward, *Cinema Studies: The Key Concepts*, second edition (London: Routledge, 2000), p. 75.

33. Landy, *British Genres*, p. 57.

34. Pam Cook, *Fashioning the Nation* (London: BFI, 1996), p. 83.

35. Tino Balio, 'The art film market in the new Hollywood', in Geoffrey Nowell-Smith and Steven Ricci (eds), *Hollywood & Europe* (London: BFI, 1998), p. 64.

36. Stephen Crofts, 'Foreign Tunes? Gender and Nationality in Four Countries' Reception of *The Piano*', in Harriet Margolis (ed.), *Jane Campion's The Piano* (Cambridge: Cambridge University Press, 2000), p. 135.

37. Ibid., p. 136.

38. Miramax was also the production company for *Enchanted April*.

39. See Claudia Eller and John Evan Frook, 'Disney Munches on Miramax', in *Variety* no. 3, May 1993, pp. 1, 60, 62. On Miramax as a 'major independent', see Justin Wyatt, 'Economic Constraints/Economic Opportunities: Robert Altman as Auteur', in *The Velvet Light Trap* no. 30, Fall 1996, pp. 59–65.

40. In 1997, a British production wing of Miramax was set up under Disney. See Adam Minns, 'The English Patient', *Screen International* no. 1133, 7 November 1997, p. 15.

41. On Miramax's marketing strategies, see Wyatt, 'Economic Constraints', pp. 62–3.

42. Balio, 'The art film market', p. 64.

43. Statistics from The Internet Movie database, www.imdb.com/. Cited for comparative purposes only, the figures are rounded to the nearest million.

44. Balio, 'The art film market', p. 64. For example, the 1995 *Pride and Prejudice* broke the long-standing record of *Upstairs, Downstairs* as the most profitable British

television series export, and also sold some 200,000 video copies in the US. (See Peter M. Nichols, 'Literary Cycle: Bookshop, Broadcast, Video Store', *The New York Times*, 7 September 1997, Arts & Leisure section, online version.)

45. On the economics of *Elizabeth*, see Nick Roddick, 'Shotguns and Weddings', *Sight and Sound* vol. 9 no. 3, March 1999, 'Mediawatch' supplement, pp. 10–13.

46. For a thorough discussion of this economic context, see Higson, *English Heritage, English Cinema* (Oxford: Oxford University Press, 2003), pp. 86–145. On British film production of the 90s see Robert Murphy, 'A Path through the Moral Maze', in Robert Murphy (ed.), *British Cinema of the 90s* (London: BFI, 2000), pp. 1–16.

47. Higson, *English Heritage*, p. 5.

48. Ibid., pp. 197–8. See also Claire Monk, 'Sexuality and the Heritage Film', *Sight and Sound*, October 1995, pp. 32–4.

49. This sequence includes *Picnic at Hanging Rock* (1975), *My Brilliant Career* (1979) and more recently John Duigan's *Wide Sargasso Sea* (1993) and *Sirens* (1994). On Australian period film, see Jonathan Rayner, *Contemporary Australian Cinema: An Introduction* (Manchester: Manchester University Press, 2000), pp. 3–93.

50. On the French superproductions of the 90s, see Ginette Vincendeau, 'Unsettling Memories', *Sight and Sound*, July 1995, pp. 30–2, and Julianne Pidduck, 'Versions, Verse and Verve: Jean-Paul Rappeneau's *Cyrano de Bergerac*', in Ginette Vincendeau (ed.), *French Film: Texts and Contexts*, 2nd edition (London: Routledge, 2000).

51. See Geoffrey Nowell-Smith, 'Introduction', in Nowell-Smith and Ricci (eds), *Hollywood & Europe*, p. 8.

52. See Claire Monk, 'Heritage films and the British cinematic audience in the 1990s', *Journal of Popular British Cinema* no. 2, 1999, p. 31. The entire article (pp. 22–38) offers a useful reading of audience trends for heritage cinema.

53. See Higson, *English Heritage*, pp. 200–17.

54. Hipsky, 'Anglophil(m)ia', p. 102.

55. This was how *Elizabeth*'s primary target audience was described in the film's British marketing plan. See Higson, *English Heritage*, p. 202.

56. Robert Stam, 'The Dialogics of Adaptation', in James Naremore (ed.), *Film Adaptation* (New Brunswick, NJ: Rutgers University Press, 2000), p. 64.

57. Ibid.

58. Ibid., p. 57.

59. Mikhail Bakhtin, *The Dialogic Imagination* (Austin: University of Texas Press, 1981), p. 84.

60. Ibid., p. 254.

61. Neale, cited in Catherine Grant, 'www.auteur.com?', *Screen* vol. 41 no. 1, 2000, p. 102.

62. See Belén Vidal, 'Classic adaptations/modern reinventions: reading the image in the contemporary literary film', *Screen* vol. 43 no. 1, Spring 2002, pp. 6–9.

63. Geoffrey Nowell-Smith, 'Minelli and Melodrama', in Christine Gledhill (ed.), *Home is Where the Heart Is* (London: BFI, 1987), p. 70. Emphasis in original.

64. Thomas Elsaesser, 'Tales of Sound and Fury: Observations on the Family Melodrama', in Gledhill (ed.), *Home is Where the Heart Is*, pp. 61–2.

65. Higson, 'Re-presenting the National Past', p. 113.

66. Linda Hutcheon, 'Theorising the Postmodern', in Charles Jencks (ed.), *The Post-Modern Reader* (London: Academy Editions, 1992), pp. 77–8.

67. Patricia Mellencamp, 'Five Ages of Film Feminism', in Layleen Jayamanne (ed.), *Kiss Me Deadly* (Sydney: Power Publications, 1995), p. 58.

68. Deleuze, *Cinema 1*, p. 2.

69. D.N. Rodowick, *Gilles Deleuze's Time Machine* (Durham: Duke University Press, 1997), p. 22.

70. Ibid., p. 42.

71. Teresa de Lauretis, *Alice Doesn't* (Bloomington: Indiana University Press, 1984), p. 118.

72. See Laura Mulvey, 'Afterthoughts on "Visual Pleasure and Narrative Cinema" inspired by *Duel in the Sun*', in Constance Penley (ed.), *Feminism and Film Theory* (New York: Routledge, 1988), and Mary Ann Doane, *The Desire to Desire* (Bloomington: Indiana University Press, 1987), pp. 70–5.

73. Deleuze, *Cinema 1*, p. 70.

74. Stephen Heath's concept of 'narrative space' describes how within classic narrative cinema, framing and spatiality are tightly restricted to a sequential narrative logic of narrative coherence and progression; extraneous elements are excluded within this 'space which is itself part of the action in its economy, its intelligibility, its own legality'. See his *Questions of Cinema* (London: Macmillan, 1981), p. 20.

75. Deleuze, *Cinema 1*, p. 65.

76. Ibid.

Part One
The Spaces of Costume Drama

Chapter One
The Woman at the Window

The recurring moment of the woman at the window captures a particular quality of feminine stillness, constraint and longing that runs through 90s film and television adaptations of Jane Austen's novels. Consider, for instance, the sequence in Ang Lee's *Sense and Sensibility* where Elinor Dashwood (Emma Thompson) sits at a writing desk facing the window. Muted sunlight streams in through the thick glass, bathing her face in a soft golden light; her startling cornflower-blue eyes exactly match her simple frock. Cut to an over-the-shoulder shot from Elinor's point of view as she glances out of the window. In a preframed vignette set in the landscaped garden, her younger sister Margaret appears with Edward Ferrars (Hugh Grant). Fencing with long sticks, they play at pirates duelling on the high seas. Edward demonstrates the 'lunge' to the precocious Margaret, who promptly guts him when he's not prepared. Elinor glances up to watch them, smiles indulgently, then returns to her letters. Reminiscent of Vermeer,[1] the film consistently uses the window as framing device and as filter for natural light.

With its frames within frames, this sequence indicates the importance of gendered interior and exterior space at work in contemporary Austen adaptations. Elinor, the responsible older sister, sits demurely indoors, attending to the small fatherless family living in genteel poverty. Meanwhile, Mrs Dashwood and her daughters commonly hover by the window, hoping for the arrival of an eligible suitor. The male characters (Edward, Willoughby, Colonel Brandon), in contrast, tend to come and go, moving

A gendered economy of interiors and exteriors: Elinor Dashwood (Emma Thompson) at the window in *Sense and Sensibility*

freely through the countryside – indeed, Brandon's robust and worldly masculinity arises in part from his military adventures abroad. This brief sketch brings into relief a gendered spatial play between a mannered treatment of interiors, and the more natural blocking of outdoor sequences (country walks, picnics, coach rides). Set against the precise dialogue and intricate human interaction condensed into Austen's parlours, libraries and balls, exterior sequences (often leavened by swelling orchestral scores) tend to create a sense of spatial and emotional expansiveness, not unlike the role of dance numbers in the musical.[2] Meanwhile, just off-screen lurk the liminal vistas of pirates, imperial adventure and profit.

A link in the overall topography, the window marks the threshold of inside and outside. For Mikhail Bakhtin, the threshold is 'highly charged with emotion and value . . . whose fundamental instance is as the chronotope of *crisis* and *break* in a life'.[3] In a cycle of works organised around female characters who are both actually and metaphorically 'housebound', windows and doors where arrivals and departures occur provide focal points of narrative interest. During the quiet embroidering days of the Misses Dashwood, the Misses Bennet, Anne Elliot, Catherine Moreland, Fanny Price, and to a lesser degree Emma Woodhouse, arrivals of potential suitors are highly anticipated events. A formal and narrative framing device, the window marks a transparent filter between the ordered, confined lives of Austen's female protagonists, and the comings and goings of visitors. From the Dashwoods, to Emma's startled rush to the window at the outset of *Jane Austen's Emma* (1997), to the Bennet girls' ongoing vigilance from their windows in the television series *Pride and Prejudice* (1995), to Fanny Price's wistful lingering at the windows in television and film adaptations of *Mansfield Park* (1990 and 1999, respectively), to Catherine Moreland's and Anne Elliot's respective confinements in Bath town houses in *Northanger Abbey* (1987) and *Persuasion* (1995), the woman at the window encapsulates a gendered structure of feeling at work in Austen and in costume drama more generally[4] – a generic spatio-temporal economy of physical and sexual constraint, a sumptuous waiting barely papering over an elaborate yet attenuated register of longing. This persistent movement-image offers a metonymic point of departure to consider interlocking power relations of class, gender and imperialism.

What then are we to make of the woman at the window, poised so graciously at this threshold? At first blush, this recurring moment often implies a lingering quality of anticipation, a poignant desire – the digressing yet inexorable pull of the romance narrative toward the inevitable double weddings concluding *Pride* and *Sense*. Indeed, the spatial compression of feminine interiors bottled up against the green 'natural' offerings of the wider world works as an audiovisual condensation of the tremendous force of repressed female desire at work more generally in costume drama. As Monk suggests of *A Room with a View*, the woman at the window may be read as a cinematic instance of 'active female sexual agency and active female looking'.[5] In the Austen adaptations, the apparently passive woman at the window, wistfully waiting, suggests a polite, yet coyly lascivious, desiring female gaze. Along with the films' predominantly female audiences, these characters fully appreciate Hugh Grant's (Ferrars's) tight breeches with that soft bulge at the crotch, Crispin Bonham Carter's (Bingley's) shapely calf, or the manly, square-shouldered cut of Ciaran Hinds's (Wentworth's) uniform.

Yet rather than undertake a psychoanalytic reading of the female gaze, this chapter traces issues of power and desire in the Austen adaptations through the audiovisual plotting of space and movement. Psychoanalysis has furnished feminist film theory with a powerful, if problematic, vocabulary for understanding the cinematic machinations of sexual difference; all too often, however, the psychoanalytic binary excludes other axes of difference. Drawing in part from the insights of literary criticism, this book's topographical analysis seeks to extend the gaze of feminist film theory toward class and colonial relations that cohabit the screen. Returning to Austen in adaptation, the camera rests undoubtedly *inside* with the female protagonist, looking out. However, to follow the trajectory of that desiring gaze *outward*, I extend the question: besides Hugh Grant, Colin Firth or the others, what *do* these women want? Recalling the inviting garden, the eye is drawn outdoors, where Norland's picturesque grounds come into sharp relief as the Dashwood daughters' rightful inheritance denied them by patriarchal law. Similarly, in *Pride*, Elizabeth finds herself gazing out of an upper window of Darcy's Pemberley estate after refusing his offer of marriage. In a classically ironic Austen moment (heightened by Andrew Davies's knowing screenplay), she muses to herself: 'Of all this I might have been mistress.'

These films highlight the precariousness of their heroines' situations through their exclusion from property ownership; in this respect, the romance's desiring narrative tug toward heterosexual courtship and marriage is inextricable from the question of historical property relations. In this sense, the gaze from the window may also be read as a retrospective yearning for the middle-class entitlements of citizenship denied Austen's female protagonists by accident of sex. From a slightly different angle, the woman at the window might imply not only social or sexual constraint, but also a certain potentiality. Within the clearly demarcated limits of Austen's social sphere, this potentiality is deeply yearned for if not realised, and represents a whole spectrum of desires for personhood, social mobility, corporeal and sexual freedom. However, I would argue that such aspirations gain resonance, whether explicitly or implicitly, only in relation to the respective positions and horizons of other social groups. With reference to *Huckleberry Finn*, Toni Morrison describes 'the interdependence of slavery and freedom' in American literature. In this context, not only is slavery understood as the worst form of human constraint, but Huck Finn's own process of becoming a social individual, of gaining agency, can only be measured against the static figure of Jim the slave: 'Freedom has no meaning to Huck or to the text without the spectre of enslavement, the anodyne to individualism.'[6] To tease out the contemporary yearnings afoot in the Austen adaptations is to bring forward the supporting characters of servants and country folk – and to consider the structuring absences of colonial peoples and places just outside the frame.

Film and television adaptations of Austen's novels can be seen as a centrepiece of recent costume drama. Made up of television serials, made-for-television movies and feminist mainstream cinema, the Austen craze exemplifies the wider industrial pattern of recent costume film. As with many classic adaptations, Jane Austen's authorship serves as a branding device that is used to market the films internationally as quality British cultural texts. The British BBC/ American Arts and Entertainment co-production *Pride* and Ang Lee's lush *Sense*, both released in 1995, offer viable precedents for two versions of *Emma* (the British television adaptation is entitled *Jane Austen's Emma*) from each of the two following years and Rozema's later *Mansfield*. Following the industrial logic of the cycle, the pattern in adaptation is to exhaust the works of bankable authors before seeking new ones. Austen, James, Wharton, Wilde and Dickens as iconic authors follow the spate of 80s and early 90s Forster adaptations. A *New York Times* article on the 'literary cycle' stresses that period drama relies on the pleasures of familiarity and repetition, where film and television adaptations are later repackaged as videos.[7]

Austen's novels have had many incarnations, from Robert Z. Leonard's 1940 *Pride and Prejudice*, featuring Greer Garson and Laurence Olivier, to the television serial of the same book scripted by Fay Weldon in 1979. While recognisably part of this tradition, the 90s Austen films and television serials share a striking stylistic and philosophical coherence. Rich production values feature heritage interiors and grounds, filmed with an eye to British and especially international markets. Film and television productions share generic spatio-temporal conventions that both reiterate and rearticulate long-standing conventions of literary adaptation. In this chapter, I read the Austen cycle through recurring movement-images: the woman at the window, the country walk and the sailing ship. The Austen adaptations offer a productive point of departure for a broader analysis of costume drama. A canonical English author, Austen's work is pivotal to the spatial imaginary of the English novel; in turn, the movement-images addressed here form discursive regularities across the wider groupings of costume drama. The woman at the window and other recurring movement-images operate as what Sue Harper calls 'a series of intense, illuminated moments, resonant with sensual meaning'.[8] Following Deleuze, I read these recurring saturated moments not as empty formal structures or clichés, but as 'images of thought'.[9] These movement-images crystallise costume drama's spatio-temporal rendering of the past – familiar cultural forms that are continually reinflected by current discourses of gender, class and individualism.

With their memorable heroines, incisive wit and complex interplay of social convention, individual choice and romance, Austen's novels offer fertile ground for contemporary feminist reworkings. A guiding worldview, which I call 'liberal feminism', understands the historical feminine condition as one of genteel social constraint which is perfectly captured by the woman at the window. This influential account tends to collapse historical differences among women into a familiar middle-class, white and Western 'quest for self' which reads remarkably like a novel by Jane Austen, the Brontës, or George Eliot. This chapter examines how the Austen adaptations project the contradictory gender, class and colonial relations of late eighteenth- and early nineteenth-century England for contemporary consumption.

Interiors and Exteriors: Reading Austen's Landscapes

> To be face-to-face in this world is already to belong to a class. No other community, in
> physical presence or in social reality, is by any means knowable. And it is not only most
> of the people who have disappeared . . . it is also most of the country, which becomes
> real only as it relates to the houses which are the real modes; for the rest of the
> country is weather or a place for a walk.[10]

Raymond Williams's class-based reading of the English novel points out the partial historical view afforded from the upper windows of Austen's great houses. Although the woman at the window may be persuasively read through a narrative of female sexual repression and desire, her very location and, by implication, her desiring gaze, is poly-semic. The confinement of Austen's interiors, so achingly and self-consciously framed by the window, gains resonance only in relation to some 'outside'. If costume drama may be read as spatio-temporal plotting of social, sexual, physical and emotional con-straint, then such constraint figures only against an implied release, movement, expres-sion. The woman at the window can be read in relation to Austen's mobile male protagonists, and also with reference to the surrounding countryside, as offering more spontaneous and meaningful human interaction, romance or contemplation. However, these iconic English landscapes also have as their referent the historical countrysides of improvement and enclosure;[11] as Williams insists, these exteriors are as manicured and carefully constructed as the interiors.

Recent adaptations characteristically render Austen's interiors dense with rich furnishings, heavy oil paintings, expensive ornaments. This *mise en scène* orchestrates a sumptuous experience of gracious nineteenth-century living – what have been called 'museum pleasures'.[12] Yet this panoply of detail also at times evokes the claus-trophobic weight of history, oppressive patriarchal laws of inheritance, and the strict codes of comportment that Austen at once problematises and upholds. A sense of confinement emerges most poignantly in the Norland sequences of *Sense*, in Fanny Price's pious confinement in the television drama *Mansfield*, and in *Persuasion*'s claustrophobic depiction of hypocritical social convention. Shot in the uninhabited Kirby Hall, the interiors of Rozema's cinematic *Mansfield* interiors eschew a lush period aesthetic, seeming 'cold, and at times scarcely furnished, and in disrepair, corrupted by the moral crime on which it subsists and on which it cannot thrive'.[13] Particularly marked in these four films, recent Austen adaptations as a whole tend to contrast mannered interior spaces with the more spontaneous interactions in the countryside (although these boundaries are fluid).

Contemporary adaptations increasingly favour picturesque exteriors over the inter-ior sound stages of earlier works.[14] Particularly noticeable in Merchant Ivory films *A Room with a View* and *Howards End* (1992), iconic English landscapes figure increasingly in 90s period drama. Indeed, the quiet countryside and peaceful Georgian houses of the Austen adaptations might be seen to exemplify what Higson calls an 'alluring spectacle of iconographic stability, providing an impression of an unchanging, traditional, and always delightful and desirable England'.[15] These are the vistas enjoyed by Austen's heroines as they gaze hopefully out of the window awaiting male suitors, or as they throw open the shutters to air their still and quiet rooms. Yet coach rides, horse rides, picnics and especially country walks are also important to the topog-raphy of these texts, and these movement-images offer respite from the pressures of social convention. From Lizzie's constitutional ramblings in *Pride*, to Emma's match-making strolls with Harriet Smith, to *Persuasion*'s seaside strolls, country walks figure centrally in the Austen adaptations. If the woman at the window dramatises feminine constraint and longing, the movement-image of the country walk draws Austen's protagonists out into the broader social space of the countryside.

Consider, for instance, the sequence in *Sense* where Elinor and Edward walk out from Norland Park. Leaving behind the prying eyes and listening walls of Norland, the pair's first private tête-à-tête transpires as they walk out into a gentle green field with the great house in the background. The line of the hill draws the eye toward

A walk in the country in *Sense and Sensibility*

the manor, nestled cosily behind a stand of trees. The film's first extended exterior sequence, this movement-image perfectly sets the nineteenth-century picturesque landscape painting into motion. The protagonists' walk through the middle ground marks out depth in the image; their trajectory into the foreground toward frame right traces a diagonal leading back to the house, which serves as the vanishing point. Marianne's piano score follows the pair outside, layering the precise banter, the romantic nuance of the scene.

Accompanied by the camera in a medium travelling shot, the pair discusses Edward's prospects. Modestly he states: 'A country living is my ideal.' Then a cut to a long shot prompts a subtle temporal ellipsis, even as the conversation continues seemingly unabated to bridge the edit. Edward and Elinor now proceed on horseback at a leisurely pace (toward the foreground, frame right, on the same diagonal as their walk) and the landscape opens up to their progress. Norland has receded into the background, and a shepherd, sheep and running sheepdog briskly cross in front of them moving in the opposite direction. In a classic cinematic technique that emphasises movement, this brief countercurrent of constrasting trajectory and tempo further emphasises the protagonists' progress. The sheep in the foreground scatter at the riders' approach. The shepherd, his dog, the sheep (Dashwood sheep, most likely) complete the blocking of the shot. Even as tiny riders in the distance, Elinor's and Edward's modulated voices project across the mute and obliging countryside.

This moment marks a subtle but important shift of location from Austen's novel, where the conversation about Edward's prospects occurs at breakfast between Edward and Mrs Dashwood. In adaptation, the scene is transported outside into the quiet countryside idealised by Edward and by the film's visual language. Scriptwriter Emma Thompson adds the following exchange to Austen's dialogue:

Elinor: 'You talk of feeling idle and useless. Imagine how that is compounded when one has no hope or choice of any occupation whatsoever.'
Edward: 'Our circumstances then are precisely the same.'

Elinor: 'Except that you will inherit your fortune. We cannot even earn ours.'
Edward: 'Perhaps Margaret is right. Piracy is our only option.'

These subtle changes from novel to film indicate both a generic interest in iconic English landscapes, and a liberal feminist update of Austen's narrative. In a moment of godsent simultaneity for the film theorist, Elinor's and Edward's near encounter with the shepherd coincides with a deliberately revisionist feminist moment. In a sense, this exchange superimposes a feminist commentary on land tenure over the mute countryside. Laid out like a feast in the background, the Norland estate is the prize at stake in Elinor's wry commentary. From her comfortable spot by the window, Thompson's script deliberately poses a critique of patriarchal laws of inheritance.

This movement-image highlights key audiovisual orchestrations of power in costume drama, namely the layering of voice (associated with a significant classbound narrative and subjective authority) with the visual dynamics of corporeal movement and historical landscape aesthetics. The cultural encoding of these 'natural' landscapes has been explored in a substantial body of scholarship that reads capitalist and patriarchal relations of ownership within the British landscape painting tradition.[16] For instance, referring to Thomas Gainsborough's painting *Mr and Mrs Andrews*, Gillian Rose writes:

> Their ownership of land is celebrated in the substantiality of the oil paints used to represent it, and in the vista opening up beyond them, which echoes in visual form the freedom to move over property which only landowners could enjoy. The absence in the painting's content of the people who work the fields . . . denies the relations of waged labour under capitalism.[17]

Rose also identifies this painting's gender relations, noting Mr and Mrs Andrews' contrasting access to physical mobility. Mrs Andrews appears rooted to the spot, under the shadow of the oak tree's symbol of generations. 'Like the fields she sits beside, her role was to reproduce and this role is itself naturalized by the references to trees and fields.'[18] In contrast with this eighteenth-century painting, we find a deliberately egalitarian shot of the couple's walk in *Sense*. Thompson's Elinor banters with Edward as they move freely through the countryside, side by side. Through the characters' voices and physical trajectories, this sequence both visually includes Elinor in the proprietary surveying of Norland's grounds and records in dialogue her exclusion from her apparent birthright.

This sequence demonstrates how the film's liberal feminist critique relies on class-specific conceptions of space and movement. Returning to the shepherd, in audio-visual terms this man, the sheep, the dog are designated as visual details of landscape that lend a backdrop, a countercurrent to the steady progression of the film's middle-class protagonists. Seemingly digressing and without purpose, the country walks and constant matchmaking of Austen's characters, as Williams points out, correspond to a historical flurry of changes in property relations. If marriage marks the culmination of the romantic narrative, juxtaposed with the embattled historical context of the Industrial Revolution, Improvement and the Enclosure Acts, these alliances cannot be separated from the ascendant fortunes of the middle classes. In this vein, Edward Said situates the narrative momentum of the nineteenth-century English novel within a broader middle-class consolidation of power.

The novelistic hero and heroine exhibit the restlessness and energy characteristic of the enterprising bourgeoisie, and they are permitted adventures in which their experiences reveal to them the limits of what they can aspire to, where they can go, what they can become. Novels therefore end either with the death of a hero or heroine (Julien Sorel, Emma Bovary, Bazarov, Jude the Obscure) . . . or with the protagonists' accession to stability (usually in the form of marriage or confirmed identity, as is the case with novels of Austen, Dickens, Thackeray, and George Eliot).[19]

My reading of Austen's landscapes suggests how the 'restlessness and energy' of Austen's protagonists is conveyed in film language. The pretty countryside affords an empty space, always already available to the eye and to the wanderings of the protagonists. To return from the country walk to the woman at the window, these audiovisual plottings of space and movement are clearly bound up in complex ways with gender. Where Williams and Said do not distinguish between male and female middle-class mobility, for a feminist reading the Austen adaptations map out the limits of historical feminine middle-class mobility and aspiration, while at the same time seeking to overcome them. Rendered through the heightened feminist sensibility of the 90s adaptations, Austen's female protagonists retrospectively long to partake in the acquisitive ramblings of their male counterparts.

A Walk in the Country: Class and Gender Mobility

Austen's writings are frequently seen as bounded miniatures closed to the outside world. For Sandra M. Gilbert and Susan Gubar,

> Austen's self-effacing anonymity and her modest description of her miniaturist art also imply a criticism, even a rejection, of the world at large. For, as Gaston Bachelard explains, the miniature 'allows us to be world-conscious at slight risk.' . . . Austen attempted through self-imposed novelistic limitations to define a secure place. . . . And always, for Austen, it is women – because they are too vulnerable in the world at large – who must acquiesce in their own confinement, no matter how stifling it may be.[20]

In the recent Austen adaptations, these qualities are frequently reworked for feminist critique. Roger Michell's *Persuasion* emphasises Anne Elliot's confinement through extended periods of anxious waiting, often by the window. In contrast, the more adventurous *Emma*, *Jane Austen's Emma*, Rozema's *Mansfield*, *Sense* and *Pride* extend their horizons and pick up the pace to break the still frame of the miniature. The extended walk in *Sense* points to a more broadly dynamic treatment of Austen's narratives, and this subtle shift in emphasis also evokes a feminist craving for female physical and social mobility that is written directly into the script.[21] Screenwriter Thompson wryly notes the problem of physicality for the Dashwood women: '[I was] pulled out of reverie by James [Schamus, co-producer] asking, yet again, what physical activities can be found for Elinor and Marianne. Painting, sewing, embroidering, writing letters, pressing leaves, it's all depressingly girlie. Chin-ups, I suggest, but promise to think further.'[22] Thompson's rewriting of Margaret as a tomboy introduces female physical movement to the restrained spatio-temporal economy of the costume drama. Margaret is continually pictured running, playing in the fields outside of Barton Cottage, mucking about in the pond. Often Elinor, Marianne or Mrs Dashwood watch Margaret play outside from the window, as in the fencing sequence with Edward mentioned above. With her tree house, her atlas, her fearless pirate games, Margaret shifts the film's immobile spatial interior balance outward into the inviting green landscape. Margaret presents a dynamic, moving detail in the otherwise posed, still shots.[23]

To briefly historicise these questions of gender and class mobility, Leonore Davidoff and Catherine Hall chronicle the emergent middle-class distinction between private and public spheres in England of 1780–1850. For these authors, demarcation of the feminine realm of the home corresponds to a broader class-based focus on 'careful regulation of spatial, temporal and social categories'.[24] This social and spatial demarcation was battled out in the countryside through the Enclosure Acts, and through the relegation of middle-class women to the private realm of the family. 'Growing constraints on the physical and social mobility of women, especially young girls, is a motif across a range of activities. Into the early nineteenth century, a great deal of enjoyment was still gained through walking, often combined with dropping in to chat with neighbours or relatives.'[25] From this, Austen's, period onward, Davidoff and Hall note how increasing social pressures made it suspect or even dangerous for a respectable young woman to travel unaccompanied through the countryside. The social and physical mobility accorded to middle-class men of the period was imagined and enacted in relation to the increasing confinement of their female counterparts – as well as the fixed existence of the working class, or, for that matter, the inviting thresholds of colonial lands and peoples.

Written in this context of embattled mobility, Austen's female protagonists tend to walk with a chaperone or in a group. In *Jane Austen's Emma*, the characteristically empty and picturesque countryside twice becomes a place of danger or at least discomfort for ladies out on a walk: when Emma and Harriet Smith are accosted by a ragged group of gypsies, and when their carriage gets stuck in the mud. On both occasions, they are rescued by men on horseback. In *Sense*, Marianne's rainy-weather ramblings precipitate melodramatic physical peril (the quintessential turned ankle and life-threatening 'chill' in two chance downpours) and rescue. Finally, in *Persuasion*, Lydia rashly throws herself over an embankment into the arms of Captain Wentworth, only to incur a concussion. A smirking Frank Churchill (played in Douglas McGrath's *Emma* by a rakish Ewan McGregor) or the inconstant Willoughby (Greg Wise) are dubious heroes, tinging these would-be romantic scenes with irony. Austen's novels, and in turn the adaptations, toy knowingly with melodramatic conventions, although ultimately these dangers constitute plot points, rather than real conditions, and do not really disturb the pastoral English landscape. What is interesting in this intertextual juxtaposition of Austen's social period with her novels, and in turn contemporary adaptations, is how the codes of middle-class femininity and corporeality are constantly reworked.

From a liberal feminist perspective, female access to mobility, even for the middle classes, is rarely self-evident. Austen's heroines, framed at the window, now resonate both as symbols of social constraint and repression and as figures of potentiality. The active female figure is most dramatic in Rozema's *Mansfield* and in *Pride*, where Elizabeth (Jennifer Ehle) strides, cheerful and apple-cheeked, through the countryside. Four out of five of the episodes of this television serial begin with Elizabeth or her sisters out on a country walk. Lizzie meets with the disapproval of the more aristocratic folk at Netherfield when she arrives for a visit with muddy shoes. At Rosings

Park, when admonished to stay inside for her health, she replies: 'I think I've stayed indoors too long. Fresh air and exercise is all I need.' Lizzie's walks evoke an audio-visual and corporeal pleasure in implied freedom of movement. Embodied in the movement-image of the country walk, Lizzie carries an independent, dynamic, freethinking force as a compelling protofeminist heroine. Set against costume drama's predominant physical compression, Lizzie's enjoyment of the walk, with its relative physical freedom, *for its own sake* is particularly poignant in a scene like this one, in which the past is viewed through present exigencies.

John Caughie notes a tension between historical verisimilitude and the contemporaneity of the actor's performance in British classic television serials: 'The furniture may be authentic nineteenth century, but the body of the actor and its gestures are our contemporary.'[26] This critic specifically cites Ehle's performance of Elizabeth. Like Thompson's Elinor, Kate Beckinsale's Emma, Amanda Root's Anne and Frances O'Connor's Fanny Price, Ehle's posture, gestures and attitude evoke a late twentieth-century white femininity. In this sense, British period films enact 'history [as] the present in costume, showing us only human continuities and lingering generalities of tone and style'.[27] If the Austen adaptations dramatise the past through the lens of a liberal feminist present, the lingering continuities of individualism and aspiration persist in these visions – even as its physical embodiment is updated to a more robust assertive 90s female physicality.

For the contemporary feminist viewer – or indeed perhaps as Lionel Trilling suggests, for the modern reader full stop – this dynamic imperative might be traced through different adaptations of *Mansfield Park*. Trilling locates the troubled historical reception of this novel in its insistence on 'cautiousness and constraint. . . . Most troubling of all is its preference for rest over motion.'[28] *Mansfield*'s stasis persists into its 1990 television adapation, easily the least compelling of the 90s Austen cycle. For Trilling, the source of the trouble is Austen's Christian heroine, who piously adheres to duty, peace and security. If the television version suffers from the novel's static pace, Rozema's later film radically transforms Fanny into a romantic feminist heroine. Wryly, critic Jonathan Romney describes O'Connor's Fanny as 'a tough, sprightly minx', where Fanny is enhanced by weaving in 'extracts from the author's own letters and journals in order to replace Fanny the desiccated wallflower with Fanny the dashing literary ironist'.[29] Fanny's wretched confinement to the chilly upstairs nursery of the novel and 1990 version is transformed by Rozema into a source of inspiration, and Fanny commonly appears at a desk by the window penning adventure stories. This romantic imperative to self-expression is paralleled in Fanny's physical transformation. Where the novel dwells on the heroine's frail health, O'Connor's Fanny is robust and energetic as she rough-houses with Edmund (Jonny Lee Miller) and gallops recklessly through the countryside on horseback. Rozema's maverick *Mansfield* crystallises the modern feminist propensity for dynamism, attributing physical, sexual and intellectual energy to its contemporary heroine.

If there is an ambivalence in these layered readings of gendered space and movement, it is deliberate. I maintain a tension between a critical reading of structural power relations and those pleasureable elements of 'movement' that captivate, and transport, the viewer. As Pam Cook suggests of historical costume drama, the sensations of fantastical identification and escape are pivotal to feminist readings of cultural texts. In this

light, the woman at the window might be read as condensing several irreducible qualities of desire: a passive desire for romance and marriage; an acquisitive desire for property and the wealth and rights it imparts; and a desire for physical and sexual freedoms.
Set within past microcosms, these feminist desires are at once complicit with historical
power relations – indeed they cannot be conceived except in relation to class-based and
colonial forms of constraint and mobility – and a form of potentiality that is at once corporeal, discursive and deeply felt.

Ships and Imperialist Movement

The spectre of colonial space lurks just beyond the pages of the nineteenth-century
novel and outside the frame of its adaptations; this space can be read through the
movement-image of the sailing ship. Said notes that 'as a reference, as a point of definition, as an easily assumed place of travel, wealth, and service, the empire functions
for much of the European nineteenth century as a codified, if only marginally visible,
presence in fiction'.[30] Even from Austen's Regency period, the colonies provided a significant register of imagined mobility and possibility in the English realist novel. By
extension, colonialism constitutes a shadowy yet essential aspect of an audiovisual
economy of constraint and movement in contemporary adaptatons. One way of con-
ceiving the place of colonialism in these emphatically domestic English texts is as an
hors champ or 'out-of-field'. Deleuze uses this term with reference to the problem of
framing to describe 'what is neither seen nor understood, but is nevertheless perfectly
present'.[31] If reinserting class into Austen demands the deconstructive tactics of reading against the grain of narrative space to amplify details within the frame, the problem of colonialism necessitates examining what lurks outside the frame altogether.

In parallel with Williams's account of the expulsion of the working class from the
English pastoral novel, the raw materials and cheap labours of the colonies were indispensable to the emergent wealth and culture of the middle classes chronicled by
Austen. Said suggests that as a source of wealth, and as an escape from the constraints
of British society, the fortunes of empire, like class, pervade the nineteenth-century
novel. In *Persuasion*, for instance, Captain Wentworth joins the navy to make his fortune when he lacks the capital to marry Anne; upon his return ten years later, he has
made his fortune of £20,000 by bringing privateers to the West Indies. With their
worldly adventures, William Price and Wentworth and the other sailors of *Persuasion*,
like Colonel Brandon of *Sense*, represent a robust worldly masculinity that contrasts
favourably with the duplicitous and idle Henry Crawford, Mr Elliot and Willoughby.

Where the British Empire figures largely in these works as a constitutive absence,
in *Persuasion* seafaring adventures offer an escape from hypocritical bourgeois morality. Consider, then, the haunting movement-image where Anne Elliot (Amanda Root)
gazes apprehensively out of a second-storey window of a townhouse in Bath. Shot
from street level outside, the character is symbolically imprisoned behind a wrought-
iron grate as she anxiously scans the street below for Captain Wentworth. The most
sombre and socially critical of this cycle, *Persuasion* conveys a profound sense of the
physical and social constraints of a certain feminine experience. Anne voices her condition explicitly, noting the devotion of the 'weaker sex' to the men who come and go
from their lives: 'We do not forget *you* as soon as you forget us. We cannot help ourselves. We live at home, quiet, confined, and our feelings prey on us. You always have

business of some sort or another to take you back into the world.' In contrast to the attenuated yet inviting possibilities offered by the idyllic countryside outside of Elinor's, Emma's, Fanny's and Lizzie's windows, Anne's confinement is much crueller. From her claustrophobic existence as the ill-favoured younger daughter, Anne looks further afield for her escape, toward the spectre of Wentworth's sailing ship. *Persuasion* pointedly foregrounds themes of class and gendered social constraint by juxtaposing the stuffy interiors of mannered society with the inviting open horizons of the sea.

In a departure from the novel, *Persuasion* opens on a rowing boat coming ashore from a navy ship. Returning from the Napoleonic Wars, Admiral Croft and Captain Wentworth, as well as the sailors at Lyme, extend the restless mobility of the emergent middle class from the English countryside out into the colonies. Besides their pointed function as foils to the decadent aristocracy, these kindly sailors offer a link with the exotic and exciting possibilities of the colonies – riches, adventure, war. The romance and promise of empire speaks through the movement-images of sailing ships that bookend the film; from the navy frigate bringing the eligible sailors home at the outset, to Captain Wentworth's ship that bears the happy newly married couple off into the sunset to a soaring romantic love aria. Whereas ships do not explicitly appear in the novel, the film resolves Anne's confinement in an egalitarian marriage that includes Anne in her husband's adventures. (Intriguingly, *Maurice*, *Angels & Insects* and *Desperate Remedies* share this resolution, where star-crossed lovers escape the constraints of society by boarding a ship bound for unnamed shores.)

An earlier sequence in the film dramatises the romantic possibility of travel for women. Speaking to a circle of intent candlelit faces crowded around the dinner table, Admiral Croft's wife Sophie recounts her seafaring adventures: 'In the fifteen years of my marriage, though many women have done more. . . . I have crossed the Atlantic four times, and have been once to the East Indies, and back again.' Like *Persuasion*'s seafaring yarns, Margaret's atlas and pirate games bring the colonial out-of-field into Thompson's feminist rewriting of *Sense*. Colonel Brandon captivates Margaret by telling her that the East Indies 'is full of spices', while the girl's cherished atlas forges an imagined link with distant vistas. Meanwhile, in *Mansfield*, Rozema evicts Fanny's seafaring brother William from her feminist adaptation, developing instead the character of sister Susan. William's adventures are inserted as Fanny's own fantasies; drawn from the young Austen's diaries and narrated by Fanny, the adventurous impetus is reinscribed as part of a nascent feminist fantasy world. These movement-images crystallise 'images of thought' for contemporary Western feminism – an emergent modern female subject who craves travel and adventure beyond her circumscribed domestic sphere.

References to seafaring adventure or the charming movement-image of Margaret Dashwood perched on the tree house surveying the landscape with her glass extend the woman's view from the window through present horizons. Uncertain, humorous, or self-conscious, these vantage points suggest positions of mastery over the view, actual or imagined. On this theme, Inderpal Grewal considers a passage from George Eliot's *Middlemarch* where Dorothea Casaubon watches the farm workers below from her window, suddenly realising that she is no mere spectator in class relations, but that her 'luxurious shelter' derives from these people's labours.[32] At this moment, Dorothea participates, however ambivalently, in the nineteenth-century aesthetic

trope: 'I am the monarch of all I survey.' Grewal suggests that Dorothea's complex alle-
giance to structures of mastery, 'a denial of domination and a parody of power', arises
in late nineteenth-century discourse to produce 'a subject position for middle-class
Englishwomen that is gendered through discourses of class and imperialism'.[33] While
Grewal's reading of Eliot evokes a later historical period, this position extends suggestively to the contradictory liberal feminist desires of the Austen adaptations, and of
costume drama more generally.

If the woman at the window evokes both constraint and potentiality, the 'outside'
to this constrained interior space – class relations, colonialism, and indeed racial and
ethnic 'others' – impinges on the costume drama's careful interiors. In *Mansfield*,
Rozema forcefully imports the colonial out-of-field into the frame from the outset,
when the young Fanny spies a slave ship en route to her new home; this moment is
marked musically by an African song (composed and performed by Salif Keita).
Meanwhile, Rozema rewrites the Oedipal struggle between Sir Thomas and his eldest
son as a moral conflict over slavery – a conflict that is resolved through Tom's collapse
and Fanny's discovery of his violent drawings of the Bertram plantations. In a strange
interpolated scene, Fanny is transfixed by these terrible images of rape and hangings,
underscored by eerie extradiegetic screams and moans. Not unlike the climax of *Jane
Eyre*, where Mrs Rochester's origins are revealed, the violent secret of the Bertrams'
wealth is uncovered as the film takes a Gothic turn. This violent imagery and the
sounds of the out-of-field disturb the contained microcosm of *Mansfield*.

Some critics commented that this film's explicit sexuality, queer erotics and references to slavery were 'heavy-handed' or 'politically correct'. Jonathan Romney writes:
'You want to cry out, as Mary archly does in this version: "This is 1806, for heaven's
sake!" Rozema's film, all superior 1990s hindsight, feels like an A-level gloss designed
to make the story "relevant" to audiences more socially and sexually enlightened than
poor Austen could have been.'[34] Like *Orlando*, *The Piano* or *Daughters of the Dust*,
Mansfield is a watershed film that brings contemporary feminist and postcolonial critique into the frame of costume drama.

Persuasion: Reprise

A series of observations on the representational significance of space and movement
are condensed in one movement-image from *Persuasion*. Reminiscent of *Sense*'s country stroll, this moment transpires during a sea walk at Lyme. Anne and Henrietta stroll
at a deliberate pace toward frame right along the sea wall. This long shot sets them
against a luminous, expansive seascape, the glorious morning animated by a lively
piano score. Away from the prying eyes of Kellynch Hall, the women's every step is
both freer and somehow more weighty with things unsaid. In the midst of this leisurely
stroll, there is a remarkable moment. The camera, almost bored with the slowness, the
agony of this romance that cannot seem to get started, deserts the narrative to follow
a ragged young boy's headlong run as he passes them, moving swiftly toward frame
right along the pier. Digressing for a moment on this detail of pure movement, the
camera briefly lights on another journey distinct from that of the narrative. In keeping
with *Persuasion*'s foregrounding of the sea and its liberating possibilities, this shot
opens up the seaside horizon as the boy runs past a tiny wooden sailing ship. As the
boy passes Captain Wentworth and Louisa walking in the other direction, the camera

Intersecting trajectories of class and movement in *Persuasion*

deserts the boy who runs off frame, instead returning to the narrative where the two pairs meet on the sea wall.

This movement-image expresses several intersecting spatial power relations. Like the scattering sheep, this boy's headlong run (what or who was he running from or to?) functions within the visual economy of the shot as a kinetic counterpoint to the class-designated perambulation of the protagonists. Austen's deliberate country walks and dinner-table conversations function visually (and also audibly) against carefully backgrounded landscapes and social groups. These narratives unfold largely through careful conversation, and in precise diction; consequently, Austen's protagonists can never move too quickly. Along with the genre's constitutive pleasures of costume and *mise en scène*, this narrative economy contributes to costume drama's characteristic stillness. For the spatial choreography of scenes, the camera commonly enters and leaves library or dinner-table conversation on the coat-tails of a servant carrying a tray. In this way, the adaptation situates the novels' rather disembodied conversations and interior monologues, inserting movement and passages between scenes. In class terms, period spectacles of beautifully choreographed balls and mouth-watering feasts are anticipated through the frenetic bustling of servants; even the pointed dinner conversations are facilitated, 'moved along', by gloved hands that reach into the frame to pour or to clear away. In one sense, all of these precise, leisurely narrative moments are brought to us, both literally and formally, by the backgrounded labours of working people.

A topographical approach to the analysis of cultural texts perceives the work of representation as the continuing charting of geographical, social, and corporeal spaces. Michel de Certeau suggests that the work of the story is constantly to mark off space, to symbolically produce (and demolish) imagined social spatial structures. More than mere description, the story becomes a creative act of delimitation.

> It even has distributive power and performative force (it does what it says) when an ensemble of circumstances is brought together. Then it founds spaces. Reciprocally, where stories are disappearing (or else are being reduced to museographical objects), there is a loss of space. . . . By considering the role of stories in delimitation, one can see that the primary function is to *authorize* the establishment, displacement, or transcendence of limits.[35]

Following de Certeau, the contemporary Austen adaptations may be seen as the latest charting of sedimented literary, painterly and audiovisual cultural traditions. At each telling, the story symbolically reconfigures the historical social spaces of late eighteenth- and early nineteenth-century England through the retrospective projections of contemporary cultural producers. In adapting Austen's novels, these films operate, in de Certeau's terms, to 'found' or even 'authorise' the exploration of gendered places and experiences within a representational field still dominated by masculine stories. Given the cultural authority and marketability of Austen's worldview for generations of audiences, especially feminine and feminist audiences, it is illuminating to consider the overlapping spaces, voices and historical trajectories that impinge on the view and desires of the woman at the window.

Coda: *Mansfield Park* and the 'Queer' Sensibility

Austen's fiction offers an influential miniature, firmly demarcating limits and norms. However, in this chapter I have analysed how the very strict limits of Austen's milieu often invite commentary (and sometimes transgression) in contemporary adaptation. Undoubtedly the most politically and formally inventive adaptation is Rozema's *Mansfield*. Often slated for decrying the violent colonial origins of the Bertrams' fortune, the film's daring sexuality stirred up even more controversy. One critic sums up the fuss: 'Despite paying lip-service to civility, Jane-ites tend to be the grumpiest of fans, and many have taken umbrage at Rozema's deviations. . . . Many readers who are usually intelligent become stupid and priggish, as if it is indecent – *indecent*, mind you – to discover sexuality in Austen's novels.'[36] *Mansfield* shares a more explicit sexuality, and an increasingly ironic address, with other Miramax period productions including *Shakespeare*, *The Wings of the Dove*, *The Golden Bowl* and *An Ideal Husband*.

Within the 90s Austen adaptations, the television serial *Pride*, with Darcy's (Colin Firth's) famous nude bathing scene, best foreshadows Rozema's maverick approach. *Pride* was scripted by Andrew Davies, whose robust touch, predilection for outdoor sequences, physical movement and sexual tension has shifted the feel of British television adaptation. With credits including *Middlemarch* (1994), *Jane Austen's Emma*, *Vanity Fair* (1998) and *Tipping the Velvet* (2003), Davies exemplifies the crossover between British television and film production styles. If *Mansfield* incorporates a critical feminist and postcolonial tendency in costume drama, Canadian director Rozema pushes the Austen cycle to new levels of self-consciousness and sexual explicitness. Fanny Price's Christian coming-of-age dilemmas are transformed into a playful economy of desire and embodied female corporeality.[37] Claudia L. Johnson comments that the ball sequence 'is not a set piece of Regency manners, but is shot as a semi-private scene to bring out Fanny's awakening to the pleasure of her body and the circulation of erotic interest between and among the principle couples'.[38] The film's economy of

Queer revisions: Mary (Embeth Davidtz) helps Fanny (Frances O'Connor) out of her negligée in *Mansfield Park*

sexuality is associated with a contemporary vision by critics: 'A thoroughly modern Fanny',[39] 'Not the girl we once knew',[40] 'Fanny Price returns as heroine for our times',[41] or 'Jane Austen's Spice Girl'.[42]

Returning to Caughie's formulation, despite the period garb, the contemporaneity of the actress's body addresses the audience *in the present*. If historical fiction negotiates the 'pastness of the aesthetic object . . . as being in some degree or in some sense *dead*',[43] the infusion of sexuality implies an immediacy and intensity of the cinematic moment. The film's most flagrant transgression of 'polite' period drama arises in an invented scene where Fanny discovers Henry Crawford in bed with Maria Bertram. In this sexually charged atmosphere, Rozema introduces a lesbian frisson between Mary and Fanny, where Mary helps a shivering drenched Fanny out of her negligée. These scenes raised the greatest critical outcry, but a generally lascivious atmosphere pervades the film. Another polymorphously perverse scene marks the arrival of two attractive new neighbours, Henry (Alessandro Nivola) and Mary Crawford (Embeth Davidtz), as they interrupt the vaguely bored Fanny and the young Bertrams at cards. The camera registers the astonishment and delight of the Mansfield Park young people, sketching in their visual appraisal of the new arrivals with two brash slow tilts up and down the visitors' attractive bodies. Then Rozema cuts to a brisk montage with accelerated music that evokes the exciting combinations of players, glances and flirtations.

The scene's non-traditional film language and brisk pace marks its formal departure from standard languid period-drama pacing. For Michele Aaron, the sequence also exemplifies *Mansfield*'s 'queer' sensibility:

> The sexuality of looking is unhooked from its normative roots, and what could be more
> normative or better bred than a costume drama? Despite its achingly straight heritage,
> in Rozema's hands *Mansfield Park* is a queer film indeed. But it is not the quasi-lesbian

encounters between Fanny Price and Mary Crawford that mark it so. . . . Instead, it is the film's creation of a polyvalency of desire, a general air of erotic objectification available to the characters and spectators, unhinged from the conventional love-story trajectory.[44]

Like many critical indictments of Austen's prudishness, Aaron suggests that the 'achingly straight' and 'normative' costume drama almost invites sexual innuendo and queer perversion. If the colonial out-of-field silently informs Austen's ordered white microcosms, the poignant (English) economy of desires unspoken gestures to an out-of-field of polymorphous sexual expression. Clearly the attraction between Mary and Fanny is only momentary, but such moments highlight the sapphic possibilities of costume film's intimate, same-sex spheres – a point that I will elaborate in Chapter Seven.[45]

Notes

1. Pamela Church Gibson points out the film's quotation of Vermeer in her article 'Fewer Weddings and More Funerals: Changes in the Heritage Film', in Robert Murphy (ed.), *The British Cinema Book*, second edition (London: BFI, 2001), p. 117.
2. Richard Dyer suggests that in the musical dance numbers offer the possibility of abundance, release and intensity as an antidote to the 'social tensions' explored in the narrative. This article and his work on 'whiteness' provide important conceptual grounding for my argument. See his *Only Entertainment* (London: Routledge, 1992), pp. 17–34, and *White* (New York: Routledge, 1997).
3. Bakhtin, *The Dialogic Imagination*, p. 248.
4. Other film theorists have also addressed the image of the woman at the window. For instance, see Mary Ann Doane, 'The Woman's Film: Possession and Address', in Gledhill (ed.), *Home is Where the Heart Is*, p. 288; and, in the same book, Elsaesser, 'Tales of Sound and Fury', pp. 61–2.
5. Claire Monk, *Sex, Politics, and the Past* (MA Thesis, Birbeck College, 1994), p. 20.
6. Toni Morrison, *Playing in the Dark: Whiteness and the Literary Imagination* (New York: Vintage Books, 1993), p. 56.
7. See Peter M. Nichols, 'Literary Cycle: Bookshelf, Broadcast, Video Store', *The New York Times* (electronic version), 7 September 1997.
8. Sue Harper, *Picturing the Past* (London: BFI, 1994), p. 132.
9. See Hugh Tomlinson and Barbara Habberjam, 'Translators' Introduction', in Deleuze, *Cinema 1*, p. xi.
10. Raymond Williams, *The Country and the City* (London: Chatto & Windus, 1973), p. 166.
11. Between 1750 and 1830, the English and Scottish countryside was subjected to extensive agricultural 'improvements' including the enclosure of open fields, commons and wastes. While agricultural yields increased, the human costs were high as these changes reduced labourers' access to common lands, effectively consolidating the control of the landowners. See Edward Royle, *Modern Britain: A Social History 1750–1997* (London: Arnold, 1997), pp. 1–3.
12. Richard Dyer, 'Feeling English', *Sight and Sound*, March 1994, pp. 16–19.
13. Claudia L. Johnson, 'Run mad, but do not faint', *Times Literary Supplement*, 31 December 1999, p. 16.

14. For instance, two influential earlier versions of *Pride* (Robert Z. Leonard's classic 1940 film and the 1979 television serial scripted by Fay Weldon) situate the drama substantially indoors, in stark contrast with Simon Langton's 1995 version.

15. Andrew Higson, 'The Heritage Film and British Cinema', in Andrew Higson (ed.), *Dissolving Views* (London: Cassell, 1996), pp. 239–40.

16. See John Berger, *Ways of Seeing* (London: Penguin Books, 1972), and Dennis E. Cosgrove, *Social Formation and Symbolic Landscape* (London: Croom Helm, 1984).

17. Gillian Rose, *Feminism & Geography* (Minneapolis: University of Minnesota Press, 1993), p. 91.

18. Ibid., p. 93.

19. Edward Said, *Culture and Imperialism* (New York: Vintage Books, 1992), p. 71.

20. Sandra M. Gilbert and Susan Gubar, *The Madwoman in the Attic* (New Haven: Yale University Press, 1979), p. 108.

21. For a phenomenological account of feminine corporeal kinesis, see Iris Marion Young, 'Throwing Like a Girl', *Throwing Like a Girl and Other Essays in Feminist Philosophy and Social Theory* (Bloomington: Indiana University Press, 1990), pp. 141–59.

22. Emma Thompson, *Jane Austen's Sense & Sensibility: Screenplay and Diaries* (London: Bloomsbury Publishing Limited, 1995), p. 208.

23. Kristin Flieger Samuelian argues that Margaret's 'healthy nonconformity' presents the most explicit protest to the injustices suffered by the Dashwood women (notably their eviction from Norland). See her ' "Piracy is our only option": postfeminist intervention in *Sense and Sensibility*', in Linda Troost and Sayre Greenfield (eds), *Jane Austen in Hollywood* (Lexington: University of Kentucky Press, 1998), p. 149.

24. Leonore Davidoff and Catherine Hall, *Family Fortunes: Men and Women of the English Middle Class, 1780–1850* (London: Hutchinson, 1987), p. 319.

25. Ibid., p. 403.

26. Caughie, *Television Drama*, p. 224.

27. Ibid., p. 221.

28. Lionel Trilling, *The Opposing Self* (London: Secker & Warburg, 1955), pp. 210–11.

29. Jonathan Romney, 'Jane Austen's Spice Girl', *The New Statesman*, 3 April 2000, p. 46.

30. Said, *Culture and Imperialism*, p. 75.

31. Deleuze, *Cinema 1*, p. 16.

32. Anthony Page's 1994 BBC adaptation of *Middlemarch* includes frequent shots of Dorothea at the window. However, her attitude is much more one of confinement than mastery, or even reverie.

33. Inderpal Grewal, *Home and Harem* (Durham: Duke University Press, 1996), p. 24.

34. Romney, 'Jane Austen's Spice Girl', p. 46

35. Michel de Certeau, *The Practice of Everyday Life* (Berkeley: University of California Press, 1984), p. 123.

36. Johnson, 'Run mad', p. 16.

37. Rozema comments: 'There is an atmosphere in this novel of sexuality, even sometimes unwholesome sexuality, that I think I'm completely justified in bringing to the fore. . . . I think there's a very good chance that a wealthy group of attractive young people with a lot of time on their hands would have been very physically aware

of each other.' Quoted in Carol Allen, 'Empowering Austen', *The Times*, Section 2, 30 March 2000, p. 24.

38. Johnston, 'Run mad', p. 17.

39. Anthony Quinn, *Independent Review*, 31 March 2000, p. 10.

40. *Evening Standard*, 30 March 2000, p. 30.

41. Adam Mars-Jones, *The Times*, Section 2, 30 March 2000, p. 22.

42. Romney, 'Jane Austen's Spice Girl', p. 46.

43. Lionel Trilling, 'Why We Read Jane Austen', in Diana Trilling (ed.), *The Last Decade: Essays and Reviews, 1965–75* (Oxford: Oxford University Press, 1982), p. 219.

44. Michele Aaron, 'The New Queer Spectator', unpublished conference paper, 'Persistent Vision', San Francisco, June 2001.

45. For a 'queer' reading of Austen's novels, see Eve Kosofsky Sedgwick, *Tendencies* (Durham: Duke University Press, 1993), pp. 109–29.

Chapter Two
Houses of Fiction

In the preface to *The Portrait of a Lady*, Henry James famously evokes 'the house of fiction', a metaphor highlighting the spatial figures in his writing.

> The house of fiction has in short not one window but a million. . . . These apertures, of dissimilar shape and size, hang so, all together, over the human scene. . . . They are but windows at the best, mere holes in a dead wall, disconnected, perched aloft; they are not hinged doors opening straight upon life. But they have this mark of their own that at each of them stands a figure with a pair of eyes, or at least with a field-glass.[1]

With its windows and watching figures, this trope foregrounds literary devices of point of view and narration. In cinematic adaptation, these qualities become compressed into dramatic interior spaces criss-crossed by watchful gazes and self-conscious framings through windows and doorways. This chapter extends James's literary trope to suggest the structuring and symbolic centrality of the 'house of fiction' to costume drama, especially the influential adaptations of Regency, Victorian and Edwardian novels. For James, the literary house of fiction has 'not one window but a million'; similarly, films set in these periods are conjoined intertextually through their reinscriptions and renovations of familiar renditions of the house of fiction: the melodrama of confinement and lingering desire (*Washington Square* (1997)), the comedy of manners (*An Ideal Husband*), upstairs/downstairs class dramas (*The Remains of the Day*), or domestic zones tainted with illicit sexuality (*Angels & Insects*). A widely intelligible and generative chronotope, the house of fiction conveys specific connotations and narrative dilemmas to audiences across disparate historical and geographical locations.

Country houses and large suburban homes offer rich sites for analysing the dramatic and symbolic stakes of contemporary costume film. On a scenic level, the houses' names and *mise en scène* convey the personalities and affective states of their occupants. For instance, in *Portrait* Gilbert Osmond's 'museum' is stuffed with desiccated art treasures demonstrating his impeccable taste, with Isabel as just another exquisite acquisition. Osmond's villa exemplifies how houses signify through historical and geographical location, social position and taste; in the Austen, Forster, Wharton and James adaptations, the characters' wealth and class status are precisely demarcated through the size, furnishings and location of their residences. The house of fiction becomes a dramatic focus for gender and class struggles over ownership and authority epitomised in the dispute over the inheritance of Norland Park (*Sense and Sensibility*) or Howards End.[2] Finally, these affluent townhouses and country manors house generic set pieces for romantic trysts, polite social interaction, and private unspoken anguish. Houses of fiction and their precisely coded rooms constitute affectively charged interiors where intimate dramas of desire and mannered social critique unfold.

If Chapter One reads from the woman at the window *outward* to demarcate the discursive limits of costume drama as microcosm, in this chapter I might begin again from the woman at the window to read *inwardly* toward interior spatial motifs as figures of subjectivity and desire. Within the house of fiction, qualities of interiority, deep feeling and desire are rendered cinematically through *mise en scène*, lighting, framing, music and duration. These qualities can be read through recurrent movement-images: the opera, the writing desk and the letter, and the ball. Borrowing from the common cultural source of the realist novel, these interior movement-images invoke the characters' private consciousness and deepest passions. As contemporary 'images of thought', these enclosed figures can be read as retrospective forms of bounded subjectivity – and, in turn, as moments in costume film's traffic of desire.

Victorian and Edwardian period films especially accentuate a repressive interior spatial economy where transgressive desires erupt within highly regulated societies. This spatial economy is often represented by oppressive houses of fiction (Howards End, Washington Square, Darlington Hall), each a material sedimentation of class and patriarchal order. Near the end of *Innocence*, for instance, Newland Archer (Daniel Day-Lewis) sits in their stuffy parlour opposite his wife May (Winona Ryder), who embroiders contentedly, seemingly oblivious to his passion for Countess Ellen Olenska (Michele Pfeiffer). In a fit of frustration, Newland strides over to the window and leans his head out. Gently, May admonishes him: 'Newland Archer, you'll catch your death.' The window is closed, the husband safely enclosed and Ellen's cosmopolitan world shut outside. The still parlour's cluttered Victorian fittings powerfully convey the stifling convention of Newland's marriage, and, significantly, it is now a male protagonist who lingers by the window.

Released in 1994 alongside Campion's *The Piano*, Scorsese's prestigious film takes its place among a series of films that recentre masculine interiority and desire within the genre. Since the 90s, costume drama has been fuelled by popular feminist projects such as *Sense and Sensibility*, *The Piano* and *Elizabeth*; in turn, politically and formally inventive films such as *Orlando*, *Daughters of the Dust*, *Edward II* and *Gosford Park* are enabled by the critical energy and popularity of the broader genre. However, another group foregrounds male protagonists through nostalgic prisms of repression and (thwarted) desire. Stanley Kubrick's *Barry Lyndon* (1975), starring Ryan O'Neal, was the first of several Anglo-American auteurist costume films featuring headlining American (and sometimes British) stars. Commonly quoting classic art films, these films are marketed on the strength of male auteurs and period spectacle. For instance, *Innocence* is celebrated in a 14-page full-colour spread in *Empire* magazine, where Scorsese is lauded as 'America's greatest living director': 'It is Scorsese's delight to enter Merchant Ivory territory and leave his unmistakable mark, as in exuberant overhead shots of ballroom strutters or dining-table schemers.'[3]

In scope, budget, marketing, distribution and star power, Scorsese's *Innocence*, Roman Polanski's *Tess* (1979), Milos Forman's *Amadeus* and *Valmont*, Stephen Frears's *Dangerous Liaisons* and Francis Ford Coppola's *Bram Stoker's Dracula* differ from the more prevalent 'miniatures' of 80s and 90s costume film. While interesting for their sensitive and suffering male protagonists, these projects share with some smaller-scale works a masculinist desiring economy of lack.[4] Women are consistently figured as receding objects of desire (the romance) and/or, as I discuss in Chapter Four, the muse (the historical biopic depicting male genius at work) in *The Remains of the Day*, *Shadowlands* (1993), *Immortal Beloved*, *Onegin*, *Pandaemonium*, *The Wings of the Dove* and *Shakespeare in Love*. This chapter addresses the house of fiction as a series of figures of bounded sites of interiority and desire. As I foreground a specific suffering and nostalgic mode of masculinity, I make reference to the male protagonists of *Innocence*, *The Remains of the Day*, *The Wings of the Dove* and *Dangerous Liaisons*.

At the Opera: Interiority and Expression

Scorsese's adaptation of Edith Wharton's *The Age of Innocence* perfectly evokes the American Victorian house of fiction. Set in the subtle but ironclad social topography of 1870s 'Old New York', Scorsese's film is a masterpiece of psychological compression. The parlour scene described above encapsulates how Newland is progressively trapped within a conventional marriage. As the director remarks in an interview: 'All the details build up, almost like building a wall, brick by brick, around Newland Archer, so that he simply couldn't escape. … It's like a prison.'[5] Scorsese's film combines the sexual and emotional constraint of this Victorian house of fiction, the romantic promise of expression and deep feeling, and a pervasive self-consciousness of address that provokes an ambivalent distantiation.

Innocence begins at the opera during a scene of Gounod's Faust. From the credit sequence of voluptuous red flowers shot in close-up with time-lapse photography laid over an intricate lace pattern, the film cuts to a bouquet of yellow roses on the opera stage. Two singers perform a passionate duet, and the film cuts to a white rose on Newland's lapel. Newland, the lover, is introduced through the flowers, signifiers of pure feeling. Flowers appear throughout the film, as unobtrusive bouquets that offset the mannered decor, and as anonymous missives of love, representing the fragile intensity of passion within a coldly calculating social order. At moments when the characters are overwhelmed with passion, the flowers' vivid primary colours fill the screen with 'vaporous red or yellow as if perception was suffused, completely coloured by emotion; rising in on the lovers and then dropping out the sound so it seems that for each of them nothing exists but the other'.[6] The opera scene demonstrates the film's overarching double address, where an initial (romantic) saturated colour and sound soon gives way to more worldly dynamics.

As is common with opera and theatre scenes in *Dangerous Liaisons* and *The House of Mirth*, the characters appear oblivious to the music or theatre as they relentlessly survey one another. Pointedly, Scorsese introduces a rapid montage of the audience's finery: necklace, waistcoat, watch chain, hair ornament. This striking montage presents a detail of visual irony where crass display and social positioning jars with the pure affective register of the music. Newland sits in a box seat with two gentlemen who tirelessly scan the audience with opera glasses, lighting on three women in an opposite box. Lawrence Lefferts (Richard E. Grant) comments waspishly to his neighbour about Countess Olenska's brazen appearance in public with May Welland and her mother. Without comment, Newland joins the three women. He talks fondly with

At the opera in *The Age of Innocence*: spectacle, surveillance and emotional constraint

his fiancée, May (clad in virginal white), and is soon introduced to the exotic Ellen, who wears a shimmering blue dress. Day-Lewis's performance as Newland is restrained and completely unreadable as he exchanges pleasantries with the countess. However, their meeting is pointedly juxtaposed with the rising climax of the love aria, setting the stage for Newland at the apex of a romantic love triangle. Finally, the camera returns to the singers to end the scene neatly on a shot of the opera house from the point of view of the performers as the audience bursts into thunderous applause.

This monumental opening scene signals a drama intense and larger than life in its emotional range. Scorsese consistently uses music, colour and *mise en scène* to evoke Newland's psychological state, even though few clear signs of the protagonist's increasing agitation can be seen in his demeanour. In fact, Newland's sensitivity and reticence renders the unconsummated extramarital passion with Ellen all the more poignant. The insistent ritual and theatricality of this opening scene also underscore how these melodramatic expressive codes are overlaid with a self-conscious visual style and narration. A preface to a tragic love story, the operatic setting, with its self-conscious editing and virtuoso travelling shots, also implies a studied artifice.[7] A related stylistic element introduced in this scene is the voice-over narration read by actress Joanne Woodward, who voices Wharton's biting authorial commentary. For instance, as the audience streams out of the hall, she comments: 'Americans want to get away from amusement even more quickly than they want to get to it.'

Scorsese's insistence on both diegetic and extradiegetic verbal and visual commentary refracts the film's address into a series of concentric and knowing frames. Intense and fleeting qualities of passion are set against the superficial conventions of the period, while a self-consciousness of form and narration presents the microcosm of tragic romance at an ironic and contemplative remove. Temporal gaps are important to this distantiation, and the film is three times retrospective: at the end, the storyline is revealed as Newland's recollections of the great lost passion of his younger life, Wharton's 1920 novel recalls her childhood 1870s New York,[8] and Scorsese respectfully adapts a classic American novel. This self-referentiality extends to the history of cinema, and *Innocence* is steeped in references to auteurist costume film. The soaring tunes of the opera's love aria and the dark reds of the curtains and seats are reminiscent of the opening scene of Visconti's *Senso*; as with *Senso*, Scorsese's film lovingly invokes the decline of a decadent era of grandeur and beauty, lingering palpably on the moment of loss. Sensuous flowers are destined to wither, the tyrannical but beautiful society is evoked in painstaking period detail on the brink of its decline. Pivotal to the film's nostalgia is a masculinist narrative that scripts Michelle Pfeiffer as the perfect receding object of desire, which can be traced through the film's sophisticated use of period detail and costume.

Part of what sets Ellen apart from her demure cousin May is the 'inappropriate' flashy blue dress she wears at the opera. Discourses of costume and comportment foreground seething undercurrents of corporeality and sexuality, for 'if dress is a social form, as surrogate for the body it also partakes of the body's relation to psyche and desire. Clothing is a compound medium and critical axis of the social (law), the sexual (fantasy), the figural (representation) and the individual (will and desire).'[9] In the opening scene, Ellen's iridescent blue dress announces Pfeiffer's star presence and accentuates her character's suspect sexuality. Unwittingly, she makes a similar gaffe at the Van der Luydens' dinner party, where a bold red dress betrays Ellen's tainted Bohemian European past; the social response provoked by the unfortunate dress piques Newland's compassion, but it also transforms Ellen into a fetish object, setting her apart as the exquisite object of the male gaze. Terence Davies's *Mirth* deploys a parallel costuming strategy where Lily Bart's red dress stands out as a visual affront to the surrounding throng of sombre clothes in a striking shot that captures the audience ascending the steps to the opera house. As with Ellen, this dress marks out Lily as a sexualised body outside the law, and indeed it is her compromised exchange with Gus Tenor after the opera that begins her social fall.

Victorian period dramas rely on a repressive sexuality that emerges not only in *mise en scène* and narrative, but through a costume fetishism 'on the cusp between display and denial, signalling as much a lack as a presence of sexual desire, through which it is especially relevant to films that depict a past, less ostensibly liberated age'.[10] This gendered play of display and denial figures centrally in *Innocence*. In contrast with Ellen's vivid attire, Newland's clothes are drab and conventional, exactly matching those of other young men down to the identical flower on the lapel.

Newland's buttoned-up clothes and performance form an integral aspect of Scorsese's careful cataloguing of Victorian repression. Events such as the opera, the Beauforts' opera ball and the Van der Luydens' dinner party encapsulate a combination of compressed spatiality, an agonisingly slow tempo of leisured bourgeois life and ritualistic codes of decorum. These elements together create an almost unbearable pressure on the lovers. Nowhere is this dynamic clearer than in a carriage journey after Newland's marriage, when the pair steal a few precious moments alone. In desperation, Newland pulls down Ellen's glove to kiss her wrist in the carriage. Within the scene's spatial and temporal compression, this kiss only briefly punctures a simmering, repressed eroticism.

The Age of Innocence: in the carriage: a moment of release in an agonising economy of spatial and emotional repression

Stella Bruzzi argues that this scene (as when Newland kisses Ellen's shoe) indicates a 'costume fetishism' that renders the past strange. In contrast with the realist strategy (exemplified by the Austen adaptations) that 'looks through clothes' to the character underneath, this film opts 'to look at clothes [in order to] create an alternative discourse, and one that usually counters or complicates the ostensible strategy of the overriding narrative'.[11] While I would concur that costume becomes a powerful mode of social commentary in *The Piano*, *Orlando*, *Daughters of the Dust* and *Angels & Insects*, Scorsese's film ultimately reinscribes the cinematic convention of the female body as fetish for the male gaze. As Belén Vidal observes, the film's romance narrative unfolds 'in the purest Lacanian sense: feminine subjectivity is conspicuously absent, and desire is triggered by a chain of partial objects. A glove, a lost umbrella, a key; they all become replacements for the unreachable female body.'[12]

In contrast with the retrospective dynamism attributed to Austen's heroines, *Innocence*'s leading women are radiant images to be cherished and frozen in time. Character development, complexity and interiority rest with the male protagonist, and the voice-over at the end of the film reveals that Newland's sacrifice as a 'dutiful and loving father and a faithful husband' preserved a conventional marriage. In a nod to the confining and ultimately comforting solidity of the house of fiction, Scorsese incorporates a 360° panning shot of the parlour in a concluding ellipsis. With this shot, the furnishings change to mark time passing, but the library remains essentially constant even as Newland has failed to break free of the convention that this room represents. Gently, the voice-over notes: 'It was the room in which most of the real things in his life had happened', including his children's christenings and marriage announcements. *Innocence* retrospectively critiques the crippling emotional costs of Victorian social conformity, but, paradoxically, it is this very suffering that elevates Newland as a figure of both identification and desire.

Innocence follows an understated costuming strategy for its hero that invites the viewer to 'look through' the clothes to the person beneath. Newland's very plainness affords a rich development of character, and the meaningful gaps, hesitations and silences of Day-Lewis's performance invite interpretation. Melodrama relies on a distinction between what is felt and what can be said in carefully monitored social situations, and its affective power emerges from what cannot be said, and from actions not taken. Ultimately, for Brooks, the dramatic energy of melodrama is bound up with a pressure and desire for 'expression' against a silencing, repressive milieu, and Newland's struggle to articulate his feelings is symptomatic of a 'text of muteness',[13] a struggle for authentic expression. Scorsese uses cinematic codes of music and *mise en scène* to evoke Newland's inner state; further, the narrator also gently probes Newland's unspoken inner feelings. If Newland's sartorial conformity and restraint connote repression, the film's drive toward emotional expression is displaced partly onto the female narrator, who reveals a vivid and unique masculine consciousness.

Newland's depth of characterisation contrasts sharply with an emphasis on display that flattens female characters into ornamental place holders in the film's love triangle. Beside Ellen's elaborate garb, May's virginal whites and pastels suggest her 'emptiness' and lack of imagination, as the narrator intones: 'But what if all her calm, her niceness, were just a negation, a curtain dropped in front of an emptiness?' It is only at the film's conclusion that May's awareness of her husband's extramarital passion, and consequently her greater complexity, is revealed. Through his passion for the unconventional Ellen, Newland is transformed and differentiated from the other men of his generation. Amy Taubin describes the most 'haunting and relevatory' image of *Innocence*: 'A slow-motion shot of a crowd of men in identical bowler hats walking towards the camera . . . Newland is about to be engulfed by these men whose hats are a sign of the conformity he fears – the conformity of men who've learned to keep it all under their hats.'[14] This scene brilliantly encapsulates Newland's struggle to forge a sensitive individuality at odds with a prevailing conformity.

Denis de Rougemont argues that the myth of true love as suffering is central to the Western psyche. For this theorist, tales of impossible love are most moving, and in this 'etymology of passions', the life-threatening trials of true love forge a path to self-awareness: 'Why is it that we delight most of all in some tale of impossible love? Because we long for the *branding*; because we long to grow *aware* of what is on fire inside us. Suffering and understanding are deeply connected; death and self-awareness are in league.'[15] Passion as an epiphany that transforms the feeling subject is a fundamental Western discourse.

> Our eagerness for both novels and films with their identical type of plot; the idealized eroticism that pervades our culture and upbringing and provides the pictures that fill the background of our lives; our desire for 'escape', which a mechanical boredom

exacerbates – everything within and about us glorifies passion. Hence the prospect of a passionate experience has come to seem the promise that we are about to live more fully and more intensely. We look upon passion as a transfiguring force, something beyond delight and pain, an ardent beatitude.[16]

In *Innocence*, the audience comes to understand Newland even as he becomes aware of himself through the great suffering of love. A romantic discourse of love promises a transformation of the self through suffering and intensity of feeling. This is one of the great pleasures of costume drama, and nowhere is the narrative more poignant than in tales of star-crossed lovers.

Day-Lewis's Newland finds a kindred spirit in Anthony Hopkins' middle-aged Edwardian men who ponder their lives in disappointment at the 'remains of the day'. Hopkins achieves a signature English masculinity painfully encumbered by social codes of emotional restraint in the Merchant Ivory films *Remains* and *Howards End* and Richard Attenborough's *Shadowlands*. Adapted from Kazuo Ishiguro's novel, *Remains* (like *Innocence*) dramatises an impossible passion between Stevens the butler (Hopkins) and the housekeeper Miss Kenton (Emma Thompson). Imprisoned by an emotionally inarticulate, 'proper' servant-class masculinity, Stevens is unable to act on his passionate feelings for Miss Kenton. The film begins in 1956 as the ageing Stevens reflects through flashback on events of the 30s leading up to the war. A common homology between the self and the house of fiction is pronounced in *Remains*, where Stevens blindly commits his life to Darlington Hall and its owners. When Miss Kenton announces her impending marriage, his distraught response is: 'The house shall miss you.' The only time that the two spend together informally is in 'the remains of the day', when they share a cup of cocoa and discuss the day's events. Within a stultifying economy of emotional repression, their mutual passion is never broached, and these encounters are even more powerful for the pressure of what is not said.

The Remains of the Day: inarticulate masculinity and the pressure of what is not said

As with *Innocence*, the filtering of these events through the memory of its protagonist produces an obsessive structure that returns insistently to moments of encounter and loss. Flashbacks are signalled with shots through windows or an oval glass in a door through which Stevens spies Miss Kenton, and this surreptitious, anguished gaze encapsulates a dynamic of desperate longing. Despite their mutual attraction, neither character is able to express their feelings. The final scene returns to the film's present of 1956, when an older Stevens visits Miss Kenton (who has now left her husband) in the West Country. At the end of the visit, the two stand together in the rain awaiting Miss Kenton's bus. As the bus arrives, the lovers are once again separated and, once again, nothing is said. John Orr notes a contemporary resonance for these scenes of loss: 'There may be a chasm of distance between us now and this brief encounter in an English country house sixty years ago. Yet the poignancy of waste goes beyond this confined world to strike a deeper chord. We all fear the wrong move that leads to emotional sterility and loss.'[17]

The wounded rigidity of Hopkins' performances in *Remains* (as in *Shadowlands* and *Howards End*) suggests an old-fashioned, unbending masculinity that becomes an object of desire and sympathy. These performances are encoded with a particular English emotional reticence described by Richard Dyer in relation to *Shadowlands* and *Brief Encounter*: 'Feeling is expressed in what is not said or done, and/or in the suggestiveness of settings, music and situation.'[18] Where Dyer associates such emotional reticence with 'Englishness', it finds parallels in James's and Wharton's American Victorians. These examples signal a widespread masculine quest for emotional expression. The drama of the 'text of muteness' is rehearsed again and again by Colin Firth's Darcy (*Pride*), Hugh Grant and Alan Rickman (*Sense*), Ciaran Hinds (*Persuasion*), Ralph Fiennes (*Onegin*), Harvey Keitel (*The Piano*), Gary Oldman (*Immortal Beloved* and *Bram Stoker's Dracula*), and Mark Rylance (*Angels & Insects*). Filtered through the prism of the past, the discourse of 'exquisite anguish' reveals, and sometimes redeems, masculinity's hidden emotional world.

But how do these treatments of masculinity function for contemporary audiences? Part of the answer to this query lies in a predominantly heterosexual female audience's desire for strong and sensitive male romantic leads. Male love interests in the Austen films (notably Colin Firth's Darcy) present perhaps the best example. The later *Bridget Jones's Diary* (2001) trades on a virtually identical performance by Firth; the successful repetition of his smouldering and inexpressive masculinity within a contemporary romantic comedy implies a concomitant projection of contemporary ideals of romance and masculinity onto period dress. Similarly, the ubiquitous Hugh Grant moves effortlessly between frequent period roles, in *Maurice* and *Sense*, for instance, and identikit bumbling male leads in *Four Weddings and a Funeral* and *Notting Hill* (1999). A related type that plays well in present popular culture is the Edwardian Englishness of *Chariots of Fire*, *Maurice*, *A Room with a View* or *A Passage to India*. Common to fashion magazines of the late 80s, for Sean Nixon this look represents 'on the one hand the assertive masculinity associated with a dominant version of Englishness and on the other the Romantic connotations of narcissistic young manhood'.[19]

Day-Lewis's and Hopkins' more 'difficult', even masochistic male characters present a much more complex challenge. *Innocence* bristles with self-consciousness, and indeed the viewer only gains access to Newland's consciousness through the narrator.

With his hesitations, and his failure as a dashing lover, Newland offers a 'failed' male lead for a classic romance. Does *Innocence* then present a parable for a contemporary (white Anglo-American) masculinity struggling to free itself from a prison of emotional reticence? Or does the film's retrospective stance project the Victorian period as an era of psychological and sexual repression that has been safely surpassed through the steady march of sexual and social liberation? *Innocence* is wryly ambivalent in its retrospective scripting of masculinity and desire, and it is in this that part of the film's fascination lies.

Costume drama affords an unapologetic account of affairs of the heart, but these films' knowing discourse mediates a contemporary postmodern scepticism toward romance. Costume drama's microcosms of the leisured past facilitate passions seemingly extinct in a cultural moment where 'the romantic self perceives itself in the halo of an ironic semiotic suspicion'.[20] If the seeds of the postmodern are often to be found in the modern, the aporia of lost innocence is also part of the knowing 'modern' address of Austen, Forster, Wharton or James. Scorsese weaves Wharton's knowing narrator into *Innocence*, just as the opening line of *Pride* transposes Austen's narrator to Elizabeth's voice-over: 'It is a truth universally acknowledged, that a single man in possession of a good fortune, must be in want of a wife.'

Innocence is exemplary in its doubled address, invoking the compression of the American Victorian house of fiction alongside a knowing vantage point somewhere outside the frame. As an ornately framed microcosm, Scorsese's film exemplifies a masculinist narrative trajectory of repression, suffering and desire. Newland's confinement within his cloying but comfortable brownstone could be seen, following Henri Lefebvre, as part of costume film's continuing 'production of space'. In the next section, I reflect further on the chronotopic significance of the house of fiction with reference to interiority and the medium of the letter.

The Writing Desk and the Letter: Spaces of the Self

For Henri Lefebvre, according to Andy Merrifield, space is 'organic fluid and alive; it has a pulse, it palpitates, it flows and collides with other spaces. And these interpenetrations – many with different temporalities – get superimposed upon one another to create a *present* space.'[21] Capitalist spatiality is comprised of three interrelated elements. First are 'representational spaces' (the *lived space* of users and inhabitants): 'This is the dominated – and hence passively experienced – space which the imagination seeks to change and appropriate. It overlays physical space, making symbolic use of its objects.'[22] Representational or lived space functions in a dialectical relationship with 'representations of space' (*conceived space*, or the vision of scientists, planners, urbanists and social engineers). Finally, the lived space of everyday life and the planners' conceived space are mediated by a third concept, 'spatial practice' or *perceived space*.[23] As a medium that both represents and produces a spatio-temporal imaginary, cinema is perhaps closest to a 'spatial practice' that mediates between structural power relations and everyday life.

Costume films are fascinated by one particular chronotope of anterior lived space, the bourgeois intimate sphere associated with Western modernity. For Lefebvre, lived space is always a social production, a fluid, dynamic realm, 'redolent with imaginary and symbolic elements [with its] sources in history'.[24] Through costume film as a mediating spatial practice, the complexity of historical lived space is bundled into the dramatic form of the house of fiction, a generic container for interiority, desire and romance. At the place and time of cinematic reception, cultural texts are vehicles for reflecting upon present lived spatial relations such as gender and domestic space, class, privilege and privacy, (post)modernity and the pastoral ideal. If lived space in any historical period is 'dominated' and 'passively experienced', for Lefebvre as for de Certeau, then the imagination fuels change, and, clearly, films and other cultural texts inform and enrich the cultural imaginary. Like Bakhtin's artistic chronotope, cinema as a spatial practice is both absorbed and transformed by its participants. In this way, the topography of costume drama participates in a continuing cultural semiosis, a dialogic production of space. These films' bounded interiors constitute an iconic and ideologically laden microcosm, both reinscribing and sometimes rearticulating traditional identities, and psychic and social relations.

Figures at the window and the writing desk convey a bounded subjectivity that values the dreamer and the realm of deep feeling. These recurring interior movement-images represent the place from which a certain model of the Western subject emerges. The conditions of possibility of the modern subject arise symbolically from a mythology of home, an interior and anterior (gendered and classed) place to be overcome and returned to. This iconic site corresponds with Jürgen Habermas's bourgeois intimate sphere of the family, an idealised site that facilitated 'the emancipation . . . of an inner realm, following its own laws, from extrinsic purposes of any sort'.[25] Arising in late eighteenth-century Europe, for Habermas the intimate sphere fosters the masculinist citizen-subject. For many theorists, the emergence of the modern Western subject corresponds with the social production of private space and the literary forms of the letter and the novel.

Ian Watt describes architectural changes in the eighteenth-century Georgian house that accompany 'a much larger change in outlook – the transition from the objective, social and public orientations of the classical world to the subjective, individualist and private orientation of the life and literature of the last two hundred years'.[26] With its construction of individual bedrooms off a long corridor, the Georgian house offered increased privacy, including a 'closet or small private apartment usually adjoining the bedroom'.[27] A place for writing desk and books, this apartment had special social significance for the increasingly leisured middle and upper classes. In eighteenth-century England and France, an associated practice of letter-writing facilitated a 'new pattern of personal relationships made possible by familiar letter-writing, a pattern which, of course, involves a private and personal relationship rather than a social one, and which could be carried out without leaving the safety of the home'.[28] Watt notes how the cult of letter-writing facilitated both 'withdrawal from society, and emotional release'. Similarly, Lovelace writes in *Clarissa*, that 'familiar letter-writing . . . was writing from the heart . . . as the very word "*Cor-respondence*" implied. . . . Not the heart only; the *soul* was in it.'[29]

A common trope in recent costume film, the letter signals cherished discourses of interiority and desire. Movement-images of letter-writing and composition are afforded duration and affective weight in many costume dramas, and the letters themselves stand in for the intimate thoughts and feelings of their writers. For instance, in *Pride and Prejudice*, the aloof Mr Darcy pours out his soul to Elizabeth Bennet in a letter. This extended sequence records the recalcitrant Darcy's suffering as he undertakes the physical torment of writing and a pile of crumpled discarded drafts grows beside his desk. Intercut with flashbacks, Darcy's letter-writing reveals his 'inner self', his childhood, family affiliations and the difficult business with Wickham. Darcy is seated at the writing desk, and the cinematic duration of letter-writing as expression lingers on the 'exquisite anguish' of desire. In *Onegin* (1999), Tatiana (Liv Tyler) places pen and ink on the floor to write a love letter to Onegin (Ralph Fiennes) by candlelight; the camera records in close-up her effort to express her feelings, words crossed out, ink blurred, hesitation, exhilaration.

These scenes are frequently shot in close-up: the hands writing, the pensive face in a darkened room illuminated by an intimate light source (*Emma, Mansfield, Onegin*) or the natural light from the window (*Sense, Pride*). The affective significance of the letter can be read through its framing of the hand or the face in close-up, redolent of Deleuze's 'affection-image', which captures an intensive moment of deep feeling. The close-up may present a 'reflecting surface' ('sometimes the face thinks about something, is fixed on an object' in wonder or admiration) or 'intensive micro-movements' ('what is called *desire*, inseparable from the little solicitations or impulsions which make up an intensive series expressed by the face').[30] For the figure at the writing desk or at the window, reflection and expression/desire are co-present – the two poles of interiority and relationality. The affection-image is also frequently used to record the expressive labour of letter-writing, composition (*Shakespeare, Mansfield, Immortal, Amadeus, Pandaemonium*), or musical performance (the romantic movement-image of the duet in *Washington* or *Emma*). These recurring movement-images highlight qualities of deep feeling and creativity that are cherished within this cycle of films.

As the antecedents of 90s costume film, English and European novels staked out a realm where intimate relationships were valued above all. Richardson, for example, perfected a formal attention to romance and sentimental detail, so that 'his readers found in his novels [a] complete engrossment of their inner feelings, and [a] welcome withdrawal into an imaginary world vibrant with more intimately satisfying personal relationships than ordinary life provided'.[31] The letter as expression links the deep feelings of the lover (the daydreamer at the window) with the beloved. If the Victorian house of fiction is a spatial milieu of repression that generates drama, desire and expression, the letter *travels* – between friends and lovers and across geographical distance. In *Innocence*, the flurry of correspondence between Archer and Ellen underscores the risk of courtship, where clandestine trysts are subject to the uncertain postal medium. The letter and its associated narrative risks, detours and delays instantiate moments of vivid sensation already in the process of being absorbed into the past.

For Roland Barthes, 'love letters' and 'waiting' are two fragments of the lover's discourse, and the letter brings with it the burden of waiting, the 'gap' in time and space that heightens desire.[32] Costume drama's slowness allows not only the leisure of sparkling conversation and lavish attention to period furnishings, but also a languorous, sometimes desperate temporality of waiting, interruption and longing. The desiring trajectory of waiting and loss in *Innocence* adheres to a Lacanian account where 'desire is predicated on lack and even its apparent fulfillment is also a moment of loss'.[33] The device of the letter that arrives too late epitomises the shimmering residue of impossible or squandered passion. Immortalised in *Letter from an Unknown Woman*, this trope recurs in *The House of Mirth* and *The Wings of the Dove, Onegin* and *The Remains of the Day*.

The most dramatic example of the devastating power of the tardy letter occurs in *The Wings of the Dove*. In this film, the acquisitive Kate Croy refuses to marry her lover Merton (Linus Roache) on financial grounds. She masterminds a plan for Merton to seduce Milly (Allison Elliott) a mortally ill American heiress, so that she will leave him her money. Merton finds the plan increasingly distasteful, and a flurry of letters among the characters enacts an economy of deceit. After Milly's death, Kate visits the profoundly shaken Merton in his dingy London flat. Unopened on his desk is a last letter from Milly, presumably a love letter announcing Merton's inheritance. He offers the letter to Kate to test her reaction, and she nonchalantly throws it into the fire to prove that her love for him is greater than her greed.

The letter signifies Milly's ghostly force in the couple's lives from beyond the grave – an influence that cannot be shaken even by Kate's offer of her body (desired by Merton from the outset) and her hand in marriage. After they make love without conviction, with the rain teeming down outside, Kate offers to marry Merton without Milly's money if he swears that he is not in love with Milly's memory. Yet Merton cannot swear, as he is destined to love Milly's memory as he could not love the living woman. The letter, Milly's gracious last gesture, rises above Kate's and Merton's cruel plot, but it destroys their love. Where the novel ends on Kate's and Merton's unhappy break, where 'nothing shall ever be again as it was', the film adds a brief denouement in which Merton returns to Venice. He is haunted by flashbacks of his time with Milly in Venice and in voice-over Milly's voice says: 'I believe in you.' This resolution underscores a narrative resolution through flashback common to *Onegin*, *Dangerous Liaisons* and *Valmont*, where the hero of each film is redeemed by the love and the loss of a good woman.

The narrative of redemption through loss recurs in Stephen Frears's *Dangerous Liaisons*. The letter constitutes both the form and the content of Choderlos de Laclos's epistolary novel, twice adapted in 1989/1990 with *Liaisons* and Milos Forman's *Valmont*. In *Liaisons*, the libertines' tendrils of deceit are disseminated in whispered confidences and through letters composed in collusion with the scheming Vicomte de Valmont (John Malkovich) and the Marquise de Merteuil (Glenn Close). Here, as I will explore further in Chapter Eight, the content of the letter is secondary to its performative capacity to manipulate and wound. This capacity is vividly illustrated in the devastating penultimate scene as Merteuil takes her place at the opera only to find the entire audience staring at her in hatred: upon Valmont's dying instructions, Dançeny has circulated her poisonous letters to reveal her ruthless machinations. In Chapter Eight, I return to the figure of Merteuil, but here I will examine Valmont as another male character who in his suffering experiences the epiphany of love.

If Close, the female villain, is humiliated, Valmont is redeemed in a humanist hermeneutic. As Guy Gautier points out: 'It is essentially Valmont who determines the others' paths and who experiences the most intensive psychological evolution. It is worth mentioning that he is the only significant male character amidst a swarm of women who are the prey to his devastating seductions.'[34] Valmont discovers true love and compassion through the loss of the angelic Madame de Tourvel (again it is Michelle Pfeiffer who plays the lost object of love). In an ending classic to the Western romantic tradition, it is only after a duel with Dançeny at the moment of his death that Valmont declares his undying love for Tourvel. This dying realisation is clinched by a montage of flashbacks that reinflect his relationship with Tourvel through the retro-spective poigancy of love discovered too late.

Letters are commonly linked with flashbacks, a cinematic device that signals loss and regret. Flashbacks structure *Remains*, and provide telling denouements to the tor-mented romances of *Liaisons*, *Wings*, *Immortal*, *Innocence* and *Dracula*. Like the double articulation of voice-over, the flashback offers an exterior (or posterior) perspective on the action that reifies desire as past. Ophuls's *Letter from an Unknown Woman* exem-plifies this trope, where a letter sent by a woman to her lover after her death prompts a series of flashbacks. The letter's effect on the errant lover Stefan (as with Valmont in *Liaisons*) is pedagogical: it is only upon his lover Lisa's death that he can remember or recognise her. As with *Onegin*, *Wings* and *Liaisons*, the letter prompts a memory through which the moment of lost possibility is continually revisited. But as Maureen Turim points out, this structure 'represents the woman as object of spectacle and the gaze, and as a lost object, confined to the past, unknown'.[35] In keeping with this chapter's focus on interiority and bounded subjectivity, this theorist links the cinematic development of the flashback with 'an amplification of the psychological subjectivity of a character'.[36]

The temporal gap afforded by the flashback allows a deepening understanding of character developing through time. Significantly, in the films addressed in this chapter, the male protagonist is afforded a depth and complexity that come with ageing and regret, whereas the female object of desire remains frozen in time. This tendency is encapsulated in the ending of *Innocence*, where, rather than visit Ellen in Paris, the aged Newland bids his son to convey a message to her that he is 'old-fashioned'. Instead of viewing an older Ellen, the film cuts to a flashback of an earlier scene where Newland had sought out Ellen at the seashore; he makes a pact with himself that he will leave May if Ellen turns to him by the time that a boat passes a lighthouse on the horizon. However, Vidal notes that Ellen 'is not going to turn around because she has been given up already for the sake of preserving *her image*'.[37] In the final flashback, Newland returns obsessively to a poignant moment of loss, but this time in his fantasy Ellen turns to him. In this way, through the nostalgic device of flashback, the film pre-serves the timeless pleasures of the female image as displayed for the male gaze.

The Ball and the Sexual Contract

Innocence, *The Remains of the Day*, *Onegin* and *The Wings of the Dove* present instances of a recent, pervasive masculinist house of fiction, where the letter encapsulates a nos-talgic and regretful economy of desire. These films present some of the most poignant (and the most clichéd) romances of contemporary costume film. Qualities of deep feeling are conveyed through recurring 'interior' movement-images of the figure at the window and in the act of letter-writing. Integral to costume drama as a 'production of space', these tropes are closely bound up with discourses of interiority, sentiment and desire. I conclude this chapter by briefly examining the ball as another significant movement-image that transpires within the house of fiction. Like the letter, the ball is deeply implicated in costume film's traffic of desire. Yet, as a semi-public orchestration of courtship and flirtation, the ball brings into relief the wider social relations of costume film.

In her study of English domestic fiction, Nancy Armstrong, like Watt, comments upon the carving out of interiority – both deep subjectivity and a specific historical configuration of class, gender and sexuality. She also claims that, within the influential medium of the novel, 'the modern individual was first and foremost a woman'[38] who 'became an object of knowledge in and through her own writing'.[39] In this account, the (literary) emergence of a bourgeois female subject corresponds with a realignment of social differences into gender differences – a realignment negotiated within the novel through rituals of courtship and an economy of polite language. This economy of sentiment and polite language are pivotal to the erotics of costume film, as is a partic-ular account of individuality and romance. Costume film reproduces these discourses of Western subjectivity and desire, and Stevi Jackson considers

> the way in which Western introspection about our 'feelings' is linked to a definition of
> individuals in terms of unique subjectivities. This is particularly pertinent to the
> emotion we call romantic love since it assumes a coming together of two such unique
> subjects, each of whom should be the 'only one' for the other.[40]

At the forefront of costume drama's pleasures is an exploration of the sensitive, expres-sive self and his/her quest for an amorous merger with another vivid individual. As we see with *Innocence*, the gendering of the vivid individual and the desiring relations of costume film are central to the films' politics. The movement-image of the ball might be seen as a metonym for the social, symbolic and aesthetic structures of costume drama, an intersection between private discourses of interiority and desire, and a broader social milieu. In the Austen adaptations, the ball is a centrepiece of visual spectacle that condenses complex social relations and erotic rivalries. If the coy romances in Austen unfold through a series of stolen trysts – country walks, letters, duets – the ball assembles all of the dramatis personae of the knowable community, encapsulating social allegiances and barriers that both produce and impede romance. For instance, in *Pride*, Darcy first expresses his desire for Lizzie by staring at her obses-sively at Netherfield Ball. Their subsequent bristling confrontation on the dance floor introduces a conflict between 'pride' and 'prejudice', and the ensuing courtship nego-tiates obstacles of misunderstanding and social convention.

Within costume drama's spatio-temporal economy of interiors, the tension between social regulation and renegade desire is played out in a spectacle of costume, music and dance in the set pieces of the ball, the society party, or a public spectacle such as the opera or the theatre. These sites of courting rituals manifest the underlying sexual and economic dynamics of exchange essential to domestic fiction. For Armstrong, Austen's plot lines exemplify how the English domestic novel converts broader social and political conflict into what she calls the 'sexual contract': 'By enclos-ing such conflict within a domestic sphere, certain novels demonstrated that despite the vast inequities of the age virtually anyone could find gratification within this pri-vate framework.'[41] *Pride* is characteristic of this process, where Darcy's and Elizabeth's class differences are reconciled, and 'their union miraculously transforms all social dif-ferences into gender differences and gender differences into qualities of mind'.[42]

The serious business of courtship, social distinction and the landed gentry's exchange of properties, sons and daughters are all orchestrated through the ball's spoken asides, musical interludes, dance, costumed display and eloquent glances. In this contained and carefully monitored social and sexual space, the lovers' tangible

Sense and Sensibility: the mannered, yet intimate movement-image of the ball: playful exchange of partners in dance

longing is heightened by prohibitions that intensify desire. Meanwhile, the mannered-yet-intimate ritual of the dances, with their exchange of partners, playfully stage the films' romantic intrigue. As with costume drama's polyvalent houses of fiction, it is possible to track comparatively the playfulness of Austen's Regency balls through to an increasing airlessness and dramatic compression in the Victorian *Angels & Insects*, *Washington Square*, *The Portrait of a Lady* and the Beauforts' opera ball in *Innocence*. Finally, in the *fin de siècle* settings of *The House of Mirth*, *Wings*, *An Ideal Husband* and *The Golden Bowl*, society parties (as well as theatre or opera scenes, as in *Innocence*) perform some of the ball's functions of narrative consolidation and audiovisual spectacle.

As cherished figures held within costume drama's houses of fiction, the figure at the window, the opera, the love letter and the ball can represent a lost economy of feeling. For Catherine Belsey, the romantic impulse promises authentic emotions that transcend consumerism.

> To the degree that the postmodern condition implies an unbridled consumerism, the cultural logic of late capitalism, pleasure for cash and a product to gratify every possible impulse . . . love is a value that is beyond the market. . . . More than ever, love has come to represent presence, transcendence, immortality, what Derrida calls proximity, living speech, certainty, everything, in short, that the market is unable to provide or fails to guarantee.[43]

Ironically, it is precisely this scarcity of authentic feeling that makes romance such a marketable commodity. Lynne Pearce and Jackie Stacey comment upon the enduring nature of the powerful ideal of romance, where 'its dilution and mass production has *not* brought about its destruction. Against all the odds (social, political, intellectual) the *desire* for romance has survived.'[44]

Costume film's obsessive return to movement-images of deep feeling and desire – the window, the writing desk, the letter – mediate a pervasive sense of loss of an originary plenitude and depth of human experience. In this chapter I have linked this nostalgia with costume films organised around masculine subjectivity and desire. In Chapter Three I once again take up the question of gendered subjectivity and desire within the Victorian house of fiction, with reference to feminist 'anti-romances' *The Portrait of a Lady*, *The House of Mirth* and *Washington Square*. In the spirit of costume film as a continuing production of space (and a site of struggle), the repressive topography of the Victorian house of fiction presents a rich point of departure for revisionism.

Notes

1. James, *The Portrait of a Lady*, p. 7.
2. For Higson, this dispute condenses much broader questions of class and gender at stake in *Howards End*, raising the symbolic question of 'who is to inherit England'. See 'The Heritage Film and British Cinema', p. 239.
3. Angie Errigo, '*The Age of Innocence*', *Empire* no. 56, February 1994, p. 54.
4. The argument in this chapter is greatly indebted to Belén Vidal's identification of a masculinist auteurist cycle of costume dramas. See her 'Classic adaptations', pp. 17–18.
5. Chris Heath, 'Good Fellows', *Empire* no. 56, February 1994, p. 61.
6. Amy Taubin, '*The Age of Innocence*: Dread and Desire', in Vincendeau (ed.), *Film/ Literature/ Heritage*, p. 65.
7. For an insightful account of this scene and of the film more generally, see Lesley Sterne, *The Scorsese Connection* (London: BFI, 1995), pp. 222–52.
8. The novel has been read as a fictionalised treatment of Wharton's parents' marriage. See Cynthia Griffin Wolff, 'Introduction', in Edith Wharton, *The Age of Innocence* (New York: Penguin Books, 1996), pp. xii–xviii.
9. Baert, 'Skirting the Issue', p. 359.
10. Stella Bruzzi, *Undressing Cinema* (London: Routledge, 1997), p. 38.
11. Ibid., p. 36.
12. Vidal, 'Classic adaptations', p. 12.
13. On melodrama's 'text of muteness', see Brooks, *The Melodramatic Imagination*, pp. 56–80.
14. Taubin, 'Dread and desire', p. 65
15. Denis de Rougemont, *Love in the Western World* (Princeton: Princeton University Press, 1956), p. 51.
16. Ibid., p. 16.
17. John Orr, 'Beyond Heritage', *Film West* no. 39, February 2000, p. 24.
18. Richard Dyer, 'Feeling English', *Sight and Sound*, March 1994, p. 16.
19. Sean Nixon, *Hard Looks: Masculinities, Spectatorship and Contemporary Consumption* (London: UCL Press, 1996), p. 191.
20. Eva Illouz, 'The Lost Innocence of Love', in Mike Featherstone (ed.), *Love & Eroticism* (London: Sage, 1999), p. 182.
21. Andy Merrifield, 'Henri Lefebvre: a socialist in space', in Mike Crang and Nigel Thrift (eds), *Thinking Space* (London: Routledge, 2000), p. 171.
22. Henri Lefebvre, *The Production of Space* (Oxford: Blackwell, 1991), p. 39.
23. Ibid., p. 38.
24. Ibid., p. 41.

25. Jürgen Habermas, *The Social Transformation of the Public Sphere: An Inquiry into a Category of Bourgeois Society* (Cambridge: Polity Press, 1992), p. 47. Lauren Berlant influentially extends Habermas's 'intimate sphere' to analysis of contemporary culture. See her 'Introduction', Lauren Berlant (ed.), *Intimacy* (Chicago: University of Chicago Press, 2000), p. 3.

26. Ian Watt, *The Rise of the Novel* (London: Chatto & Windus, 1963), p. 176.

27. Ibid., p. 188.

28. Ibid.

29. Cited in Watt, *The Rise of the Novel*, p. 191.

30. Deleuze, *Cinema 1*, p. 88.

31. Watt, *The Rise of the Novel*, pp. 195–6.

32. See Roland Barthes, *A Lover's Discourse* (London: Penguin, 1979), p. 37.

33. Catherine Belsey, *Desire* (Oxford: Blackwell, 1994), pp. 38–9.

34. Guy Gautier, '*Les liaisons dangereuses: Le livre*', *La Revue du cinéma* no. 448, April 1989, p. 4. [My translation.]

35. Maureen Turim, *Flashbacks in Film* (New York: Routledge, 1989), p. 156.

36. Ibid., p. 149.

37. Vidal, 'Classic adaptations', p. 12.

38. Nancy Armstrong, *Desire and Domestic Fiction* (Oxford: Oxford University Press, 1987), p. 8.

39. Ibid., p. 98.

40. Stevi Jackson, 'Women and Heterosexual Love: Complicity, Resistance and Change', in Lynne Pearce and Jackie Stacey (eds), *Romance Revisited* (New York: New York University Press, 1995), p. 51.

41. Armstrong, *Desire and Domestic Fiction*, p. 48.

42. Ibid., p. 51.

43. Belsey, *Desire*, p. 72.

44. Lynne Pearce and Jackie Stacey, 'The Heart of the Matter', in Pearce and Stacey (eds), *Romance Revisited*, p. 11.

Chapter Three
For Love or Money

Ralph: 'You were the last person I expected to see caught.'

Isabel: 'I don't know why you call it "caught".'

Ralph: 'Because you're going to be put into a cage.'

Isabel: 'If I like my cage, that needn't trouble you.'

Ralph: 'You must have changed immensely. A year ago you valued your liberty beyond everything. You only wanted to see life.'

Isabel: 'I've seen it. And it doesn't look to me now such an inviting expanse.'

Ralph: 'I had treated myself to a charming vision of your future. I had amused myself with planning out a high destiny for you. There was to be nothing of this sort in it. You were not to come down so easily or so soon.'

Isabel: 'Come down?'

Ralph: 'It hurts me – it hurts me as if I had fallen myself.'

Henry James places Isabel Archer, the eponymous heroine of *The Portrait of a Lady*, within a paradoxical and cruel situation aptly described by her cousin Ralph as a cage. The terrible irony of Isabel's trap is that the tremendous breadth of her intellect, aspirations and desires are exactly matched by the massive subtlety of the walls that enclose her. But Isabel is no ordinary fool for love. After refusing two ideal suitors in Caspar Goodwood and Lord Warburton, she sets out to pursue what the latter calls her 'mysterious purposes – vast designs'. Fuelled by Ralph's well-intentioned gift of his inheritance, Isabel's pursuit of an unconventional life leads her to Madame Merle, and eventually into a crushingly conventional marriage to Gilbert Osmond, a man who hates her and seeks to control her. In the face of these obstacles, Isabel emerges as a troubling Jamesean heroine – an expansive and naive 'American girl' whose forthrightness and dynamism are confounded by the complications of romance and marriage within the perilous milieux of England and Continental Europe.

Two present-day feminist dilemmas are encapsulated in Jane Campion's 1996 adaptation of *Portrait*: Isabel's quest to live her life on her own terms, and the pursuit of autonomous female desire. Young, middle class or even rich, attractive and educated – James's heroines explore the horizons opened up by the New Woman[1] in the latter half of the 19th century. Isabel Archer, Catherine Sloper, Milly Theale and Kate Croy each embody the potentiality of middle-class opportunities for education and travel extended to young ladies of the period. Yet each, in her own way, eventually finds herself in the Jamesean cages of marriage, romantic desire, poverty, or social convention. The tremendous resilience of these bars is that they are forged both by external forces and by the characters' deepest desires. James's and Wharton's heroines are rendered in 90s feminist cinema as portraits of complexly contained femininity.

In an influential reading of nineteenth-century women's writing, Gilbert and Gubar trace a pervasive 'spatial imagery of enclosure and escape, elaborated with what frequently becomes obsessive intensity'.[2] In this account, Jane Austen, Emily Dickinson, the Brontë sisters and Charlotte Perkins Gilman share a tradition of using 'houses as primary symbols of female imprisonment . . . to enact their central symbolic drama of enclosure and escape'.[3] While most frequently this topography is a way of dramatising feminine experience, these authors also point out that male writers such as Dickens, Poe, James and the English Romantics also use dramatic imagery of containment. For these authors, 'the distinction between male and female images of imprisonment is – and always has been – a distinction between, on the one hand, that which is both metaphysical and metaphorical, and on the other hand, that which is social and actual'.[4] Although this account rests on essentialist notions of gendered expression, this distinction neatly distinguishes between the spatial compression of *Innocence* and the 'trapped femininity' that is the subject of this chapter.

Against the levity of Austen romances or the poignant romanticism of *Liaisons*, *Onegin* or *Immortal Beloved*, James's recalcitrant 'anti-romances' challenge the pleasures of romantic closure. While, as Armstrong asserts, Austen's novels convert vast social differences into the 'sexual contract' of the domestic sphere, James's house of fiction (romance, marriage, family relations) is tainted with money and power relations. It is this aspect of James that has proven so germane to the feminist adaptations addressed in this chapter: *Portrait* and Agnieszka Holland's *Washington Square*. Edith Wharton shares much literary ground with James, and in this chapter I also address Terence Davies's adaptation of *The House of Mirth* as another film that grapples with the problem of woman as both subject and object of the text. These films share the auteurist ambitions of *Innocence*, and similarly probe the desiring relations within a Victorian house of fiction, but they challenge the pervasive masculinist script of woman as (lost) object of desire. In contrast with the preceding chapter's psychoanalytic account of a dominant form of repressive spatiality that produces (masculine) desire, I turn here to Deleuze's 'action-image'; here, the microcosm becomes a field of force, within which struggles unfold over the gendered organisation of agency and desire.

James's writings have been widely adapted into prestigious films including William Wyler's classic *The Heiress* (1949), Jack Clayton's *The Innocents* (1961), Peter Bogdanovich's *Daisy Miller* (1974) and the Merchant Ivory productions *The Europeans* (1979) and *The Bostonians* (1984). Subsequently, following the logic of the branding of authors of classic literature, in the wake of Forster and Austen, many of James's novels have been taken up in the 90s.[5] Along with *Portrait* and *Square*, 90s James feature-film adaptations include Softley's *The Wings of the Dove* and James Ivory's *The Golden Bowl*. James's 'melodramas of consciousness' are notoriously difficult to adapt for the screen.[6] These problems arise most obviously in Merchant Ivory's failed *Bowl*. In general, the 90s James films are uneven, with *Wings* as perhaps the most coherent and accomplished of the cycle. (As neither *Wings* nor *Bowl* is especially feminist, they are analysed in Chapters Two and Four respectively, while *The Bostonians* is examined in Chapter Seven.)

Prestige productions featuring bankable directors and actors, *Square*, *Portrait* and *Mirth* share little of the international popularity of the Austen and Forster adaptations, or the critical acclaim and commercial success of *Innocence* and *Liaisons*.[7] *Square* was received indifferently by critics and audiences alike, while Campion's eagerly awaited successor to *The Piano* was a box-office flop; widely reviewed, *Portrait* was also commonly read as an interesting but failed experiment. In spite of its tiny budget,[8] *Mirth* garnered the most consistent critical accolades, at least in the UK, as an accomplished auteurist production. Paradoxically, some of the reasons for their uneven reception at the box office make these three films particularly interesting for this book. Sharing *Innocence*'s repressive Victorian house of fiction, each of these films grapples with cinematic *form* to convey attenuated accounts of feminine desire and agency against powerful constraining forces.

In the Jamesean Cage: *Washington Square*

Charles Anderson suggests that James's characters are 'fleshed out' in relation to places and things – landscapes, buildings, national settings, objects and possessions.[9] Not only are economic fortunes and social position encoded through property, but James's dwellings express the distinctive personalities, quirks and secrets of the occupants. If, on a psychoanalytic reading, the house of fiction produces a scene of psychic and sexual repression, it is also demarcated by more worldly relations of money, power and influence. While Adam Verver, Lord Darlington, the Touchett men or Osmond revel in their homes, their wives, daughters, servants and itinerant relatives remain only by the patriarch's consent. If a man's house is his castle, James's recurring metaphor of the cage suggests the claustrophobia of domestic space for its female inhabitants.

Campion's inimitable *mise en scène* brilliantly conveys female entrapment, from *Sweetie*'s (1989) tangled psychodrama, to *The Piano*'s concentric frames, shadows and barriers (corsets, windows, doors, the rainforest). In *Portrait*, Campion consistently shoots through grids and bars. The scene noted above, in which Ralph names Isabel's entrapment, is shot in a stable bathed in blue light. The bars of Isabel's 'cage' are etched in shadows across Ralph's face, and in the stable bars behind Isabel. After her marriage, Isabel is cornered in the resplendent Italian villa bought with the Touchetts' money and furnished with Osmond's precise, cloying taste. For his female protagonists, James's house of fiction becomes a trap. In Campion's film, Isabel struggles against the controlling logic of the male gaze and patriarchal laws of marriage and money.[10] In another cinematic study of confinement, Davies's *Mirth* reiterates a spatio-temporal economy of stillness and constraint. Disinherited by her aunt and thrown out of the home where she had always remained a visitor, Lily Bart is overcome by the encroaching forces of poverty, social betrayal and predatory men.

In Holland's claustrophobic *Square*, the cage is rendered literal. Catherine first appears as a child framed within an upper-storey window, with a birdcage suspended beside her. As Catherine matures, the child actress is replaced by a mature Jennifer Jason Leigh, Morris Townsend (Ben Chaplin) replaces Dr Sloper (Albert Finney) in Catherine's affections, and finally she breaks with them both. Yet the bird persists, a visible marker of Catherine's confinement within her father's house. *Square* often uses the spatial metaphor of a bourgeois home as a prison – a spatial figure familiar from 40s woman's films *The Heiress* or *Now, Voyager* (1942).

> Home . . . brings out the characteristic attempt of the bourgeois household to make time stand still, immobilise life and fix forever domestic property relations as the model of social life and a bulwark against the more disturbing sides in human nature.

The Jamesean cage expressed literally in *Washington Square*: Catherine Sloper (Jennifer Jason Leigh) confined to her father's house

> The theme has a particular poignancy in the many films about the victimisation and enforced passivity of women – women waiting at home, standing by the window, caught in a world of objects into which they are expected to invest their feelings.[11]

The house on Washington Square epitomises how James's houses stand in for their owners. Dr Sloper's investment in propriety, money and control of his daughter's life emanate from a seat of comfort and respectability (as borne out in his evening rituals of port and cigars in the rich dark woods and heavy furnishings of the airless library). The pinnacle of his achievement as a respected, wealthy physician, the father's castle becomes Catherine's prison. After sabotaging her love affair with Morris, Dr Sloper ultimately wills his daughter the house but not the oft-mentioned inheritance of $30,000 per annum. Intended as a prison of genteel limited means for his 'old maid' daughter, the brownstone instantiates the doctor's attempt to control his daughter from beyond the grave.

As in her earlier Victorian adaptation *The Secret Garden*, Holland incorporates Gothic motifs in *Square*, including recurring shots of staircases, *noir* lighting, oppressive *mise en scène* and oblique camera angles. Indeed, the disembodied camera of the opening sequence makes a startling and disturbing preface to the film. From a bird's-eye view of Washington Square, the camera swoops rapidly down to ground level, through the square, up the front steps and through the Slopers' front door. A baby can be heard wailing as the Steadicam shot races up the stairs, around corners, along the hallway and into the master bedroom. Here, the camera dollies over to the bed where a woman, clad in white, lies dead in a pool of blood, the residue of childbirth. A servant holds out the wailing child to its father but, overcome with grief, he pushes past the child to cradle his dead wife. Invented by Holland to explain Dr Sloper's bitter antipathy toward his daughter, this opening scene uses Gothic motifs to frame the Sloper family home as 'a place rendered threatening and uncanny by the haunting return of past transgressions and attendant guilt on an everyday world shrouded in strangeness'.[12]

From an ominous close-up on the infant's abandoned, upset face, cut to Catherine as a plump child of about eight at an upper window, awaiting her father's return from work. She clatters noisily down the stairs to meet him at door, where the father's face registers his distaste at his unrefined daughter. From this moment, all of Catherine's efforts to please her father – a surprise birthday party, a thwarted singing performance, her first formal dress – fail miserably. Patterned into a series of passages up and down the stairs, Catherine's anticipations and disappointments punctuate the film. When Catherine rushes down the stairs to her father, he calls out sharply, 'Catherine!' to slow her progress to a ladylike pace. Struck dumb by her father's scathing verbal bullying, Catherine is an inarticulate character, and in a nod to *The Heiress* Holland uses the wordless device of the stairs to dramatise the battle of wills between father and daughter. After her father's refusal of Morris's proposal, Catherine's dramatic ascent resembles a funeral dirge. At the landing, she stumbles in terrible grief, but catches herself rather than submit to an 'unladylike' demonstration of raw emotion.

Yet Catherine's submission is not total. Mark Le Fanu suggests that the core drama of the novella arises from the discovery that 'underneath this compliant and patient exterior is harboured an individual will, however tentative and unsure. . . . The slow process of this unfolding is at once the book's interest and excitement.'[13] In the bleak ending of *The Heiress*, Olivia de Havilland's Catherine coldly ascends the stairs leaving the returned Morris to pound desperately at the door. If Holland's protofeminist project invents a beginning for her adaptation, she also changes the ending. Catherine's final gesture is no longer the 'no' of a bitter old maid, but a gesture toward the future. Jason Leigh's Catherine literally picks herself up out of the mud after she falls in the street pursuing Morris's departing carriage. This 'transformed' Catherine is not consumed with bitterness and condemned to eternal solitude (as in *The Heiress*), but rather transforms the house into a crèche. In the final shot, after refusing Morris's final offer, she sits at the piano with the child Edith, who gazes at her adoringly – an emblem of a feminine, or even feminist future. In a final redemptive gesture by Holland, the broken mother-daughter bond is restored, even as the Gothic Victorian family is joyfully reconstituted at the end of *The Secret Garden*.

From the opening scene, Holland uses figures of interiority, thresholds and passages (doors, windows, stairs) to represent Catherine's psychological and emotional development. If the Austen adaptations are characterised by the window's mannered transparency, James's and Wharton's houses of fiction emphasise the door. Gaston Bachelard describes a phenomenological dialectic between inside and outside, with the threshold as a sacred and densely significant figure: 'An object, a mere door, can give images of hesitation, temptation, desire, security, welcome and respect.'[14] Georg Simmel distinguishes between bridges, windows and doors. The window offers 'a connection of inner space with the external world. . . . The teleological emotion with respect to the window is directly almost exclusively from inside to outside: it is there for looking out, not for looking in.'[15] Meanwhile, 'life flows forth [in either direction] out of the door from the limitation of isolated separate existence into the limitlessness of all possible directions'.[16] If the dialectic of inside and outside distinguishes between a bounded subjectivity and the outside world, Bachelard contrasts doors open, half-open or closed. Sometimes appearing half-open, the doors of James and Wharton are ultimately barred shut to imprison their protagonists and to exclude those of lower class origins (Morris Townsend, Merton Densher in *Wings*) or tainted sexuality (Ellen Olenska, Olive Chancellor in *The Bostonians*). If thresholds mark symbolic sites of risk and transformation, the closed figure of the door is a powerful trope for stagnant Victorian houses and arrested development.

For Love or Money: *The House of Mirth*

Square's stylised camera work generates a furtive spatial economy, where the camera's passage through the dark shadowy house is strangely unanchored in character point of view. This self-reflexive cinematic narration underscores a watchful distance from outside the house of fiction. Virtuoso camera work is common to auteurist costume drama in *Barry Lyndon*, *Innocence* or Ophuls's works. And while in Scorsese's and Kubrick's films, this camerawork combines with the voice-over to distance the spectator, Holland's use of Steadicam borders at times on the hysterical: the opening Steadicam shot exemplifies a violent rupture between diegesis and a retrospective narration that is only partially mended in the utopian closing scene. As with the television series *The Tenant of Wildfell Hall* (1996), *Angels & Insects*, *Sister My Sister* or Campion's films, Holland's Gothic *mise en scène* and camerawork in *Square* and *The Secret Garden* create an emotionally resonant account of female entrapment.

In *Mirth*, Remi Adefarasin's cinematography, in conjunction with the director's distinctive scenic sense, creates a controlled environment. Balanced compositions freeze Lily's (Gillian Anderson's) face or figure in concentric frames with heavy door frames, windows, stairwells and marble columns. Slow zooms and crawling pans emphasise a precise framing that transforms each moment into a perfect still life. *Mirth* deploys ornate red, green and gold interiors and red-stone high Victorian architecture, dwarfing the diminutive heroine with its draughty grandeur. Progressing at a snail's pace, the film's restrained aesthetic (likened by critics to Strindberg or Bergman)[17] is accentuated by the actors' precise diction and an exceedingly spare use of diegetic sound and music. An expressionistic lighting scheme illuminates faces and figures with directional (often natural) lighting, leaving the ornate surroundings in gloom. This device is used increasingly as the film progresses and the palette of colours becomes increasingly sombre.

As she is distanced from society, Lily is more and more isolated in the frame and engulfed in darkness. For instance, a desperate appeal to her Aunt Julia for financial assistance is filmed in a high-angle shot with only Lily's pale face illuminated; the pale oval of the face is heavily framed by a high-necked black cloak and hat that fade into the inky background.[18] Davies's spare aesthetic could be partly attributed to a limited budget, but the film's carefully choreographed, episodic quality resembles his earlier works *Distant Voices, Still Lives* (1988) and *The Long Day Closes* (1992). Each scene is distilled to restrained performances within sketchy sets, and a stilted dialogue prevails, with every word weighted, each consonant pronounced. In this respect, *Mirth* differs both from the Merchant Ivory realist period aesthetic and Scorsese's play on period detail as fetish.

The House of Mirth: Lily is increasingly isolated in the frame and engulfed in darkness

Davies's formal strategy dramatically foregrounds Lily's predicament, with deliberate framing and performances highlighting the theatricality of this treacherous world. As both subject and object of Wharton's protofeminist morality tale, Lily's cinematic reduction to the role of aesthetic object underscores her explicit status as object of exchange within the narrative. In 1899, six years before Wharton's novel, Thorstein Veblen published *The Leisure Class*, the study of American life that coined the term 'conspicuous consumption'.[19] Veblen's account of a materialist economy of surplus wealth describes a society gorged with ornamental and luxury possessions. Within this milieu, Lily, who lacks inherited wealth and is not trained to earn a living, is destined to become a human 'decoration', to be cast aside when she fails in the marriage market and the value of her beauty expires. Lily's decorative role is reinforced by frequent framing, portrait-like, in doorways, windows and in mirrors. Where the window implies 'a connection of inner space with the external world', Lily's horizons shrink dramatically through poverty and social exclusion, until she dies alone in her tiny apartment with the curtains closed. *Mirth*'s frequent use of mirrors could have plumbed silent depths of suffering, but (unlike in *Innocence*, *Onegin* or *Liaisons*) Lily's interiority is not revealed to the audience through suffering. Although the character is not presented or performed as mere

In *The House of Mirth*, Lily becomes an aesthetic object, a human 'decoration' within a wealthy, materialistic society

surface (as are Ellen and May in *Innocence*), the real stakes of the drama trace how a complex and contradictory character is somehow 'flattened' into a decorative object.

Mirth dwells on long balanced still shots of Lily's face and posed body, and Davies uses a cluttered, claustrophobic *mise en scène* and expressionistic gloomy lighting to create a twilight world of obscure motivations. Within this eerie realm, Wharton's and James's complex physical and social landscapes include the play of desire, but desire and especially marriage are always closely imbricated with other 'desiring relations' of power and money.[20] The literal force of wealth and power are concealed beneath polite conversation and ironclad social convention until they gradually emerge through Lily's predicament. For instance, in her encounter with Gus after the opera (where, as noted in Chapter Two, the provocative red dress marks her out as a sexualised body outside the law), the underlying brutality of this mannered society is disclosed. On a ruse, Gus invites the gullible Lily to his house and literally corners her in the library, demanding that she repay a loan through sexual favours. As with Dr Sloper's seat of power in *Square*, this is a solid, masculine room, lined with books and heavy furniture, where business ventures are secured. Lily realises the full meaning of their 'contract' as Gus explicitly confronts her with the language of exchange, even as he assaults her physically: 'The man who pays for the dinner is generally allowed a seat at the table. . . . You're dodging the rules of the game, Lily, and now you have to pay.' This scene demonstrates how, within Wharton's critique of *fin de siècle* New York high society, human relations are dominated by the logic of the marketplace.

> The power of the marketplace, then, resides not in its presence, which is only marginal . . . but in its ability to reproduce itself, in its ability to assimilate everything else into its domain. As a controlling logic, a mode of human conduct and human association, the marketplace is everywhere and nowhere, ubiquitous and invisible. Under its shadow, even the most private affairs take on the essence of business transactions, for the realm of human relations is fully contained within an all-encompassing business ethic.[21]

In *Mirth*, as in the James adaptations, the cinematic orchestration of desire and repression is polluted by an increasingly explicit reference to money. Where in *Innocence* Newland's life comes to be defined by his desire for Ellen, the melodramatic 'pressure on the surface of reality' in *Mirth* refuses a pure language of romance. Each exchange is made ambivalent by dynamics of power, influence and money. Even with Lawrence Selden, her 'true love', Lily engages in elaborate negotiations that are thwarted by Selden's limited means and his emotional reticence. During a walk in the park at Bellomont the pair find themselves alone, and Lily asks Lawrence if he wants to marry her. Laughingly, he replies: 'No, I don't want to – but perhaps I should if you did.'[22] Selden's calculating response confounds the romantic expectations attached to the country walk. In *Mirth*, as in *Wings*, where Kate gambles Densher's love on a lucrative future, courtship follows a logic of speculation. In the end, Lily pays with her life while Kate sacrifices both Milly's friendship and Merton's love.

In a society of conspicuous consumption, Lily finds widespread financial, social and emotional cheapness. Lily's interview with her Aunt Julia is only the first of several encounters where this lack of generosity is manifested. Within a relentlessly stilted and 'polite' social milieu, it is only Lily's 'unseemly' poverty that pierces the film's stifling composure. Pale, drawn, her face puffy from sleeplessness and chloral, in her final meeting with Selden, Lily breaks down in tears: 'Life is hard. And I have tried hard. But I am a useless person. And now I am on the rubbish heap.' Within the film's emotionally reticent world, however, Lily's outburst barely pierces the surface of repression. James Morrison notes that moments where undercurrents of repression are released (the explosions of violence in *Howards End*, the sex scenes in *Wings*, the exposed wrist in *Innocence*) are common to many costume dramas. However, Lily's pitiful outburst, greeted by an unresponsive Selden, refuses melodramatic release in *Mirth*: 'Davies wants to reveal these undercurrents without ever manifesting them directly because, his film suggests, social repression doesn't just short-circuit true expression temporarily before it finally comes out – it kills the feelings it smothers.'[23]

Mirth chronicles the relentless suffering and punishment of its female protagonist as an indictment of both the patriarchal double standards of turn-of-the-century New York, and the infiltration of the market into every aspect of social exchange. Following her disastrous encounter with Gus Trenor, Lily adheres to a strict code of honour where she refuses assistance from Sam Rosedale and Selden that might be compromised by sexual expectations. In this morality tale, Lily functions as example, and her abjection is complete in the closing scene of her suicide. And where Wharton allows her heroine to drift off in an ambiguous haze, Davies opts for a clear suicide. The passive heroine consistently turns her face away from dishonourable solutions, and her only decisive acts in the entire film are paying her debts and taking her own life. While the sacrifice of the moral heroine underscores Wharton's moral intervention in 1905, Lily's complicity in her own fate sits uncomfortably within a contemporary feminist context.

An aspect of the discomfort engendered by *Mirth* is similar to the problematic stasis of Austen's Fanny Price discussed in Chapter One: if the modern novel prefers an active 'opposing self' (Trilling), popular feminist costume films prefer a sprightly and independent heroine (such as Elizabeth Bennet or Rozema's updated Fanny) to a silently suffering one. Questions of entrapment and agency (as foregrounded by Deleuze's action-image) prove part of the formal and thematic power of these works.

Agency and the Action-Image

For Deleuze, within the dominant narrative logic of the action-image, the 'milieu' is a specific location or environment which the protagonist wrestles to transform. For D.N. Rodowick,

> within the action-image, qualities and powers are determined as forces acting in a given milieu or *mise en scène*. Action properly speaking is motivated by a protagonist, whose actions and reactions are constituted as physical movements in a struggle with the milieu. The milieu and its forces construct a situation that englobes the protagonist, defining the challenge to which he or she must respond. . . . The milieu is individuated as a determined space-time with a determining situation; the protagonist, individual or collective, is individuated as actant, locus of the required action. . . . The action in itself is conflict – with the milieu, with others, with itself.[24]

Catherine's struggle with her father within the milieu of the house on Washington Square exemplifies a psychological and physical struggle of the action-image. The series

of ascents and descents of the stairs illustrate how her physical and psychological vitality are crushed by her father – and how she eventually transforms the brownstone into
her own protofeminist enclave. Further, like the carefully observed interiors of
Innocence, this house of fiction stands in for a specific order of affluent American
Victorian society.

This account of *Square* suggests that the motor of the action-image is human
agency and transformation (of the self and of the surrounding world). Expressing the
American 'ideology of will', dominant narrative cinema dramatises a physical and psychological struggle with the milieu as 'determined space–time with a determining situation'.[25] As mentioned in the Introduction, the action-image has two forms, large and
small. Progressing from an initial situation through explosive action (the gunfight, the
car chase) to a modified situation, the large form exudes confidence in the transformative powers of protagonists and decisive action in milieux such as the American
Frontier. Early Westerns were based on a clear separation between figure and ground,
the 'ground' of the frontier and the town offering a stable mythic milieu within which
the moral dilemmas of the genre unfold. But in the small form of the action-image this
clarity of milieu and action breaks down. Here, 'it is the action which discloses the situation, a fragment or an aspect of a situation, which triggers off a new action. The action
advances blindly and the situation is disclosed in darkness.'[26] In *Mirth*, for instance, the
heroine blunders naively through a mannered milieu where an underlying market logic
of exchange is only gradually revealed.

The Deleuzian action-image opens up new avenues for thinking about costume
drama, and cinema more generally. In Chapter Two I described a 'repressive' psychoanalytic spatial economy that follows a Lacanian modality of desire as lack. While this
theoretical paradigm maps well onto nostalgic films such as *Innocence*, *Remains* or
Wings, the feminist adaptations of Wharton and James wrestle with both cultural and
theoretical narratives that position 'woman' as object of the male gaze. These films
bring into relief how desire and marriage are complicated with economics and social
relations of power. In contrast with a purely psychoanalytic approach, Deleuze's
action-image invokes a psychological and physical battle for agency, a struggle against
historical milieux represented cinematically by solid, confining houses of fiction. This
mode of film analysis investigates not only what Deleuze calls 'Oedipal' lines of force,
but also broader material struggles that unfold symbolically through the cinema as a
'spatial practice'. The action-image as used here rearticulates postmodern narrative as
'force'. Andrew Gibson traces this concept through Nietzsche, Derrida, Deleuze and
Guattari, noting an emphasis on 'becoming rather than being, force rather than form'[27]
grounded metaphysically within the body.

Thus, for a Deleuzian reading of narrative cinema as 'movement-image', 'movement is not appended or added to [the cinematic image] but is endemic to it as an
immediate given, as force. . . . We understand movement in itself, as force or the play
of forces.'[28] This approach rearticulates feminist film scholarship according to a much
more *literal*, *material* epistemology of the image. Cinematic 'images of thought' are no
longer '"concepts of", understood by reference to their external object. They are
"exactly like sounds, colours or images, they are intensities".'[29] To understand narrative as force or intensity parallels feminist scholarship around narrative. Notably,
Teresa de Lauretis examines the work of difference in narrative: 'Its movement seems

to be that of a passage, a transformation, predicated on the figure of a hero, a myth-ical subject;'[30] in contrast, 'female is what is not susceptible to transformation . . . she (it) is an element of plot-space, a topos, a resistance, matrix, matter'.[31] Within the logic of the action-image, the body of the protagonist can be read as a vector of becoming and force. Unlike the powerful female protagonists projected into the large form of the action-image (*Thelma & Louise* (1991), *Alien* (1979) or *G.I. Jane* (1997)), physical and psychological agency prove elusive for the heroines of costume film. This, for me, is part of the ambivalent fascination offered by these films.

The (feminist) protagonists of *Square*, *Mirth* and *Portrait* struggle physically and psychologically within the grip of constraining Victorian costumery and tangled milieux; these scenic elements themselves signify a complex series of sexual, social and economic obstacles. Campion's films illuminate this tangled web. Her work critically interrogates agency, costume and *mise en scène*, from *Sweetie*'s tangled tree roots and family ties to the Victorian cage of clothes in *The Piano*. Lizzie Francke points out how Isabel's very physical *progress* in *Portrait* is impeded by elaborate set decoration and costumes.

> Campion's heroines have been truculent individuals, tripped up by their desires (and one may sweepingly suggest her films can be measured by how they keep their footing among all the treading of water and land). . . . [Isabel's] path is beset by things for her perhaps to stumble on, bringing her down to the primordial level of some of those around her. But (as she claims), 'I will not crawl.'[32]

Confounded by Romance: *The Portrait of a Lady*

The theme of a woman's struggle for autonomous desire and subjectivity across diverse historical and geographical locations runs through Campion's *oeuvre*. In *An Angel at My Table* (1990), Janet Frame's later-life voyages to England and Spain facilitate artis-tic and personal self-realisation. Subsequently, *The Piano* begins with Ada's emigration from Scotland to the New Zealand rainforest, and her struggle for self-expression and autonomous desire are framed against the tensions between 'white settler' and Maori sexual mores. In *Holy Smoke* (1999) Australian teenager Ruth Barron (Kate Winslet) is converted to an unnamed Indian cult. The opening scenes record Ruth's 'conver-sion' in India, but the film's true cross-cultural showdown unfolds between Ruth and an American 'cult deprogrammer' (Harvey Keitel) in the Australian outback. *Portrait*, possibly Campion's least-loved film, explores an American woman's progressive entrapment in a claustrophobic marriage within a disorienting European setting. The film is long and at times painful to watch as it systematically unravels Isabel's agency, autonomy and vitality. What is so corrosive in Campion's work, especially in *Portrait*, is a relentless dismemberment of the expectations of romance and a liberal feminist pref-erence for female agency and redemptive closure.

Portrait's period film is prefaced by a mock documentary sequence about present-day Australian teenage girls. Standing out stylistically and temporally from the rest of the film, this preface breaks the closed period-film microcosm, insisting on a dialogic relationship between literary classics and the feminist present. In contrast with a pre-dominant realist costume drama that addresses 'the present in costume', Campion's explicit reframing – as with the Victorian Gothic of *The Piano* – is both more directly distanced from Isabel's Victorian experience and more critically engaged with it. The preface begins with a sound montage of young women's voices projected over a black screen with white opening titles:

> *First Speaker*: 'The best part of a kiss . . . '
> *Fourth Speaker*: 'I'm addicted to that being entwined with each other, whether it's really positive, as it was in the beginning . . . '
> *Fifth Speaker*: 'I believe in fate. So I believe that person will just find me, or we'll find each other some day.'
> *Fifth Speaker*: 'It means finding a mirror, the clearest mirror, and the most loyal mirror. And that so when I love that person, then they're going to shine that back to me . . . '

The theme tune, a courtly chamber-music number, is cued to a cut from the black screen to an overhead shot of a circle of girls lying in the grass looking upwards. Cut to a series of wordless, black-and-white portraits of modern young women. Photographed in a forest or grove, singly or in groups of twos and threes, the girls sometimes dance strangely as if in a trance; they do not speak, but gaze candidly or defiantly into the camera. The forest setting, shot primarily in lush black-and-white film stock, along with the girls' white shifts and innocent demeanour, evokes a temporal frame that is both current and mythic. This montage of voices with disjointed portraits suggests the enduring clichés of romance.

From the film's present-day preface, the period film opens on an extreme close-up of Isabel (Nicole Kidman), her eyes red from weeping. Her hairstyle and dress indicate the 1870s period, but the entangled garden setting suggests a continuity with the preface. Hearing a noise, she gives a sudden start, and the camera cuts to a medium shot of the protagonist sitting on a low-lying bough in a leafy grove. Ominously, a man's boots can be seen advancing, and Lord Warburton (Richard E. Grant) approaches, pushing leaves aside to face Isabel. With the two characters standing awkwardly face to face, the tree branches form a cage around what would normally offer an idyllic, romantic setting. Campion's trademark whirling camera accentuates a dramatic sense of vertigo and enclosure. Apparently, Isabel's tears have been caused by Warburton's offer of marriage. Overcome with quiet emotion, he returns to plead his case, offering himself through his houses: 'You know, if you don't like Lockleigh . . . there's no difficulty whatever about that, I have plenty of houses.' The suitor's perfect manners and social standing emanate from his property – as with *Square*, *Mirth* and *Wings*, the language of love is a language of exchange.

Warburton's speech expresses an identifiably 'English' restrained depth of feeling that conventionally marks an eminently desirable suitor (exemplified by Hugh Grant's or Anthony Hopkins' politely inarticulate leading men). Isabel, however, is unable or unwilling to respond in kind, and brusquely departs. The picnickers on the lawn pause to watch as she strides purposefully past them toward the house. A brief shot from Ralph Touchett's (Martin Donovan) point of view renders Isabel's passing in slow motion. At key moments, Campion employs a few seconds of slow motion to underline risky narrative moves: Isabel's refusal of Warburton; her rejection of Goodwood at Ralph's club in London; her vertiginous descent after Osmond's proposal in Rome; her uncertain defiance of Osmond when she returns to England; and, finally, the concluding sequence, where she tears herself away from Goodwood's embrace to face an uncertain future.

Significantly, the 'period' film begins and ends with failed trysts in a tangled garden, with Gardencourt as a flawed version of what Lynne Pearce calls the 'romantic love chronotope'. This chronotope 'exists apart from the "historical" lives of the characters, but into which they all are liable to be swept as into a black hole. This chronotope of romantic love . . . [occurs in what Bakhtin calls] "empty time": a spatio-temporal corridor running "outside" or "beyond" the diachronic processes of the material world.'[33] In *Portrait* the grove as romantic-love chronotope is pointedly rewritten as a site of entrapment and disappointment. The clichéd grove, Warburton's proposal, Goodwood's relentless pursuit, even Ralph's dying vows of love offer stock romantic plot lines that never come to fruition. Meanwhile, the heroine's progress is constantly interrupted by sinister or interfering encounters with male admirers: Warburton, Goodwood, Osmond, and Ralph – each in turn tries to sway her progress.

Isabel manages to evade these clutching hands, these would-be prescribed romances – all except Osmond, whose strange power over the heroine is cemented as he surprises her alone in a Roman catacomb. Here Isabel is first framed from Osmond's point of view, the frame dominated by a twirling parasol in the foreground creating a hypnotic effect. Osmond circles Isabel mockingly, now at a distance, now in close to whisper in her ear. When he declares his love, there is a jump-cut to a long shot, followed by a rushing Steadicam shot that swoops through the space toward them, generating an unpleasant, wrenching motion. Isabel tries to break away physically as she has done with the other suitors, but Osmond grasps her parasol. In James's and Campion's view, love is like any other transaction, and Osmond uses the parasol as a bargaining chip.

As a last gesture toward independence, Isabel embarks on her world travels. Announced with the intertitle 'My Journey 1873' and shot in black-and-white grainy film stock, this sequence combines stylistic features of early cinema, surrealism, the home movie and orientalist documentary. Beginning aboard ship, shots of waves are intercut with images of Isabel looking out to sea, with Madame Merle looking over her shoulder. Fragments of travelogue footage depict Isabel in Egypt, looking at the pyramids, surrounded by Arab children. Jumpy, grainy film stock with disparate elements spliced randomly together evoke a dream or a diary. The departure from realist codes of continuity and narrative seem to signify an 'interiority', an inscription of female subjectivity and fantasy. Yet even this journey is invaded by Osmond. His haunting presence in Isabel's fantasies is indicated by disorienting surrealist imagery including the whirling parasol and a fade from Osmond's mouth to a plate of kidney beans that become little mouths, muttering: 'I am absolutely in love with you.' For Vidal, this sequence erases the possibility of female subjectivity.

> Although the whole sequence replicates the grainy texture of a silent film, 'My Journey' is in fact a false silent film that gives us that impression of loss because voice, the second most important marker of spatial control after the gaze, appears as a fluctuant, disembodied entity. The soundtrack contains a miscellany of music and sounds; however, there is only one shot where the voice is in synch: the extreme close-up of Osmond's mouth. . . . The Mouth utters, 'I'm absolutely in love with you'. The Mouth thus becomes the radical signifier of male desire that stands at the origin of all historical

Isabel Archer (Nicole Kidman) entrapped by Osmond (John Malkovich) in *The Portrait of a Lady*

narratives. . . . The end of the sequence pushes this [identification with the Other's desire] to the limit and Isabel's body is literally engulfed by Osmond's gaze and voice. Isabel faints, and there is a fade-out.[34]

The sudden ending of 'My Journey' is the film's turning point, where Isabel is 'caught' by Osmond. This moment is cemented in the recurring gesture of the male hand encircling Isabel's waist, to signify possession, as Isabel becomes simply another object for Osmond's collection. The film poster reprints a similar image of a woman's headless torso grasped by a large proprietary male hand. The discomfort of this narrative image arises from Campion's masochistic lingering on the moment of capture. (However, Campion's casting of Malkovich as Osmond is amiss. A reprise of his role as Valmont in *Liaisons*, Malkovich's performance of Osmond is so odious that his seduction of the naive but intelligent Isabel stretches credulity.)[35] Overwritten by masculine desire and voice, Isabel's own motivations and desires remain opaque. Her inner state is indicated but barely revealed through framing, *mise en scène*, costume and a curiously stilted bodily and facial expression. A disturbing disjunction between female body and voice runs through *Portrait*, beginning with the preface, where the girls' voices are not synchronised with their portraits. In this film, Campion produces a perfect portrait of masculine tyranny and control in which Osmond breaks the will and desires of her heroine. As with *Mirth*, the film tracks Isabel's entrapment in lighting and *mise en scène*, from the saturated greens of England, to Florence's tangled and harshly sunny gardens, to an increasingly dark palette where the heroine is engulfed in shadow and gloom in the Roman villa that she occupies with Osmond.

Francke identifies a recurring streak of female masochism in Campion's work that 'taps into the most perverse part of the female psyche, unafraid to deal with women who are the undoing of themselves'.[36] Indeed, the mesmerising and disturbing power of her films lies in a relentless interrogation of female entrapment that is both socially produced and self-inflicted. As with Kidman's Isabel, in *The Piano* Ada (Holly Hunter) must rely on male protectors, even as she struggles awkwardly to invent a language for self-expression. Both heroines conduct a series of explicit economic, emotional and sexual negotiations in order to somehow enable their nascent desires. For Campion, this problem of inventing a language of autonomous female sexuality is a dilemma for contemporary feminism that finds cinematic resonance within a Victorian milieu.

Changing the Ending

Campion's films construct wordless but eloquent interlacing 'cages' of costume, *mise en scène*, marriage and economic reliance. However, as contemporary feminist allegories, these intricate Victorian prisons cannot but pose the question of escape. Steeped in ambivalence, Campion's resolutions refuse a simple feminist positivism: after lingering in the depths of the ocean with her piano, Ada struggles reluctantly to the surface only at the last moment of *The Piano*. James's novel concludes with Isabel returning to Osmond in Rome, but Campion's film ends as it began, in the grove at Gardencourt. In contrast with the opening scene's lush summer foliage, *Portrait* concludes in bleak winter. In the last of a series of escapes, Isabel tears herself away from Goodwood's passionate kiss in the tangled grove to run full tilt toward the camera.

The Portrait of a Lady: left out in the cold? Isabel at the door of Gardencourt

Revisiting the opening scene, a Steadicam shot captures her flight in slow motion, tracking her dress hem as it drags through the snow. The slow motion signifies a final moment of risk in Isabel's trajectory, and the film closes on an ambivalent shot framing Isabel with her hand on the door of Gardencourt.

With the door as indicative threshold in the James and Wharton adaptations, Bachelard distinguishes between the significance of open, half-open or closed doors. In one reading, the door to Gardencourt might be locked with Isabel left outside in the cold, excluded from the comfort and social position of the Touchett house. Alternately, if the door is half-open, Isabel is left on a threshold of risk and potentiality where 'life flows forth [in either direction] out of the door from the limitation of isolated separate existence into the limitlessness of all possible directions'.[37]

Francke reads *Portrait* as a sequel to Gillian Armstrong's Australian feminist classic *My Brilliant Career* (1979): Kidman's red-haired Isabel even resembles Judy Davis's Sybylla, both 'awkward sorts, with a determined stride that would have horrified the deportment tutors of the day'.[38] If both films offer portraits of 'vivid individuals' characterised by potentiality, Campion's work adroitly depicts the multifaceted 'cage' that entraps Isabel. Challenging the positivist trajectory of *Career* – a trajectory consonant with the confidence of the large form of the action-image – Campion's films insist on how the female subject 'trips herself up'. *Square*, *Mirth* and especially *Portrait* insist on the structuring power of the patriarchal house of fiction, the insidious determining power of money, and the intransigence of women's entanglement within the expectations of romance. Through their struggle with narrative conventions and their refusal to attribute heroic agency to historical female characters, these films dwell on the slowness of social change and the painful contradictions in the transformation of the (female) self.

These gnarled accounts of late-Victorian culture are deeply antithetical to contemporary Anglo-American mores of individualism, agency, emotional and sexual expression. *Mirth* takes the social critique of woman as 'decoration' to its logical conclusion of death, with Davies's slight concession of rescripting Lily's suicide as a choice. Like

Holland's update to James's novella, and also *The Heiress*, *Portrait*, with its modification of James's ending, offers a small opening. Concluding the film on a moment of uncertainty foregrounds the contemporary resonance of the classic text implied by the film's preface. This preface alerts the viewer to a *dialogic* (female or feminist) address, as do Tilda Swinton's and Frances O'Connor's asides to the camera in *Orlando* and *Mansfield*. With their attention to the nefarious forces of money and power within the 'pure' realm of desire, the 'anti-romances' examined in this chapter undertake a difficult feminist rearticulation of the romance narrative that addresses the stakes of female agency both inside and outside the text.

Rozema's *Mansfield* also undertakes to reinflect Austen's novel. An ironic narration offers a running commentary on the conventions of period drama, including the romance formula. As endings are often read as the sites of ideological closure, the film's brisk, postmodern denouement highlights Rozema's feminist revisionism. From Tom's sick bed, the camera flies rapidly out of the window past Fanny, into the countryside, resting on a series of vignettes to resolve various plot lines. The film's narration (read by O'Connor, who plays Fanny) recounts the fate of each character:

> In good and perfect time, Tom's health did improve. Henry Crawford decided not to marry Maria. Mrs Norris, who Sir Thomas came to regard as an agent of evil, went to devote herself to her 'unfortunate' niece. It may be reasonably supposed that their tempers became their mutual punishment. It could have all turned out differently, I suppose. [The action freezes in a scene of an unhappy Maria and Mrs Norris in a kitchen together.] But it didn't. [Action continues.]

From this scene, the camera wends its way rapidly through the countryside to find the Crawfords settled in Westminster, finally returning to find Fanny and Edmund sitting by a pond outside of Mansfield Park. Inexplicably, the great house is now pictured in ruins, as Rozema fancifully decimates the Regency house of fiction as seat of class, patriarchal and colonial power. The voice-over continues: 'And as you may have guessed, at exactly the time when it was quite natural that it should be so . . . Edmund came to speak the whole, delightful and astonishing truth.' A brief scene briskly depicts Edmund's proposal, and the lovers embrace as Fanny looks directly, triumphantly into the camera. The voice-over and Fanny's look (reminiscent of Tilda Swinton's direct looks and addresses to the camera in *Orlando*) forge a complicity with the audience, signalling the pleasure of stock endings, with a qualifier that 'things might have turned out differently, I suppose'.

Mansfield slyly 'updates' Austen without spoiling the fun. What Rozema's film shares with the more dour *Portrait* and *Square* – as well as art-house films *Orlando* and *The Piano* – is an interest in female narration, agency and expression. Through the movement-image of the girl at the writing desk and Fanny's voice-over narration, Rozema creates a hybrid between the writings of the young Jane Austen and her heroine Fanny. Consequently, part of the feminist update of *Mansfield* is a celebration of female authorship. *Portrait* and to a lesser extent *Square* share this preoccupation, where their harsh accounts of the limits of agency and expression for their female subjects are to some degree attenuated by a virtuoso feminist authorship updating the classic literary text. To change the ending, add contemporary prefaces, direct addresses to the camera, interpolated scenes or 'queer looks' (*Mansfield*) to the canonical text is part of the pleasure of feminist costume drama. Within genre and adaptation, what Bakhtin calls the 'deep generative series' of literature (and film), auteurist film-makers intervene in formative narratives of gender, sexuality and desire.

Up to this point, this book has focused primarily on the gender relations within the house of fiction and its environs. However, the case of James's 'American girl' emphasises how gendered itineraries of identity and desire are also centrally engaged with travel and cross-cultural encounter. If Deleuze attributes the velocity of the large form of the action-image to an American 'ideology of will', vectors of agency and desire are clearly inflected by national discourses of travel and location. Depicting historical contexts and literary texts fully engaged in international travel and exchange, English-language costume drama is imbricated with discourses of 'Englishness', 'Europe' and 'America'. These discourses are the subject of the next chapter.

Notes

1. For an account of Victorian discourses of femininity as explored in James's novels, see Elizabeth Allen, *A Woman's Place in the Novels of Henry James* (London: Macmillan, 1984); Martha Banta, 'Men, Women, and the American Way', in Jonathan Freedman (ed.), *The Cambridge Companion to Henry James* (Cambridge: Cambridge University Press, 1998), pp. 21–39; and Jessica Berman, 'Feminizing the Nation: Woman as Cultural Icon in Late James', *The Henry James Review* no. 17, 1996, pp. 58–76.

2. Gilbert and Gubar, *The Madwoman in the Attic*, p. 83.

3. Ibid., p. 84.

4. Ibid., p. 86.

5. On cinematic adaptations of James, see Philip Horne, 'The James Gang', in Vincendeau (ed.), *Film/Literature/Heritage*, p. 85.

6. See Horne, 'The James Gang', and Suzie Gibson, 'The Terror of Representation: The Difficulty of Filming the Novels of Henry James', *Metro Magazine* vol. 117, 1998, pp. 47–50, and Robin Wood, *The Wings of the Dove: Henry James in the 1990s* (London: BFI, 1999), pp. 9–15.

7. *Innocence* achieved a US gross of US$32 million, while *Liaisons* earned $34.7 million. In contrast, *Square* ($1.7 million), *Portrait* ($3.7 million) and *Mirth* ($3 million) had much smaller takings. Statistics are taken from the Internet Movie Database, www.imdb.com. Cited for comparative purposes only, the figures are rounded to the nearest hundred thousand.

8. Produced by British Granada Films with funding from Channel Four and Canal 5, *Mirth* was limited to a stringent $US7.5 million budget. See Graham Rae, '*The House of Mirth* Navigates a Vicious Circle', *American Cinematographer* vol. 82 no. 2, February 2001, p. 12.

9. Charles R. Anderson, *Person, Place, and Thing in Henry James's Novels* (Durham, NC: Duke University Press, 1977), pp. 3–4.

10. Isabel Archer's fate is reminiscent of that of her namesake Newland Archer, and Wharton's *The Age of Innocence* shares many themes with James's *Portrait*, written some forty years earlier. Both characters are literally and symbolically trapped by

convention and marriage. However, Newland achieves a respectable life (even as he nurses a secret desire for Ellen), while Isabel is entirely disenfranchised.

11. Elsaesser, 'Tales of Sound and Fury', pp. 61–2.
12. Fred Botting, *Gothic* (London: Routledge, 1996), p. 11.
13. Mark Le Fanu, 'Introduction', in Henry James, *Washington Square* (Oxford: Oxford University Press, 1982), pp. xi–xii.
14. Gaston Bachelard, *The Poetics of Space* (Boston: Beacon Press, 1969), p. 224.
15. Georg Simmel, 'Bridge and Door', in David Frisby and Mike Featherstone (eds), *Simmel on Culture* (London: Sage Publications, 1997), p. 173.
16. Ibid.
17. See James Morrison, '*The House of Mirth*', *Film Quarterly* vol. 55 no. 1, 2001, p. 51, and Philip Horne, 'Beauty's slow fade', *Sight and Sound*, October 2000, p. 16.
18. This framing draws from painters of the period James McNeill Whistler and John Singer Sargent, where 'the backgrounds are just impressions and not celebrated'. See Rae, '*The House of Mirth*', pp. 12, 14.
19. Cynthia Griffin Wolff, 'Introduction', in Edith Wharton, *The House of Mirth* (New York: Penguin Books, 1985), p. xxi.
20. Gilles Deleuze and Félix Guattari's analysis of James's novella *In the Cage* is useful here. The authors emphasise first the 'molar' lines of containment (class; powerfully circumscribed 'cage' where the telegraphist works), 'molecular' lines of Oedipal desire that allow the heroine to fantasise a different life, and deterritorialising 'lines of flight'. These three 'lines of force' intermingle, and Deleuze and Guattari are careful not to reduce the analysis either to the unconscious, or to the structuring grid of class, money or the banal constraints of repetitive, boring work. See their *A Thousand Plateaus* (Minneapolis: University of Minnesota Press, 1987), pp. 195–8.
21. Wai Chee Dimock, 'Debasing Exchange: Edith Wharton's *The House of Mirth*', in Shari Benstock (ed.), *The House of Mirth* (Boston: St Martin's Press, 1994), p. 375.
22. For a more complete discussion of Selden's 'stinginess', see Dimock, 'Debasing Exchange', pp. 379–82.
23. Morrison, '*The House of Mirth*', p. 49.
24. Rodowick, *Gilles Deleuze's Time Machine*, p. 68.
25. Ibid., p. 69.
26. Deleuze, *Cinema 1*, p. 160.
27. Andrew Gibson, *Towards a Postmodern Theory of Narrative* (Edinburgh: Edinburgh University Press, 1996), pp. 34–5.
28. Ibid., p. 51.
29. Tomlinson and Habberjam, 'Translators' introduction', Deleuze, *Cinema 1*, p. xi.
30. de Lauretis, *Alice Doesn't*, p. 113.
31. Ibid., p. 119.
32. Lizzie Francke, 'On the Brink', in Vincendeau (ed.), *Film/Literature/Heritage*, p. 84.
33. Lynne Pearce, 'Another Time, Another Place: The Chronotope of Romantic Love in Contemporary Feminist Fiction', in Lynne Pearce and Gina Wisker (eds), *Fatal Attractions* (London: Pluto Press, 1998), p. 99.
34. Belén Vidal, *Textures of the Image* (València: Departament de Filologia Anglesa i Alemanya, Universitat de València, 2002), pp. 120–1.

35. Robin Wood also critiques Malkovich's casting (*The Wings of the Dove*, p. 15) as does Karen Michele Chandler ('Agency and Social Constraint in Jane Campion's *The Portrait of a Lady*', *The Henry James Review* no. 18, 1997, p. 193). Francke is in the minority in describing Malkovich's performance as 'terrifyingly persuasive' ('On the Brink', p. 84).

36. Francke, 'On the Brink', p. 84.

37. Simmel, 'Bridge and Door', p. 173.

38. Francke, 'On the Brink', p. 83.

Chapter Four
The Idea of Europe

Henry James's novels often feature an 'American girl', a nineteenth-century 'new woman' who has the world at her feet. A layering of vivid characterisation and national type, James's heroines Isabel Archer and Milly Theale encounter foreign milieux steeped in sensuality and ancient cultural traditions. As the house of fiction opens out onto the world of nineteenth-century travel, the protagonists' voyages of desire and aspiration take them out into English and European image space. Crucial to the appeal of the works of James and Forster for contemporary adaptation are their cosmopolitan settings. Cinematic treatments of James's novels chronicle the experiences of American travellers in Britain (*Portrait*, *Innocence*), as well as British and American sojourns in Europe (*Portrait*, *Wings*, *Bowl*). Meanwhile, the Forster adaptations *A Room with a View*, *Maurice* and *Where Angels Fear to Tread* (1991) stage ritual encounters between British protagonists and Southern European landscapes and cultures.

Sightseeing in Florence: the retrotourist gaze in *A Room with a View*

Part of the successful formula established in Merchant Ivory's 1985 *A Room with a View* was to situate the sensual awakening of Forster's leisured English protagonists within the settings of Florence and Tuscany. Much has been written about Englishness in heritage cinema, but the relationality of national and regional identities has been largely overlooked, with the notable exception of Pam Cook's work which I return to below. If the colonial out-of-field functions as a constitutive absence in recent costume drama, European image space forms a significant element in costume drama's narrative space and intertext. Embedded in character point of view and scenic cinematography, a contemporary 'retrotourist' gaze is gratified through cinematic sightseeing expeditions to Venice, Rome, Florence, Tuscany, Paris and London.

These films reference a contradictory set of discourses sometimes called the 'idea of Europe'.[1] Overwhelmingly, British and European heritage cinema draws upon the 'oldness' of Europe 'as residing in common, ancient cultural roots'.[2] Even as the house of fiction presents a residual cultural form representing an emergent Western subjectivity, iconic travel destinations project cultural roots: Italy as 'cradle of the Renaissance'; nineteenth-century England as cultural and political precursor to present-day Western culture. Another crucial discourse of Europeanness is a celebration of high-culture traditions and artistic genius. Authorship itself is the subject of a series of historical biographies (*Amadeus*, *Shakespeare in Love* and *Topsy-Turvy*) that return to the making of classic texts of Western culture. In this chapter, I argue that through ritual treatments of artistic creation and an implicit 'retrotourist gaze', contemporary costume films reinscribe nineteenth-century ways of viewing and experiencing the past. Highly structured relations of looking are encoded through romantic and touristic discourses, and what is produced here is not only an 'idea' or 'image' of Europe, but also a discerning, worldly Anglo-American spectator.

If lush images of Europe are central to the narrative image of costume film, the spectre of America as a dominant cultural force looms large within the films and in the critical discourses surounding them. Implicit within the British heritage cinema critique is the claim that American finance and American taste overdetermines British audiovisual production. Increasing numbers of American co-productions within an industry tailored to American tastes means that British costume films are often produced with American audiences in mind. For example, the title of Alan Bennett's play, 'The Madness of King George III', was altered to *The Madness of King George*; this change was prompted by survey findings that many filmgoers 'came away from Kenneth Branagh's film of *Henry V* wishing they had seen its four predecessors'.[3] This industry anecdote points to a broader set of debates about cultural autonomy and American dominance.

Geoffrey Nowell-Smith notes that contemporary European film production is gripped by a threefold dependence: television/video financing and presale agreements, European co-productions, and Hollywood; this latter dependence 'is experienced not at the level of production but at that of distribution and competition for market share'.[4] The consequence of these dependencies for European (and virtually all other) national cinemas is an increasing reliance on American-led conglomerates for financing and distribution. Stuart Hall posits that global mass culture is built on the markets and cultural traditions of imperialism, indicating two of its salient features: first, 'it remains centered in the West [using] Western technology, the concentration of capital, . . .

techniques, . . . advanced labour in the Western societies, and the stories and the imagery of Western society'. Secondly, this is 'a homogenizing form of cultural representation, enormously absorptive of things', and it 'always speaks English'. However, Hall qualifies this assertion with the observation that

> the homogenization is never absolutely complete. . . . It is not attempting to produce little mini-versions of Englishness everywhere, or little versions of Americanness. It is wanting to recognize and absorb these differences within the larger, overarching framework of what is essentially an American conception of the world.[5]

Hall's account is useful for its insistence on the embedded relations of domination intrinsic to global mass culture. Yet within an 'essentially American' worldview, the residual cultural authority of canonical English culture persists in classic adaptations and quality cinema.

The relationship between production capital and cultural content is a vexed one, and at times the films themselves are self-reflexive in their treatment of national identity. For instance, Altman's *Gosford Park* incorporates a sub-plot of American cultural invasion. Paralleling Altman's own outsider's incursion into British period drama, a Hollywood director (Bob Balaban) and American actor (Ryan Phillippe) are included in the weekend shooting party. Their presence prompts a series of pithy exchanges lampooning both American populism and the elitism of the English aristocracy. Obsessed with his new film *Charlie Chan in London*, the director remains oblivious to the murder of his host Lord McCordle. The following telephone conversation between the director and his producer plays over the visual depiction of the police inspector's arrival:

> I'm looking for a kind of *realistic* Charlie Chan movie. That isn't out of the question. . . . We can't just do the same old shit over and over again. . . . Alan Mowbray, I mean *that's* a butler, I like that. [On the image track Gosford Park's butler (Alan Bates) opens the door for the police inspector.] These people look like Alan Mowbray, they're sort of tall and they don't talk too much, and they have fucking British accents, right. They talk like they're from England.

As I will discuss in Chapter Six, this sly juxtaposition is characteristic of the film's ironic critique. Pitched as a cross between Renoir's *Rules of the Game* (1939) and Agatha Christie's *Ten Little Indians*, *Gosford* is marketed both on its American art director and its 'best of the British' all-star cast. Backed by the British Film Council, Altman's film represents an exceptionally canny case of transatlantic co-production.

Hailed by critics as a fresh treatment of British period drama by outsiders, *Gosford* signals the generative possibilities of international collaboration in an era where American mass culture dominates indigenous local and national film production. Yet the very self-consciousness of *Gosford*, *Shakespeare in Love*, *Orlando* and *The Madness of King George* is integral to their 'quality' international appeal. Like more conventional films, these innovative postmodern projects are marketed in part as mannered experiences of nineteenth-century or Renaissance Britain or Europe. These films convey little about British or European history, but rather a lot about perceptions of Europe that are guided both by American and British worldviews.

The Tourist Gaze

John Urry's concept of the 'tourist gaze' is useful for discussing the cultural dynamics of viewing distant places and times. Heritage critics suggest that costume drama's account of the past intersects with social practices of work and leisure, and I would suggest that these films' virtual journeys through time and space correlate closely with tourism.

> Tourism is about consuming goods and services which are in some sense unnecessary. They are consumed because they supposedly generate pleasurable experiences which are different from those typically encountered in everyday life. And yet at least a part of that experience is to gaze upon or view a set of different scenes, of landscapes or townscapes, which are out of the ordinary. . . . In other words, we gaze at what we encounter. And this gaze is as socially organized and systematized as the gaze of the medic.[6]

Costume film plays on escape from ordinary life into vivid microcosms of 'elsewhere' and 'elsewhen'. Iconic British and European locations are foregrounded in the films' commercial intertext through trailers, reviews and press coverage of heritage locations.[7] These cinematic landscapes and cityscapes are encoded through discourses about the past and tourism.

With its celebrated view, *Room* exemplifies how nineteenth-century tourism was bound up with a quest for an authentic pre-industrial environment unsullied by modernity. Tourism has been historically associated with changing apparatuses of vision, including the framing of landscapes through painterly compositions: 'What picturesque seeing yielded was not only a scene that "looked like" a painting, but a *scene*, balanced and complete.'[8] In England, the Lake District was reconfigured as 'picturesque' through the Romantic vision of the Lake poets. Associated with this picturesque mode of perception is stillness, and these spatio-temporal qualities perfectly encapsulate the gardens and countrysides of the Forster and Austen adaptations. In a slightly different project, Julien Temple's *Pandaemonium*, a biography of Coleridge and Wordsworth, deploys the romantic landscapes of the Lake District as setting and inspiration for Coleridge's increasingly psychedelic creative vision.

Prevalent within contemporary costume film is a privileged, retrotourist cinematic gaze that is increasingly inflected toward, if not reducible to, a dominant Anglo-American 'idea of Europe'. While global mass culture follows an essentially American worldview, most of the characters and many of the actors in these films are British. English and sometimes American characters and actors signal a preferred white Anglo-American axis of identification that is strongly differentiated from European traditions and characters. Intermingling English, American and European characters and vistas, James's cosmopolitan novels enact a pervasive play of sameness and difference between British and American protagonists against European backdrops.

Significantly, these narratives unfold during the expansive period after the Civil War when American tourist excursions to Europe became more common.[9] At stake in James's 'international scene' was

> the *relationality* of national feeling at the moment of international intermingling. It is only when they travel to Europe, after all, that James's Americans are able to define

their own national identity. And James's Englishmen and Europeans are by that very same process forced to recognise their own transmutation: their transformation into objects of exotic touristical interest.[10]

Deborah Parsons situates James's treatments of European travel in relation to late nineteenth-century modernity, discourses of consumerism and taste, and the identity of Europe contrasted with the rising cultural and industrial power of the US. Following the eighteenth-century Grand Tour of the cultural elite, the 19th century witnessed the 'production' of Europe as a consumable entity for a broader group of affluent British and American tourists. In this mythological and geographically indistinct 'Old World', it is ' "the note of Europe," rather than the hard facts of specific artifacts or architectural stones themselves, that the visitor seeks'.[11] Many costume dramas including the Forster and James adaptations, *Amadeus*, *Immortal Beloved*, *Impromptu* (1991), *Enchanted April*, *Tea with Mussolini* (1999) and *The English Patient* harness this 'note of Europe' for cinematic retrotourism. Far removed from actual historical locations and events, 'Europe' offers itself as the cultural capital of literature, art, music and architecture – and catalyses emotional and sexual awakenings for Anglo-American travellers.

James's *The Portrait of a Lady* exemplifies the 'complexity of Europe's nineteenth-century cultural image as both Old World and the centre of modernity. The locus of taste and high culture in *Portrait* is Italy, museum of the Renaissance.'[12] Historically, British and American tourist discourses of an 'authentic' Europe were based on a Romantic response to industrialisation and the growth of capitalism:

> As the critics of utilitarianism described it, foreign travel readmits into human life the imaginative and moral energies – the poetry – sacrificed in a Benthamite workaday world. . . . Physical departure from one's busily modernizing society could take on the ideological appeal of a temporary, revivifying departure from compromised social existence. Invested with a pent-up psychic energy, that which lay across any appreciable boundary (Atlantic, Channel, Alps) could be shaped into a vessel for deferred wishes. Britons constructed the 'Continent' in this way, Americans a larger 'Europe' that included Great Britain. . . . Britons and Americans agreed that Italy possessed the greatest concentration of the valuably different in Europe, the greatest density of Europeanness.[13]

These resilient nineteenth-century tropes are revisited in *Room*, *Portrait*, *Wings* and *Where Angels*, where American and English protagonists are first captivated then finally overwhelmed by Italy, cradle of the Renaissance. Reminiscent of orientalist tropes, Southern European locations provide a horizon of fear and fascination.

With reference to the (primarily female) spectators of 30s and 40s Gainsborough melodramas, Cook points out how cinematic fantasies of travel and cross-cultural encounter can prompt a productive destabilisation of 'home' and (national) identity.[14] While critics claim that heritage cinema shores up a stable, implicitly conservative Englishness, Cook finds a fluid exploration of identity in this genre's exotic locations, travel and masquerade. Crucial to this play is a drama of Anglo-American selves lost and found, and a cinematic rendering of disorientation is central to the Forster adaptations *A Passage to India*, *Where Angels* and *Room*. Cross-cultural encounter, especially with southern European or 'Asian' cultures and individuals, proves profoundly disorienting for some characters (for instance, Judy Davis's hysterical Harriet Herriton in *Where Angels*), but proves profoundly liberating for culturally sensitive English travellers such as George Emerson (*Room*) or Philip Herriton (*Where Angels*). The sensation of disorientation is rendered dramatically in *Portrait*, where Isabel's first view of Florence is marked by a strange canted shot from a horse-drawn carriage ascending a ramp into the hazy city. The canted shot is repeated later to record Isabel's first impression of the Colosseum in Rome. Campion's idiosyncratic camera angles register Isabel's first bewildered impression of Florence, as the unfamiliar scenes literally upset the equilibrium of her gaze. Osmond's seduction of Isabel in the San Apollinare Nuovo in Ravenna also plays on the residual unsettling power of an ancient civilisation.

If Italy often represents refinement and high culture, the expatriate American Osmond's relationship to Italian culture is parasitic. With his tasteful collection of European art objects, Osmond exemplifies one Jamesean type of American-in-Europe. Buildings and art objects rendered as collectibles and placed in museums dramatise the commodification of European culture and tradition by American capital. Collections enhance the collector's cultural capital, and Europe is rendered as an object for consumption and exchange. In *Remains*, Senator Lewis (Christopher Reeve), the wealthy American, purchases Darlington Hall after the war, but the most dramatic example of this phenomenon is in *Bowl*, where American industrialist Adam Verver (Nick Nolte) acquires warehouses full of European treasures. The collection is destined for a museum in 'American City' – a momentous project destined as a monument to Verver himself.

Verver also purchases an Italian castle, to which is attached its occupant, Prince Amerigo (Jeremy Northam), who marries Verver's daughter Maggie (Kate Beckinsale). In James, the objectification of Europe extends to people, where the powerless (especially women or people without means) become pawns or objects of exchange for the rich. In *Portrait*, Osmond adds Isabel (and the inherited Touchett fortune) to his collection, and in *Bowl* Verver marries the beautiful and penniless Charlotte (Uma Thurman), his daughter's childhood friend. The appropriation of people and objects in James is largely associated with unsympathetic male characters. Osmond and Verver perfect a controlling and acquisitive gaze that is backed up with buying power. In contrast, female characters often have a less aggressive gaze; they do not seek to possess, but rather to fully 'experience' Europe as tourists. Indeed, the James and Forster adaptations project a nuanced gendered ethics of looking and cross-cultural encounter.

In *Portrait*, Isabel's friend Henrietta Stackpole (Mary-Louise Parker) represents the crass gaze of mass tourism. At the National Portrait Gallery in London, the impressionable Isabel is engrossed in the artworks while a visibly bored Henrietta plagues her friend with idle chatter. A writer of travelogues, Henrietta is shown ironically to lack any real curiosity for her British and Italian surroundings. Similarly, in *Innocence*, during the Archers' short European honeymoon, May's lack of curiosity about European places, complex ideas and people underscore her inner emptiness. The Archers' travels are intercut with classic paintings of London and Paris that point to the flattening of 'Europe' into a series of tourist spots, as the narrator intones: 'They travelled to the expected places that May had never seen.' The mismatch between Newland and May is emphasised by their differing cultural horizons, while Ellen, the sophisticated expatriate, awakens Newland's passions.

Parsons notes that nineteenth-century tourist discourses of the self-consciously cultural élite constructed 'women and Americans, and most anathema of all, female Americans … as patronising "vulgar" tourists'.[15] Isabel and Henrietta both represent American 'new women', but, with her curiosity and sensitivity to her surroundings, Isabel is singled out as superior from her 'vulgar' friend. This contrast corresponds to Urry's distinction between the collective tourist gaze and a romantic gaze characterised by 'solitude, privacy and a personal, semi-spiritual relationship with the object of the gaze'.[16] Sightseeing visits in *Wings* and *Portrait* also adhere to this value system, where 'art is to be possessed through the impressions that it makes on the human consciousness, not through actual ownership'.[17] James's value system is echoed in many contemporary costume films, where this romantic mode of seeing is preferred above all. By extension, for these products framed by claims of 'quality', the films' knowing address and breadth of cultural reference similarly construct the cinematic spectator as discerning, sensitive and worldly.

Discourses of taste and perception within the films can be instructively juxtaposed with recent debates about the audiences of heritage cinema. Noting that British costume drama enthusiasts are commonly assumed to be female and 'older', Monk points to a dismissal of this assumed demographic within a British context.[18] Her point is borne out by Higson's influential claim that heritage cinema audiences are mesmerised by cinematic spectacle that overwhelms narrative social critique. Caughie extends Higson's argument to an international context, where the tailoring of British period film and television drama for American audiences leads to productions where 'irony and wit are rendered as English quaintness, and the national past is captured like a butterfly on a pin in a museum of gleaming spires, tennis on the lawn, and the faded memory of empire'.[19] This notion that English literary irony is subsumed by the view coincides with the idea of an undiscriminating mass-tourist gaze – a type most recognisable as female and/or 'American'.

Interestingly, critical discourses about audiences resonate with distinctions drawn within the films, where the viewer (or critic) may choose to inhabit the high ground of critical sophistication while deprecating less 'cultivated' modes of spectatorship – or, indeed, ideas of 'Europe'. This contested field of taste corresponds with Dean MacCannell's account of 'touristic shame', where tourists are 'reproached for being satisfied with superficial experiences of other peoples and places'. However, for MacCannell this disdain

> is not based on being a tourist but on not being tourist enough, on a failure to see everything the way it 'ought' to be seen. The touristic critique of tourism is based on a desire to go beyond the other 'mere' tourists to a more profound appreciation of society and culture.[20]

Diegetic and intertextual differentiations in modes of perception are inseparable from assumptions about gendered and national audiences. These competing claims are not easily resolvable, but the discussion can be productively reframed around broader practices of visual culture and consumption. Modernist critics raise the troubling phenomenon of those instances where the specificity of history and geography are flattened into images for rapid consumption. Rather than interrogating hegemonic accounts of national or European pasts and their link with the present, the heritage simulacrum often reproduces mythological and conservative representations of national and European pasts. However, Dimitris Eleftheriotis argues that this modernist critique relies upon a European hermeneutic or depth model of art appreciation and social critique.[21] In keeping with the European discourses of high art and art cinema, the romantic tourist gaze prefers profound and searching modes of looking and understanding. The hermeneutic is profoundly distrustful of postmodernist accounts of the past that are perhaps too easy, popular or superficial.

Europe and the *'Mise en scène* of Desire'

One controversial mythology that has flourished in costume film from the mid-90s draws on long-standing discourses of Europe as a zone of illicit sexuality, and costume film's retrotourist gaze is bound up with ambivalent gendered fantasies and desires. Viewed against a cinematic apparatus that traditionally structures the gaze as male, the foregrounded diegetic gaze here is often female. Painterly views, sightseeing expeditions or the appreciation of male objects of desire are pleasureable modes of looking available to female characters. Yet, as noted previously of the view from the window, this gendered gaze not only connotes mastery, but also stasis and powerlessness. The romantic tourist gaze of British and American female characters implies both cosmopolitan mobility and a certain vulnerability. Travel is associated both with risk and with self-transformation through experiences distinct from the modern and the familiar. The pleasures and perils of travel are extended not only to female protagonists, but also to their male companions. At a remove of time and space, these journeys are extended to international audiences.

Italy's special significance as heady repository of Renaissance culture makes it a favourite destination for nineteenth-century novels and their adaptations. In *Wings*,

Venice as the European *mise en scène* of desire in *The Wings of the Dove*

Venice as city of the Renaissance profoundly affects not only Milly the impressionable 'American girl', but also the more worldly Londoners Kate and Merton. As Milly's illness and her romance with Merton progress, the heiress's reckless state of mind is dramatised through an ascent to the dizzying parapet of St Mark's cathedral; a series of quick cuts indicate Milly's unsteady state. Later, she scales a rickety scaffolding to view a partially restored fresco. The beauty of the painting, which we barely glimpse through the drapery, moves Milly to embrace Merton, who has followed her. A comparable scene occurs in *The English Patient* where Kip accompanies Hannah to a local Italian chapel late at night to show her the frescoes. Suspended on a pulley to view the lofty paintings, Hannah swings from one to the next, holding a smoking flare that illuminates each image in turn. An accompanying swelling orchestral score combined with the characters' palpable delight and the swaying hazy light convey a vertiginous experience.

These scenes suggest the capacity of Renaissance art to spark a romantic intensity of feeling in the Anglo-American protagonists. Literally, they swoon. Sensations of disorientation and vertigo relate to the picturesque as a spatial scenic sense that is also temporal, an epiphanic moment that evokes an 'authenticity effect' in the viewer 'when the unified aesthetic essence of the place shines forth'.[22] As with Isabel's seduction in Ravenna, these movement-images convey something of the sublime, where encounters with classical ruins or Renaissance art are both terrifying and exhilarating. A dying Milly is overcome by her own mortality when viewing the Renaissance painting, and part of the power of the sublime is an encounter with death.

The sensual potency of Venice figures differently in the carnival sequence of *Wings*. Invented by the film-makers, this sequence employs the mysterious Venetian locale to dramatise the complex love triangle. Milly, Merton and Kate dress in character (as princess and pirates, respectively) to join a local night of revelry. Shot at night by flickering torchlight, this scene 'reveals' the characters' agendas through their costumes, but also implicates them in the ancient Italian *commedia dell' arte* and the rough sensuality of an Italian street scene. In contrast with the languor and repressed desires of the Anglo-American characters, the Italians' sexual potency and physical dynamism galvanises Kate and Merton to finally consummate their relationship.

Where James's novel transpires mostly in London, the adaptation opts primarily for exotic Venetian locations. *Wings* director Iain Softley states in interview that these 'updates' were deliberate for this Miramax production: 'It's a modern experience, not all buttoned-up and corseted. . . . The costumes are much more sexy and we have taken the older characters out and left the younger, fresher ones to be intoxicated by this dark place.'[23] In keeping with an increasingly sexual turn in mid-90s costume film, literal sexuality creeps into the later James adaptations: Kate's fantasy of an illicit encounter with Merton in the underground that prefaces *Wings*, Isabel's sexual fantasy of an orgy with her suitors in *Portrait*, and Charlotte and Amerigo's adulterous liaison in *Bowl*.

The Italian 'density of Europeanness' is associated with a dangerous eroticism for Anglo-American travellers. Along with Milly's and Isabel's adventures, in the Merchant Ivory production *Where Angels*, rich English widow Lilia Herriton (Helen Mirren) marries Gino Carelli (Giovanni Guidelli), a much younger Italian man of limited means. Mirren's brilliant performance conveys both the imperious attitude of a wealthy Edwardian Englishwoman, and her vulnerability as an older woman in love with a beautiful younger man. Tragically, Lilia dies in childbirth, surrounded by the unfamiliar language and customs of Gino's family. When her in-law Philip (Rupert Graves) and her companion Caroline (Helena Bonham Carter) travel to Tuscany to retrieve Lilia's child, they are similarly bewitched by the charm of the village, the opera and, most of all, by Gino himself. Steeped in Latin stereotypes, Gino's childlike character is almost irresistible to the repressed Edwardian English characters, both male and female. All of these English characters experience a spiritual and sexual awakening in the simple Tuscan village.

Italy as a zone of passion and danger can also be found in *Wings*. From the epiphanic heights of the cathedral, Milly, Merton, Kate and Susan proceed to the dark earthy canal. Milly is overwhelmed by the press of bodies, the clatter of the unfamiliar sounds of the market. Like the exotic bazaars and inscrutable desert vistas of orientalist literature, European places and people function primarily as ciphers for the tourists' fears and desires. *Wings* plays on a long-standing Western lore of Venice as a place of disease, death and shadowy, ill-understood folk culture, reminiscent of Thomas Mann's *Death in Venice*. Cinematic precursors for this vision of Venice include Visconti's *Senso* and his 1971 adaptation of Mann's novella. Images of delusional wanderings through Venice recur in *Don't Look Now* (1973) and *The Comfort of Strangers* (1990). A related association of Eastern Europe with death and illicit sexuality appears in *Bram Stoker's Dracula*, where Dracula's Transylvanian castle hosts a startling series of orgies and violent deaths.

These treatments of Venice and Tuscany correspond with a widespread use of French and Italian locations to evoke a '*mise en scène* of desire' for Anglo-American spectators. This notion is borrowed from Patricia White, who suggests that 'genres and cycles are industrial and consumer categories, but they are also another level of cinema's inscription of fantasy as *mise en scène* of desire'.[24] As Anglo-American costume drama of the 80s and 90s delves further and further into the more intimate recesses of the house of fiction, explicit sexual content is often signalled by French or Italian settings or pre-nineteenth-century periods in films including *Elizabeth*, *Shakespeare*, *Restoration*, *Caravaggio* and *Edward II*. In Chapter Eight I further explore the corporeal and sexual dimensions of recent costume film.

European High Culture and the Biopic

If the 'idea of Europe' creeps into English-language costume film as object of a retro-tourist gaze and a *mise en scène* of desire, its association with European high-art traditions is also crucial. European art cinema forms an important industrial and cultural antecedent for contemporary costume drama, and Jarman's, Potter's and Greenaway's films arise from the British avant-garde. Stephen Heath describes the art film as follows:

> Art films tend to be marked by a stress on visual style (an engagement of the look in terms of a marked individual point of view rather than in terms of institutionalised spectacle), by a suppression of action in the Hollywood sense, by a consequent stress on character rather than plot and by an interiorisation of dramatic conflict. . . . Art films are marked at a textual level by the inscription of features that function as marks of enunciation – and, hence, as signifiers of an authorial voice (and look).[25]

Most costume dramas are best described as crossover products (the works of Campion) or popular cinema (*Sense, Elizabeth*) rather than art film. Yet part of their appeal springs from the renewal and popularisation of the expectations of European art film – notably an attention to character and interiority and a preoccupation with signifiers of authorship. As mentioned previously, authorship as a 'brand' features prominently in the films' commercial intertext, where films are marketed both through their literary sources (Austen, James, Shakespeare, Wilde) and on the basis of prestige directors and production teams (Merchant Ivory, Altman, Forman, Scorsese, Coppola, Davies, Jarman, Potter, Campion).

The inscription of authorship within the films and their intertext signals a fascin-ation with moments of (European) cultural creation most evident diegetically in a series of historical biographies of composers, writers and painters including *Amadeus, Caravaggio, Impromptu, Shakespeare, Total Eclipse, Vincent & Theo, Immortal Beloved, Wilde, Topsy-Turvy, Quills* and *Pandaemonium*. An often denigrated mode of film-making, recent biopics have mostly proven critically and commercially unremarkable, with the exceptions of *Amadeus, Caravaggio, Shakespeare* and *Topsy-Turvy*. Even so, they are intriguing as a group for their fascination with (male) 'creative geniuses' of Western civilization: Shakespeare, Beethoven, Mozart, Van Gogh, Rimbaud. As with the 30s British historical biopics, these films frequently turn on an interrogation of an embat-tled masculinity and the challenges and hardships for creativity.[26]

The pivotal narrative image of these films is of embattled romantic genius, tortured artists suffering from an unsustainable physical or emotional intensity: Rimbaud's and Verlaine's high-octane sexual and creative relationship in Agnieszka Holland's *Total Eclipse*; Mozart, engrossed in his work and harried to death by poverty and profes-sional sabotage; Coleridge's opium-generated writing marathons, where the words seem to be physically torn out of him. These are prestigious roles for actors, intensely physical and sexual bravura performances where the momentum of thought, music, painting and verse is conveyed physically through a ravaged, expressive and often highly sexualised masculine corporeality. Joseph Fiennes' title role in *Shakespeare* play-fully captures a common correlation of abundant physical energy and virility with creativity. Stoppard's script playfully equates Will's 'quill' with his sexuality. Writer's block is diagnosed by a seer as sexual frustration, and an antidote appears in the form of a new love (Gwyneth Paltrow) who becomes Will's muse.

Shakespeare, as a high-velocity biopic, is indebted to Milos Forman's influential *Amadeus*. Based on Peter Shaffer's play, the film portrays Mozart (Tom Hulce) as an overgrown child genius with a scatalogical sense of humour and a ridiculous, giggling laugh. There is an interesting fault line in *Amadeus* between Hulce's petulant, adolescent masculinity and the powerful, moving score; this non-identity of composer and compos-ition undercuts a common biographical match between music and the inner life of its composer. Through its energetic and parodic tone, and its sense of entertainment-as-spectacle (spectacular set pieces of orchestral music and operas choreographed by Twyla Tharp), Forman's singular film reanimates the turgid tradition of historical biography. Shot in Prague as a stand-in for eighteenth-century Vienna, *Amadeus* ritually re-enacts Mozart's works for contemporary audiences. In keeping with a late-twentieth-century repopularisation of Western classical music, the film soundtrack was also widely marketed.

A spectacular set piece in *Amadeus*: recreating the excitement of the original performance

Nora Lee writes of *Amadeus* that 'there has rarely, if ever, been a film that deals so perfectly with the frustrations of mediocrity'.[27] The film is narrated by the powerful court composer Antonio Salieri (F. Murray Abraham), who is torn between bitter jealousy and an intense admiration of Mozart's genius. As narrator, the lesser composer offers a privileged point of identification, a diegetic character who bears witness to the maestro's genius. This device recurs in *Immortal*, where Beethoven's devoted follower Schindler (Jeroen Krabbé) takes on the film's hermeneutic task of uncovering the maestro's 'immortal beloved' – the lost love tormenting the great composer. Even as the tourist gaze of the sightseeing tours offers a vantage point for European locations, narrators act as ordinary interlocutors who help navigate distant historical periods and unfamiliar historical content. Creative rivalries and partnerships recur in *Shakespeare*, with a competition between Marlowe and the bard, and in *Total Eclipse* and *Pandaemonium*. In the latter two films the lesser poet (Verlaine, Wordsworth) is both inspired and repelled by the other's incontrovertible originality. Ultimately, however, the contrast between mediocrity and genius shores up the mythology of the 'great man'.

Based on Christopher Hampton's 1968 stage play, *Total Eclipse* was panned by critics: *Empire* called it a 'tawdry enterprise'.[28] Here, the teenage genius Rimbaud (Leonardo DiCaprio) is caught in a destructive relationship with the older married poet Paul Verlaine (David Thewlis). The sadism of their sordid relationship is played out most directly against the older man's wife (Romaine Bohringer); Verlaine beats her while she is pregnant, and later sets her hair on fire. *Total Eclipse* exemplifies a common homosocial creative bond, where women are depicted with ambivalence. For instance, male genius is frequently enabled by women who are muses (*Immortal Beloved*, *Shakespeare*) or nurturing mother figures (*Amadeus*, *Pandaemonium*, *Wilde*), but never creative agents in their own right. *Pandaemonium* poses the question of gender inequality, where

Wordsworth is shown to steal ideas and inspiration from his sister Dorothy. But these quibbles are footnotes in a film that explores, typically, the protagonists' expression of deep interiority and singular creative vision. These depictions of musicians and writers correspond with Christine Battersby's account of masculine genius as perceived by the Romantics:

> in terms of a personality-type (an outsider, near-to-madness, degenerate, shamanistic, etc.). A second (related) idea of 'genius' comes to us from the pre-Romantics – who explained it as a specific mode of consciousness: variously (and conflictingly) described as passion, imagination, instinct, intuition, the unconscious, reason. A third [related] strand . . . describes 'genius' in terms of energy (usually sublimated sexual energy).[29]

These terms are eminently recognisable within the contemporary biopic. The diegetic inscription of authorship through movement-images of character at the writing desk, or through heightened attention to camera work and the look, is common to the group as a whole. Even as the contents of the letter, read aloud, 'fill in' the feelings of its writer, the dramatisation of musical classics (the Mozart 'Requiem', Beethoven's 'Ode to Joy') transports the audience to the artist's moment of inspiration. Conventionally, the music (*Immortal*, *Amadeus*) or play (*Shakespeare*, *Topsy-Turvy*) fades in over the scene of the writing, so we are offered both the freshness of the moment of creation, and the satisfaction of a finished composition. For the finale of *Immortal*, film-maker Bernard Rose also attempts to visualise the source of Beethoven's symphony. At the work's premiere, the ageing, deaf Beethoven (Gary Oldman) climbs onto the stage, his back to the audience. From a close-up of his face, a cut to an extended flashback conveys the source of the epiphanic emotions of 'Ode': late one night, the boy Ludwig climbs out of the window in his nightshirt to escape his abusive father; he runs through the forest to a pond and strips down to his breeches to float on his back, contemplating the stars. A cut to an overhead shot reveals the boy in a pond full of reflected stars; finally, the camera pulls back and back so that the young Ludwig appears afloat in the heavens.

Deleuze's affection-image is the preferred cinematic sign for expression, a cinematic sign akin to Peirce's 'firstness':[30] 'Firstness is difficult to define, because it is felt rather than conceived: it concerns what is new in experience, what is fresh, fleeting and nevertheless eternal. . . . Firstness is thus the category of the possible.'[31] 'Firstness' in these films is akin to the Romantic epiphany and authenticity effect projected by the films: the power of music, poetry, art, theatre to move the audience. Depictions of cultural creation dialogically bridge time and space to reach out toward a contemporary viewer who might be moved by the Mozart 'Requiem' or Beethoven's 'Ode to Joy'. As explored in Chapter Two, the close-up on the hand often conveys the difficult business of self-expression through letter-writing. Similarly, in the interests of heightened drama, the biopic presents a highly physical depiction of creative expression, and the pouring out of the soul onto paper is a sweaty, smudged affair. An example of this can be found in *Pandaemonium*'s writerly 'duelling, banjos', where Wordsworth (John Hannah) and Coleridge (Linus Roache) sit down to compose the 'Lyrical Ballads' in an all-night session. Wordsworth, eternally afflicted with writer's block, watches in frustration as Coleridge (fuelled by his first dose of laudanum) furiously scrawls 'The Rime of the Ancient Mariner'.

Troubled masculine genius and the moment of literary creation: Coleridge (Linus Roache) writing 'The Rime of the Ancient Mariner' in *Pandaemonium*

Here, Temple's film moves into pure romantic imagery, taking us into Coleridge's fevered imagination. Roache's voice-over reading of the poem bridges a transition from the affection-image of hand and face bent over the lamplit pages to the visual exposition of the poem. In this fantasy sequence, Coleridge clings to the icy mast of the death ship, swaying in the wind and scanning the stormy horizon for the albatross. During this, the best part of a disjointed film, the viewer is transported, literally, into the poem and into the head of the poet. In a later sequence, *Pandaemonium* tracks the hallucinating poet into the orientalist kingdom of Kubla Khan, then flashes forward in time. The Mariner's prophecy about the destruction of nature comes to pass as the poet moils through seaside muck; a nuclear power station appears behind him while seabirds struggle feebly in an oil spill. An awkwardly literal rendition of the poem's imagery, this laboured sequence indicates the challenge of the biopic: to enliven and make relevant the weighty classics for present viewers. While *Pandaemonium* succeeds at moments, like many biopics it often suffers from cliché.

With its witty script and agile choreography, *Shakespeare* is the film that perhaps best enlivens the process of literary creation. The script delights in virtuoso appropriation and rewriting, drawing from the practice of Renaissance artists to pilfer earlier classics for dramatic material. A palimpsest of plays within plays, and a sly coupling of historical and fictional figures, Stoppard's clever script fences with the audience over the genre of the play ('Romeo and Ethel the Pirate's Daughter') and the outcome of the love affair: is this a comedy or a tragedy? Through Fiennes' dynamic physical performance, and a fanciful return to its writing and premiere performance, the play comes back to life: rather than pedagogical Shakespeare – the petrified classic, its outcome and every word set in stone – the film casts the viewer bodily into the creative process. *Shakespeare*'s knowing address aligns it with Jean-Louis Comolli's account of historical fiction as a spectacle that 'is always a *game*. It requires the participation of the spectators not as consumers but as players, accomplices, masters of the game, even if they are also its stakes.'[32]

Far surpassing the box-office takings of recent 'straight' adaptations of the bard's plays, *Shakespeare* offers a populist biopic threaded through a behind-the-scenes glimpse into the genesis of *Romeo & Juliet*. Explicitly incorporating the 'gaming' spirit of historical fiction, *Shakespeare* achieves a popular success while retaining a series of clever commentaries for spectators versed in Shakespearean lore. In fact, Stoppard's witty script intersperses the film's blatant populism with a series of running gags about pleasing all tastes. For example, in response to Shakespeare's lofty literary aspirations about theatrical merit, theatre manager Philip Henslowe sagely remarks, 'Love and a bit with the dog. That's what they want.' Meanwhile, a grubby and leering young John Webster comments, 'I like it when they cut heads off. And the daughter, mutilated with knives . . . plenty of blood, that's the only writing'. Of course, part of the joke is that this Miramax British/American co-production (winner of the Oscar for best picture of 1999) exemplifies a profitable rewriting of British high-culture traditions for international (especially 'American') consumption. Meanwhile, *Elizabeth*, another flagrantly ahistorical and 'spectacular' biopic released in the same year, fulfils Webster's taste for gore.

Like *Shakespeare*, Mike Leigh's *Topsy-Turvy* uses the device of a play within a play. Here, the odd couple of dour W.S. Gilbert (Jim Broadbent) and light-hearted Arthur Sullivan (Allan Corduner) struggle to revive their flagging creative partnership with *The Mikado*. As with *Shakespeare*, enticing scenes from the operetta are cut into the narrative, and the film culminates in an explosion of costume, song and dance. Leigh's script cannily doubles Gilbert and Sullivan's problem of artistic freshness with his own revival of a much-loved light-opera classic. He takes a stab at 'high art' values in this celebration of light opera: where Sullivan strives mightily throughout the film to produce a 'serious' musical composition, the epilogue titles note that his 'one grand opera, *Ivanhoe* . . . is now mostly forgotten, and isn't as fun as *The Mikado*'. Finally, characteristically, this democratic director ends *Topsy-Turvy* not with the 'great men', but rather on a solo performance of 'The Moon and I' by Yum-Yum (Sukie Smith). The camera begins with a close-up on Yum-Yum, and gradually pulls back, craning upward to reveal first the orchestra, then the operetta's audience, retrieving the audience from the past to situate them in the (theatrical) present.

Biopics use different strategies to mediate the gap between the (diegetic) past moment of the author and his spark of creation, and the present of the film's reception. Following the logic of Jean-François Lyotard, as postmodern cultural productions these works engage implicitly with the (European) aesthetic project of modernism – the acknowledgment of the 'unpresentable' within representation. This theorist identifies two modes of artistic response to this dilemma. The first emphasises 'the powerlessness of the faculty of presentation [and] the nostalgia for presence felt by the human subject'.[33] Relying on a modernist lament for an imagined moment of lost plenitude and species-being, this mode is crystallised in *Immortal Beloved*. This film is fuelled by a tremendous sense of loss, from the mysterious 'immortal beloved' as receding figure of desire, to the clumsy visual lexicon of the sublime used to illustrate 'Ode to Joy'. Clearly, this mode also corresponds with the nostalgic masculinity and lingering poetics of regret explored in Chapter Two.

In contrast, Lyotard's second (and preferred) mode highlights 'the increase of being and the jubilation which result from the invention of new rules of the game'.[34] This postmodern approach is exemplified by the energy and playfulness of *Shakespeare*, *Topsy-Turvy* and *Amadeus*. These postmodern works retain a knowing distance, while *Immortal Beloved*, *Total Eclipse*, *Pandaemonium* and *Vincent & Theo* enter fully into Romantic tales of artistic genius.

Modernity and the Microcosm

Lyotard's distinction between nostalgic and exuberant postmodern aesthetics places late-twentieth-century cultural forms in dialogue with European modernism. Even as postmodern cultural production takes up modern cultural forms and reinvents them, 90s costume film ambivalently negotiates the European modernity that fostered Beethoven's compositions and Rimbaud's poetry. Contemporary costume film rests on a structuring difference between perceptions of 'Europe' as the (Western) past and 'America' as the industrial and capitalist future. Notably absent from costume drama is an associated perception of Europe as perceived source of Western modernity, democracy and industrialisation. Aside from films set in early modern times (*Shakespeare*, *Restoration*), costume film overwhelmingly prefers the ordered interiors of the houses of fiction to the noise, dirt and crowds of the modern city. Perched ambivalently on the cusp of modernity, the films only offer brief, often unpleasant glimpses of the squalor of the modern city (1870s Paris, London and Brussels of *Total Eclipse*; revolutionary London of 1788 in *Pandaemonium*).

With the cinematic and literary pastoral prevailing over urban space far into the Edwardian period, the European motor of industrialisation comes into the frame only through leisure transportations such as ocean liners (*Portrait*, *The Piano*, *Square*, *Bowl*) and trains (*Mirth*, *Where Angels*). These modern conveyances appear only briefly to sketch in the passage between narrative (and scenic) locations. Exceptionally, in Winterbottom's *Jude* and the 1900 segment of *Orlando*, the steam engine appears as an interruption – a noisy harbinger of the Industrial Revolution disrupting the peaceful English countryside. In *Orlando*, the rushing train surprises Shelmerdine and Orlando as they gallop through misty fields. Hearing the train whistle, the startled Shelmerdine asks: 'What's that?' and Orlando responds, 'The future!' *Orlando* is anomalous in its welcome of the train as dynamic promise of modernity. Characterised by speed, industrialisation and urbanisation, the ontological experience of modernity is often linked with instability, rapid change, and a dislodging of 'authentic', organic premodern experience.

The rushing train is an apt metaphor for modernity as associated with industrialisation and a series of rapid changes in communication, transportation and the everyday structures of time and space. Amidst these processes of destabilising social change, social theorists often posit epistemic ruptures spanning subjective experience, forms of cultural production and the economic infrastructure. Henri Lefebvre describes such a rupture in spatial terms:

> The fact is that around 1910 a certain space was shattered. It was the space of common sense, of knowledge (*savoir*), of social practice, of political power, a space thitherto enshrined in everyday discourse, just as in abstract thought, as the environment of and

channel for communications; the space, too, of classical perspective and geometry,
developed from the Renaissance onwards on the basis of the Greek tradition (Euclid,
logic) and bodied forth in Western art and philosophy, as in the form of the city and the
town. . . . Euclidean and perspectivist space have disappeared as systems of reference
along with other former 'commonplaces' such as the town, history, paternity, the tonal
system in music, traditional morality, and so forth.[35]

Whether such epistemic breaks are located with World War I, the Industrial Revolution
or with the postmodernity of the 60s, a landscape of rupture and change is endemic to
modern and postmodern cultural discourses.

Against these accounts of subjective fragmentation and disorienting social change,
the 'continuous spatial and temporal experience'[36] of the novel, and in turn period
drama, presents intelligible microworlds and distinctive, vivid characters who interact
within them. Within contemporary global image space, picturesque and historic settings, buildings and works of art represent what MacCannell calls 'sacralization', where
identifiable sites are marked off with an 'aura' that sets them apart from the everyday.[37]
These sites are commonly filmed in contemporary costume drama. As with the Anglo-
American house of fiction or Italy as 'cradle of the Renaissance', these films frequently
return to symbolic sites of emergence for Western subjectivity and culture. In keeping
with recurring 'European' signifiers, such sites of return for modern ritual are bound
up with questions of authorship, genius and Romantic vision.

*   *   *

In the first half of this book, I have mapped out the topography of conventional costume drama. This section has mapped out a series of structuring 'interior' and 'exterior' movement-images including the woman at the window, the writing desk and the
letter, the opera and the ball, the sightseeing tour and the moment of artistic creation.
Many of the films analysed in the first four chapters combine a dramatic microcosm
and self-conscious framings, while retaining a formal integrity that I call the house of
fiction. This densely symbolic chronotope evokes the modern subject as a bounded
and deep-feeling self situated within the bourgeois intimate sphere. Isabel and
Newland Archer of *Portrait* and *Innocence* respectively encapsulate the dilemmas of literary protagonists in dialectical struggle with constraining and carefully circumscribed
milieux (the English country house, the New York brownstone or the villas, landscapes
and tourist sites of Italy).

Following the logic of the action-image, these films trace the hero or heroine's trajectory of becoming and desire, and this same logic relegates the contradictions and
social struggles of the broader historical milieu to the landscape or the out-of-field. In
the book's second half, 'Costume Drama Reassembled', I turn to a series of revisionist and formally innovative works that open up the house of fiction to questions of
class, colonialism, transgressive sexuality and the body.

Notes

1. On the 'idea of Europe', see Brian Nelson, David Roberts and Walter Veit (eds), *The Idea of Europe* (New York: Berg Publishers, 1992); Dimitris Eleftheriotis, *Popular Cinemas of Europe* (New York: Continuum, 2001), pp. 3–4; and Antoine Compagnon, 'Mapping the European Mind', in Duncan Petrie (ed.), *Screening Europe* (London: BFI, 1992), pp. 106–13.

2. Richard Dyer and Ginette Vincendeau, 'Introduction', in Richard Dyer and Ginette Vincendeau (eds), *Popular European Cinema* (London: Routledge, 1992), p. 6.

3. Joseph H. O'Mealy, *Alan Bennett: A Critical Introduction* (New York: Routledge, 2001), p. 142.

4. Nowell-Smith, 'Introduction', *Hollywood & Europe*, p. 10.

5. Stuart Hall, 'The Local and the Global: Globalization and Ethnicity', in Anthony D. King (ed.), *Culture, Globalization and the World System* (London: Macmillan, 1991), p. 28.

6. John Urry, *The Tourist Gaze*, 2nd edn (London: Sage Publications, 2002), p. 1.

7. For instance, a two-page illustrated spread in the 'Escape' (travel) section of the *Observer* offers 'a guided tour of cinema's famous locations' for *Shakespeare*, *The Madness of King George*, *Shadowlands*, *Braveheart* and *Emma* (among others). See Robin Barton and Sarah Jacobs, 'Where to find the film action', the *Observer*, 23 July 2000, 'Escape' section, pp. 12–13. Popular press coverage of period drama locations is important to heritage critics' linkage of heritage cinema and tourism. See, for instance, Higson, *English Heritage*, pp. 56–63.

8. James Buzard, *The Beaten Track* (Oxford: Clarendon Press, 1993), p. 188.

9. Ibid., p. 219.

10. Jonathan Freedman, 'The Moment of Henry James', in Freedman (ed.), *The Cambridge Companion to Henry James*, p. 8.

11. Deborah L. Parsons, 'The Note/ Notion of Europe: Henry James and the Gendered Landscape of Heritage Tourism', *Symbiosis* vol. 2 no. 2, 1998, p. 229.

12. Ibid., p. 230.

13. James Buzard, 'A Continent of Pictures: Reflections on the "Europe" of Nineteenth-Century Tourists', *Publications of the Modern Language Association of America* vol. 108 no. 1, 1993, p. 32.

14. Cook, *Fashioning the Nation*, pp. 2–4.

15. Parsons, 'The Note/ Notion of Europe', p. 229.

16. Urry, *The Tourist Gaze*, p. 150.

17. Adeline Tintner, cited in Buzard, *The Beaten Track*, p. 225.

18. Monk, 'Heritage films and the British cinematic audience in the 1990s', p. 31.

19. Caughie, *Television Drama*, pp. 208–9.

20. Dean MacCannell, *The Tourist* (New York: Schocken Books, 1989), p. 10.

21. Thanks to Dimitris Eleftheriotis for his helpful comments about this European tradition. For a discussion of the European art/popular cinema divide, see his *Popular Cinemas of Europe*, pp. 68–80.

22. James Buzard, 'A Continent of Pictures', p. 33.

23. Louise Tutt, '*Wings of the Dove* production notes', *Screen International* no. 1069, 2 August, 1996, p. 18.

24. Patricia White, *unInvited* (Bloomington: Indiana University Press, 1999), p. 111.

25. Steve Neale, 'Art Cinema as Institution', *Screen* vol. 22 no. 1, 1981, pp. 14–15.

26. Landy, *British Genres*, pp. 58–9.

27. Nora Lee, 'Miroslav Ondricek and Amadeus', *American Cinematographer*, April 1985, p. 95.

28. See Kenneth Geist, '*Total Eclipse*', *Empire* vol. 47 nos. 1/2, Jan/Feb 1996, p. 69.

29. Christine Battersby, *Gender and Genius: Towards a Feminist Aesthetics* (Bloomington: Indiana University Press, 1989), p. 156.

30. For a useful account of Deleuze's references to Charles Sanders Peirce's semiotic terms 'firstness', 'secondness' and 'thirdness' in *Cinema 1*, see Rodowick, *Gilles Deleuze's Time Machine*, pp. 55–9.

31. Deleuze, *Cinema 1*, p. 98.

32. Jean-Louis Comolli, 'Historical Fiction: A Body Too Much', *Screen* vol. 19 no. 2, 1978, p. 46.

33. Jean-François Lyotard, *The Postmodern Condition* (Minneapolis: University of Minnesota Press, 1999), p. 79.

34. Ibid., p. 80.

35. Lefebvre, *The Production of Space*, p. 25.

36. Margaret Morse, 'Paradoxes of Realism', in Ron Burnett (ed.), *Explorations in Film Theory* (Bloomington: Indiana University Press, 1991), p. 158.

37. See MacCannell, *The Tourist*, pp. 43–8.

Part Two
Costume Drama Reassembled

Chapter Five
Radical Form, Radical Pasts

Two important films of the early 90s, Sally Potter's *Orlando* and Julie Dash's *Daughters of the Dust*, open up costume drama's microcosm to broader social formations. In the process, each film interrogates the critical possibilities and limitations of generic form. *Orlando* presents a stunning instance of 'costume drama reassembled', brilliantly rewriting formal codes of narrative/time, *mise en scène*/filmic space, and costume/character. Potter's film can be read as an allegorical journey based upon an influential mode of Western liberal feminist discourse; significantly, Orlando literally 'stumbles' when s/he reaches the British Empire. If imperialism and the colonial encounter present discursive limits for *Orlando* and feminist costume film, Dash's singular film offers a rejoinder to these limits. *Daughters* begins from a very different place, on the Gullah sea islands with the collective protagonist of the Peazant family descended from slaves. Incorporating a dense intertextual field of African American cultural references into the iconography of costume drama, Dash's film mediates past violence, present struggle and a utopian future.

With close attention to *mise en scène*, tempo, costume and performance, I have argued so far in this book that many costume films dwell upon a particular quality of white, bourgeois social constraint. This emblematic repressive economy enables a journey into the modern self framed through past/present discourses of gender, sexuality, expression and transformation. In contrast with the hegemonic spatio-temporal cohesion of the house of fiction, *Orlando* and *Daughters* use space and time innovatively in the service of the 'radical past'. Along with works such as *The Piano* and *Edward II* (addressed in the next chapters), these films challenge a prevalent account of costume drama as intrinsically conservative, nostalgic or outside of history. Deliberately reassembling costume drama's formal elements, these films interrogate the very terms of 'politics' and 'history'. As Meaghan Morris writes, feminist historical discourse

> is skeptical but *constructive*. . . . Feminist discourse often stammers when it comes to validating action with a logic of events; it is not that this logic is renounced, or history deemed chaotic, but that there is a struggle to name a different temporality . . . that might make a *feminist* concept of eventfulness historically intelligible. More exactly, feminism makes political discourse 'stammer'.[1]

Orlando: Chronotope and Costume

As mentioned previously, Teresa de Lauretis identifies a structuring narrative economy of gendered stasis and movement that scripts the male subject as dynamic hero who strides through narrative time and space, where the female character stands for stasis, home and hearth. The female character represents social and narrative constraint – a threshold or destination for the male protagonist's inner and outer journeys of self-realisation and social transformation. Doane extends this gendered economy to spatio-temporal patterns of genre, suggesting that more dynamic narratives and open landscapes signifying freedom of movement correspond to male address; meanwhile cluttered interiors and constraint correspond to female address.[2] Female narrative constraint is manifested textually and historically in gendered codes of corporeal and geographical mobility – differential gendered access to real and imagined social space and agency.

With its meandering, detail-rich, languorous quality of event, costume drama is a quintessentially 'female' genre. In relation to structuralist terms of gendered (narrative) movement (as well as Deleuze's action-image), what fascinates me about *Orlando* is the attenuated dynamism of a protagonist who changes, at least on the surface, from male to female. If narrative corresponds conceptually with a journey, Orlando's trajectory is unusual, with his/her audacious time travelling through 400 years of English history. The slowness and uncertainty of *Orlando*'s progress coincides with an explicit play (in both Virginia Woolf's source novel and Potter's adaptation) with gendered conventions of narrative. According to de Lauretis, feminist film criticism and film-making have sought to produce new forms of discourse and narrative in order to 'construct the terms of reference of another measure of desire and the conditions of possibility for a different social subject'.[3] Potter's *Orlando*, like her earlier projects *Thriller* (1979) and *The Gold Diggers* (1984), takes up this challenge.

Bakhtin's chronotope connects spatio-temporal forms of genre and narrative with the historical contexts where the work is produced and read. Thus, in the 'deep generative' work of culture, historical relations of power and difference are embedded into the very form of narrative: 'Spatial and temporal indicators are fused into one carefully thought-out, concrete whole. Time, as it were, thickens, takes on flesh, becomes artistically visible; likewise, space becomes charged and responsive to the movements of time, plot and history.'[4] Where the Deleuzian movement-image offers a cinematic approach to the image in and through time, I return here to Bakhtin who (like Lefebvre and de Certeau) works from a Marxist account of the historical continuity of cultural form as a site of struggle. Given costume drama's predominantly literary 'sources', and indeed the broadly literary antecedents of cinematic narrative and genre, Bakhtin's chronotope, with its roots in literary criticism, is useful for investigating *Orlando* as a deliberately time-travelling and intertextual adaptation.

A classical Greek chronotope, the 'adventure novel of everyday life' evokes the spatio-temporal machinations of plot in *Orlando*. This form twins a biographical narrative of human identity, crisis and metamorphosis with an adventure structure. Here, the 'empty' epic adventure time of the Greek romance is intermingled with the everyday time of human biography: 'The factor of the journey itself, the itinerary, is an actual one: it imparts to the temporal sequence of the novel a real and essential organizing center. In such novels, finally, biography is the crucial organizing principle for time.'[5] In fact, Orlando follows a highly selective journey through 400 years of English aristocratic gender and social relations. A considerable critical and commercial success[6] for an art film, *Orlando* capitalises on Woolf's novella as an iconic feminist text. The subtitle of Woolf's novel, 'a biography', hints that *Orlando* was written as a *roman-à-clef* shadowing the life of Woolf's friend and lover Vita Sackville-West.[7] Stylised and self-conscious,

Orlando's journey evokes an allegorical (English) feminist trajectory, transporting the modern viewer into the past for a feminist 'history of the present'.

Potter's film follows a narrative structure of segmentation and passage. Intertitled signposts mark off a sequence of seven semi-autonomous episodes: '1600 DEATH', '1610 LOVE', '1650 POETRY', '1700 POLITICS', '1750 SOCIETY', '1800 SEX', and 'BIRTH' (not dated). Bold white capitals on a black screen, these intertitles effectively frame, foreground and methodically interrupt the narrative. Crass episodal tags from death to (re)birth mark formative moments in Orlando's life according to traditional biographical developmental stages. Meanwhile, Orlando passes through stylised periods delineated by the dates. The protagonist, then, literally moves through clearly differentiated tableaux, from the dotage of Elizabeth I (1600) to an ambassadorial appointment in the Orient (1700) and into the late 20th century (the present day of Woolf/Potter). [8]

I shall call these segments 'tableaux' or, even better, 'movements'. As with musical compositions, each movement carries its own colorations and mood – a stylistically and narratively semi-autonomous segment that encapsulates an aesthetic/historical milieu. Visually, the tableaux are set apart by a distinct array of period costumes and decor. The Elizabethan grounds of the great house, the Duchess's drawing room, or the magical ice court, each fragment of filmic space metonymically invokes an era using stylised non-realist signifiers. In keeping with the film's theme of property holding, Orlando continually returns to the family seat, the great house. The bold black-and-white flagstones of the great hall, the manor's exterior architecture, and the great oak tree in the field that bookends the film ('enduring old England') remain constant. Yet the rooms (like Orlando) are 'made over' to signal temporal transitions. Sandra Gilbert suggests that this structure crystallises Woolf's 'alternative' history: 'Orlando *is* history, if only because the light of her mind is the lamp that lights up time . . . and her stately mansion is the house whose endurance-through-change is the metaphor that Woolf gives us for human duration.'[9]

Bakhtin's adventure novel chronotope is structurally episodic, a series of ordeals against 'a very broad and varied geographical background'.[10] Potter adapts Woolf's modernist text using a postmodern spatiality characterised by pastiche and fragmentation. Through Orlando's distinctive asides and looks into the camera, the bounded parameters of the house of fiction are scrutinised. Rather than a realist 'narrative space' created by continuity editing, *Orlando* is comprised of a series of mannered, theatrical *tableaux*. With its stylistic excess and a 'flat' postmodern scenic sense, this theatrical spatiality is reminiscent of other British 'anti-heritage' auteurist projects such as Peter Greenaway's *The Draughtsman's Contract*, Derek Jarman's *Caravaggio* and *Edward II* or Isaac Julien's *Looking for Langston* (1989). On set decoration, Potter comments:

> I always said to the design teams: this is not a costume drama, this is not a historical
> film. It's a film about now that happens to move through these periods. Research and
> find out all the things we can and then throw them away. We're going to stylize, we're
> going to leave out, exclude certain colours or textures or shapes. . . . The usual
> approach to costume drama is through . . . realism, where a room is made to look like
> a room as it is thought to have looked then. But the premise of *Orlando* is that all
> history is imagined history and leaves out all the most important bits anyway.[11]

The fantastical setting of each movement calls attention to the film's irreality. The encounter with the Muscovites transpires not in a castle, but in the magical space of the ice court; Orlando's ambassadorial mission to Asia occurs within a grove of pillars, or in the windblown desert. Balanced compositions and static long shots emphasise theatrical *tableaux* where the actors go through their painstakingly choreographed, if meaningless, paces. Superb costumes and a performative attention to exaggerated ritual offer a visual satire of bourgeois English manners, gender and, less rigorously, empire.

Innovative set design is echoed in Sandy Powell's virtuoso costumes, described as 'citational interpretations as opposed to realistic productions'.[12] The sheer crippling unmanageability of Orlando's bourgeois female attire in the latter half of the film brilliantly conveys feminine physical and social constraint as 'image of thought'. Shortly after her sex change, a newly corseted Orlando minces with difficulty around the dust-draped furniture in what had been her own parlour in a voluminous stiff white gown; the whiteness and volume of her skirt liken her to the furniture, which has been draped awaiting the return of the lord of the manor. Orlando's ambivalent debut as a member of the 'fairer sex' in 1750 corresponds loosely with the onset of the Industrial Revolution in England. Clothing historians have associated the late eighteenth century with gendered and classed changes in clothing where, within the emergent middle class, women's attire became increasingly elaborate: 'The conspicuous display of finery by women of the rising bourgeois class served as an advertisement of their husband's (or father's) prosperity, the unwieldliness of the increasingly pumped up and elaborate clothing itself a sign of the freedom of women of this leisure class from the physical requirements even of household labour.'[13] This phenomenon is brilliantly evoked in the SOCIETY movement, where Orlando is costumed like an elaborate, frosted blue cake and perched on a love seat. Complete with a sculpted headdress, in her huge blue dress Orlando resembles a porcelain figurine, hampered from moving or responding to the routine snubs by the male 'wits'.

Orlando (Tilda Swinton) entrapped in feminine attire

Meanwhile, in this period men of the upper and middle classes gradually abandoned their earlier dandy phase – styles depicted exaggeratedly in *Orlando* with stiff Elizabethan collars, a voluminous lace shirt with a huge bow at the collar, and satin male fripperies. From the mid-eighteenth century, clothes becoming increasingly more sombre, purposeful, corresponding with the emergent masculine 'virtues of industry, self-control, and renunciation'.[14] These qualities are captured in Newland's sartorial conformity in *Innocence* and William Adamson's sombre clothes in *Angels & Insects*. Eventually, Orlando dons the more unisex garb of the liberated twentieth-century woman, entering the 'present' in a pair of practical brown trousers and a white shirt, her hair pulled back. Travelling clothes equip her to set off into the future on a vintage motorcycle with her daughter in the sidecar. A voice-over notes with satisfaction that she is 'no longer trapped by destiny' – nor is she trapped by her attire.

Feminist Narrative Movement

Potter vehemently rejects dominant realist conventions for costume film. Devising a radically different formal language for the past, she deploys strategies often associated with postmodernism: pastiche, irony, citation, performativity; further, Potter's stylised period spectacle generates a disjointed and fragmented filmic space, which overwhelms narrative drive. Intriguingly, some of these very qualities, notably the flattening of the past into postmodern spectacle, are central to the critique of heritage cinema. For instance, Fredric Jameson's influential critique of 'postmodern historicity' describes 'an approach to the "past" through stylistic connotation, conveying "pastness" by glossy qualities of the image and . . . by the attributes of fashion'.[15] Drawing from Jameson, Higson suggests the social critique and irony of dialogue and narrative are often overwhelmed by the spectacle of heritage locations and *mise en scène*.

Within the parameters of this argument, what would constitute a 'critical' or 'radical' period drama? A modernist response to this problem might prescribe Brechtian distantiation to unsettle the codes of realism. These formal strategies can be found within a British auteurist anti-heritage tradition that includes Greenaway, Julien and Jarman; accordingly, Potter's reassemblage of the house of fiction does more than rearrange the furniture. Rather than a realist narrative space, the various conventions of agency, event, referentiality and milieu are deterritorialised. Potter replaces 'the Orient' with Uzbekistan, symbolically reconfiguring the 'imagined geography' of Britain/Europe/Asia. In a related example, for Colin MacCabe Jarman's *The Tempest* (1980) challenges a dominant 'representational space' that developed within English theatre in the early seventeenth century and continues to the present day. Shakespeare's play emerged in a period when a populist and politically engaged Elizabethan theatre shifted to a more aesthetically, socially and sexually contained tradition, directed toward increasingly privileged audiences. For MacCabe, *The Tempest* fractures this hegemonic representational space by situating the play 'not on an island but in a ruined aristocratic house, an imperial monument'.[16]

Returning to *Orlando* and the problem of radical costume film, it is important to remember that Jameson's critique exceeds questions of form. For this author, the postmodern simulacrum of the past signals 'the loss of the radical past': 'This mesmerizing new aesthetic mode itself emerged as an elaborated symptom of the waning of our historicity, of our lived possibility of experiencing history in some active way.'[17] Undoubtedly, Orlando is buffeted by the winds of change – the nineteenth century arrives with a great gust of wind and a locomotive, and she stumbles while pregnant through the trench warfare of World War I. However, the film eschews causal chronology, and these events are not conventionally historical, but rather filtered through stylised tableaux and Orlando's idiosyncratic perception. Ultimately, Potter's film is resolutely presentist. After all, as stated above, 'the premise of Orlando is that all history is imagined history and leaves out all the most important bits anyway'.

The problem of the 'openness of history' raises the crucial Marxist question of history as time and transformation. How might this languid and often conservative filmmaking tradition, caught up in the inconsequential detail of costume and setting, understand social change and the 'openness of history'? Pushed to the extreme in Orlando, costume drama's characteristic torpor stands in paradoxical relation to the great modernist paradigms of historical transformation and change. Narrative is a key measure of time in cultural texts, and Orlando's idiosyncratic plot structure indicates the film's treatment of subjective and social change.

For de Lauretis, 'the semantic structure of all narrative is the movement of an actant-subject toward an actant-object',[18] and the movement of narrative 'seems to be that of a passage, a transformation predicated on the figure of a hero, a mythical subject'.[19] This gendered division of narrative labours describes

> the fundamental opposition between boundary and passage; and if passage may be in either direction, from inside to outside or vice versa, from life to death or vice versa, nonetheless all these terms are predicated on the single figure of the hero who crosses the boundary and penetrates the other space. In so doing the hero, the mythical subject, is constructed as human being and as male; he is creator of differences. Female is what is not susceptible to transformation, to life or death; she (it) is an element of plot-space, a topos, a resistance, matrix and matter.[20]

Confounding the binary gendering of movement and agency (and the structural logic of narratology), Orlando becomes mobile, almost in spite of him/herself, as s/he moves through different historical circumstances. But this is a fickle quality of agency, reliant on the whims of chance. Eschewing a psychological motor of character development, Orlando progresses according to Bakhtin's 'logic of chance': 'This logic is one of random contingency, which is to say, chance simultaneity [meetings] and chance rupture [nonmeetings], that is, a logic of random disjunctions in time as well.'[21] Orlando's immortality springs from his fortuitous meeting with Queen Elizabeth I who, upon her deathbed, simply wills away the ruins of time. Subsequently, he happens to meet Sasha (the daughter of the Muscovite ambassador) amongst the pomp of the ice court – only to court her for only the time granted by the insubstantial ice that so beautifully suspends the skaters.

Intriguingly, Orlando's biographical journey differs from Bakhtin's adventure novel of everyday life, where the hero must weather crisis and emerge transformed, a better (or worse) version of himself. Rather, Orlando proves a lethargic hero who fails most of the 'ordeals' of manliness (or womanliness). In this way, the closure of typical narrative convention is constantly denied: our hero does not get his girl; he proves a mediocre 'dabbling' poet; faced with the enemies at the gate of Khiva, Orlando fails the test of manly valour and flees; Orlando parts with Shelmerdine. This frustration of each segment's micronarrative recursively defies conventional narrative resolution in the film as a whole – both the heterosexual closure of marriage and the capitalist drive toward regaining what was owned and lost, Orlando's property. Moreover, where metamorphosis is central to Bakhtin's biographical passage, Orlando does not change fundamentally, even though he changes sex.

Through such a contradictory account of gendered agency, *Orlando* confounds a structuralist account of narrative. Indeed, Woolf and Potter set out to usurp such narrative conventions. In the film, Orlando's transformation is registered superficially at the level of costume and hairstyle. Upon realising her change of sex, Orlando comments dryly to the camera, 'Same person. No difference at all. Just a different sex.' Woolf and Potter remind us that gender is insignificant; at the same time, however, the film's irony arises from its demonstration that gender is made to matter immensely through social and legal convention. In this vein it is absolutely pivotal that Orlando is played by a woman, not a man. While *Orlando* is commonly treated as a 'cross-dressing' film, I read Orlando's enigmatic address to the camera as female, and feminist. In this deliberately allegorical feminist project, what de Lauretis calls 'desire in narrative' is vested in *Orlando*'s allegorical journey. This impetus corresponds to Rosi Braidotti's 'ontological desire': 'the desire to be, the tendency of the subject to be, the predisposition of the subject toward being'.[22]

For Braidotti, psychoanalysis and Deleuzian theory both deploy desire as a challenge to Enlightenment thought. However, Deleuze decentres normative desiring-movements of heterosexual desire and Oedipal narratives towards a more dispersed account of affects and intensities. 'Ontological desire', as a trajectory toward an 'embodied female feminist subject', exceeds the psychoanalytic desire explored in Chapter Two and is emphatically social: 'Not only is it intersubjective but also it transcends the subject.'[23] Explicitly confounding conventional narrative resolutions of marriage and ownership, *Orlando* does not follow the causality of the action-image – the psychological progession of characterisation – but rather projects a 'female feminist subject' who witnesses and comments upon the historical milieux of costume drama.

The Limits of Western Feminism

Orlando's 'look' provides a chronotopic link between the text and the meaning-making processes of situated historical subjects. By evoking Woolf's iconic feminist text and authorial voice, Orlando speaks from an iconic source of Western, English-speaking feminism. Hardly disturbing the times through which she travels, Orlando bears witness to the absurdity of these quasi-historical tableaux, pausing periodically to 'report back' to the 90s audience. Through the prism of Deleuze's affection-image as close-up, these looks forge a dialogic bridge, seeking a recognition in the audience that exceeds diegetic 'identification'. Akin to Braidotti's 'ontological desire', this look communicates the possibility for a feminist future emerging from a shared understanding of past oppression.

Potter's changes to key aspects of Woolf's plot offers clues to the 90s feminist exigencies informing her adaptation. Woolf's novella, a wish-fulfilling spoof biography of Vita Sackville-West, ends with green lights on all counts. Potter's film also ends on a hopeful note, but renounces the romantic closure of married life with Shelmerdine, gives up the bourgeois privilege of property, and trades a daughter for the son.

Replacing the conventional closure of the 'sexual contract', in Potter's vision the symbolic achievement of female artistic self-expression is crucial to a utopian feminist future. The film closes in the field under the oak tree where it began with the unbearded youth trying to write poetry. Only now, in the present, Orlando stares coolly into the camera in a final lingering close-up, as her daughter plays with a camcorder (a symbol of feminist self-representation). The field, the oak tree (solid, enduring old England), Somerville's otherworldly angelic falsetto, bookend the film, enclosing it in the pleasing wrapper of 'once upon a time' and 'happily ever after'.

As with Campion, Rozema and Holland, who rewrite the endings for *Portrait*, *Mansfield* and *Square* respectively, the gesture toward the future resides implicitly with the feminist auteurs. Returning to the problem of the 'openness of history', *Orlando*'s look does not bring an implied audience into the past itself, as s/he is always framed as a bystander, a visitor. Potter's is a textual project that sets out to rework the cinematic conventions of the past. However, in evoking the transformative power of authorship, Potter's film shares some ground with the romantic biopics explored in the last chapter. Moreover, *Orlando* is firmly embedded in an English feminist project that includes Woolf as an iconic figure.[24] The film's desiring movement toward female authorship invokes an intertextual superimposition of three generations of cultural producers: Woolf, Potter, and Swinton.[25] The juxtaposition of these three faces suggests both the power and the limits of Potter's project as a radical costume drama.

The white bourgeois English face as iconic point of identification stands in for an influential Western feminist tradition. For Gayatri Spivak, 'what is at stake, for feminist individualism in the age of imperialism, is precisely the making of human beings, the constitution and "interpellation" of the subject not only as individual but as "individualist".'[26] At its most explicitly 'feminist', costume drama is taken up with the (re)production – and the marketing – of female (and protofeminist) individuals: the 'vivid individual' or character (Isabel Archer, Ada McGrath), the bravura performance (Tilda Swinton, Holly Hunter), the feminine and feminist auteur (Woolf, Potter, Campion). As I suggested of the Austen and James adaptations, many feminist costume dramas script the dilemmas and desires of the present through the prism of the past. In this respect, *Orlando*'s dialogic look makes explicit the allegorical journey that joins *Mansfield Park*, *Washington Square*, *The Piano*, *Sense*, *Portrait* and *Orlando*.

I argued in Chapter One that imperialism marks a discursive limit for the Austen adaptations and costume drama generally; this dynamic can also be found in the self-conscious *Orlando*. Empire is commonly depicted as a romantic destination to escape the constraints of Old World society (*Persuasion*, *Maurice*). When the films venture into the 'contact zone',[27] they are fraught with danger and exotic sexuality (*Angels & Insects*, *The Piano*, *A Passage to India*). Woolf's novella deliberately satirises that convention of the English novel where privileged young men are sent to sow their wild oats in the colonies. The gentle irony of *Orlando*'s sojourn in Khiva (shot in Uzbekistan) is conveyed through the stock trope of the adventure novel, the encounter with the Other.

Khan: 'Why are you here?'
Orlando: 'I am here as a representative of His Majesty's government –'
Khan: 'Yes. It has been said to me that the English make a habit of collecting . . . countries.'

The contact zone: the Khan of Khiva (Lothaire Bluteau) has heard that the English make a habit of collecting . . . countries

This scene, as well as the Khan's elaborate exchange of toasts with Orlando, incisively parodies the imperial encounter. The Khan is resplendent in a blue 'Arab' outfit,[28] flanked by his twin turbaned lieutenants with columns aligned perfectly behind. Orlando is clad even more outrageously in an enormous white flowing wig, backed up by his effeminate soldiers. The theatricality of these matched shots, the stasis of both camera and actors, concisely satirises the imperial encounter with strategies similar to those Potter employs elsewhere to address gender.

Orlando is symptomatic of imperialism as a discursive limit for feminist costume drama, and in turn for Western feminism. How is an English film-maker to critically represent the project of empire? What exactly is/was Orlando doing in Khiva? Following Woolf, Potter focuses on empty ceremonious detail and luxury, representing the lassitude of Orlando's oriental mission through the constant parading of the Ambassador and his henchmen through the dusty streets of the walled city. After a time, Ambassador Orlando is pictured posed in rapturous meditation beside a 'Turkish' bath, wrapped in a middle eastern shift, his hair up in a towel. Apparently, Orlando has 'gone native', fulfilling the cliché of Westerners who 'discover' themselves in the Orient. However, Brenda Longfellow's caution about Ulrike Ottinger's disavowed orientalism through postmodern pastiche in *Johanna d'Arc de Mongolie* (1989) also applies to Potter's film: 'The caricatured nature of the orientalist signifier . . . functions to deny any ontological status of the referent, [but] this reflexivity does not entirely liberate the gesture from the orientalist scenario.'[29]

In imperialist literature, the encounter often facilitates some deeper knowledge of self. The Other (like the female term in de Lauretis' equation), marks a threshold for the protagonist's passage. Although Orlando is pointedly framed as narcissistically alone in Khiva (a rendezvous with self as the logical fruition of the colonial encounter), such a critique can only be about Englishness. As in *A Passage to India*, the colonial encounter ultimately reinstates the gap between self and Other, bringing Orlando back to her 'true' (female and English) self. Personal and political crisis strikes for Orlando only with the Khan's enemies at the city gates when the English visitors are called upon to prove their mettle. Significantly, an incomprehensible battle between heathen forces becomes backdrop and catalyst for Orlando's sex change. At this key juncture in the film, the site of critique shifts from the awkwardness of the colonial encounter back to issues of gender, as Orlando is abruptly transported back to SOCIETY on the back of a camel. Crisis of empire becomes crisis in masculinity, a timely disengagement from distasteful matters of statesmanship and empire.

Woolf's point, of course, is that British women have historically been excluded from the public life of Orlando's country. As a limit case, *Orlando*'s expedition to Khiva reveals the contested quality of imperial space as a vanishing point for a critical feminist costume drama. Orlando's journey of becoming through the ages brings into relief the allegorical trajectory of the individual white bourgeois subject. A radical costume drama addressing class, race and colonialism must begin somewhere else altogether, and this is precisely the achievement of Julie Dash's 1991 *Daughters of the Dust*. Dash's work emerges from a radical contingent of Black film-makers at the UCLA film school, and needs to be understood within the context of African American self-representation. Despite a languorous pace and unconventional form, Dash refuses the category of 'experimental' film, insisting that the primary intended audience for *Daughters* was Black women.[30] *Daughters* can also be read as a rejoinder to contemporary costume drama. As with *Orlando* and *The Piano*, the contemporary spectator is challenged to think about the history of women's oppression through reconfigured narrative space and unexpected articulations of *mise en scène*, costume and the body.

Daughters of the Dust: The Past as Living Memory

Daughters brings African American experience into the very white frame of costume drama, celebrating a tradition of Black women's resistance to oppression. Influenced by the Black independent cinema tradition, the film uses distinctive 'communal' spatial and narrative structures and refers to a rich intertextual field of African American cultural forms. Dash works from precise spatial and temporal coordinates, portraying one day of a Gullah island family in 1902. Descended from slaves, the Peazant family lives on one of the sea islands off the coast of South Carolina and Georgia. The major drop-off point for Africans brought to North America during the transatlantic slave trade, the Gullah islands retained strong elements of African culture.[31] One generation after slavery, the Peazants prepare to leave 'Ibo Landing' with its associations with slavery and the 'old ways' to pursue the American dream on the mainland. *Daughters* generates a rich materiality of history, place and memory that interrogates cultural identity as a *shared* 'matter of "becoming" as well as of "being." It belongs to the future as much as to the past'.[32]

Daughters chronicles a family gathering called by great-grandmother Nana (Cora Lee Day) on the day before the planned departure. Nana tries to persuade the younger generations to stay and to heed the wisdom of African traditions and spirituality. The film is shot in 35mm and reduced to 16mm to enhance resolution; it favours long takes and careful compositions resembling 'iconic portraits [where] the images resonate beyond their duration on the screen'.[33] Indeed, *Daughters* is deliberately photographic in composition, and the importance of Black self-representation is signalled through the photographer Mr Snead, who documents the family's departure. Working with cinematographer Arthur Jafa Rogobodian, Dash's 'layered dissolves' are a conscious tribute to Harlem photographer James Van der Zee. A series of carefully composed shots capture groupings of characters rather than individuals – an imaging strategy that portrays the matriarchal Peazant clan as a multiple protagonist with different personalities, ages and religious convictions.

Daughters is characterised by lush cinematography, careful compositions and an extremely slow pace. Along with Julien's *Looking for Langston*, the film has been critiqued as 'too beautiful' for a radical Black aesthetic.[34] Such a view associates politicised Black self-representation with a gritty inner-city milieu favoured by 80s and 90s film-makers such as Spike Lee and David Singleton. However, Karen Alexander insists that 'the retelling of history is a fundamental concern of almost all significant black cinema and culture. Spike Lee's *Malcolm X* and Isaac Julien's *Looking for Langston* could each be dismissed as a costume drama, but each is also a history lesson.'[35] Following from her earlier *Illusions* (1982), Dash presents a critique of racial representation in American cinema; in this respect (as with *Orlando*) the 'history lesson' is inextricable from the history of representation. From its opening shots *Daughters* subtly undermines pictorial traditions of racism and colonialism:

> The landscape in the opening shots is hot, green, and sluggish. A boat glides into view.
> Embedded in the Black spectator's mind is *that* boat, *those* ships. As this boat cuts
> through the green, thick waters, we see a woman standing near the prow. She wears a
> veiled hat and a long, white dress. Embedded in the memory of millions is the
> European schoolmarm-adventuress-mercenary-disguised-as-missionary woman who
> helps sell the conquest of Africa. ... But this is not that woman. She's standing
> hipshot, chin cocked, one arm akimbo.[36]

This figure evokes Katharine Hepburn in *The African Queen* (1951), but as Toni Cade Bambara notes, 'that hipshot posture says, Africans will not be seen scrambling in the dust for Bogie's tossed away stogie. Nor singing off-key as Hepburn plunks Anglican hymns on the piano.'[37] This opening sequence indicates the arrivals and departures that structure this film. The woman with the hipshot posture is Yellow Mary (Barbara O. Jones), returning to her home from the mainland with her friend Trula (Trula Hoosier); the women are resplendent in elegant white gowns with dramatic veiled hats that mark them off as outsiders, city dwellers and 'fancy women'. Reminiscent of Impressionist painting, the film's carefully composed *mise en scène* incorporates picnics, expansive beaches and sunny glades. Dash's Black characters in period costume and painterly compositions disrupt these white European aesthetic traditions. *Innocence* evokes the same painterly tradition to frame Michelle Pfeiffer in a white dress and parasol on the park bench, with the effect of freezing the female figure in time as an objet d'art and object of desire. In contrast, the Peazants' body language, gestures and language challenge these representational codes and insist on the co-presence of African American lives in the historical frame.

Yellow Mary is the truant Peazant who has left the island for the city. Dressed in city clothes, she is judged harshly by the islanders as 'yellow' (half-breed), a prostitute, and possibly a lesbian (her relationship with Trula is ambiguous). Through the family's harsh

Daughters of the Dust: The boat arrives at Ibo Landing

judgments, Dash portrays a streak of parochialism, highlighting differences within the community. In turn, the city women offer outsiders' perspectives on island customs that guide the film's investigation of this fragile community. Yellow Mary and Trula were scripted according to Dash's research findings that many prostitutes of this period were lesbians and bisexual women who travelled together;[38] these characters also inscribe different historical patterns in Black women's lives into the film's allegorical family.[39]

Where the conventions of costume film (and narrative cinema more generally) would focus on a single character and love story – perhaps Yellow Mary's return to an old lover – Dash creates a shared cinematic space that allows for multiple perspectives. In the barge opposite Mary and Trula sits Viola Peazant (Cheryl Lynn Bruce), a zealous Christian clad in sombre missionary clothes. A forward-looking Christian woman, Viola comments on the Peazants' upcoming migration: 'What's past is prologue . . . I see this day as their first steps towards progress, an engraved invitation, you might say, to the culture, education and wealth of the mainland.' Viola, like her sister Haagar, who scorns Nana's superstitions and 'old ways', favours a 'modernising' strategy for Black development. This dream of progress is encapsulated in brief early film footage of a bustling city cut in as one of the children looks at photographs of the North.

Upon her arrival, Yellow Mary shares Hagaar's and Viola's scepticism toward the past: 'Here it is folks! Ibo Landing, reflecting the muddy waters of history. . . . I don't look for my reflection in no muddy water, you know. The only way for things to happen or for people to change is to keep moving.' This declaration suggests an ambivalence within the film toward modernity and 'progress'. Viola and Hagaar ascribe to the promise of modernity, industrialisation and 'the North' as the future for African Americans. Yet Mary's experience of the wider world is marked by exploitation. Later in the film, she recounts she worked as a wet nurse for a white family after the stillbirth of her own child; taken along as a servant to Cuba, she was not permitted to leave until 'fixing' her breasts so that she could no longer nurse. Like Eula's rape by an unnamed (presumably white) man that precedes the film's narrative,

Mary's story details Black women's oppression. But these are not only tales of suffering, but also of resistance and coming to terms with a violent past. In the course of the day, Yellow Mary comes to value the traditions represented by Nana and the Unborn Child.

The film is bookended by these two voices, the matriarch Nana embodying the memory of the 'old souls' who have come before, and the Unborn Child, a promise of the future sent by the ancestors to heal the rifts in the Peazant family. For instance, there is a deep gulf of hurt and anger between the Unborn Child's mother Eula (Alva Rogers), who has been raped, and her husband Eli (Adisa Anderson), who is troubled by the paternity of the baby. In a fit of rage, he attacks one of the 'bottle trees', trees hung with bottles that function as spiritual safeguards. In his rage and frustration, Eli's attack on the tree represents a crisis of faith in Nana's old ways. As the guardian of the family's memories, Nana pleads with him: 'Eli . . . Eli! There's a thought . . . a recollection . . . something somebody remembers. We carry these memories inside of us . . . Eli, . . . I'm trying to teach you how to touch your own spirit. I'm fighting for my life, Eli, and I'm fighting for yours. Look in my face! I'm trying to give you something to take north with you, along with all your great big dreams.'[40] Here, the matriarch's pleas extend dialogically beyond the diegesis, admonishing the wider community, and African American men in particular, to lay aside violence and anger to seek a greater faith in shared cultural memories.

Nana carries the family's 'scraps of memories', including a lock of her mother's hair, the only trace she retains of a mother sold away from her during slavery. Nana represents a living link with the history of slavery, but this connection is also preserved in custom and in folklore. For instance, the tale of the Ibo is told three times in the course of the film. Eula first tells the mythic form of the tale: upon their arrival at the sea islands, the members of the Ibo tribe brought from Africa on a slave trip took a good look around them and walked back out to sea. As Eula tells it, the water held them, and they walked all the way back to Africa. Toward the end of the film, old Bilal the Muslim retells the story, insisting that no one can walk on water, and that the shackled Ibo walked into the water and chose to drown together rather than submit to slavery. The Ibo legend imbues the sea islands with a sense of the living past. The island's utopian landscapes, reclaimed from Western aesthetic traditions, are full of reminders: the wooden Ibo carving that floats just off the shore at Ibo Landing; the simple but well-tended gravestones in the forest; the bottle tree as a 'reminder of who's come and gone'.

Dash's film sets in relief the ethical and material historicity of the cinematic image. Deleuze claims that narrative cinema (the 'movement-image') unfolds in a perpetual present governed by a vision of human intentionality and agency. In contrast, *Daughters* evokes the regime of the time-image: 'There is no present which is not haunted by a past and a future, by a past which is not reducible to a former present, by a future which does not consist of a present to come.'[41] Rather than a narrative of individual becoming (the action-image), this film explores the ethical burden of the past upon present and future generations. In his rejoinder to the 'spirit' of Marx, Jacques Derrida asserts that the contemporary ethical project – simply 'to learn to live, finally' – means learning to live with the 'spectres' of the past through 'a *politics* of memory, of inheritance, and of future generations'.

Without this *non-contemporaneity with itself of the living present*, without that which secretly unhinges it, without this responsibility and this respect for justice concerning those who *are not there*, of those who are no longer or who are not yet *present and living*, what sense would there be to ask the question 'where?' 'where tomorrow?' 'whither?'[42]

Daughters transpires at a transitional moment for the Peazants; as 'peasants', ordinary African Americans on the cusp of the 20th century, their dilemmas and dreams are deeply allegorical. The vital importance of memory for imagining the future is captured in the Unborn Child. Dash uses slow motion to mark the ghostly passages of the Unborn Child, who runs headlong through the frame clad in a white shift.

Significantly, Ibo Landing shelters no white people. In a rare reversal, the American mainland and the history of slavery forms the out-of-field of this microcosm. The film's only non-African American character is St Julien Lastchild, the Native American Sea Island labourer who is to marry Iona Peazant. Iona and Mary opt to stay behind with Nana, but the matriarch worries about the safety of her family as they leave the safety of Ibo Landing. The association of Nana with roots, home and safety, evokes bell hooks' insistence on the importance of 'homeplace': 'Historically, African-American people believed that the construction of a homeplace, however fragile and tenuous (the slave hut, the wooden shack), had a radical political dimension. . . . Black women resisted by making homes where all black people could strive to be subjects, not objects.'[43] This account challenges universalised Western discourses of public and private space underlying the house of fiction. Rather than costume drama's usual tropes of confinement or stylised interiors of opulence, the shanty interiors of *Daughters* are fragile, porous and makeshift. Most of the film transpires out-of-doors, invoking a communal homeplace through the shared space of the island, with Nana at the emotional and spiritual centre.

Dash layers different voices, which weave together as a squabbling, diverse and allegorical community. Following Bakhtin, Robert Stam suggests that texts may be read as 'a polyphonic play of voices',[44] where 'a voice is never merely a voice; it also relays a discourse'.[45] Dash's insistence on dissonance among the Peazants refuses to privilege a single voice or discourse, and this strategy extends to the film's preference for shared framings rather than the idealised or delineated space of realism:

In *Daughters*, the focus is on shared space (wide-angled and deep-focus shots in which no one becomes backdrop to anyone else's drama) rather than dominated space (foregrounded hero in sharp focus, others Othered in background blur); on social space rather than idealized space (as in Westerns); on delineated space that encourages a contiguous-reality reading rather than on masked space in which, through close-ups and framing, the spectator is encouraged to believe that conflicts are solely psychological not, say, systemic, hence, can be resolved by a shrink, a lawyer, or a gun, but not, say, through societal transformation.[46]

As with Campion's sculpted images, Dash works within a temporal economy of stillness and considered, choreographed movement. Fragments of dialogue, often mythic in content and delivery, are carefully rendered in 'Gullah' dialect interspersed

The living past: the young women of the island are taken into spiritual possession

with English. For Bakhtin, voices carry 'accents' and 'intonations' as indicators of difference and power, and *Daughters* reveres language as a material trace of the fragile living past. Dialogue is layered with subtle, non-verbal elements. For example, inter-cut with Nana and Eli's exchange cited above ('We carry these memories inside of us') is the remarkable sequence where Myown, Iona and several other girls dance on the beach. Beginning as a simple ring-and-line game the girls are, according to the script, 'taken into spiritual possession'. Clad in simple white shifts, their braids flying around their faces, they dance with abandon on the sand, framed in medium shot against the wide-open horizon. Like all spiritual moments, this sequence is shot in slow motion. Based on African cultural and film-making traditions, the girls' simple game on the beach marks the presence of the 'old souls' in the repetition of ritualistic gestures and movements.

A common attention to inherited gesture, games, food preparation and hairstyling can be read through a preoccupation with hands in *Daughters*. The face forms a privil-eged point of identification in costume drama (and most film) – as accentuated in *Orlando*'s dialogic looks and addresses to the audiences. In *Daughters*, hands are fore-grounded in order to explore a radically different affective link between the film and its 'interpretive community' of Black women. The film opens on a striking close-up of Nana Peazant's hands. This shot is described in the script as follows:

CLOSE ON
The rough, INDIGO, BLUE-STAINED hands of an African American woman,
YOUNG NANA PEAZANT. She is wearing an indigo-colored dress and holding Sea
Island soil within her hands. There is a great WIND blowing. The soil, like dust, blows
from her hands and through her fingers.[47]

As matriarch of the Peazant clan, Nana's body forms a tangible link with her people's slave past, and with their almost-forgotten African forebears. The winds blowing in this opening shot represent the winds of change at the turn of the twentieth century, along with the eternal cycle of birth and death, slavery and the continuing migrations of the African diaspora. Like most other costume dramas, *Daughters* is figured significantly around female relationships and activities. But where in other texts such as *Pride* and *Sense*, hands are filmed in the intimate leisured activities of writing or embroidery, the Sea Island women's hands are worn with labour. They are taken up with the tasks of sustaining community, food preparation, weaving baskets, braiding hair, caring for children. The film culminates in a feast on the beach to celebrate before the clan's departure. A scene where Viola teaches the children old African words for the ingredients is intercut with close-ups of the chopping of the okra. This sharing of food evokes Bakhtin's 'idyllic chronotope'[48] which, through the feast, evokes community, bounty and intergenerational links with past and future.

Nana embodies the source, the living memory of African spirituality and oral traditions. Dash constantly returns to Nana's strong blue-stained hands. Only in flashback, late in the film, do we learn the source of the blue stains. Born a slave on an indigo plantation, Nana's hands were stained by a poisonous indigo dye. In voice-over she states: 'Our hands, scarred blue with the poisonous indigo dye that built up all those plantations from swampland.'[49] Nana's hands bear the marks of years of labour – labours imposed and labours of love. While hands as affection-image in conventional costume drama forge an affective link with imagined literary and leisured histories, the hands of *Daughters* connect materially with a corporeal history of struggle and suffering.

The film closes on a long shot as Nana, Yellow Mary and Eula stroll along the beach against the glittering horizon. As their figures 'dissolve' into dust, the Unborn Child once again runs headlong across the frame. In her closing voice-over the child states: 'We remained behind, growing older, wiser, stronger.' The Unborn Child's run is not oriented toward the conventional linear future of the twentieth century, but rather rests suspended somewhere between a reckoning with the past, an acknowledgment of the importance of staying (of 'homeplace') and the collective possibility of a common future for the African American people.

Orlando and *Daughters* present two very different reassemblages of costume drama. In these two utopian projects, traditions of struggle enable a liberating vision of the future. As with Campion's *The Piano* (which I will return to in Chapter Eight), these films end symbolically on daughters as the inheritors of Western feminist and African American traditions of political struggle and artistic production. In these films, innovative form is integral to a radical revisioning of costume film. However, *Daughters* breaks from the vast majority of costume films, including *Orlando*, by insisting on the materiality of memory in a return to the 'radical past'. In addition to the intersecting questions of race, gender and colonialism explored here, class struggle is central to the radical past of costume film. The next chapter explores class relations through perspectives of framing and voice.

Notes

1.   Meaghan Morris, *Too Soon Too Late* (Bloomington: Indiana University Press, 1998), pp. xiv–xv.

2.   Doane, *The Desire to Desire*, pp. 70–95.

3.   de Lauretis, *Alice Doesn't*, p. 155.

4. Bakhtin, *The Dialogic Imagination*, p. 84.

5. Ibid., p. 104.

6. With a small budget of US$5 million, *Orlando* grossed $5.3 million in the US. Figures from the Internet Movie Database (www.imdb.com), with statistics rounded to the nearest hundred thousand.

7. See Sandra M. Gilbert, 'Introduction', in Virginia Woolf, *Orlando: A Biography* (London: Penguin Books, 1993), pp. xi–xv.

8. At the end of her novel, Woolf brings the text into her 'present' in recording the exact time of its completion: 'And the twelfth stroke of midnight sounded; the twelfth stroke of midnight, Thursday, the eleventh of October, Nineteen hundred and Twenty Eight.' (Woolf, *Orlando*, p. 228). In Potter's denouement, Swinton's final Amelia Earhart-style flying gear, worn as she drives an old motorcycle, approximates Woolf's period, but the setting is contemporary London. This typically non-realist periodisation further 'updates' Woolf's text into the present day of the film-maker and the audience.

9. Gilbert, 'Introduction', Woolf, *Orlando*, p. xxvii.

10. Bakhtin, *The Dialogic Imagination*, p. 88.

11. Penny Florence, 'A conversation with Sally Potter', *Screen* vol. 34 no. 3, 1993, pp. 276–7.

12. Bruzzi, *Undressing Cinema*, p. 195. For a reading of *Orlando*'s costumes, see pp. 192–8.

13. Baert, 'Skirting the Issue', p. 355.

14. Ibid.

15. Fredric Jameson, 'Postmodernism, or the Cultural Logic of Late Capitalism', *New Left Review* no. 146, 1984, p. 67.

16. Colin MacCabe, 'A Post-national European Cinema', in Petrie (ed.), *Screening Europe*, p. 13.

17. Jameson, 'Postmodernism', p. 68.

18. de Lauretis, *Alice Doesn't*, p. 112.

19. Ibid., p. 113.

20. Ibid., p. 119.

21. Bakhtin, *The Dialogic Imagination*, p. 92.

22. Rosi Braidotti, *Nomadic Subjects* (New York: Columbia University Press, 1994), p. 196.

23. Ibid., p. 203.

24. For an exploration of how Woolf travels as a textual, photographic and 'star' figure through literary and popular culture, see Brenda R. Silver, *Virginia Woolf Icon* (Chicago: University of Chicago Press, 1999).

25. Interestingly, Woolf and different incarnations of her characters appear in other recent feminist films. In Marleen Gorris's adaptation of *Mrs Dalloway* (1997), Vanessa Redgrave plays Clarissa Dalloway, and in *The Hours* (2002) Woolf herself is played by Nicole Kidman, while a modern-day 'Clarissa' is played by Meryl Streep.

26. Gayatri Chakravorty Spivak, 'Three Women's Texts and a Critique of Imperialism', *Critical Inquiry* no. 12, Autumn 1985, p. 244.

27. This term for 'the space of colonial encounters' is borrowed from Mary Louise Pratt's *Imperial Eyes* (London: Routledge, 1992), p. 6.

28. Surely the casting of Québécois actor Lothaire Bluteau as 'Khan' of a generic oriental kingdom can be no coincidence? Potter slyly sets the breadth and arbitrariness of British imperialism in relief, as one colonial subject is made to stand in for another.

29. Brenda Longfellow, 'Lesbian phantasy and the Other woman in Ottinger's *Johanna d'Arc of Mongolia*', *Screen* vol. 34 no. 2, 1993, p. 130.

30. Jacqueline Bobo, *Black Women as Cultural Readers* (New York: Columbia University Press, 1995), pp. 195–6.

31. Julie Dash, *Daughters of the Dust: The Making of an African American Woman's Film* (New York: The New Press, 1992), p. 32.

32. Stuart Hall, cited in Gloria J. Gibson-Hudson, 'The Ties that Bind: Cinematic Representations by Black Women Filmmakers', *Quarterly Review of Film & Video* vol. 15 no. 2, 1996, p. 25.

33. Bobo, *Black Women*, pp. 133–4.

34. See Jacquie Jones, '*Daughters of the Dust*', *Cineaste* vol. 19 nos. 2/3, December 1992, pp. 68–9.

35. Karen Alexander, '*Daughters of the Dust*', *Sight and Sound*, September 1993, p. 21.

36. Toni Cade Bambara, 'Reading the Signs, Empowering the Eye: *Daughters of the Dust* and the Black Independent Cinema Movement', in Manthia Diawara (ed.), *Black American Cinema* (New York: Routledge, 1993), p. 129.

37. Ibid.

38. See Bobo, *Black Women*, p. 146.

39. For Bambara, 'Yellow Mary's walk, posture and demeanour are in stark contrast to that of the Christianized cousin Viola. The careers of women blues singers in the twenties and thirties showed that Black women need not repress sexuality to be acceptable to the community.' See Bambara, 'Reading the Signs', p. 126.

40. Dash, *Daughters of the Dust*, p. 96.

41. Gilles Deleuze, *Cinema 2* (Minneapolis: University of Minnesota Press, 1989), p. 37.

42. Jacques Derrida, *Spectres of Marx* (New York: Routledge, 1994), p. xix.

43. bell hooks, *Yearning: Race, Gender, and Cultural Politics* (Boston: South End Press, 1990), p. 42.

44. Robert Stam, 'Bakhtin, Polyphony, and Ethnic/Racial Representation', in Lester D. Friedman (ed.), *Unspeakable Images: Ethnicity and the American Cinema* (Urbana: University of Illinois Press, 1991), p. 255.

45. Ibid., p. 257.

46. Bambara, 'Preface', in Dash, *Daughters of the Dust*, p. xiii.

47. Dash, *Daughters of the Dust*, p. 75.

48. Bakhtin, *The Dialogic Imagination*, p. 225.

49. Dash, *Daughters of the Dust*, p. 105.

Chapter Six
Upstairs/Downstairs

In costume drama's recurring set piece of the formal dinner party, servants are a silent yet essential part of the scene: white-gloved hands efficiently offer up sumptuous dishes, refill wine glasses with prime vintages, whisk away empty dishes and clear up spillages. Although they are crucial to the visual economy of costume drama, domestic servants rarely impinge on the dramas of romance and self-discovery of the middle and upper classes whom they serve. These disembodied hands correlate with a common trope in Western literature, where working people are figured through their 'working hands': 'Instead of full representations of the life of the people, literary tradition has typically offered only servants, mere appendages of their masters. Moreover, all that has been represented of these prefabricated tropes is their effects, their momentary performance of useful functions.'[1] As with Nana's slave's hands in *Daughters*, the servants' utilitarian hands contrast starkly with costume drama's usual depictions of the hand in close-up – the privileged figure of artistic expression or desire conveyed through the love letter.

Adaptations of Austen, Forster, Wharton and James painstakingly chronicle distinctions of wealth, social standing and cultural capital within their cosmopolitan middle- and upper-class milieux. Yet the symbiotic connections between these leisured microworlds and working-class labour and experience are largely suppressed. In Chapter One I suggested that the burgeoning desires of Austen's heroines must be understood in relation to the backgrounded figures of servants and working people. Extending this analysis, this chapter uses the tools of topographical criticism to analyse class relations – both through imaging (what is included and excluded from the frame) and through voice (the aural register of difference). The detail of the disembodied hand encapsulates the domestic servant's pervasive visual role as facilitator and scenic detail. Further, if the middle-class and upper-class protagonists are visually centred in the frame, their foregrounding is also aural. Carefully encoded indicators of language and speech further differentiate between deep-feeling protagonists and supporting roles.

Through voice and image, the generic form of costume film reinscribes cultural traditions that have historically rendered working-class characters invisible and inaudible. Against this pervasive erasure, it is American director Robert Altman who has developed recent costume drama's most sophisticated class critique with *Gosford Park*. As with *The Remains of the Day* and *Angels & Insects*, Altman returns to the Edwardian 'upstairs/downstairs' house of fiction. In the opening scene of *Gosford Park*, long-suffering lady's maid Mary Maceachran (Kelly Macdonald) stands by a 1926 Rolls Royce in the driving rain. Before entering the car, she must wait for her mistress Countess Trentham (Maggie Smith) to be ushered out to the car by a butler who shelters her with an umbrella. Both servants are drenched in their deferral to their mistress, and as the car departs the camera holds for several seconds on the butler standing on the steps. Emphasising the duration of Mary's wait and the enduring presence of the butler, this scene inaugurates *Gosford*'s methodical scrutiny of the strange conflictual symbiosis between servants and their masters in the Edwardian house of fiction.

Gosford is one of a series of recent revisionist films that foreground working-class characters and experience within the frame. *Gosford* is based on an original screenplay by Briton Julian Fellowes and Altman, while *Angels & Insects* and *The Remains of the Day* are based upon recent revisionist writings by A.S. Byatt and Ishiguro respectively; finally, *Jude* and *Sister My Sister* critique class oppression and normative morality. All of these films interrogate costume film's class relations from the explicit vantage point of the present (or in the case of *Remains*, the recent past), and in this respect they offer presentist, often ironic and postmodern commentaries on the past. Strategies of critique deployed in these works include on the one hand humanist dramas of class oppression, and on the other the use of Gothic stylistic features and themes to make strange the normative bourgeois house of fiction.

Class Erasure, Class Aspiration

In *Persuasion*, when the elitist Sir Walter Elliot formally departs Kellynch Hall for Bath, the footmen and gardeners line up formally along each side of the walk to mark the occasion. Rather than filming Sir Walter's departure in a conventional medium or long shot, the film-maker chooses to pan along the faces of the footmen as Sir Walter walks past them, oblivious. Elliot's leaving marks a stock narrative event in Austen's story, but these brief shots imply the constancy of the servants' lives, for as one master departs surely another will soon arrive. If the close-up registers an individual subject, a character, then *Persuasion*'s attention to the footmen's and labourers' faces fleetingly acknowledges the co-presence of the working classes in the frame. Here, they are projected out of the corner of the parlour or the landscape to which they are conventionally consigned as scenic elements. A similar subtle reframing occurs in the British television adaptation *Jane Austen's Emma*, which begins with an attempted theft of the Woodhouse chickens.[2] The film's companion volume notes how scriptwriter Andrew Davies

> chose to start the film with an incidental detail from the book: the image of a group of
> chicken thieves breaking into the Woodhouses' poultry house. . . . The next morning,
> Mr Woodhouse is unsettled by the break-in and wonders how safe his world is . . .
> for the French Revolution is still very recent history to Mr Woodhouse's generation.
> As they ride to the church, they pass tumbledown cottages that aren't fit for habitation,
> but we see families in them. 'I would have been in one of those cottages,' says Andrew,
> 'and so would most of the audience. I think it's an interesting aspect of this book, the
> fears and evasions of the aristocracy and gentry, living in such close proximity to the
> great unwashed.'[3]

Deliberate framing decisions on the part of the scriptwriter and director address the limits and nuances of audiovisual presence, visibility and audibility. Deleuze's perception-image is useful for analysing these interrelated axes of difference within the frame. Correlated with the long shot, the perception-image describes a 'set [ensemble] of elements which act on a centre, and which vary in relation to it'.[4] For Deleuze, perception is a process of subtraction, and the set implies selection or framing, which in turn indicates how costume drama images difference. Narrative movement is a vital force that 'overcodes' the cinematic field through 'segmentarity' – capital accumulation, the consolidation of the middle class and oedipal heterosexual sexuality. However, the cinematic system is never closed, always including deterritorialising 'lines of force' – 'a whole micro-segmentarity, details, possibilities, tiny movements that cannot be over-coded at all'.[5]

Visual detail as an integral element in costume drama's digressing narrative economy was explored in the last chapter. Here, however, I link these 'lines of force' to secondary bodies and trajectories that intersect with or even interrupt cinema's dominant narrative space. The chicken thieves who set the stage for *Jane Austen's Emma*, the footmen and labourers who silently survey Sir Walter Elliot's departure in *Persuasion*, the shepherd and sheep who cut across Elinor and Edward's path in *Sense* (see Chapter One), the listening presence of the servants in *Gosford* and *Angels* – these visual details reinscribe working-class characters as a silent counterpoint to the concerns of the bourgeois protagonists. Pleasing scenic elements or instances of deliberate visual irony, these fleeting cinematic interruptions reflect upon an overwhelming erasure within the pastoral literary and cinematic tradition. Momentarily self-reflexive, contemporary film and television adaptations still largely reinscribe a systematic erasure of working people from the frame – a rhetorical violence evoked poignantly by Raymond Williams with reference to the English novel's landed gentry arriving in the city:

> What they brought with them, and what they came to promote, rested on the brief and aching lives of the permanently cheated: the field labourers whom we never by any chance see; the dispossessed and the evicted; all the men and women whose land and work paid their fares and provided their spending money.[6]

Working-class characters in costume drama rarely disturb the dominant English literary chronotope of the 'neo-pastoral'. For Williams, the neo-pastoral is embodied in the English country gentleman as a figure of 'natural order' (the 'correct' authority of Knightley, Mr Darcy or Colonel Brandon). From the late seventeenth century onward in English literature, the country gentleman became 'an ideal of a rural society, as against the pressures of a new age' where 'the social order is seen as part of a wider order: what is now sometimes called a natural order, with metaphysical sanctions'.[7] Part of the legacy of the neo-pastoral is an exclusion of modernity, urbanisation, indus-trialisation and the industrial worker from the pages of the novel. This dominant cultural discourse strongly informs contemporary costume film, where the working class figures almost exclusively as domestic servants (rather than, for example, the factory worker emerging with industrialisation).[8]

Class exclusion and misrepresentation is at the root of the heritage cinema critique. As Craig Cairns puts it, 'the issue of affording a room is never in question, only the quality of the view'.[9] For these critics, these films offer a retrospective belonging to conservative myths of privileged Englishness that glosses over class struggle, past and present. Tana Wollen suggests that national mythologies of the past (the neo-pastoral, the glorious past, British endurance) offer an escape from a contemporary 'dislocating experience of modernity': 'But whether these fictions were dismissed or embraced, they bind together questions of the past and of belonging: at the heart of their narratives the pleasures of belonging and of identification are on offer.'[10] Interestingly, these films rarely offer an unproblematic affinity with the 'natural order', but commonly mediate belonging through outsiders. In *Chariots of Fire*, for example, the Jewish runner Abrahams endures ethnic slurs at Cambridge, and only through their sporting achievements do he and Scotsman Liddell achieve a tenuous status as 'British' heroes.[11] Similarly, in *Maurice*, the middle-class homosexual protagonist strives to join the exclusive Cambridge set and to fit into his lover Clive's aristocratic circle.

Middle-class aspiration is a primary desiring 'line of force' in 90s costume drama. In Rozema's *Mansfield Park*, the sprightly Fanny challenges the 'natural order' of slavery in a protofeminist rebellion against the patriarchal order headed up by patriarch Sir Thomas Bertram. A poor cousin, Fanny exemplifies the vantage point of less powerful occupants of the house of fiction – children (*The Secret Garden*, *Mansfield*), governesses (*Jane Eyre*, *Angels*, *The Governess*) and poor relations (*Persuasion*, *Sense*, *Angels*, *Portrait*, *Mirth*, *Nicholas Nickleby* (2002)) – who wryly observe the decadent ways of the upper classes while enjoying improved social status under their roofs. Thus, the topography of the house of fiction facilitates not only a repressive narrative of desire, but also a spatial architecture for class aspiration. The vast majority of these films reward their protagonists' efforts to achieve a 'respectable' social standing and income, and a rewarding marriage or family relationship. Narrated from the perspective of an ambitious working man, Michael Winterbottom's adaptation of Thomas Hardy's novel *Jude the Obscure* is exceptional as a relentless tale of defeat and despair.

Jude begins in black and white, as a young Jude Fawley is pictured in a fallow field feeding the crows that he has been hired to frighten away. Suddenly, the angry farmer bursts into the frame, beating Jude about the head and shoulders. As the ragged urchin runs off, three dead crows suspended on a pole foreshadow the woes to come. A far cry from the rolling green fields of the Austen adaptations, Jude's village of Marygreen is dirty, wet and full of hardship. When his schoolmaster Mr Phillotson (Liam Cunningham) leaves the village to attend the ancient university in Christminster, Jude accompanies him along the road. They halt at a high point on the road where man, boy, horses and cart are silhouetted against the horizon. The boy listens to Phillotson's advice in rapture as the sun breaks through the clouds to illuminate Christminster in the distance:

> You see it, over there? That's Christminster. If you want to do anything in life, Jude, that's where you have to go. Even if it means giving up everything else for awhile. You have to read your books when your friends are out playing, get out of bed early in the morning even when it's freezing cold, study every chance you get. One day, it'll all pay off, I promise you. Once you're there, everything's open to you. . . . You can choose your future.

Jude (Christopher Eccleston) grows up to become a stonemason, but still hopes to become a scholar. Still following his teacher's advice, Jude is frequently pictured at the table, reading and reciting Greek and Latin passages out loud. In contrast with the leisured affection-images of letter-writing and repose, study in *Jude* is an arduous process followed with a kind of fanaticism. Yet Jude's ambitions are dogged by adver-

The road to success: Young Jude accompanies his schoolmaster toward Christminster in *Jude*

sity. First, believing that his sweetheart Arabella (Rachel Griffiths) is pregnant, he is trapped into a loveless marriage. With his loftier ambitions, Jude is disgusted by his primitive life with the daughter of a pig farmer; depicted in gruelling detail, the grim slaughter of the pig that had been a wedding present sends Jude packing, and Arabella leaves him to emigrate to Australia.

Finding himself free, Jude sets out for Christminster in the first of the film's many peregrinations. Here, he finds work and camaraderie among the stonemasons, and studies by night. By coincidence, his beautiful and unconventional cousin Sue Bridehead (Kate Winslet) also lives in Christminster, and the two soon become inseparable. Jude's and Sue's meeting provides a joyous interlude in this stark film, as the pair wander the streets of Christminster (shot in Edinburgh) in rapt conversation, trying their luck at a country fair. Such depictions of ordinary nineteenth-century working-class life are exceptional within costume film, and these sequences have a quasi-documentary feel. Sue encourages Jude in his studies, and he writes to the university requesting admission. Unconventional in both his ambitions and in a growing infatuation with his cousin, his two greatest desires are soon thwarted. After learning that the schoolmaster Phillotson is courting Sue, Jude receives a letter of rejection from the dean of admissions. Curtly, the letter states: 'Judging from your description of yourself as a working man, I think you have a much better chance at success in life by sticking to your own trade than by adopting any other course.'

Jude drowns his sorrows with his stonemason friends in a pub where workers rub shoulders with university men. Claiming loudly to be able to recite the creed in Latin, Jude is overheard by a scholar and dismissively challenged to demonstrate his acumen publicly. The noisy pub falls silent as he climbs up on a bar stool and recites the passages emphatically for all to hear. Shaking, the Latin words seem to be dredged from his very depths, as this will be Jude's only chance to share his knowledge. As he finishes, the pub noise resumes, and Jude climbs down in disgust. Thwarted in his dream of a university education, Jude single-mindedly pursues his cousin Sue even after she reluctantly marries Phillotson. Jude's and Sue's love prevails, and she leaves her husband to live with Jude. Soon afterwards, Arabella tells Jude that she has borne him a son in Australia, and that Little Jude must now live with his father. Initially, the little family is happy, but as Sue bears two children of their own they are beset by hardship. When their extramarital relationship is discovered, they become outcasts who are refused lodgings and work everywhere they go.

The climax of this tale of woe transpires in Christminster, when the family is once again turned out of their lodgings. Overhearing his parents' distress, Little Jude is convinced that their troubles arise from having too many children. Soon afterwards, even though he has found work again, Jude returns home with Sue to discover that Little Jude has strangled their two small daughters and hung himself. This scene of horror is depicted in a terrible silence, as a handheld camera shakily documents the parents' frenzied grief over the small corpses. For Sue, the death of the innocents is a punishment for their immoral relationship, and she leaves Jude. Winterbottom renders cinematic Hardy's social critique of the period, where the three small coffins in the snow are an indictment of Victorian hypocrisy and class oppression. More than any other recent costume film, *Jude* reveals the hard labour of class mobility.

Upstairs/Downstairs

A powerful humanist critique of nineteenth-century class relations, Winterbottom's film stands out within recent costume film for its labourer protagonist. Another mode of class critique can be found in recent 'upstairs/downstairs' dramas framed through the experience of domestic servants. An 'upstairs/downstairs' architecture for the house of fiction invites an interrogation of class difference. The landmark example is *Upstairs, Downstairs*, the popular 70s British television drama that was successfully exported to the US,[12] a series important for its 'active presence of three-dimensional working-class people'.[13] Subsequently, this structure has been strikingly rare amidst this proliferating genre. With the critical and creative energy of 90s costume drama much more engaged with rewriting gender and sexuality, the few upstairs/downstairs films of the 90s and early 2000s are *The Remains of the Day*, *Sister My Sister*, *Angels & Insects* and *Gosford Park*.

Like *Jude*, *The Remains of the Day* is a humanist working-class tragedy, but it operates at the register of emotional repression. Anthony Hopkins, as Stevens the butler, is a difficult protagonist, lacking voice and agency in the film's arenas of courtship and politics. Several scenes dramatise the butler's objectification. In the most pointed of these, a visiting dignitary interrogates him for his opinions on the pressing political matters of the day. Stevens, mortified, responds repeatedly: 'I'm afraid that I can't be of any assistance in this matter, Sir.' The gentleman ridicules the butler in order to make the point that 'ignorant' working people should be excluded from political debate. At a later point, when Lord Darlington dismisses two Jewish refugee maids, the visibly troubled Stevens remains silent, even when Miss Kenton (a much more modern and outspoken young woman) challenges him. Miss Kenton's relatively more expressive femininity proves an apt foil for Stevens' emotive silence, and a narrative of English repression displaces the problem of class conflict.

Stevens is portrayed as a stunted human being who overidentifies with his 'place' as butler at the cost of his humanity, and this tragedy is conveyed most powerfully through his relationship with his father. Although clearly too frail for servants' duties, Stevens Sr (Peter Vaughan) is employed as under-butler in Darlington Hall. With the exertion, the old man takes to his bed. During an important house event, Stevens chooses to attend to his duties rather than sit with his father, who is clearly dying. John Orr comments on the film's 'fascination of the ritual and the decorum of the country house [where] the culture of formality lends itself to an aesthetic of restraint'; for this critic, such formality and restraint leads to a compelling and disturbing quality of 'complete emptiness'.[14]

The film's resounding hollowness arises not only from Stevens' compulsive attention to the empty ritual of the servant's tasks, but also from the character himself. Arguably, *Remains* 'fails' as a satisfying romantic narrative,[15] for the film's repression produces no emotional release, no sign of the butler's inner life. Hopkins' performance generates only a mask, an emptiness. Part of the film's hollow quality arises from Stevens' verbal and emotional inarticulateness – a mode of traditional English masculinity inflected in this case with his class status. The scene of Stevens at his father's bedside confirms a tradition of service – and an absence of inner life – passed from father to son. In Chapter Two, I discussed *Remains* as one of several recent films concerned with an emotionally inarticulate 'conservative' masculinity. Here I extend this analysis to suggest that this film also exemplifies a reticence and inarticulateness about working-class life in an otherwise verbose cycle of films.

The mannered power relations of costume drama are sustained in part through language. To address language as a privileged register of narrative in period drama is to shift from relations of visibility to the aural register of voice. For Austen, the condition of full subjectivity, of narrative presence, lies in the command of a class-based art of conversation. Austen's characters are 'contained' within the domestic sphere, but also centred in narrative space through their mastery of language and manners. Armstrong sees 'Austen's novels [as] striving to empower a new class of people – not powerful people, but normal people – whose ability to interpret human behavior qualifies them to regulate the conduct of everyday life and reproduce their form of individuality through writing'.[16] 'Ordinary' (middle-class) people announce themselves in the English novel and again in costume drama through modulated expression as a normative quality of middle-class English speech. The dialogue and narration of adaptation are brought to life by 'quality' English actors (and by Australians and Americans who emulate this mode of expression).

Bakhtin's concept of 'heteroglossia' posits that power and difference are conveyed aurally through accent, intonation, dialogue and voice. The novel is seen as a dialogic medium characterised by 'centripetal forces in socio-linguistic and ideological life'[17] such as the 'unitary language' of the nineteenth-century English novel. Such a 'unitary language' is not monolithic, but comprises an element of heteroglossia – a multiplicity of accents and discourses that operate as 'centrifugal, stratifying forces'. Historical material utterances woven into the novel, these forces correspond with Deleuze's 'lines of segmentarity' and 'lines of force'. If the ideological nature of the nineteenth-century novel is reinscribed in adaptation through a class-based 'unitary language',

> the task of the Bakhtinian critic . . . is to call attention to the voices at play within a text, not only those heard in aural 'close-up,' but also those voices distorted or drowned out by the text. . . . A voice is never merely a voice; it also relays a discourse, because . . . an individual voice is itself a discursive sum, a polyphony of voices.[18]

In the last chapter I argued that *Daughters of the Dust* revives fragile African American discourses erased from popular representation. Heteroglossia embraces not only individual texts, but culture as a whole, where 'stratification and heteroglossia widen and deepen as long as language is alive and developing'.[19] In this light, even as innovative feminist discourses have flourished in costume film, *Daughters*, *Jude* and *Gosford Park* extend costume drama's critical parameters to 'speak' race and class differently. Christopher Eccleston's gaunt Jude Fawley stands up in outrage in the Christminster pub to stubbornly claim his right to speak, howling forth his hard-earned knowledge to the deaf ears of the university men. Hardy's nineteenth-century outsider hero voices the rage of being excluded from the world of thought and learned discourse. In contrast, the great tragedy of the butler in *Remains* is his silence – a silence which provides no evidence of class resistance but can only point to an aporia around working-class expression in costume film.

Like *Remains*, *Gosford Park* is a class-conscious portrait set at the twilight of the Edwardian era. Yet where Stevens stands as a melancholic residue of a past era, Altman's film is resolutely polyphonic and lacking in nostalgia. Altman depicts 'below stairs' as a babble of humour and conflict, a beehive of activity contrasting sharply with the lassitude of the upstairs characters. This contrast is dramatised through the demanding Countess Trentham and her maid Mary from *Gosford*'s opening vignette noted above, where the maid shelters her mistress in the rain. At a later point, the Countess confides to two ladies as they sit comfortably in the drawing room: 'I'm breaking in a new maid, I'm simply worn out with it. There's nothing more exhausting, is there? . . . The amount I have to do for her, she should be paying *me*!' The uncomplaining Mary is shown to bear the brunt of the Countess's selfishness. On the evening before the shooting party, for instance, the Countess petulantly opts to wear the same blouse the next day, even though it is soiled. As a result, Mary is shown labouriously scrubbing the shirt late that night. The next morning, the oblivious Countess announces, 'Mary, I don't think I'll wear that shirt after all.'

Gosford shares with *Remains* a fascination with the ritual of servants' tasks. Publicity materials for the film highlight how the film-makers undertook considerable research into the 'below stairs' practices,[20] including the practice of calling lady's maids and valets by their employers' names. In the course of the film, a complex servant hierarchy emerges, with the butler Jennings (Alan Bates), Mrs Wilson (Helen Mirren) the housekeeper and Mrs Croft (Eileen Atkins) the cook firmly in charge of their respective domains. Through an array of superb character performances, a dense weave of jealousies, conflicts and passions emerge. This account of servant life delves into the lives normally excluded from costume film. For instance, Emily Watson's Elsie is capable, generous and loyal to her co-workers, and highly class-conscious, yet is still a bit in love with her odious employer McCordle (Michael Gambon). As younger, more outspoken characters, Elsie and Robert Parks (Clive Owen) are the servants most openly critical of their employers. When Mary asks Robert to describe Lord Stockbridge, he replies: 'He thinks he's God Almighty. They all do.'

Dissonance, critique and humour in the below stairs dialogue emerge from servant roles that are not merely visual place-holders or victims, but articulate commentators on the class system. Moreover, an unusual range of perspectives emerges through Altman's 'improvisatory approach to dialogue and narrative, his camera flitting from character to character as if in search of the most memorable snatch of conversation'.[21] Two mobile cameras tirelessly track all events in the house, placing the audience in a creeping, surreptitious, peering position.[22] Indeed, Fellowes wrote the screenplay entirely from the servants' point of view, where 'the camera can't be on the posh people unless a servant is present. . . . You may hear an argument inside a room, but if a servant enters it'll stop. . . . This may not be that evident . . . but the story is transmitted through downstairs gossip, through what the servants know.'[23]

Altman has a unique capacity to assemble ensemble casts. In casting actors with the status of Derek Jacobi, Helen Mirren, Alan Bates, Richard E. Grant and Emily Watson as servants, these roles are weighted at least on equal footing with the upstairs characters (Maggie Smith, Michael Gambon, Kristin Scott Thomas, Charles Dance, Jeremy Northam). The camera's constant movement parallels the servants' discreet steps, and early in the film the first footman, George (Richard E. Grant), happens upon Freddie Nesbitt (James Wilby) and Isobel McCordle (Camilla Rutherford) in an adulterous tryst. Startled, Isobel reprimands him: 'You shouldn't sneak up on people like that.' Carelessly, Freddie comments: 'Hey don't worry, it's no one.' This moment elicits an intertextual irony, as George is a distinct character in the film; also, many spectators know perfectly well that this is Richard E. Grant of *Withnail & I* (1987) and a score of other films including *Innocence* and *Portrait*.

As the film shifts genres from comedy of manners to whodunnit, poetic justice is served through the upstairs characters' disregard of the servants, who are not considered either as 'witnesses' or as possible perpetrators. In contrast with Stephen Fry's bumbling police investigator, Mary, the little lady's maid, proves the film's true sleuth. It is through her naive vantage point that the true murderer, and her motive, are revealed. Just before leaving Gosford Park, Mary visits Mrs Wilson's room to ask her why she poisoned McCordle, and how she knew that Robert (her son fathered by McCordle out of wedlock, given up by Wilson for adoption) would try to kill his father. Efficiently sorting linen all the while, the housekeeper responds that like all good servants she has the gift of anticipation:

> *Mrs Wilson*: 'I'm a good servant. I'm better than good, I'm the best, I'm the perfect servant. I know when they'll be hungry and the food is ready. I know when they will be tired and the bed is turned down. I know it before they know it themselves.'
> *Mary*: 'What if they find out what's happened?'
> *Mrs Wilson*: 'Not much of a crime to stab a dead man, is it? They can never touch him. That's what's important, his life.'
> *Mary*: 'And your life?'
> *Mrs Wilson*: 'Didn't you hear me, I'm the perfect servant. I have no life.'

In this moment, even the 'perfect servant' reveals the feelings and life experience behind the mask, and she achieves a self-effacing heroism. It is only after Mary leaves the room that the housekeeper breaks down and wails out her sorrow at the loss of her son. In a moment epitomising the melodramatic 'text of muteness', Wilson's 'inarticulate cry' pierces decades of enforced silence to reveal a terrible underlying 'moral occult'.[24] Mirren's splendid performance remedies a slightly clichéd denouement, as it is revealed that McCordle's indiscretions have been commonplace. The film's tragedy

The centrepiece of *Gosford Park*: Ivor Novello (Jeremy Northam) performs a medley of songs in the drawing room while a murder is committed in the library

'The Land of Might-Have-Been': the kitchen staff gather in the stairwell to listen to Ivor Novello

is the plight of the below-stairs women who sexually service their masters, only to lose their reputations and their children.

McCordle's murder symbolises the imminent demise of this topography of power. McCordle has two attackers: his upstart bastard son Robert, and Mrs Wilson who strikes the moral blow. *Gosford* revels in the revenge of unseen and all-seeing servants: Elsie is sacked for answering back to Lady Sylvia, but this may be the best thing that ever happened to her, as she departs with the Hollywood director. Meanwhile, Robert smiles radiantly as he bids Mary farewell, getting off scot-free. Like Renoir's *Rules of the Game*, and *Remains*, *Gosford* is set in the 30s on the brink of World War Two, an era marking the twilight of the leisured English landed gentry. Yet where *Remains* is couched in an ambivalent melancholy, Altman's film, like Renoir's, is full of energy, humour and tragedy.

Gosford depicts not only the strict divide between upstairs and downstairs, but their interdependence, and how the narcissistic culture of the upper classes is fated to give way to the greater vitality and awareness of the below-stairs characters. For this film is also a coy parable about the cross-fertilisation of British and American characters and cultural production. In a centrepiece scene, Altman dramatises the magnetic capacity of popular entertainment to invade the snobbish enclave of the Edwardian landed gentry. Ivor Novello (Jeremy Northam) performs popular 30s songs at the piano, temporarily bridging the film's structuring upstairs/downstairs division. The matinee idol Novello, an actual British actor, songwriter and playwright of the period, is adored by both the middle-class Mabel Nesbitt and the servants. Novello performs a medley of songs for the guests in the drawing room, as McCordle's murder transpires in the library. Novello's honey tenor is ostensibly intended for the cynical upstairs characters, who play cards and chatter over his singing, but Altman continually cuts to the servants, transfixed in the wings. Skiving their duties, two maids dance the jitterbug in an ill-lit hallway, while the kitchen staff gather reverently in the stairwell to listen. It is as if Novello's songs, including the whimsical 'The Land of Might-Have-Been', usher Gosford Park into a more utopian and egalitarian era.

Gothic Social Critique

The concluding section of this chapter shifts from the humanist critique of *Jude*, *Remains* and *Gosford* to explore the tangled Gothic milieux and landscapes of *Angels & Insects* and *The Secret Garden*. If *Remains* and *Gosford* adjust the genre's point of view and site of enunciation toward the servants, the use of Gothic motifs and themes allows perverse sexuality and the twisted decadence of the class system to creep into the frame. A little-known gem, Philip Haas's inventive *Angels & Insects* scrutinises the Gothic underside of the Victorian 'natural order'. The film is set in 1859, when biologist William Adamson (Mark Rylance) returns to England from his fieldwork in the Brazilian rainforest. Sir Harald Alabaster, a wealthy country gentleman with a keen interest in the natural sciences, employs William to classify his collection of exotic flora and fauna. William subsequently marries Sir Harald's daughter Eugenia (Patsy Kensit), but soon the quiet hero notices disturbing parallels between an ant colony he is studying and unusual Alabaster family traditions.

The film opens with a brief tribal-dancing sequence in Brazil. To the sound of primal drumming, William is shown by flickering torchlight dancing in wild abandon with a 'native' woman. Provocatively, Haas fades directly from the tribal dance to a Victorian ball at Bredely, Sir Harald's English country manor. Here, a much more demure William is overwhelmed by a dizzying array of brilliantly costumed women dancing with men in plain sombre costumes. In the place of realist period costume, the women's gowns are decorated with vivid colours and bold, insect-like patterns. These costumes connote the bright display of the mating rituals of insects and birds,[25] and the classic movement-image of the ball is fractured through a disorienting series of close-ups, blurred motion and an accelerating editing pattern. In this way, a stylised comparison is established between the Amazon Indians and English country life. Returning to his native land from the tropics, Yorkshire commoner Adamson ('everyman') speaks eloquently of having missed the beauty of the English countryside.

> When I was in the Amazons ... I was haunted by an image of an English meadow in spring – just as it is today, with the flowers, and the new grass, and the early blossom, and the little breeze lifting everything, and the earth smelling fresh after the rain. It seemed to me that such scenes were truly Paradise – that there was not anything on

earth more beautiful than an English bank in flower, than an English mixed hedge, with roses and hawthorn, honeysuckle and bryony.[26]

Yet William's nostalgia is short-lived as the spoilage and injustice underlying this pastoral fantasy gradually emerge through the systematic pollution of costume drama's stock movement-images: the ball, the picnic, the country walk and, finally, the bedroom. One perfect summer's afternoon, 'cream tea' in the garden becomes an orgy of overeating as the pregnant Alabaster women stuff themselves with rich, creamy desserts. Gorging themselves on the (unearned) fruits of the land, these attractive 'butterflies' rapidly morph into matronly baby factories, 'ant queens' producing a steady stream of identical pale, blue-eyed Alabaster babies. Within Bakhtin's 'idyllic chronotope', food and feasting signify an organic bond between agricultural labour and the rural family, but in *Angels* the Victorian natural order is vexed, the picnic overrun by ants.

The perverse underbelly of the lily-white Alabasters is unveiled from the vantage point of their bustling servants and educated employees (Adamson and governess Matty Crompton played by Kristin Scott Thomas). Excluded from Bredely's sexual economy, William as the frustrated and ineffectual husband cannot help but notice that the Alabaster males are completely useless, nothing but drones. Meanwhile, Eugenia shuts him out of her bedroom at night, and William later discovers her continuing incestuous relationship with her brother. If the bedrooms of the landed gentry and their lavish feasts are zones of perversion, the country walk becomes more purposeful, its findings sinister. The educational perambulations of William, governess Matty and the Alabaster brood are charged with the project of scientific discovery. William is persuaded by Matty to undertake a close study of the natural life of the ant colony, with the help of the identical little girls costumed like insects. At first the red and black ant

Angels & Insects: the natural life of the ant colony as allegory for the bizarre habits of the Victorian landed gentry

colonies coexist peacefully, but one day without warning the black ants mount an attack, kidnapping the black ant babies for servants. Painstakingly recorded in William and Matty's books, the ant world strangely parallels Bredely's mode of reproduction and its silent class struggle.

For Susan Stewart, 'the miniature presents us with an analogical mode of thought, a mode which matches world within world'.[27] The detail of the miniature suggests a series of concentric allegorical frames in *Angels*: the ant colony, the country estate, and, finally, the colonial 'exotic' world of the Amazon basin. The microcosm of the insect world and the macrocosm of the out-of-field (the Amazon basin that bookends the film) provide two allegorical frames for Bredely. Tiny and gigantic worlds merge visually and symbolically through restless cycles of reproduction, violence and decomposition. Ultimately, through the film's reference to discourses of natural history, the behaviour of the aristocracy is revealed to be the most bizarre of all. The rotting core of Bredely, and the Alabasters' bizarre family traditions, are made manifest by the beetles that suddenly pour out of every nook and cranny. As with *Remains* (and to a lesser degree *Mansfield*) the corrupt landed gentry are depicted as authors of their own demise.

Angels also enacts a parodic depiction of the servants as menacing worker ants who threaten to take over the estate. Scores of female servants dressed alike in sombre dresses and insect-like braided hair shuffle silently through the servants' corridors and back stairways. Here, the omnipresent servants of conventional period drama are transformed eerily into a faceless throng that buzzes methodically behind Bredely's peaceful façade. The servants overpopulate the backroom spaces normally hidden from view. Buglike, they swarm. Byatt's novella incorporates imagery from the Gothic tradition, an excessive form that shadows the eighteenth- and nineteenth-century discourses of the Enlightenment, Romanticism and realism. For instance, the film's visual parallels between humans and insects borrow from 'Darwinian models of evolution, researches in criminology and physiological science [which] identified the bestial within the human'.[28] The film's structuring analogies compare both servants and the landed gentry with insects, producing ambivalent class commentaries.

If Gothic textual excesses negotiate the fears of an era, within this postmodern work the visual metaphor of servants-as-insects parodies a nineteenth-century fear of working-class aspiration. Meanwhile, the film's revisionist imagery inverts nineteenth-century class discourses of eugenics, equating the ever-so-white Alabasters with craven sexuality, incest and frantic breeding. In *Angels* Gothic forms and themes call into question the transparency and natural order of costume drama's pastoral landscapes and well-run country houses. However, the question remains as to what degree this imaginative cinematic parody challenges or reinscribes hegemonic class and colonial discourses. The servants are attributed an eerie behind-the-scenes power to stage events, to convey information. After William is led back to the house to discover Eugenia in bed with her brother Edgar, Matty explains:

> There are people in the house, you know, who know everything that's going on –
> invisible people, and now and then the house simply decides that something must
> happen – I think your message came to you after a series of misunderstandings that at
> some level were quite deliberate. . . .

Ultimately, the privileged point of view and enunciation in this film rests with the middle-class characters William and Matty. These educated employees offer a vantage point between the decadent gentry and the servants' subhuman rustlings. As the film gradually uncovers Bredely's labyrinth of back passageways and stairways (visually reminiscent of interlocking ant tunnels), the servants are attributed an indirect agency. A visual similarity between the servants and the ants and beetles who overrun the picnic and the house respectively implies an inevitability (if not necessarily a justice) in the working people taking over Bredely. In keeping with costume drama's ritual narrative of middle-class aspiration, however, the pivotal attributes of desire, aspiration, narrative energy, enquiry and thought are attributed to William and Matty. *Angels* concludes as the couple opt to abandon the rotten English natural order, setting their sights instead on the knowledge and adventures offered by the tropics. As with *Persuasion* and *Maurice, Angels* ends romantically with William and Matty sailing off into the sunset. Finally, this narrative closure is doubled with publications – both William's scholarly study of the ant colonies, and Matty's drawings and fantastical tales based on the same subject. As with the coda to Rozema's revisionist *Mansfield*, where Fanny publishes her 'fanciful tales', William and Matty are literally given the last word.

As with *Angels & Insects*, in many recent adaptations of Gothic novels (two versions of *Jane Eyre*,[29] *Wuthering Heights* (1992), *The Piano, Wide Sargasso Sea, The Secret*

Governess Matty Crompton
(Kristin Scott Thomas) as
artist and author: middle-class
ascendancy

Garden, The Tenant of Wildfell Hall), the protagonists are outsiders – orphans placed within the homes of indifferent wealthy relatives, or governesses working in menacing lonely mansions. These characters negotiate the homes of the rich, desiring their trappings or persons while disapproving of their madness and lascivious sexuality. Through the eyes of these characters, the aristocracy is seen to be in decline, often giving way to the meek yet insistent middle classes. Nancy Meckler's *Sister My Sister* narrates the Gothic house of fiction from the point of view of two maids, Christine (Joely Richardson) and Lea (Jodhi May), who are sisters and lovers. Based on actual events in 1933 France, this film resolves class conflict differently as the maids beat their employer and her daughter to death.[30] The film begins with a disembodied camera floating eerily down a shadowy stairwell, revealing streaks of blood on the floor and a motionless foot at a strange angle. From this murder scene, the film reconstructs how incestuous passion and class rage led to the murder of Madame Danzard (Julie Walters) and her daughter Isabelle (Sophie Thursfield).

From the murder scene, the film cuts to the film's present, where the pretty and shy younger sister Lea arrives at the Danzards' house to work with her elder sister Christine. From its ominous beginning, *Sister My Sister* is organised around an increasing claustrophobia and hostility among the four women confined to the Danzards' provincial home. The house is divided between the Danzards' living space downstairs and the sisters' private enclave in the attic. Madame Danzard proves a harsh taskmaster, donning white gloves to check the furniture for dust. Christine and Lea are fully taken up with servants' tasks that are documented in detail through a montage of the two girls scrubbing the floor, preparing food, serving food, washing and sewing clothes. Yet, even as Madame Danzard seeks to implement complete control in the house, the two girls become increasingly embroiled in an obsessive and jealous mutual passion in the privacy of their attic room. As they become increasingly silent, Christine and Lea's erotic attachment begins to interfere with their duties downstairs.

The tide turns when the girls take the risk of making love in a shadowy corner in the kitchen, making Madame Danzard suspicious. These tensions come to a head when Lea burns a blouse while ironing, and the iron blows a fuse. When her mistress finds the house in darkness, she crosses the upstairs/downstairs boundary to confront the girls at the top of the stairs. The dispute over the blouse soon escalates at Madame Danzard's accusation that the two girls are lovers. When she threatens to have them separated and begins to call them names, the girls fall on their employee in a frenzy, beating her and her daughter to death. With its oblique shots of staircases and *noir* lighting, *Sister My Sister* evokes stylistic elements of the Gothic house of fiction. Within this disturbing realm, a class rage boils over to decimate the controlling bourgeois Danzards. But this is no redemptive tale, and the closing titles reveal that Christine died four years later in a mental institution, while Lea was imprisoned for twenty years before returning to work as a maid until her death.

In *The Secret Garden*, undoubtedly Agnieszka Holland's most accomplished period drama, the protagonist is a traumatised young orphan who is sent to live with her uncle in a forbidding Yorkshire mansion. This adaptation of Frances Hodgson Burnett's well-known children's story begins in India, where the upper-class English child Mary Lennox (Kate Maberly) loses her parents in an earthquake. In keeping with *Jane Eyre*, *The Tenant of Wildfell Hall*, *The Piano* and *Mansfield Park*, *The Secret Garden* negotiates a broken and troubled family in a pattern common to Gothic fiction, where 'the family became a place rendered threatening and uncanny by the haunting return of past transgressions and attendant guilt on an everyday world shrouded in strangeness'.[31] Kate is supervised by the unsympathetic housekeeper Mrs Medlock (Maggie Smith), while her uncle Lord Craven (John Lynch) is distant and strange, haunted by his wife's death. A difficult and unlovable child, Mary finds playmates in a servant's brother Dickon (Andrew Knott) and her crippled cousin Colin (Heydon Prouse), who has been confined to a secret room.

Mary and Colin seek solace from their troubled family in 'the secret garden', a place of respite associated with their dead mothers, who had been sisters. Hidden in the middle of a maze, the garden offers a 'liminal space' of magic and healing within the mansion's forbidding grounds. Whereas the house and its grounds are eternally winter – grey, cold and overgrown – when the children enter the garden, spring arrives with green shoots, flowers and young animals. Mary is guided to the garden by a robin, and aided by Dickon, who can speak to animals and birds. Dickon, the brother of the kindly servant Martha, is a solid, salt-of-the-earth character, and the Yorkshire servants' simple kindnesses contrast starkly with the 'unnatural' coldness of Colin's and Mary's upper-class families. As benign helpers and sympathetic witnesses, the wholesome servants present a counterpoint to the corruption of the aristocratic family; they facilitate the healing of the troubled children. When Colin is reunited with his troubled father in the garden, Dickon looks on joyfully, wiping tears from his eyes. Finally, the servants gather in delight at the window of the mansion to watch Colin (who has only just learned to walk) returning to the house with his father and Mary as part of a reconstituted family.

Similarly, in *Maurice* the earthy servant heals the middle-class protagonist. Undergamesman Alec Scudder's (Rupert Graves) unselfconscious same-sex desire proves an antidote to Maurice's (James Wilby) tortured asexual relationship with the aristocratic and repressed Clive (Hugh Grant). I will further address this important gay costume drama of the 80s in the next chapter, but within the present discussion *Maurice* correlates with a pattern where working-class characters facilitate the desires and development of more privileged protagonists. In contrast with the supercilious and anonymous servants of *Angels & Insects*, Dickon and Scudder are sympathetic one-dimensional characters, 'helping hands' who come into partial view in the frame of costume film – and, in a limited capacity, into language as speaking characters. It is left to revisionist texts *The Remains of the Day* and *Gosford Park* to investigate the inner lives and behind-the-scenes dynamics of the 'good servants'.

This chapter has examined class dynamics within contemporary costume film. I argue that where middle-class aspiration and aristocratic lassitude are common, complex representations of working-class characters are rare. My analysis has juxtaposed a recurring narrative trajectory of class mobility with the overwhelming erasure of working-class subjects from the frame. Of particular interest has been the complex articulation of 'visibility' and 'audibility' – how class difference is negotiated (and often reinscribed) through the backgrounding of non-hegemonic bodies and voices. Of course, it is hardly ground-breaking to describe costume drama's extraordinarily limited attention to working-class experience. But I hope to have demonstrated how these figures and voices serve to amplify and consolidate – and occasionally complicate – a hegemonic middle-class subjectivity. Costume drama has proven eloquent and inventive in its revisionist interrogation of gender relations, and to some degree sexuality, as I will explore in the next chapter. However, with regards to class critique, the momentary openings offered by *Jude*, *Gosford Park*, *Angels & Insects*, *The Remains of the Day* and *Sister My Sister* are all the more remarkable as exceptions that prove the rule.

Notes

1. Bruce Robins, *The Servant's Hand* (Princeton: Duke University Press, 1993), p. x.
2. Thanks to Ginelda Alverêdo for her comments on the chicken episode.
3. Sue Birtwhistle and Susie Conklin, *The Making of Jane Austen's Emma* (Harmondsworth: Penguin Books, 1996), p. 13.
4. Deleuze, *Cinema 1*, 'Glossary'.
5. See Gibson, *Towards a Postmodern Theory of Narrative*, p. 52.
6. Williams, *The Country and the City*, p. 54.
7. Ibid., pp. 28–9.
8. See Robins, *The Servant's Hand*, p. xi.
9. Cairns, 'Rooms without a View', p. 10.
10. Wollen, 'Over our shoulders', p. 180.
11. Ibid., p. 182.
12. In 1990, *Upstairs, Downstairs* (1971–77) was the most successful television series ever exported from Britain. See D.L. Le Mahieu, 'Imagined Contemporaries: cinematic and televised dramas about the Edwardians in Great Britain and the United States, 1967–1985', *Historical Journal of Film, Radio and Television* vol. 10 no. 3, 1990, p. 246.
13. Ibid., p. 248.
14. Orr, 'Beyond Heritage', p. 24.
15. Richard Dyer slates this film as 'lifeless', with its 'emotionally inexpressive people being emotionally inexpressive in films'. See his 'Feeling English', p. 19.
16. Armstrong, *Desire and Domestic Fiction*, p. 136.
17. Bakhtin, *The Dialogic Imagination*, p. 271.
18. Stam, 'Bakhtin, Polyphony, and Ethnic/Racial Representation', pp. 256–7.
19. Bakhtin, *The Dialogic Imagination*, p. 272.
20. A feature article in *The Times Weekend* profiled Violet Liddle as an informant for *Gosford Park*; this woman had worked as a maid for George Bernard Shaw and Winston Churchill. See Christina Hardyment, 'The maid, the playwright and the Prime Minister', *The Times Weekend*, 4 August 2001, pp. 1–2.
21. Geoffrey Macnab, '*Gosford Park*', *Sight and Sound*, February 2002, p. 46.
22. For details on camera, *mise en scène* and lighting, see Eric Rudolph, 'Upstairs, Downstairs', *American Cinematographer* vol. 83 no. 1, January 2002, pp. 72–84.
23. Robert Altman, cited in David Gritten, '"You rang, Mr Altman?"', *Daily Telegraph*, 1 September 2001, p. A7.
24. On the 'articulate cry' and the 'text of muteness', see Brooks, *The Melodramatic Imagination*, pp. 65–6.
25. Within the insect and bird rituals, it is most often the male of the species with the vivid display.

26. A.S. Byatt, 'Morpho Eugenia', *Angels & Insects* (London: Vintage Books, 1992),
     p. 30.
27. Stewart, *On Longing*, p. 74.
28. Botting, *Gothic*, p. 12.
29. These include Franco Zeffirelli's 1996 version starring William Hurt and Charlotte
     Gainsbourg, and Robert Young's 1997 television film with Samantha Morton and
     Ciaran Hinds.
30. These events were the basis of Jean Genet's play *The Maids*, which was adapted in
     1974 by Christopher Miles starring Glenda Jackson and Susannah York. Meckler's
     film is also based on a theatre piece by Wendy Kesselman. See Lizzie Francke, '*Sister
     My Sister*', *Sight and Sound*, December 1995, pp. 51–2.
31. Botting, *Gothic*, p. 11.

Chapter Seven
Queer Costume Drama

The scandalous lesbian intrigue of Rozema's *Mansfield Park* and the cross-dressing girl-on-girl romance of the telly series *Tipping the Velvet* are only the tip of the iceberg. Since the 80s, costume film and television have been brimming with queer content and innuendo. This genre dramatises the intimate sphere of bourgeois gender and romance, and this realm is replete with same-sex passions and ambiguously 'queer' sexuality. Films with lesbian and gay themes include *Picnic at Hanging Rock* (1975), *Another Country*, *A Month in the Country* (1987), *Maurice*, *The Bostonians*, *Caravaggio*, *Edward II*, *Total Eclipse*, *A Room with a View*, *Wilde*, *The Wings of the Dove*, *Desperate Remedies*, *Mansfield Park*, *Looking for Langston* and *Sister My Sister*. In addition to explicit and implicit 'queer textuality', lesbian, gay and queer discourses are ubiquitous within the creative and commercial intertext of contemporary costume drama as portrayed by authors (film-makers, authors of source novels and plays, scriptwriters), their characters and the actors who play them.

If costume drama is almost coterminous with heterosexual romance, its complex choreography of desires also extends to same-sex romantic friendships (*The Bostonians*, *Picnic at Hanging Rock*, *Brideshead Revisited*, *Mansfield Park* and *Daughters of the Dust*) and non-normative 'queer' masculinities (*Carrington*, *Where Angels Fear to Tread*, *A Room with a View*, *Wilde*). In 1987, *Another Country* and *A Month in the Country* explored explicit same-sex desires set in the past, and this increased gay visibility culminates in *Maurice*, from the same year, as a bona fide 'coming out' narrative. These films raise contentious issues about representing the queer past for a homophobic present. Along with the 1981 television serial *Brideshead Revisited*, the three films of 1987 represent one prevalent 'White Flannel' formula. Here, depictions of homosexual youths set in Edwardian Oxbridge and public-school settings rest on stereotypes of the English upper classes. John Lyttle attacks a *Brideshead*-style conservative 'heritage' homosexuality that relies on a 'seductive visual surface . . . complete with endless tracking shots and just the right tweeds'; he claims that this legacy situates 'contentious' sexualities safely in the past.[1]

Maurice particularly fulfils the gay liberation agenda for gay visibility and positive images of homosexual identity, but Lyttle's critique points to a new 80s and 90s 'queer' preference for unapologetic representations of 'contentious' sexualities. Following these debates, Forster's humanism and the 80s White Flannels can be read against Derek Jarman's anti-heritage avant-garde works *Caravaggio* and *Edward II*. Finally, the *Wilde* biopic and adaptations *An Ideal Husband* and *The Importance of Being Earnest* present a very different, parodic mode of critique associated with a camp sensibility. Following on from preceding discussions of feminist and radical costume, this chapter explores these very different aesthetic and political strategies for lesbian, gay and queer representation. To begin, however, I turn to the spectre of lesbian desire in the James adaptations.

Lesbian Innuendo in the James Adaptations

In Michel Foucault's influential account, the seemingly sexually repressive Victorian era actually generates the 'dissemination and implantation of polymorphous sexualities'.[2] With its normative social and sexual codes, the Victorian period presents a rich field for cinematic narration of sexual repression and transgression. In *The Age of Innocence*, Newland's expansive desires constrained by a dutiful marriage find an outlet in extra-marital passion, while in *Angels & Insects* a bestial incestuous sexuality seethes beneath Bredely's orderly facade. In turn, the James adaptations, with their oblique and sinister passions, are haunted by what Eve Sedgwick calls an 'epistemology of secrets'.[3] The indicative chronotope for the Jamesean house of fiction is the door half-open, and these films are replete with whispers, innuendo, things unsaid, secrets 'behind closed doors': Aunt Lavinia's delight in secrets, Madame Merle's and Osmond's treachery; Kate's and Merton's designs on Milly's fortune. Some of these are ghost stories – classically, *The Turn of the Screw*, or Milly's residual influence after death in *Wings*. Implicit within this epistemology of secrets is the spectre of illicit sexuality, including same-sex desire.

James's novel *The Bostonians* was adapted by the Merchant Ivory team in 1984. Set in 1870s Boston, the film depicts a love triangle between the mature wealthy spinster Olive Chancellor (Vanessa Redgrave), her young protégée Verena Tarrant (Madeleine Potter) and Olive's cousin Basil Ransom (Christopher Reeve). A charismatic advocate of women's rights, Verena is another a dynamic Jamesean 'American girl' who will be ensnared in a traditional marriage. Verena gives rousing speeches about the 'woman question', and it is through the feminist cause that she meets the older Olive, who is transfixed by her. Redgrave's Olive is a reprise of her earlier role as the enigmatic Julia engaged in a passionate same-sex friendship in *Julia* (1977). As in *Julia*, in *The Bostonians*, the relationship between the two women is not named as a love affair, yet the two women are frequently pictured in intimate embraces, and Olive continually strokes Verena's hair and kisses her. Olive's feelings for Verena clearly exceed friendship, but the younger woman's sentiments are less clear.

From a poor family, Verena is soon persuaded to live with the wealthy Olive. Eventually, Olive's cousin Basil arrives brusquely into this cloying Victorian feminine house of fiction. Early on, Basil sets his sights on Verena, and their courtship is framed from the jealous Olive's perspective. In one agonising sequence, Olive pretends to write letters in an upstairs room by the window, as Verena and Basil meet in the garden below her window. As the couple disappear for hours on a long walk, Olive can only wait anxiously. *The Bostonians* centres on Verena's indecision and duplicity, and a bitter struggle ensues between Olive's unnamed desire for Verena and Ransome's insistent claim as a legitimate suitor.

In the film's climax, all of the players gather at a hall where Verena is to give a speech. As the audience becomes increasingly restless, a battle takes place behind the scenes. Olive and the event's organisers encourage Verena to speak, while Basil pressures his bride-to-be to leave with him immediately. In the women's final agonising separation, Verena reaches out to Olive and the older woman's anguish is framed in a long reaction shot. Ransom emerges as an overpowering brute hostile to the feminist cause, and the cruel eradication of Verena's feminist autonomy is made even more chilling by the women's violent separation.

The Bostonians conjures up an unstated lesbian desire then enacts its violent defeat. Despite the novel's ambiguity about the nature of Olive's and Verena's friendship, the implication of a lesbian relationship in *The Bostonians* is perfectly legible within 80s cinema. In this respect, Olive's cruel defeat is particularly disturbing as it corresponds with a long-standing tendency for lesbian and gay film characters to be vilified or symbolically 'punished'. In *The Killing of Sister George* (1968), *The Children's Hour* (1962) and *Personal Best* (1982), older or less 'attractive' lesbian characters are humiliated by lovers who leave them for men. Given the paucity of lesbian visibility in the cinema, the narrative closure of *The Bostonians* is problematic.

Yet a less schematic reading is possible. Terry Castle argues that Redgrave's dignified performance frames Olive Chancellor as a tragic lesbian heroine.[4] Castle's view is supported by the film's closing scene where, after Verena's departure, Olive takes Verena's place at the podium, and heroically manages a rousing speech despite her obvious distress. Although there is something tawdry about Olive's cloying obsession with Verena, the film is narrated largely from the older woman's perspective and, ultimately, its tragedy is Olive's anguish. I return below to 80s period film, but to complete this discussion of the James adaptations, I now turn to the 1997 *Wings of the Dove*.

Wings appeared in 1997, when explicit sexuality had become much more common in period film and lesbian, gay and 'queer' elements much more commonplace (and bankable) in Anglo-American popular culture. As part of the film's sexually charged atmosphere, Softley's film develops a web of same-sex attachments that complicate the core love triangle of Linus Roache's Densher as contested object of desire between Kate and Milly. Even as the worldly Madame Merle holds a fascination for the younger Isabel in *Portrait*, there is an indeterminate bond between Milly and her constant companion, Susan 'Shepherd' (Elizabeth McGovern). For Wood, McGovern's performance 'quietly suggests a lesbian attachment that makes no demands, is content simply to contribute to the comfort and tranquility of the woman she clearly adores'.[5] However, the major same-sex attraction transpires between Milly and Kate.

From the first, there is a mutual fascinaton between Milly and Kate. They first glimpse one another at a formal dinner party, where Kate is seated beside Lord Mark. She continually exchanges glances with Milly, even before she meets her or learns about her fortune.

> *Lord Mark*: 'Has anyone ever told you not to stare?'
> *Kate*: 'Do you know her well?'
> *Lord Mark*: 'I wish I knew her better.'
> *Kate*: 'Why is everyone so fascinated with her?'
> *Lord Mark*: 'She could be queen of America if they had one. She's worth millions.'
> *Kate*: 'So why aren't you sitting next to her?'
> *Lord Mark*: 'Your aunt Maud wouldn't let me.'

Screenwriter Hossein Amini's taut dialogue synthesises the complex attractions and interests at work at Lancaster Gate, and Milly's allure arises clearly both from her fresh 'Americanness' and her inheritance. In the women's first encounter, Kate is pictured moving through the crowd, dressed characteristically in black. She is framed in close-up

Milly (Alison Elliott) and Kate's (Helena Bonham Carter) mutual attraction in *The Wings of the Dove*

staring off into the distance, when suddenly we hear Milly, voice off screen: 'I've finally caught you alone. Lord Mark's been monopolising you all evening.' Kate replies provocatively: 'But he's been staring at you. So have I.' This oblique triangle recurs subsequently when the two women visit Lord Mark at his country manor. When the drunken host disturbs a sleeping Kate in her bedchamber, she finds refuge in Milly's bed, and the two women are pictured nestled intimately in bed together.

Another ambiguous tryst between Milly and Kate takes place in their shared Venetian lodgings. Whispering together, the two women are key-lit in white shifts in the middle of the darkened room. With a soft romantic musical overlay, the camera circles the pair, who are posed among several ornate classical sculptures. Milly arranges Kate's hair, while Kate gently dabs rouge on her friend's lips. Exotic art decoration and sapphic overtones signify a European *mise en scène* of desire, where transgressive erotic attractions surface in a heady Italian milieu. Eschewing the intimate close-ups and two-shots used to frame the women's friendship in earlier scenes, the restless, circling camera work frames their intimacy as erotic spectacle. Reminiscent of the semi-pornographic lesbian eroticism of *Picnic at Hanging Rock* (1975) and *Henry & June* (1988), the scenes between Kate and Milly invite a voyeuristic male gaze.

Same-sex eroticism in *Wings* parallels the lesbian innuendo in the 1999 *Mansfield Park*, and both films are products of a polymorphously perverse 'post-heritage' trend in film-making. However, I would distinguish Rozema's film from *Wings* (and from the 1984 *The Bostonians*) on the strength of its strongly feminist plot line. The glimmer of attraction between Fanny and Mary Crawford forms part of Fanny's broader sexual awakening to a field of erotic possibilities. Nonetheless, eroticism between women in this film, as in costume cinema generally, is confined to innuendo and stolen moments within heterosexual plot lines. Against a relative abundance of gay male characters in period productions from the 80s, lesbian appearances have been less frequent. Feminist and queer art cinema are the exception, with Nancy Meckler's *Sister My sister*, *Orlando*, *Daughters of the Dust* and Ulrike Ottinger's German film *Johanna d'Arc de Mongolie*. British public broadcasting has facilitated lesbian period television including *Portrait of a Marriage* (the 1990 BBC series about Vita Sackville-West's affair with Violet Trefusis) and *Tipping the Velvet* (the television adaptation of Sarah Waters' savvy *fin de siècle* lesbian novel).

Forster's Humanism

For Sedgwick, the Jamesean 'epistemology of secrets' extends to suggest the peculiar discursive configuration of homosexuality in the West since the late nineteenth century as 'the epistemology of the closet' or 'the reign of the telling secret'.[6] Hovering on the cusp of the intimate and public spheres, the notion of the 'open secret' illustrates the strange half-presence of same-sex desire in costume film. The regime of the telling secret still holds for lesbian representation, while explicitly gay male characters are common in period film and television from the 80s. In fact, two gay critics wryly observed in the 80s that in heritage cinema, 'rugby and homosexuality are compulsory [for] upper-class Edwardian youth, "often at the same time" '.[7] Far from the spectre of same-sex attachments in the James adaptations, Forster's writings explore more utopian figures of non-normative masculinity.

As mentioned above, the gay 'White Flannel' trend of *Brideshead*, *Another Country*, *A Month in the Country* and *Maurice* is tarred by some critics with the brush of heritage conservatism, but I would argue these films' importance as popular gay works of the Thatcher period. The Merchant Ivory adaptation of Forster's *Maurice* is of particular interest as an explicit and influential 'coming out' story, and the Forster adaptations are interesting for their homosocial milieux and same-sex desires. In *Where Angels Fear to Tread*, Philip Herriton is an asexual young lawyer from a family of women who is 'seduced' by the 'glamour of Italy'. As noted in Chapter Four, like the English female characters, he falls in love with Gino, the handsome Italian. Philip's transformative experience is inspired in part by the romantic Tuscan landscapes, and the capacity of natural landscapes to facilitate sexual liberation recurs in *A Room with a View*.

Although it foregrounds a heterosexual romance, Monk points out that the film is marked by an 'excessive femininity' and 'a certain gender disturbance'.[8] *Room*'s idio-syncratic characters are not immediately intelligible within normative heterosexual relations: Lucy's unmarried chaperone Miss Charlotte Bartlett (Maggie Smith), the freethinking Emersons and the kindly vicar of indeterminate sexuality, Mr Beebe (played by openly gay actor Simon Callow).[9] Through this range of characters, the film opens up discursive and real 'places' for the exploration of non-normative gender and sexual identities. In *Room*'s famous male nude bathing scene, for example, heterosexual structures of desire and courtship are joyously jumbled as Mr Beebe, George and Freddy (Rupert Graves) cavort nude at Sacred Lake. Eric Haralson comments: 'As a narrative hot spot, the bathing scene conveys Forster's sense of the male body, in especial, as a "restless captive of culture" that "animates and disrupts the social order" and that the social order only struggles to contain.'[10] The nude bathing scene suggests a Foucauldian 'heterotopia'[11] – a 'space outside' (*du dehors*), or site of possibility, away from the repressive house of fiction. The secret garden in Holland's film is another example of a heterotopia, and, like the secluded magical garden, Forster's heterotopias are often associated with outdoor settings.

The heterotopia of the English pastoral recurs in *Maurice*, and in this film the same-sex desires implicit in *Room* and *Where Angels* are rendered visible and placed at the centre of the narrative. The film follows the relationship between two young men, Maurice Hall of the 'suburban classes' and the aristocratic Clive Durham. Meeting at Cambridge, the two young men's love affair unfolds through a series of stock scenes: bonding over Tchaikovsky in a romantic movement-image at the piano, punting on the Thames, sprawled together in the long grass. The spontaneity of their romance jars with the imposing formality of the institution invoked by a series of imposing long shots and high-angle shots. In chronicling its hero's difficult (and ultimately triumphant) 'coming out' within a homophobic and moralistic Edwardian milieu, *Maurice* fulfils a gay liberation agenda of visibility and positive images.

In keeping with a broader phenomenon described by Richard Dyer within European heritage cinema, *Maurice* is premised on 'a broadly positive view of homosexuality – which is to say that [these films] take such a view while depicting pasts that did not'.[12] In contrast with the frequent demonisation or violent punishment of lesbian and gay characters (*The Bostonians*, *Carrington*, *Sister My Sister* or *Another Country*), the film has a utopian ending. Finding true love with Scudder the under-gamesman, Maurice's journey of self-discovery contrasts pointedly with Clive's decision to suppress his feelings.

> Forster's novel ends . . . with the opposing consequences of repressing and activating desire. Clive opts for the comforts of his class and position in a loveless marriage; Maurice 'risks everything' by following a course of action dictated by his sexuality; he and the underkeeper Alec Scudder choose to vanish and live as outlaws. Such an end satisfies as wish-fulfilment ([Forster insisted that] 'a happy ending was imperative') and rigorously invokes the implications of Forster's dedication ('To a happier year').[13]

After ninety minutes of frustration in a sexless liaison with Clive, Maurice finds love and sex in the arms of Alec in the heterotopia of the boathouse. Their liaison is pointedly juxtaposed with a shot of Clive indoors, firmly closing the shutters to keep out the 'natural' evening air, and offering his wife a chaste goodnight kiss. The film develops an explicit topography where interior space figures repression against the outdoors as release. Hence, as in costume film generally, windows feature centrally in *Maurice* as literal openings for 'free' sexual expression in the Edwardian house of fiction: at Cambridge, Maurice climbs impulsively through the window at night to kiss Clive in his chambers; this moment recurs later in the film when Scudder scales a ladder to enter Maurice's window, seducing him in his bed.

Maurice was released in Britain at the time of the Thatcherite Section 28 legislation (an injunction against the use of municipal funds for the 'promotion of sexuality'). In the context of the AIDS crisis and a broader homophobic backlash by the New Right, popular and affirmative 'coming out' narratives such as *Maurice* were and are essential. And where the film follows the standard arc of individual liberation, it suggests a continuum of homosexual persecution that links the 1910s with the 80s. In an invented sub-plot, Maurice's and Clive's homosexual Cambridge friend Risley is prosecuted in 1911 for soliciting a soldier. 'Sent down' for gross indecency, Risley's trial refers intertextually to the 1895 Wilde trials. Dramatised explicitly in *Wilde*, these trials mark a historical moment of 'moral panic' where homosexuality was brought into public discourse. By framing Maurice's and Clive's understanding of their sexuality through legal discourses of the period, *Maurice* situates these personal fictions within historical struggles over homosexual identity.

Derek Jarman's Queer Erotics

Jarman's non-realist aesthetics and queer epistemology of the past are at odds with *Maurice*'s bourgeois humanism. Avant-garde film-maker, artist and writer, Jarman bitterly lambasted the 'Brideshead recidivism'[14] of 'heritage cinema', reserving a special scorn for the 'revival of Empire epics' such as *Brideshead* and *Chariots of Fire*. Within the 80s British film industry, Jarman was one of a group of film-makers (Terence Davies, Stephen Frears, Sally Potter, Isaac Julien, Neil Jordan, Julien Temple, Mike Leigh) to explore oppositional terrains of gender, race, class and sexuality during the Thatcher period. Interestingly, many of these film-makers have since directed innovative costume films. In contrast to the Merchant Ivory mode of production, Jarman worked with relatively limited resources, developing an oppositional period aesthetic,

> an imaginative treatment of the historical which breaks away from the polished actorly
> artifice of so-called 'classical' quality cinema. His own period films only gesture
> towards re-creating the past. Rather, they modernise it, making it rough and
> immediate, disjointing it with anachronisms, resisting the fetishistic ['Establishment']
> aesthetic of mainstream 'heritage' cinema.[15]

Caravaggio and *Edward II* refuse realist period detail. Jarman places a typewriter in Caravaggio's seventeenth-century Rome and dresses the villains of *Edward II* in modern British army garb.

This provocative queer aesthetic refuses a respectable 'positive images' mode of gay representation. If *Maurice* as a humanist tale of self-discovery calls for a ritual 'unbuttoning' of the clean and proper Edwardian bourgeois body, Jarman deliberately excavates ambiguously queer sexualities from the more distant past. He opts for Renaissance, medieval and classical periods, and brings dirty, violent, suffering and highly sexual bodies to the screen. While *Maurice* largely respects a restrained realist period aesthetic, Jarman's films explicitly approach the queer past as pastiche, a history of the [political] present, where 80s OutRage! activists bring their placards to *Edward II*'s medieval England.

Jarman's work is emphatically 'queer' in two ways. Anglo-American activist circles of the 80s and early 90s reclaimed this pejorative term to indicate an emergent angry and unapologetic political and aesthetic strategy. With its eroticised criminal underground and transgressive desires, the 1986 *Caravaggio* belongs to this creative impulse, as does the 1990 *Edward II*, a film explicitly connected to a cycle of 'new queer cinema', as I discuss below. Jarman's work is also queer in its fascination with oblique historical sexualities. Whereas 70s gay liberation celebrated the process of 'coming out', culminating in a stable lesbian or gay identity, queer identity is a much more liminal affair.

Refusing a straight/gay binary, queerness embraces an array of non-normative gender identities and sexual practices. In keeping with this vision, Jarman's treatments of Renaissance, medieval and classical periods seek out uncharted, sometimes disturbing sexual practices and desires.

Jarman's *Caravaggio* reclaims as 'queer' the life and art of Italian Renaissance painter Caravaggio. Along with Pasolini, this painter represents for Jarman a queer artistic legacy that inform his own artistic practice.[16] Jarman is fascinated by these men's art and by their lives, which were edged with erotic intensity and violence: Pasolini was murdered by a young boy in a sexual encounter, while Caravaggio was accused of killing a man in Rome, only to die alone in exile on a beach in Lazio. On this theme, Jarman writes in the preface to the published script of *Caravaggio*:

> Chiaroscuro, light and dark, the living in the throes of death, violent subjects painted with classical restraint, sinners as saints, always the contrast, painting on the run. The last sodomite of a dying tradition, parodying Michelangelo and stealing the dark from Leonardo yet surpassing them both in emotion.[17]

Caravaggio is a poetic reflection on the life and art of Michelangelo Merisi di Caravaggio (1571–1610). Only a few fragments are known of the painter's life. As a young man he moved from Milan to Rome, where he produced many well-known canvasses, and was forced to flee after a murder charge in the early 1600s.[18] From these fragments, Jarman assembles a fictive and impressionistic portrait, using scenic and dramatic elements to evoke an era and an artistic vision. The film opens on the artist on his deathbed, and a fragmented account of his life unfolds in flashback. Jarman does not venture a realist depiction of late sixteenth-century Rome – a project that in any case far exceeded the film's budget.[19] Instead, the film was shot in an empty warehouse on the outskirts of London, and Caravaggio's distinctive chiaroscuro lighting is used throughout. *Tableaux vivants* figure centrally, where paintings are restaged with models, and an elliptical narrative emerges using the models as dramatis personae.

For Jarman, Caravaggio's sexuality holds a key to his creative genius, and from the canvasses a triangle of desire and betrayal emerges between Caravaggio (Nigel Terry), Ranuccio (Sean Bean) and Lena, the prostitute who is also Ranuccio's lover (Tilda Swinton). As with many other historical biographies, the film painstakingly recreates the scenes of painterly creation. Yet *Caravaggio* differs in its explicit attention to the dark erotic and economic forces underlying the conditions of production. As Ranuccio poses as the executioner in *The Martyrdom of St Matthew* (1599–1600), Caravaggio tosses him coins which he stows in his mouth. This sequence insists on the traffic of desire as inextricable from money, social position – and, ultimately, violence. This love triangle is rife with jealousy and betrayal, as the wealthy painter buys Ranuccio's and Lena's time as models and showers them with gifts. Eventually, Lena leaves Ranuccio for a rich man, and the jealous Ranuccio murders her. After finding Lena's body in the canal, Caravaggio slits Ranuccio's throat. Bleeding, the man falls into the painter's arms in an orgasmic dying embrace.

A witness to these charged events with an angelic and expressive face, Caravaggio's deaf-and-dumb helper Jerusaleme (Spencer Leigh) constantly grinds pigments for his master. The film's spare set and shadowy lighting are heavy with vio-

A spare set heavy with violence and desire: Caravaggio (Nigel Terry) and his muse Ranuccio (Sean Bean) in a knife fight

lence and desire, and Caravaggio's crimsons are tinged with blood. For Jarman, the intermingling of desire, death and art can be read from Caravaggio's paintings. Indeed, part of Caravaggio's painterly achievement was a new realism in painting the human body, where 'skin, flesh, and pigment blend into reality. Painting is acknowledged as an act and as a physical fact, but immediately afterward, almost simultaneously, the presence of the human figure is felt as real, touchably there.'[20] Caravaggio was a controversial painter in his time, and critics were shocked by his use of identifiable rough characters from the streets of Rome as models for religious paintings. In turn, Jarman's fascination with Caravaggio is linked with this injection of the profane into religious tableaux.

A continuing fascination with Christian imagery, homoeroticism and death informs *Caravaggio*, where Jarman substitutes characters with figures in the paintings to signify suffering, redemption and divinity. After painting the murdered prostitute Lena in *The Death of the Virgin* (1606), Caravaggio cradles her corpse in his arms – a disturbing shot that strangely reconfigures the pietà. Subsequently, Caravaggio is forced to flee Rome, and the persecuted painter is ultimately depicted as a Christlike figure, as Jarman substitutes Caravaggio/Nigel Terry's face for Christ's in the *tableau vivant* of *Entombment* (1602–1604). For Leo Bersani and Ulysse Dutoit, Jarman depicts Caravaggio as a gay martyr, just as Jarman himself will later die of AIDS.[21]

Queer martyrs recur in Jarman's adaptation of Christopher Marlowe's play *Edward II*. Released in 1991 after Jarman's public announcement of his HIV+ status, the political context of the pandemic is much more explicit in this later film. *Edward II* presents King Edward II (Steven Waddington) and Gaveston (Andrew Tiernan) as star-crossed lovers. Their passion provokes a right-wing conspiracy between the lords, bishops and Queen Isabella (Tilda Swinton), who exile Gaveston the 'commoner', then

Jarman places 1990s AIDS activists in the medieval frame of *Edward II* to suggest a parallel
between contemporary and historical homophobia

depose and execute the king. The legendary circumstances of the monarch's death – a
red-hot poker inserted in the anus – underscores Jarman's premiss that this was political execution fuelled by homophobia. Yet here, as with *Caravaggio*, the murders are reap-
propriated through the imagery of homoerotic desire: Caravaggio's and Ranuccio's
intimacy at the point of death is echoed in an erotic tenderness between Edward and
Lightborn, his executioner (played by Jarman's lover Keith Collins). On screen, the
murder scene dissolves into an ellipsis, and Lightborn discards the poker to kiss Edward.

Edward II deliberately intermingles medieval and modern dress in its final scene,
which depicts a crowd of contemporary AIDS activists, heads bowed. In voice-over,
Edward's voice states: 'I know not, but of this I am assured/ That death ends all, and
I can die but once.' Somewhere between a demonstration and a wake, this scene insists
on an activist response to Thatcherism and the AIDS crisis. Juxtaposed with a violently
homophobic past, the film portrays a present characterised by political resistance. What
links the two moments is a history of transgressive desire, reprisals and resistance – and
the intimacy of eroticism and death.

José Arroyo situates *Edward II* within a late 80s and early 90s cycle of 'new queer
cinema' that includes *My Own Private Idaho* (1991), *Poison* (1991) and *Swoon* (1992).
For this critic, new queer cinema expresses a dystopic gay worldview in the context of
AIDS. Riddled with pain, suffering and death, films like *Edward II* also display 'a priv-
ileging of romantic homosexual desire'. Where this desire often leads to death, these
deaths are charged by a utopian romanticism.[22] When Gaveston and Edward are
parted for the last time, they dance together in their matching Marks & Spencer pyja-
mas under a spotlight in a darkened cavernous space; in the background, Annie
Lennox sings a heart-rending version of Cole Porter's 'Every Time We Say Goodbye'.

Insisting on redemption for sinners and sodomites, Jarman returns again and again to a powerful, stylised staging of death and eroticism. For Arroyo, AIDS is the 'political unconscious' of the new queer cinema, and the imagery of blood, sex and death offer powerful cinematic and painterly allegories for the pandemic.

Jarman's dystopic queer aesthetic parts ways with *Maurice* as a triumph for positive image representation. Yet these films share a utopian belief in the liberating power of masculine same-sex passions. Another common thread that connects these very different film-making practices is an interest in gay male authorship and creative expression. Published posthumously, Forster's semi-autobiographical novel *Maurice* has an intertextual resonance as a personal account of Edwardian homosexuality. In Jarman's films, sexuality and creativity are closely linked, and this artist, writer and film-maker situates himself within a renegade tradition of artists reclaimed as 'queer': Anger, Eisenstein, Pasolini, Genet, Orton, Cocteau, da Vinci, Caravaggio and Marlowe. As a celebrated novelist, playwright and critic, Oscar Wilde is another important queer author who finds his way into contemporary costume film. Wilde's parodic social critique belongs to a very different aesthetic tradition from Forster's humanism and Jarman's anachronistic pastiche. Yet the case of 'Wilde' as foundational gay martyr[23] and writer crystallises the intertextual dynamics of queer authorship.

Oscar Wilde: Authorship and Intertext

An invented sub-plot in *Maurice* references the Wilde trials, and Wilde himself is mentioned explicitly later in the film when Maurice confesses to the family doctor: 'I'm an unspeakable of the Oscar Wilde sort.' Wilde carries a complex intertextual significance as infamous homosexual, a particular type of 'queer wit', and a classic author epitomising an ambiguously queer 'camp' sensibility. Wilde's plays were the sources of Oliver Parker's two adaptations, *An Ideal Husband* (1995) and *The Importance of Being Earnest* (2002), and the latter part of the writer's life is chronicled in the biopic *Wilde* (1997). Where themes of 'alternative' or 'queer' masculinities are evident in the Forster films, the Wilde adaptations do not directly address homosexuality. Clearly, the writer's sexuality is central to the biopic, but the gap between Wilde as a notorious Victorian homosexual and his plays pinpoints the interpretive problem: where do we locate the 'queerness' in costume drama?

Returning to the idea of the 'epistemology of secrets', I would contend that queerness is manifested implicitly through intertextual codes of authorship and the ambiguously queer sensibilities of camp and theatricality. I argued in Chapter Five that authorship is crucial to *Orlando*'s female and feminist address, and the recognition of lesbian, gay or more obliquely queer authors extends similarly to lesbian and gay minority audiences. Within the terms of gay liberation and queer artistic production, visibility becomes crucial to discourses of authorship, and Jarman deliberately reclaims a historical legacy of queer artists. Costume film's romantic discourse of authorship as contained (male) genius is extended to queer authors with *Caravaggio*, *Wilde*, *Waiting for the Moon* (the 1987 film depicting Gertrude Stein), *The Hours*, *Looking for Langston* and John Maybury's 60s period film *Love is the Devil: Study for a portrait of Francis Bacon* (1999).

But queer authorship also figures through cultural and commercial intertexts via the branding of creators of source texts, directors, actors and other creative personnel.

In adaptations of Wilde, Forster and James, and in Jarman's films (as in *The Madness of King George*, *Orlando*, *Carrington* and *Gods and Monsters* (1998)), the *mise en abyme* of authorship, intertextual reference and character form part of an ambiguously 'queer' pattern of reference. In fact, an aspect of the continuing lesbian and gay fascination with historical figures like Woolf, James, Carrington or Forster is rooted in a retrospective investigation of the 'telling secret' of an indeterminate sexuality.

John Caughie states that within a post-structuralist account of authorship, 'the author, rather than standing behind the text, as a *source*, becomes a term in the process of reading or spectating'.[24] Where realist narrative suppresses authorial discourse to allow identification and immersion for the spectator in the story world, there is also a performative aspect to cinematic narration:

> The play of subjectivity in the classic narrative is a play of relocations, most typically intensifying our pleasure in a moment of admiration and delight in performance. . . . Within this concept of the film as performance, the figure of the author seems to function in a complex but important way. It seems frequently to be the recognition of the marks of a supposed (or real) author which allows the spectator a moment of admiration (or, indeed, in an awareness of clumsiness), to give up his/her position within the fiction without losing possession of it. I admire (or criticize) from outside the fiction.[25]

The textual and intertextual markers of authorship so predominant in costume drama can be read as a dispersion of the cinematic pleasures of identification and voyeurism. For Caughie, 'within a certain possession of the film (the performance is for me), and, where the performance is expert or familiar, my pleasure is intensified from a new position'.[26] This account encapsulates an important aspect of costume drama's persistent 'knowing' or 'doubled' address. If the branding of authorship attributes cultural value or prestige to costume drama, the films are themselves evaluated by individual spectators and critics with reference to an original text, author or performance.

The spectator's awareness of authorial figures – figures not always named in social discourse – is particularly significant for social groups commonly excluded from a position of enunciation in social discourse. Interestingly, Wilde as author is interpolated into *An Ideal Husband*, where the characters attend a performance of *Lady Windermere's Fan*; after the play, Wilde himself appears on stage. By inserting Wilde into the scene, even as a detail in the background of the Chilterns' dialogue, the director plays on the performative pleasures of authorship. However, 'Wilde', as a famously persecuted homosexual, is also a loaded intertextual signifier. The appearance of a recognisable homosexual does not interrupt the film's heterosexual narrative trajectory, but it does discreetly reference the ambiguity of 'queer space', or the 'place of the homosexual', within the text, intertext and in the audience.

A very similar scene appears in the biopic *Wilde*, this time at the opening of *The Importance of Being Earnest*. Indeed, these three films contributed to the widespread US/UK 90s Wilde revival.[27] The ubiquity of the iconoclastic 'Wilde' in a shadow play of author, play and historical figure highlights the intertextual horizon of intelligibility for the Wilde trio. This book has argued that costume films are frequently taken up with quests for lost origins, and Wilde is revered within Western gay culture as an author and as gay martyr. Queer historians claim that the Wilde trials were pivotal in the discursive production of same-sex desire as a recognisable *identity* (rather than a set of discrete acts). For Alan Sinfield, Wilde crystallised a specific mode of identifiable effeminate homosexuality:

> The trial helped to produce a major shift in perceptions of the scope of same-sex passion. At that point, the entire, vaguely disconcerting nexus of effeminacy, leisure, idleness, immorality, luxury, insouciance, decadence and aestheticism, which Wilde was perceived, variously, as instantiating, was tranformed into a brilliantly precise image.[28]

It is this signature dandy image that forms a figure for queer reference and identification within the 'Wilde' films. Finally, I would argue that the camp mode of expression pivotal to Wilde's plays and to his historical persona can present a parodic critique of heterosexuality and bourgeois conventions more generally.

Early in *An Ideal Husband,* the dandy Lord Goring (Rupert Everett) appears at the mirror as he completes his toilette for the Chiltern ball. Inserting a white flower in the lapel of his tuxedo, Goring gazes appreciatively at his reflection, while his servant Phipps (Peter Vaughan) hovers at his elbow:

> *Goring:* 'You see, Phipps, fashion is what one wears oneself. What is unfashionable is what other people wear.'
> *Phipps:* 'Yes m'lord.'
> *Goring:* [smoothing back his hair] 'Other people are quite dreadful. The only possible society is oneself.'
> *Phipps:* 'Yes m'lord.'
> *Goring:* 'To love oneself is the beginning of a life-long romance.'
> *Phipps:* 'Yes m'lord.'

Lord Goring (Rupert Everett) with Phipps (Peter Vaughan) in *An Ideal Husband*: 'To love oneself is the beginning of a life-long romance'

As Goring turns to Phipps to deliver the classic Wilde line, there is a cut to a medium shot framing the two men in profile. As Goring strides away, the camera holds on Phipps who straightens his bow tie thoughtfully in the mirror; from Phipps, cut to a close-up of the butler announcing the guests at the Chiltern ball. As with the instances of visual irony noted in the last chapter, it is the butler, not Goring, who gets the last word. This scene parodies the master–servant relationship, playing upon the the contrast between Goring's witticisms and Vaughan's deadpan responses. Wilde's critique is never earnest, but relies on an excessive performance of the sloth and uselessness of his aristocratic characters. As a mild form of class critique, Wilde's play does not overturn the master–servant relationship, nor does it give a distinctive voice to Phipps. But the film's running commentary – irony and parody both visual and spoken – lampoons all aspects of bourgeois social life.

The scene at the mirror suggests a parodic mode where the depth model of interiority is refracted onto a multiplicity of surfaces. On a queer reading, this sequence pinpoints the discourse of homosexuality as narcissism or desire for the self. Goring, the film's most eligible bachelor, is played by the openly gay Everett.[29] This canny casting underscores the character as a diegetic double for the queer dandy Wilde. Goring's finishing touches at the mirror complete a brisk montage depicting the various characters' elaborate sartorial preparations for the Chilterns' society party. This montage highlights the preening that precedes the party (or the ball) as movement-images of deadly serious courtship and political intrigue. Also at work in this montage is the film's (and the play's) attention to surface rather than depth, the costume rather than the wearer. Character and identity are explicitly products of role-playing and masquerade.

As comedies of courtship and marriage, *Earnest* and *Husband* retain the pleasures of the narrative form of romance and marriage, while producing an elaborate parody through excess. The characters are seen to be engaged in explicit performances of 'ideal' masculinity and marriage. These self-conscious practices of masquerade are reminiscent of Judith Butler's account of identity as 'tenuously constituted in time, instituted in an exterior space through a *stylized repetition of acts*'.[30] This performative account of gender identity well describes the theatrical sensibility of Wilde's work. Indeed, *Husband* foregrounds its theatricality in the opening scene. Phipps opens the curtains to reveal the 'scene' of Goring sprawled half-naked on his bed, while a naked young woman discreetly exits, stage left. Part of the play's narrative work is to transform this incorrigible bachelor into an 'ideal husband' like his friend Lord Chiltern (Jeremy Northam). Yet the deliberate intertextual play of Everett/Wilde/Goring produces an insistent flippancy rather than the deep transformation of 'true love'.

This comedy of manners turns on both the imperative and the absurdity of marriage. An intertitle announces: '1885 The London Season', where 'people are either hunting for husbands . . . or hiding from them'. The film's second plot explores a rift within an 'ideal' marriage, where the misunderstanding between Gertrude (Cate Blanchett) and Robert Chiltern arises from the wife's idealised view of her husband. Their marriage is only saved when Gertrude learns that her husband (like everyone) has 'feet of clay'; this plea for the acceptance of human imperfection offers a pleasing resolution to the comedy of manners, but also, subtly, undercuts the Victorian ideal of marriage. The Chiltern marriage is so praised within the film that it becomes a parodic account of marital bliss. Meanwhile, the Chilterns' fall from grace is cleverly juxtaposed with Goring's reluctant steps toward marriage. Both narrative lines play on the (narrative) inevitability of marriage, and its flaws.

After pursuing Lord Goring relentlessly throughout the film, Mabel (Minnie Driver) finally corners Goring into proposing, but she insists stringently on the event's proper form: it must take place 'in the conservatory, under the second palm tree on the right . . . the *usual* palm tree!'. This emphasis on form and performance undercuts the romantic expectations of the proposal. Slyly exposing the formula and theatricality of the conventions of courtship, ideal marriage and masculinity, *Husband* undercuts the 'depth' model of romance as deep feeling. For Jonathan Dollimore, Wilde's camp sensibility

> undermines the depth model of identity from inside, being a kind of parody and mimicry which hollows out from within, making depth [of desire and romantic 'feeling'] recede into its surfaces. Rather than a direct repudiation of depth, there is a performance of it to excess. . . . The hollowing-out of the deep self is pure pleasure, a release from the subjective correlatives of dominant morality (normality, authenticity, etc.).[31]

This parody of romantic love and marriage presents a rhetorical rejoinder to the prevalence of earnest costume romances. Oscar Wilde's work exemplifies 'camp' as a distinctive aesthetics and sensibility, 'a way of seeing the world as an aesthetic phenomenon' that foregrounds artifice and stylisation.[32] Although not exclusively 'queer', camp is often associated with a gay sensibility which, for Dyer, 'holds together qualities that are elsewhere felt as antithetical: theatricality and authenticity . . . intensity and irony, a fierce assertion of extreme feeling with a deprecating sense of its absurdity'.[33] This doubled address pinpoints both the appeal and the critical possibilities of Wilde's works. It is possible to enjoy *Husband* and *Earnest* purely as comedies of manners that conclude resoundingly on a celebration of marriage and conjugal bliss. Yet these films also delight in a parodic critique of the rituals of courtship and gender performance so essential to the 'sexual contract'. Wryly performative but nonetheless resolutely heterosexual romantic comedies, the vitality and playfulness of the adaptations contrasts starkly with the biopic's more difficult depiction of a contradictory 'queer' life.

An early scene in *Wilde* economically celebrates the writer's iconoclastic effeminate masculinity as a foil to normative Victorian society. Here, the writer (played by openly gay writer and actor Stephen Fry) 'takes to the street in a sumptuous butter-colored outfit that advertises his neo-dandy look. As Wilde walks through a square he runs into a group of barristers that part for him like a school of dull fish encountering a barracuda. The irony, of course, and it is all visual, is that Wilde will find himself head-to-head with the legal establishment in a few years' time.'[34] *Wilde* begins at the height of the writer's fame and chronicles his subsequent obsession with the young aristocrat Alfred Lord Douglas or 'Bosie' (Jude Law), concluding on his trials, conviction and imprisonment. This biography is strangely unsatisfying as it hardly addresses Wilde's writing, and its treatment of the writer's life verges on the sordid. By presenting Wilde as an absent husband and father and abused lover at the hands of the manipulative, selfish Bosie, *Wilde* portrays a contradictory intimate life that jars with the adaptations' mannered pleasures.

Andy Medhurst argues that *Wilde* relies on a tradition of 'Queer Wits' including

Noël Coward, Joe Orton, Quentin Crisp and Julian Clary: 'Are such figures simply licensed jesters, permitted to poke fun at the straight world but kept safely at its margins as little more than amusing pets, or do their barbs – exposing the limitations of conventionality with the clod-clear eyes of the outsider – carry the seeds of a real exposing?'[35] This query pinpoints the limits of a camp critique that is only implicitly gay or queer. For Medhurst, the stumbling block of Wilde's trademark parody within popular culture is the horizon of explicit gay sexuality, perhaps an 'erotic visibility'. While Wilde's first sexual relationships with young men are depicted in *Wilde* as a gentle sexual awakening, the latter part of the film seals Wilde into an abusive dynamic with Bosie that is painful to watch.

Perhaps this discomfort with *Wilde* arises from a residual desire for heroic queer martyrs and heroes, and for positive images of gay lives. It is as if Wilde's famous sparkle is extinguished, at least until he finds himself in court, where he defends himself with eloquence and dignity.

> The love that dare not speak its name in this century is such a great affection of an elder for a younger man as there was between David and Jonathan, such as Plato made the very basis of his philosophy, such as you may find in the sonnets of Michelangelo and Shakespeare. It is in this century misunderstood, so much misunderstood that it may be described as 'the love that dare not speak its name'. And on account of it I am placed where I am. It is beautiful, it is fine, it is the noblest form of affection.

Wilde's speech is drawn from the trial's transcripts, and the solemnity of the moment is underscored by a complete silence in the courtroom as the camera cuts between Wilde, the prosecutor and different members of the audience. This soliloquy of a tragic figure gives an eventful resonance to the scene that stands out from an uneven narrative. If Wilde's relationship with Bosie undercuts the nobility of the love that dare not speak its name, Wilde's defence recuperates his public persecution into a heroic moment of resistance.

Significantly, Wilde mounts his defence of the 'love that dare not speak its name' on the evidence of homosexuality as intrinsic to the cultural origins of Western myth, erudition and creativity. Similarly, in *Maurice*, the young men of Cambridge realise that their classic Greek texts are steeped in references to 'unspeakable' passions. Jarman's work evokes a parallel, less respectable tradition of sodomites, saints and murderers. Despite this chapter's honorary attention to James's lesbian innuendo, costume drama's same-sex passions occur primarily between men, and are often filmed under the sign of iconic gay male authorship. *Caravaggio* and *Edward II*, like *Wilde*, *An Ideal Husband* and *The Importance of Being Earnest*, and also *Maurice*, are marketed crucially on the auteurist brands of 'Caravaggio', 'Marlowe', 'Jarman', 'Wilde' and 'Forster'.

Viewed in relation to Anglo-American popular culture as a whole, the range of gay and queer expression in period film is striking, especially in the 80s. The films discussed in this chapter bring out aspects of costume film associated with (but not limited to) queer culture. For instance, the intertextual web of the Wilde films and of Jarman's roster of historical homosexuals form part of the genre's broader playful knowing address. Finally, as I will explore further in Chapter Eight, the performative and camp qualities associated with Wilde and the insistent corporeality of Jarman are part of costume drama's wider turn toward explicitly erotic and corporeal pasts.

Notes

1. John Lyttle, 'Knights in White Flannel', *City Limits,* no. 443, 29 March 1990, p. 19.
2. See Michel Foucault, *The History of Sexuality Volume 1: An Introduction* (New York: Vintage Books, 1990), p. 12.
3. See Sedgwick, *Tendencies*, pp. 73–103.
4. Terry Castle, *The Apparitional Lesbian* (New York: Columbia University Press, 1993), p. 183.
5. Wood, *The Wings of the Dove*, p. 67.
6. Eve Kosofsky Sedgwick, *Epistemology of the Closet* (Berkeley: University of California Press, 1990), p. 67.
7. Mark Finch and Richard Kwietnioski, 'Melodrama and *Maurice*: Homo is where the het is', *Screen* vol. 29 no. 3, 1988, p. 73.
8. See Monk, *Sex, Politics, and the Past*, pp. 16–26.
9. Finch and Kwietnioski, 'Melodrama and *Maurice*', p. 79.
10. Eric Haralson, ' "Thinking about Homosex" in Forster and James', in Robert K. Martin and George Piggford (eds), *Queer Forster* (Chicago: The University of Chicago Press, 1997), p. 67.
11. See Michel Foucault, *Aesthetics, Method, and Epistemology* (London: Penguin, 1994), pp. 175–85.
12. Dyer, *The Culture of Queers*, p. 206. On gay men in European heritage cinema, see the entire essay 'Homosexuality and Heritage', pp. 204–28.
13. Finch and Kwietnioski, 'Melodrama and *Maurice*', p. 73.
14. Andrew Moor, 'Spirit and matter: romantic mythologies in the films of Derek Jarman', in David Alderson and Linda Anderson (eds), *Territories of Desire in Queer Culture* (Manchester: Manchester University Press, 2000), p. 57.
15. Ibid., p. 57.
16. Michael O'Pray includes in this legacy Christopher Marlowe, author of *Edward II*, as 'an active, passionate man who was not only gay, but died in a fight inside a Deptford tavern'. See Michael O'Pray, '*Edward II*: Damning desire', *Sight and Sound*, October 1991, p. 8.
17. Derek Jarman, *Derek Jarman's Caravaggio* (London: Thames and Hudson, 1986), p. 7.
18. On Caravaggio's life and work see Howard Hibbard, *Caravaggio* (London: Thames & Hudson, 1983), and Peter Robb, *M* (London: Bloomsbury, 2000).
19. Jarman struggled for seven years to find financial backing for this film, which was eventually financed by the British Film Institute. See Tony Rayns, 'Unnatural Lighting', *American Film* vol. 11 no. 10, September 1986, p. 59.
20. Frank Stella, *Working Space* (Cambridge, MA: Harvard University Press, 1986), p. 11.
21. Leo Bersani and Ulysse Dutoit, *Caravaggio* (London: BFI, 1999), p. 47.
22. José Arroyo, 'Death Desire and Identity: The Political Unconscious of "New Queer Cinema" ', in Joseph Bristow and Angelia R. Wilson (eds), *Activating Theory* (London: Lawrence & Wishart, 1993), p. 93.
23. See Shelton Waldrep, 'The Uses and Misuses of Oscar Wilde', in John Kucich and

Dianne F. Sadoff (eds), *Victorian Afterlife* (Minneapolis: Minnesota University Press, 2000), p. 50.

24. John Caughie, *Theories of Authorship* (London: Routledge & Kegan Paul, 1981), p. 200.

25. Ibid., p. 204.

26. Ibid., pp. 204–5.

27. This revival included Sir Peter Hall's 1992 theatre production of *An Ideal Husband*, a 'Wilde' character in Tom Stoppard's play *The Invention of Love*, Liam Neeson's depiction of Wilde in *The Judas Kiss* on Broadway, and Moises Kaufman's off-Broadway play *Gross Indecency: The Three Trials of Oscar Wilde*. See Waldrep, 'Uses and Misuses', p. 51.

28. Alan Sinfield, *The Wilde Century* (London: Cassell, 1994), p. 3.

29. Everett also appeared as the gay spy Guy Burgess in *Another Country* and more recently in the high-profile role of gay best friend to the bride in *My Best Friend's Wedding* (1997).

30. Judith Butler, *Gender Trouble* (New York: Routledge, 1990), p. 140.

31. Jonathan Dollimore, 'Post/modern: On the Gay Sensibility, or the Pervert's Revenge on Authenticity', in Fabio Cleto (ed.), *Camp: Queer Aesthetics and the Performing Subject* (Edinburgh: Edinburgh University Press, 1999), p. 224.

32. Susan Sontag, 'Notes on "Camp"', in Cleto (ed.), *Camp*, p. 54.

33. Dyer, cited in Dollimore, 'Post/modern', p. 225.

34. Waldrep, 'Uses and Misues', p. 55. Richard Dyer notes the visual significance of dandy clothes as asserting 'queer' codes of masculinity. See *The Culture of Queers*, p. 214.

35. Andy Medhurst, 'Licensed to Cheek', *Sight and Sound*, October 1997, p. 32.

Chapter Eight
The Queen's Bodies

An exploration of the intimate sphere of the nineteenth-century house of fiction – or indeed the private lives of monarchs and artists from earlier periods – insists on a dramatisation of desire and sexuality. Writing of the 'abstract space' of Western modernity (the rationalisation of space, the accumulation of capital), Henri Lefebvre describes a psychic and material organisation of interior and exterior space through the 'bourgeois apartment' and the rise of the middle classes.

> In the inhabited space a moralizing solemnity is the order of the day . . . an atmosphere of family and conjugal life – in short, of genitality – all of which is nobly dubbed an *intimité*. If the outside dominates the inside–outside relationship, this is because the outside is the only thing that really matters: what one sees and what is seen. Nevertheless, the interior, where Eros dies, is also invested with value – albeit in a mystifying and mystified way. Heavy curtains allow inside to be isolated from outside, the balcony to be separated from the drawing-room, and hence for 'intimacy' to be preserved and signified.[1]

Lefebvre rewrites Habermas's intimate sphere as a 'production of space'. The divisions between public, private and intimate sphere are still resonant, even as they are constantly being refashioned. And while costume film eschews the 'outside' as conventional historical event, it increasingly probes the folds and inner recesses of the boudoir.

As I have previously indicated, recent costume film has become increasingly sexually explicit. This tendency includes 90s British 'post-heritage' films such as *Carrington*, *Angels & Insects*, *The Wings of the Dove*, *Elizabeth*, *Mansfield Park* and *Shakespeare in Love*, as well as several Hollywood productions dating back to the 80s including *Amadeus*, *Dangerous Liaisons*, *Interview with the Vampire* and *Bram Stoker's Dracula*. Also, I have argued that pre-nineteenth-century periods and European sites invoke a '*mise en scène* of desire'. Finally, the popular form of the biopic tends to explore the psychosexual aspects of historical figures rather than their political or artistic endeavours.

In this chapter I address four distinctive stylistic and historical treatments of sexuality and the body. First, I examine *The Piano*'s rearticulation of Victorian eroticism, which situates a feminist sexual awakening with a colonial context. Secondly, I turn to *Quills*, *Dangerous Liaisons* and *Valmont*, three films set in late eighteenth-century France among the sexually adventurous libertines. In the last part of the chapter, I turn to the royal biopic, beginning with *The Madness of King George*, which is set in 1780s England, the period parallel to *Dangerous Liaisons*. Finally, I turn to *Elizabeth* and

Shakespeare in Love as physical and sexually charged Renaissance spectacles. Threaded through these different sections is a meditation on costume, performance and the epistemology of the self that develops earlier themes of 'interiority' and 'performativity'.

Victorian Flesh

The current fascination with the buttoned-up and repressive house of fiction correlates with a more general return to a broadly Victorian structure of feeling. Less a precise historical setting than a vivid articulation of sexuality, repression and the body, for Garrett Stewart the 'Victorian' is simply the other side of the coin from 'the present drift toward commercialized nudity': 'Each media form is preoccupied with corporeality, the weight and curve of flesh, whether intriguingly draped or tantalizingly unwrapped.'[2] As discussed in Chapter Six, an attention to perverse sexuality and the seedy underside of Victorian life can be found in *Angels & Insects*, *Bram Stoker's Dracula*, *The Secret Garden*, *Mary Reilly* (1996), two versions of *Jane Eyre*, *Wuthering Heights*, *Wide Sargasso Sea* and *Sister My Sister*. *The Piano*, one of the most influential costume films of the 90s, develops an extraordinary vocabulary of costume, framing and *mise en scène* to probe Victorian sexuality.

A free adaptation of Emily Brontë's *Wuthering Heights*, Campion's film transposes the Gothic romance into a New Zealand context. The film brilliantly problematises many prevalent themes of costume film, including the drive toward individual expression. The film begins with the premise that Ada (Holly Hunter) has simply decided not to speak because she recognises that women's voices are not heard. In contrast with her outpouring of expression through the piano, Ada's wilful silence presents a curious departure in a cycle of films taken up with verbal expression:

> A film about silence and expression beyond language, *The Piano* resonates with the silences embedded deep in the texts of such 19th-century women writers as Emily Brontë or Emily Dickinson. . . . In *The Piano*, Jane Campion feels her way around those echoing caves upon which they build their haunted houses of fiction. It is a virtuoso interpretation of the literary sensibility in a cinematic form, truer than any doggedly faithful adaptation of, say, *Wuthering Heights*.[3]

Like *Orlando*, this film inaugurates 90s costume drama as an international 'woman's genre'. These 'thinking women's' films use familiar texts and genres from the past to scrutinise contemporary (Western) women's psychic, social and sexual experience. Campion transposes the literary dilemmas of voice, expression and desire into a striking cinematic language of costume, gesture and *mise en scène*.

A cluttered, dank, brooding atmosphere arises from the film's New Zealand-bush setting. When Ada and her daughter Flora (Anna Paquin) arrive at their new home, the cabin of Ada's new husband Stewart (Sam Neill) is first depicted in the driving rain in a muddy clearing scored with the harsh verticals of charred, dead tree trunks – the imperial devastation of the land made manifest. Campion comments that 'the bush has got an enchanted, complex, even frightening quality to it. . . . It's mossy and very intimate, and there's an underwater look that always charmed me. I was after the vivid, subconscious imagery of the bush, its dark, inner world.'[4] This 'dark, inner world' doubles an exotic colonial milieu with an investigation into the awkward recesses of the Victorian body.

Our first clear view of Ada (in Scotland) finds her crouched at the foot of a huge tree; as she rises, the camera rises with her and travels up the tree trunk, pivoting to look down on her as she walks away; tracking along a huge overhanging bough, the camera follows her movements from above. A contributing factor to *The Piano*'s disorienting atmosphere is this distinctive stealthy and voyeuristic camera work that delves into dark corners as 'a witness directing the viewer's attention in a very intimate way'.[5] For instance, Stewart spies Ada and Baines (Harvey Keitel) having sex together through a peephole in Baines's cabin. As in *Sweetie* and *The Portrait of a Lady*, Campion employs objects as screens to eerily cloud our vision. When Stewart enters Ada's and Flora's room, for instance, he must fight through a tangle of suspended petticoats and corsets. This veiled economy of vision heightens a pervasive fascination for what is hidden and unspoken.

Perhaps the film's most striking stylistic feature lies in its innovative use of costume to evoke Victorian corporeal and sexual unease. Stella Bruzzi identifies two cinematic costuming strategies for exploring women's history: the 'liberal' and the 'sexual'. Within the liberal approach, clothes 'are merely signifiers to carry information about country, class and period'.[6] Films like *Sense and Sensibility* or *My Brilliant Career* forge a 'political and ideological affinity between the struggles of women in the present and figures from the past'.[7] The realist period aesthetic (costume, *mise en scène*, landscape) seeks to create an 'actual' historical look and accentuate continuities in historical experience. In contrast, the 'sexual' approach foregrounds the work of representation, offering 'a more elliptical way of examining the past – one based on complex, hard-to-define emotions and attractions rather than concrete events'.[8]

In parallel with *Orlando*'s use of costume to evoke the elaborate constraints of eighteenth-century femininity, Ada's and Flora's clothes are densely meaningful:

> Women's clothes are presented as constricting, ugly, absurd; the multiple skirts which trip Ada and Flora as they trudge through the mud, and which make it ludicrously difficult for Aunt Morag to relieve herself when 'caught short' in the woods. Clothes seem liberating only when they come off, as when Flora dances and cartwheels across the beach in her petticoat.[9]

With its elaborate restrictions of lace, undergarments, petticoats and corsets, the Victorian female body is constrained, but also protected. Yet the prohibition of complete coverage is also an invitation, and, in his pursuit of Ada, Baines finds a single hole in her stocking through which he touches her leg. As with the carriage scene of *Innocence* where the exposed wrist evokes such excitement, *The Piano* plays on the sexual charge of Victorian sexual reticence. This dynamic emerges most powerfully in the elaborate bartering over the piano, where Ada buys back one key of the piano for each article of clothing that she removes. This elaborate exchange lays bare the interdependence of sexual and economic relations, a theme frequently emphasised in feminist revisionist works like Campion's own *The Portrait of a Lady* and *The House of Mirth*. In fact, *The Piano* is steeped in references to the exchange of women's bodies, for Ada is sent to New Zealand because her father has promised her in marriage to Stewart.[10]

Campion's interest in erotic and economic exchange is intertwined with an investigation of the corporeal sensations of emigration and colonial contact. Unlike the utopian images of sailing ships as romantic escape from the Old World in *Persuasion*, *Maurice* and *Angels & Insects*, Ada does not choose to migrate, she is sent. Ada and Flora's landing upon a remote New Zealand beach is precarious. First, there is a shot of four pairs of hands silhouetted dark against the moody sky, reaching upward to lift Ada, Flora and their possessions (especially the bulky, heavy piano) into the pitching rowing boat. After wading through the surf, Flora collapses on the shore to vomit on the white sand. Cut to a strange shot from Ada's point of view as she looks down on her two small feet with their tightly buttoned high black boots in the surf. Then in a quick close-up of her face (framed in a severe bonnet) she looks up, birdlike, at her surroundings. Finally, in a long shot, her tiny figure is silhouetted dark against the broad white beach, a looming outcrop of black rock, the moody sky behind.

Part of the film's narrative-image – variations of this shot appear on the film poster and in the published screenplay – this scene ushers in the imperial encounter. Costume drama's sophisticated play of gesture and language is to some degree polyphonic in *The Piano*. The Maori people are constantly present, watching, sometimes commenting upon, the European characters. In the beach scene where Ada and Flora first encounter Stewart, Baines and the Maori guides, there is a remarkable ironic doubling through gesture. Even as Anna Paquin's Flora constantly mimes Ada's gestures (the birdlike manner in which she cocks her head to one side), when Ada and Stewart first meet, a Maori man stands just behind each of them, shadowing their gestures. Stewart (wearing a black top hat) is singled out for particular ridicule, as the Maori man behind him (also wearing a tall black hat) mimics his brusque, impatient mannerisms. Stewart is the butt of a number of jokes, where the Maori guides sometimes ignore his orders, referring to him as 'old dry balls'. In a film taken up with illicit watching, the gaze of the Maori people as ironic observers is pointedly foregrounded, a strategy similar to the watchful gaze of the servants in *Gosford Park*.

Mary Louise Pratt uses the term 'contact zone', to describe 'the space of colonial encounters, the space in which peoples geographically separated come into contact with each other and establish ongoing relations, usually involving conditions of coercion, radical inequality, and intractable conflict'.[11] Where some critics find in *The Piano* a liberal critique of imperialism, Lynda Dyson calls it a 'narrative of reconciliation' with New Zealand's troubled colonial past:

> This romantic melodrama is set in a landscape where 'natives' provide the backdrop
> for the emotional drama of the principal white characters. The Maori are located on
> the margins of the film as the repositories of an authentic, unchanging and simple way
> of life: they play 'nature' to the white characters' 'culture.' . . . 'Indigenous' people and
> their cultures have been privileged as the keepers of spiritual and authentic values.
> Their perceived mystical attachments to the land and to nature are idealized,
> symbolizing all that has been lost through modernity.[12]

For this critic, Baines, the sympathetic Scot who has 'gone native', offers a contemporary reconciliation between conflictual Maori and European cultural perspectives. In contrast with Stewart's inhibited Victorian morality and violence, Baines is sensual,

The Maori gaze in *The Piano*

gentle and understanding. One sequence pictures him in the nude, polishing the piano with his shirt. Beautifully lit from above with natural sunlight, this scene evokes a 'natural' eroticism implied by Baines's association with Maori culture. Baines's characterisation evokes a problematic colonial trope where Europeans discover nature, spirituality, and sensuality through their contact with 'primitive' cultures.[13]

While tattoos and an ease with Maori language and customs place Baines in a privileged relationship to the Maori, Pihama argues that his 'partial moko' appropriates Maori identity. Moreover, she suggests that the film is structured through a colonial gaze, fixing the Maori through stereotypes from 'the "happy-go-lucky native" to the sexualized Maori women available at all times to service Paheka ('white') men'.[14] Hira, a Maori woman, cooks and cleans for Baines, and has an ambiguous sexual relationship with him. As with the servants in *Angels & Insects* and *The Secret Garden*, they provide a simple and benevolent counterpoint to repressive, patriarchal Victorian norms. By choosing to collide feminist and colonial trajectories, Campion deliberately complicates her feminist Victorian costume drama with a parallel colonial history. Yet this juxtaposition rests on a problematic contrast between the Victorian 'white settlers' and the romanticised Maori 'natives'.

The Piano is part of a cinematic resurgence of Victoriana including *The Age of Innocence*, *The Secret Garden* and *Bram Stoker's Dracula*. For Stewart, these films explore a Victorian cultural fantasy 'concerned less with the historical than with the personal, the intimate or the psychosexual'.[15] Often this reflexive look back at the Victorian microcosm portrays it as a world happily since transcended, contemporary Western sexual and emotional freedoms contrasting favourably with this repressive society. Yet Stewart also notes 'a certain yearning for the sureties of the Victorian era, especially for the period's different understanding of the erotic body and its social commerce'.[16] If the repressive Victorian house of fiction inspires a series of eloquent cinematic accounts, the earlier historical setting of the late eighteenth century provokes another distinctive body of costume films. Set in a period characterised by elaborate wigs, powders and costumes, and mannered gesture and *mise en scène*, these films depict a decadent aristocracy and their boudoir politics and lascivious sexuality.

The Mirror and the Boudoir

Peter Brooks suggests that the mystified 'privacy' of the intimate sphere associated with the English and the French novel produces discourses of confession and exposure through writing: 'The dynamic of privacy and its invasion may suggest why the novel, no doubt from its inception, and notoriously in the eighteenth century, gave a large place to the erotic and the pornographic.'[17] Exemplifying European settings as a *mise en scène* of desire, *Dangerous Liaisons*, *Valmont* and *Quills* bring to the screen the erotic libertine writings of eighteenth-century France. Here, writing does not prompt the revelation of an 'authentic self' or 'true love' (as explored in Chapters Two and Four) but instead explicitly evokes the duplicity of desire and the performative power of language to manipulate, to provoke desire and to wound.

The perversity of writing is exemplified in Philip Kaufman's *Quills*, a fictionalised account of the exploits of the notorious Marquis de Sade (Geoffrey Rush), by that time in his life confined to a madhouse. While the institution is under the liberal management of the Abbé du Coulmier (Joaquin Phoenix), Sade lives in luxury and manages to smuggle his writings out of the prison with the help of a sympathetic chambermaid (Kate Winslet). After his scandalous writings appear in print, Sade is deprived of writing materials, but the prohibitions of the madhouse and state censorship only provoke him to write more lascivious and violent fantasies. For Brooks, the goal of Sade's texts 'is to make the body the scene of discourse. Sade's libertines must articulate fully the outrageous acts they perform on and with the body.'[18] This compulsion to narrate sexual acts is rendered literally in *Quills* as Sade, after his writing materials are confiscated, continues to scrawl pornographic prose all over his body and clothes and on his bedsheets.

The madhouse itself is a topography of whispered secrets and voyeurism, where Sade's cell is subject to inspection through a slot in the door, and the thick walls are full of peepholes. This titillating economy of voyeurism and partial vision is repeated in the disclosure of tantalising fragments of Sade's scurrilous scribblings. The audience's fascination is piqued, but we are not given a complete story until the film's climax one stormy night. Deprived of quill and ink, Sade recounts his tale orally in fragments to the inmate in the next cell, who passes it on to the next inmate, and so on, until it reaches the ears of Madeleine, who records it on paper. As the violent tale is slowly revealed, the inmates are increasingly aroused, even as the audience is bound into the suspense. Finally, as the tale culminates in the violent murder of its prostitute protagonist, a fire breaks out and the inmates are released. In the confusion, the burly inmate Bouchon attacks Madeleine, acting out Sade's depraved tale on her body. Later, Madeleine's broken body is found floating in a washtub, alongside the transcribed story holding the gruesome record of what has been done to her.

Quills morphs genres from comedy of manners to horror film. Only slightly less extreme is the dramatic range of comedy, seduction and dire consequence in *Valmont* and *Dangerous Liaisons*, two adaptations of Choderlos de Laclos' 1782 libertine epistolary novel. In Chapter Two, I included *Liaisons* within a group of nostalgic films that carve out a masculine interiority of deep feeling. The regret brought by the letter that arrives too late and the nostalgic flashback encapsulate a Lacanian formula of (masculine) desire as lack and loss. But another reading of *Liaisons* is possible.

Close's bravura performance of Merteuil in *Liaisons* sets in relief a veritable 'war of the sexes' that takes place within the film. If costume drama's affection-image often inscribes subjective interiority, in *Liaisons* character depth is supplanted by a performative account of character as surface and masquerade. Frears' film is drawn from Christopher Hampton's theatrical adaptation of Laclos' novel. Hampton's script and Frears' direction produce a heightened precision of language and performance much more theatrical than Forman's energetic and at times almost slapstick *Valmont*. The theatrical source, as well as the pre-Revolutionary French setting, distinguishes the film stylistically from the realist Merchant Ivory productions and Austen adaptations.

Liaisons begins and ends with another interior movement-image ubiquitous in costume film, the woman at the mirror. The mirror points to a play of identity, masquerade and duplicity that is one of the great pleasures of costume drama. At the outset, the Marquise de Merteuil (Glenn Close) applies a 'mask' of thick chalky makeup. Although she wins the bet with Valmont, in the end she loses Valmont himself (whom she clearly still loves) and her social position. The film also ends at the mirror, as Merteuil mechanically wipes away the mask, her face smudged and racked with grief and shame. These matched scenes efficiently mark out the terrain (the face, the body, emotions) and effects (complete emotional and social annihilation) of a cutthroat battle. These eloquent close-ups indicate Frears' strategy of underplaying period fittings in favour of story and character, and cinematographer Philippe Rousselot consistently shoots in close to the face, often framed against mirrors.[19] Close-ups illustrate character, and it is in the powdered, controlled faces that character and motivation flickers across the screen in bravura performances by Close and Malkovich.

The sequences at the mirror suggest a feminine behind-the-scenes powerplay laid bare by Merteuil's extraordinary direct address to the camera. A little way into the film, Merteuil is pictured poised on one end of a settee while Valmont sprawls on the other end, listening. Merteuil's self-revelation is shot in mesmerising close-up, the camera zooming slowly closer, as if trying to uncover the essence of the woman under the mask:

Valmont: 'I often wonder how you managed to invent yourself.'

Merteuil: 'Well, I had no choice, did I? . . . Women are obliged to be far more skilful than men. You can ruin our lives with a few well-chosen words. So of course I had to invent not only myself but ways of escape no one has ever thought of before. And I've always succeeded because I've always known I was born to dominate your sex and avenge my own.'

A film of faces: Merteuil (Glenn Close) and Valmont (John Malkovich) square off in a battle of the sexes in *Dangerous Liaisons*

Valmont: 'Yes, but what I asked was how.'
Merteuil: 'When I came out into society I was fifteen. I already knew that the role I was condemned to – namely to keep quiet and do what I was told – gave me the perfect opportunity to listen and observe. Not to what people told me, which naturally was of no interest, but to whatever it was they were trying to hide. I practised detachment. I learned how to look cheerful while under the table I stuck a fork into the back of my hand. I became a virtuoso of deceit. It wasn't pleasure I was after, it was knowledge. . . . And in the end I distilled everything to one wonderfully simple principle: Win or die.'

While Frears foregrounds Valmont as the male protagonist transformed through the power of love, the use of Merteuil/Close's face to bookend the film reveals her as puppeteer, winner, and, ultimately, tragic figure in this war of words, bodies and hearts.

Yet this sequence does not reveal the character's essence, but rather points to layer upon layer of careful construction. Like the movement-image of the woman at the window, the film's frequent use of mirrors invites a psychoanalytic reading following a Lacanian problematic of identity. In the mirror stage, premised on the recognition of lack or absence of the (m)other, the child forms 'an illusory corporeal cohesion, founded on a (mistaken) identification of the child with its visual *gestalt* in the mirror'.[20] The mirror stage inaugurates a process of identity formation in relation to others and one's own body image. Significantly, this drama of subject formation takes place, for Lacan, 'at the threshold of the visible world'. Virginia Blum and Heidi Nast point out that, prior to the mirror stage, the nascent subject is continuous with its surroundings, and 'the visible world is then differentiated from the "I" only as a secondary effect of mirroring. . . . In other words, the "visible world" is constituted as such through its sub-ordination to the subject's emergence.'[21]

The ubiquity of mirrors in films such as *Liaisons*, *The House of Mirth* or *An Ideal Husband* could be interestingly read through the psychodrama of the splitting of the self, formulations of narcissism and the ambivalent processes of desire and identification. But is there another reading of the woman at the mirror? Lefebvre concurs with Lacan that the mirror is a figure that 'discloses the relationship between me and myself, my body and the consciousness of my body'.[22] However, he goes on to rearticulate the mirror as a material object through which the subject locates itself in social space.

> The mirror is thus an object among others, and an object different from all others, evanescent, fascinating. In and through the mirror, the traits of other objects in relationship to their spatial environment are brought together; the mirror is an object in space which informs us about space, which speaks of space. In some ways a kind of 'picture,' the mirror too has a frame which specifies it, a frame that can be either empty or filled. . . . The mirror introduces a truly dual spatiality: a space which is imaginary with respect to origin and separation, but also concrete and practical with respect to coexistence and differentiation.[23]

Lefebvre critiques the Lacanian mirror phase for flattening the materiality of the body and social space into a set of two-dimensional specular relations. Lacan's is ultimately a narcissistic account, where the drama of the subject's emergence obscures the three-dimensional spatial and temporal relations of social and physical space. Like Lacan, Lefebvre begins 'by presenting us with a subject looking out upon a "mirror"; unlike Lacan, though, the mirror is not a human form or image, but a complex physical and social landscape'.[24]

A movement-image strikingly similar to *Liaisons'* woman at the mirror can be found in *Wings*. Kate appears at the mirror in an early scene that is a *trompe l'œil*. The scene begins with an extreme close-up of Kate's eyes as a hand applies a thick mask of white make-up and eyeliner to her face. This close-up is only revealed as a mirror shot when the camera pulls back, and we see that the hand applying the make-up is not Kate's but that of her Aunt Maud (Charlotte Rampling). As in *Liaisons*, a masklike effect is palpable, as is the subtle feminine powerplay waged through appearance and obligation. The wealthy Maud clasps an ornate necklace around her niece's neck, stating: 'Try to look as though you've worn it all your life, it's yours.' The seemingly offhand nature of the gift belies its powerful hold on Kate. While Maud, presumably, has many necklaces to offer, Kate clearly is caught by this gift, and the camera holds on her face as she stares into the mirror, fingering the necklace. This skilfully polysemic movement-image, like the woman at the window, holds in tension several interrelated lines of force: a drama of narcissism and desire; the terrible price of female subjectivity flattened into image/object; and the subtly corrosive power of class and money to poison intimate relationships.

These elements are all present in *Liaisons*, where the mirror gestures to a play of appearances. Hollander notes that in eighteenth-century baroque and rococo interiors, 'decorative impersonal' mirrors were used for room panelling that 'reduced the living people themselves moving about in the room to the status of decorative figures'.[25] Small mirrored rooms were also popular, and Hollander comments that 'the decorative mirror repels too close an examination, as it repels too intense an eye for pictorial meaning'.[26] This account of the mirror as reflective surface repelling a hermeneutic meaning prompts a different reading of subjectivity in *Liaisons*. Where the film's drama of faces might suggest an intensified narcissistic drama of 'the Ego contemplating itself in the glass',[27] Laclos' witty demolition of libertine society cloaks a critique of the hypocritical pre-Revolutionary French aristocracy.

The historical specificity of Laclos' critique is perhaps diffused for contemporary audiences in *Valmont* and *Liaisons*, but its dramatic stakes are transfigured into a contemporary lexicon of 'the war of the sexes'. Significantly, the film's decorative mirrors hide the invisible entrance to Merteuil's most private inner enclave; the door to her boudoir is embedded in a wall of tiny mirrors. This hard, decorative and reflecting surface rebuffs hermeneutic depth and toys with the symbolism of the 'door as threshold': sometimes the door is seductively half-open, often firmly shut. If the familiar narrative of desire as loss is evident in *Liaisons*, this romantic discourse is at odds with a performative mode of costume film that projects the materiality of the body and the discursive force of desire. At stake here is not only the gender of the protagonist, but also a different epistemology of subjectivity and desire. Rather than being a guarantor of authentic interiority and expression, the face becomes a mask, the body a weapon and the events a mannered battlefield of sexual intrigue.

The casting of Close as Merteuil chimes with her role in *Fatal Attraction* (released in 1987, the year before *Liaisons*) as a psychotic homewrecker; the film was lambasted by feminists as anti-feminist backlash for its vilification of sexually powerful and successful single women.[28] Close's star image adds another dimension to the polysemic and *allegorical* capacities of costume drama. Recent thrillers *Fatal Attraction* and *Basic Instinct* (1992) dramatise (male) social fears about female power and sexual autonomy through the generic milieu of violent sexuality. Exploring a related arena of sexual intrigue, costume drama deploys its own rich lexicon of rapier dialogue and volatile, sexualised bodies seething under period costume. In this vein, Pascal Pernod describes the opening scene of *Liaisons*, where Frears intercuts the elaborate robing of the two lead characters – a ritual 'girding of the loins'.

> Following generic convention, he depicts the harnessing of Merteuil and the powdering of Valmont, insisting on their respective weapons: for one, the body (where the principal weapon, her breasts, are compressed [into an forward-thrusting *décolleté*]), and for the other the face (and the tongue that he uses for verbal and erotic duels). A battle of egos is about to begin.[29]

Merteuil describes this field as a war, a vicious game of treachery, deceit and desire. *Dangerous Liaisons*, *Valmont*, *The Wings of the Dove*, *The House of Mirth* and *Elizabeth* render the cruel stakes of feminine power and desire most forcefully. In each of these films, the heroine risks not only her reputation and social position, but also the chances of love and, at times, her life. With its mannered costumes, wigs and powders, and stylised performances, *Liaisons* displays an epistemology of character where gender is not an essence, but a performance. Joan Rivière's notion of 'womanliness as masquerade' encapsulates this mode, where 'womanliness could . . . be assumed and worn as a mask'.[30] Rivière's account foregrounds issues of disguise and 'passing', where femininity is revealed as a difficult and painful stylised production.

As discussed in the last chapter, *An Ideal Husband* also deploys a heightened performativity of character and social milieu. Yet where Wilde's camp sensibility works through the parodic mimicry of an ideal Victorian marriage, Merteuil, Kate, Lily and Elizabeth I are playing for keeps, and their survival rests on their passing performances of appropriate femininity. And where the seemingly light-hearted artifice of *Liaisons* conceals a disturbing, bloodthirsty psychosexual realm, *The Madness of King George* takes the momentous theme of a mad monarch and makes light of it.

Spoof and Passing

Delighting in surface over essence, the mannered masquerade that plays deep feeling off against artificiality, is a pivotal element in costume drama. Evident even in playful 'realist' works like *The Wings of the Dove*, *Emma* and *Mansfield*, this tendency is amplified in queer costume (*An Ideal Husband*, *Desperate Remedies*), mannered eighteenth-century milieux (*Quills*, *Dangerous Liaisons*, *Valmont*, *The Madness of King George*, *Barry Lyndon*), and explicitly experimental or theatrical projects (*The Draughtsman's Contract*, *Orlando*, *Edward II*, *Topsy-Turvy*, *Shakespeare in Love*). *The Madness of King George* begins with a montage similar to the duelling wardrobes of *Liaisons*, presenting the elaborate robing of King George III (Nigel Hawthorne) in preparation for the 1788 opening of Parliament. Based on Alan Bennett's hit play, this film (like *Husband*) opens with a nod toward its theatrical source, as a hand opens a heavy oak door to reveal the royal family awaiting the king. The hand belongs to king's new equerry Greville (Rupert Graves), and it is through his eyes that we are introduced to the royal family.

Set to Handel's brisk music of pomp and circumstance that will punctuate the film, the king's robing is intercut with a flurry of domestic exchanges: a fat, dissolute Prince of Wales (Rupert Everett) takes a swig of spirits from a hip flask under the disapproving eye of Queen Charlotte (Helen Mirren); a small princess, one of the king's fifteen children, plays with a small wooden horse on the floor and bursts into tears as it is kicked over. Anticipation builds as the ceremonious robing proceeds through cutaways to details of royal regalia that do not reveal the king's face. Finally, just as the crown is placed on his head, a servant spots a blemish and hastily spit-polishes it before crowning the king. Next, there is a quick cut to a close-up of the king's face as his small daughter runs up to him; the diminutive Nigel Hawthorne is now 'in character', and his kindly, weather-beaten face cracks into a huge smile.

As with the montages of elaborate toilettes in *Husband* and *Mirth*, this sequence foregrounds role-playing, where even the command of power becomes a performance. This opening sequence introduces a structuring tension between the trappings of monarchy and a surprisingly intimate portrait of a man struggling with insanity. *Madness* careens along at a brisk pace that refuses an elegiac treatment of royalty and history. After the king's robing, the royal family hurtles at full tilt through the corridors of power toward Parliament with the dignitaries forced to walk briskly backward in front of them. As they arrive at Parliament, the king casts around for the speech: 'Who's got the speech? Lord Chancellor? Come on then, let's get it over with.' This abrupt opening that punctures the solemnity of affairs of state encapsulates director Nicholas Hytner's

The Madness of King George maintains a brisk pace that refuses an elegiac treatment of royalty and history

use of physical comedy and momentum. The film's breathless pace – including the signature image of the king racing up a hill at dawn in his undershirt, servants trailing behind him – breaks the characteristic torpor of period drama.

With its accelerated parody, *Madness* fits into a tradition of British period spoof noted by a journalist upon the release of *Shakespeare in Love*:

> Did those OTT flounces [in *Elizabeth*] damage the picture? Not a bit. We expect a slice of ham served up with our screen history now. Two generations of gleeful parody – from *Up Pompeii* and Morecambe and Wise to *Blackadder* and beyond – have wrapped all costume drama in a swathe of farce that serious intentions (or serious acting) alone can never wish away.[31]

For this journalist, the spoof tendency has left period drama teetering on the edge of self-parody. Perhaps recent high-profile productions *Madness*, *Elizabeth* and *Shakespeare* embrace an irreverent style in order to court a more popular audience. But parody does not preclude innovation and social commentary, and *Madness* turns cleverly on self-conscious performances of masculinity and monarchy. When the king is first taken ill, the sensible Greville scandalises the royal physician by remarking: 'But the king is only a man!' George III appears as an appealing character left to cruel and incompetent physicians, ambitious politicians and his increasingly impatient heir. Significantly, the king's personal drama is set in a period of crisis for the English monarchy and its conservative Tory regime, when in the wake of the French Revolution and American independence, the opposition Whig party sought massive reform in Parliament.

King George's 'madness' is a corporeal metaphor for the infirmity of the idea of royalty in the Age of Revolution and Reason. As Craig Tepper suggests, *Madness* is set in the transition from an absolute monarchy to the modern state; pointedly, the king's body is subjected to the cold scrutiny of science (an endless examination of 'the king's (blue) water') and the 'discipline and punishment' of the madhouse.[32] At the end of the film, during a reading of the scene from *King Lear* when Lear regains his acumen, George III follows suit. At this point, the likeable monarch notes: 'I have always been myself, even when I was ill. Only now I seem myself. That's the important thing. I have remembered how to seem.' *Madness* ends on the vital importance of *seeming*, and like *Liaisons* the dangers of the loss of appearances are all too apparent. *Madness* is scathing in its parodic reiteration of the forms of performance of power, whether royal, parliamentary, or medical. Ultimately, however, Bennett's script retains a fondness for a simple man proud to be known as Farmer George, and who tenderly calls his wife Mrs King. The film is pitched on Hawthorne's bravura performance and, as with *Shakespeare* and *Amadeus*, much of its momentum arises from the sheer physicality of the lead performance. Where one might expect a complete demolition of the figure of the monarch, this film chooses spoof rather than tragedy, and retains a sympathy for the humanity of the king under the crown.

Madness is often grouped with *Mrs Brown* and *Elizabeth* to form a trio of recent royal biopics. Following the formula of the 30s Korda studio historical biographies, these films deftly combine historical spectacle with the private life of the historical person. This structure serves 'the function of mythologizing monarchs (or any upperclass individual), while it also humanizes them'.[33] These films' irreverrence for British royalty is sometimes associated with a current crisis in the British monarchy, and Bennett's 1991 play and 1994 screenplay make allusions to the struggling Windsors.[34] The most obvious parallel can be found between Prince Charles and the film's ineffectual Prince of Wales, played by Rupert Everett with brilliant lassitude. The Prince waits endlessly in the wings, pleading with his father to 'give him something to do'; in another speech, he complains that his is 'not a position, it's a predicament'.[35]

Clearly, an international fascination with royalty as celebrity heightens the international appetite for British royal biopics. Both released around the time of Princess Diana's death, *Mrs Brown* and *Elizabeth* both explore the tensions between the personal lives and the state roles of these iconic queens.

The Renaissance Biopic

Elizabeth presents a maverick, distinctly violent, sexual and inauthentic chronicle of the young Elizabeth I.[36] Like *Madness* and *Mrs Brown*, *Elizabeth* approaches English royalty not through the solemnities of state, but rather through affairs of the heart and body. Influenced by Patrice Chéreau's *La Reine Margot* (a biography of the sixteenth-century Marguerite de Valois), *Elizabeth* reinvents the Renaissance through a hybrid aesthetic – part medieval thud and blunder, part *Godfather*, part Bollywood. Kapur remarks that his vision of English history is inflected by an Indian perspective: 'By being Eastern, I could play up the melodrama in its colors, light, behaviour patterns, storytelling and sense of chaos – I could make it a little mythic.'[37] Kapur deploys a distinctive aesthetic of saturated colours, vertiginous camera angles and rapid editing works to destabilise the familiar Tudor tale. This sense of historical estrangement is amplified by Remi Adefarasin's camera, which stalks the action, commonly shooting through filters, gauzes, windows and lattices, creating an atmosphere of intrigue.

This film style displaces the prosperous and relatively stable reign of 'Good Queen Bess' into a moment of risk, suspense, uncertainty. Here, the stable heritage genre of historical fiction careens toward the sexual thriller, and Elizabeth I is reframed through the lens of youth, desire and passion. Screenwriter Michael Hirst remarks:

> I wanted to show her as a young woman – the young woman arrested for treason and
> afraid for her life; the young woman passionately in love with Robert Dudley – and not
> the white-faced, pearl-encrusted icon of her later years, and of historical memory.
> Indeed, I was intrigued to know how and why that iconograph had been created; what
> and where the motivations, political and personal, behind the Virgin Queen? What did
> Elizabeth, as a Queen, gain by its creation and what, if anything, did she lose as a
> woman?[38]

Clearly, a queen who is *not* a virgin makes for more interesting cinema. In a (post)feminist era intrigued by the articulation of femininity, sexuality and power (the exact stakes of *Liaisons*), the film's portrait of a young Elizabeth adroitly confronts some of the dilemmas of contemporary liberal feminism: how can women navigate the conflicting pressures of social decorum, sexual desire and power? Through a tangle of deadly factions, the film traces how the unformed young Elizabeth is propelled (and propels herself) toward power. The film's marketing and critical reception in the US and the UK were often associated with 'girl power' – the struggles of a woman trying to make her way in a man's world.[39]

The friction between the historical figure and her biopic appearance might be posed as 'the problem of the queen's bodies'. Comolli suggests that, in historical fiction, 'the historical character, filmed, has at least two bodies, that of the imagery and that of the actor who represents him for us. There are at least two bodies in competition, one body too much.'[40] To raise the issue of the body's referentiality in historical fiction is to consider the frisson between the contemporaneity of the body of the actor and the imputed 'pastness' of the cinematic milieux. In Tudor legal parlance, the king was seen to have two bodies, the immortal 'body politic', and the mortal 'body natural'. For Foucault, 'around this duality, which was originally close to the Christological model, are organized an iconography, a political theory of monarchy . . . and a whole ritual that reaches its height in the coronation, the funeral and the ceremonies of submission'.[41]

Foucault's emphasis on ceremonies highlights their mediating role, both historically and within these films, between the biographical trajectory of individual (mortal) bodies, and their eternal symbolic place on the time line of the nation. In *Madness*, this problem is quickly resolved in the literal fact that 'the emperor has no clothes'. Amusingly, 'Dame' Judi Dench plays a mature monarch both in *Mrs Brown* and in *Shakespeare in Love*, in the process rendering her actorly persona and the cinematic queens she plays almost indistinguishable. But *Elizabeth* dwells on the female monarch as a vulnerable sexual body begging for completion in marriage; the queen's incomplete body offered a conduit, a 'vessel' for the succession.[42] Sir William Cecil pointedly reminds Elizabeth's ladies-in-waiting that 'Her majesty's body and person are no longer her own property. They belong to the state.'

For Comolli, the actor fills in the shell of the historical figure, whose body is 'an *empty mask*, and the character will appear later and bit by bit as effects of this mask, effects in the plural, changing, unstable, never quite achieved, thwarted, incomplete'.[43] This process is revealed in the film's conclusion, where the Queen steps out of a blinding light to appear in court powdered and elaborately coiffed, her body crustacean-like with embroidery, lace and jewels. Immobilised into her own portrait flanked by the coat of arms, Elizabeth has become the mask Britannia. As with *Liaisons* and *Wings*,

By the end of the biopic, Elizabeth has become the mask Britannia

the outcome of this feminist parable of power and desire is bleak. With the funereal Mozart 'Requiem' as soundtrack, this concluding mask is deathlike – the death of desire, the death of spontaneity. The mask reminds us of Elizabeth's mortality, her pastness, and the film's finale reinscribes her into the museum of history. But the story doesn't end there, for if Elizabeth has become Britannia, she has also become Margaret Thatcher.

To add still one more body to the mix, Comolli insists also on the 'presence' and 'contemporaneity' of the body of the actor. Relatively unknown when the film was released, the Australian Cate Blanchett negotiates a sensibility that is in some ways emphatically contemporary against the crusty iconography of history. Threaded through Kapur's mythic melodrama and monumental scenes of official history is a contemporary protofeminist discourse about women's pleasure, power and right to control their own bodies. *Elizabeth* (like *Madness* and *Mrs Brown*) foregrounds the passion play of the secular (and sexual) 'body natural'. Elizabeth's most vivid moments are shared with her lover Robert Dudley (Joseph Fiennes). Hirst's script scandalously puts the Virgin Queen in bed with Dudley, and on this reading the movement-images of dance best highlight the audacious sensuality retrospectively attributed to Elizabeth. In the festivities following the coronation, Elizabeth halts all proceedings, declaring, 'Play a volta!' A space is cleared in the middle of the ballroom and a ritual courting dance takes place with the camera spiralling around the couple. Intercut with titillated responses from the crowd, the voluminous stiffness of the brightly coloured costumes and the volta's ritualistic gestures make for a highly erotic moment. In slow motion, Robert lifts Elizabeth, and the arc of her body and the dress are suspended in midair.

Madness, *Elizabeth* and *Shakespeare in Love* mark a postmodern turn in British period drama. A playful, performative sensibility overtakes the realist mode, as *Shakespeare* and *Elizabeth* seek to capture a freshness of Renaissance politics and artistry: the monarch not yet crowned, the play (and the love story) not yet written. History is no longer dead, but filmed for us in the making, on the run. Distinct from BBC and RSC 'official' Shakespeare and Branagh's standard adaptations, *Shakespeare*

'Play a volta!': *Elizabeth* insists on the passion play of the 'body natural'

reimagines the English Renaissance, the sparring and mutual plagiarism of Marlowe and Shakespeare, as fresh, indeterminate and energetic. Madden uses Joseph Fiennes's stagey performance style to advantage, setting him constantly in motion – sprinting through the dirty streets of South London, nimbly dodging offal underfoot and slops from above, fencing Colin Firth's Lord Wessex with a toy foil. With the help of rapid-fire editing, the physical energy and dancing wordplay of the theatre are projected on screen. Yet choreographed grace dissolves into slapstick as Will's ardent ascent to Viola's balcony ends in a clumsy fall.

Against a British heritage tradition premised on precise dialogue, pastoral *mise en scène* and subtle dramas of love and class distinction, these Elizabethan films employ the lexicon of corporeality and sensuality. *Shakespeare* is marketed not only on the standard heritage fare, but on a lusty 'Will' whose 'quill' is lubricated by long nights with his 'Juliet' (Gwyneth Paltrow) – a young woman who passes as a young man in order to appear on stage. Sex, intrigue, cross-dressing, a raw physicality (and, in the case of *Elizabeth*, violence) distinguish these films from a largely demure British tradition. Interrupting a steady diet of nineteenth-century politesse, the crucial difference of *Elizabeth* and *Shakespeare* could be distilled down to costume and what lies underneath. The face framed by bristling lace ruffs, elaborate gowns encrusted in gold embroidery and jewels, slim hose and square doublets – these stiff geometrical shapes belie an underlying raw sexual energy. Sumptuous hems seem destined to be dragged through the mud, while tightly laced bodices are rife for the ripping. These films present the early-modern English as creatures of passion and tragic romance, of slapstick humour and bawdy worldliness. Finally, and crucially, in an affront to costume drama's tender sensibilities, the costumes come *off*.

This chapter has considered several distinct modes of sexual and corporeal representation within recent costume film. Even as the distinctive 'movements' in *Orlando* evoke particular periods through highly selective costumes and *mise en scène*, the distinctive cinematic eras addressed here reject the apparent transparency of realist period detail and humanist modes of performance and costume. Instead, these films opt for more immediate stylised 'memory-images' concerned with 'the quest for immediacy, the search for a past which is palpably and visibly present'.[44] In a genre often charged with torpor and nostalgia, this sense of 'liveness' or immediacy is conjured through corporeality, eroticism and 'the weight and curve of flesh'.

Notes

1.   Lefebvre, *The Production of Space*, p. 315.
2.   Garrett Stewart, 'Film's Victorian Retrofit', *Victorian Studies* vol. 38 no. 2, 1995, p. 167.
3.   Lizzie Francke, '*The Piano*', in Margolis (ed.), *Jane Campion's* The Piano, p. 170.
4.   Jane Campion, *The Piano* (London: Bloomsbury, 1992), p. 139.
5.   Cinematographer Stuart Drysburgh, cited in Campion, *The Piano*, p. 141.
6.   Stella Bruzzi, 'Jane Campion: Costume Drama Reclaiming Women's Past', in Pam Cook and Philip Dodd (eds), *Women and Film* (Philadelphia: Temple Press, 1993), p. 234.
7.   Ibid., p. 233.
8.   Ibid., p. 235.

9. Ibid., p. 240.

10. On the 'exchange of women', see Sue Gillett, 'Lips and fingers: Jane Campion's *The Piano*', *Screen* vol. 36 no. 3, 1995, pp. 282–5.

11. Pratt, *Imperial Eyes*, p. 6.

12. Lynda Dyson, 'The Return of the Repressed? Whiteness, Femininity and Colonialism in *The Piano*', *Screen* vol. 36 no. 3, 1995, p. 268.

13. Parallels to Keitel's white man 'gone native' can be found in Kevin Costner in *Dances with Wolves* (1990), Daniel Day-Lewis in *The Last of the Mohicans* (1992) or Gary Oldman in *The Scarlet Letter* (1995).

14. Leonie Pihama, 'Ebony and Ivory: Constructions of Maori in *The Piano*', in Margolis (ed.), *Jane Campion's The Piano*, p. 128.

15. Stewart, 'Film's Victorian Retrofit', p. 153.

16. Ibid., p. 154.

17. Peter Brooks, *Body Work* (Cambridge: Harvard University Press, 1993), p. 32.

18. Ibid., p. 47.

19. Nora Lee, '*Liaisons*: Feint, Parry & Thrust', *American Cinematographer* vol. 70 no. 5, 1989, p. 64.

20. Elizabeth Grosz, *Jacques Lacan: A feminist introduction* (London: Routledge, 1990), p. 32.

21. Virginia Blum and Heidi Nast, 'Lacan's Two-Dimensional Subjectivity', in Crang and Thrift (eds), *Thinking Space*, p. 186.

22. Lefebvre, *The Production of Space*, p. 185.

23. Ibid., pp. 188–9.

24. Ibid., p. 194.

25. Hollander, *Seeing Through Clothes*, p. 403. For a broader social history of the mirror, see Sabine Melchior-Bonnet, *The Mirror: A History* (London: Routledge, 2002).

26. Hollander, *Seeing Through Clothes*, p. 403.

27. Lefebvre, *The Production of Space*, p. 189

28. For a discussion of *Fatal Attraction* as a 'backlash text', see Susan Faludi, *Backlash: The Undeclared War Against American Women* (London: Vintage, 1992).

29. Pascal Pernod, 'Le galop des libertins', *Positif* no. 338, April 1989, p. 5 (my translation).

30. Joan Rivière, 'Womanliness as Masquerade', in Victor Burgin, James Donald and Cora Kaplan (eds), *Formations of Fantasy* (London: Methuen, 1986), p. 38.

31. Boyd Tonkin, 'A pox upon those men in tights', *Independent Review*, 21 January 1999, p. 11.

32. See Craig Tepper, '*The Madness of King George*', *Film Quarterly* vol. 49 no. 3, Spring 1996, pp. 46–50.

33. Landy, *British Genres*, p. 61.

34. Kara McKechnie, 'Mrs Brown's Mourning and Mr King's Madness: Royal Crisis on Screen', in Deborah Cartmell et al. (eds) *Retrovisions: Reinventing the Past in Film and Fiction* (London: Pluto Press, 2001), p. 108.

35. Graeme Kay highlights this speech in his aptly titled article 'The Monarchy's In A Mess . . .', *Empire* no. 70, April 1995, p. 72.

36. Significantly, *Elizabeth* lacks the solemnity of influential earlier biopics *The Lion in Winter* (1968), *Mary, Queen of Scots* (1971), the telly series *Elizabeth R* (1971) or the 2000 television docu-drama *Elizabeth*.

37. Michele Lowery, 'For Queen and Country', *American Cinematographer* vol. 79 no. 12, 1998, p. 16.

38. Michael Hirst, The Script of *Elizabeth* (London: Boxtree, 1998), p. 7.

39. See Higson, *English Heritage*, pp. 217–20.

40. Comolli, 'Historical Fiction', p. 46.

41. Michel Foucault, *Discipline and Punish* (New York: Vintage Books, 1979), pp. 28–9.

42. In 1561, during the reign of Elizabeth I, the 'body politic' was legally enshrined within the 'body natural' of the monarch. For an analysis of the legal particularities of the queen's two bodies, see Mary Axton, *The Queen's Two Bodies* (London: Royal Historical Society, 1977).

43. Comolli, 'Historical Fiction', p. 43.

44. Samuel, *Theatres of Memory*, p. 175.

Concluding Remarks

The most recent film considered in depth in this book is *Gosford Park*, which I would count as a ground-breaking socially engaged work alongside *Orlando*, *Daughters of the Dust*, *The Piano* and *Edward II*. These stunning projects exemplify a small but influential wave of critical revisionism that prises open the frame of costume drama to critical perspectives on gender, class, race, colonialism and sexuality. My agenda is strongly informed by a perhaps old-fashioned Marxist conviction that radical form is integral to the transformation of cultural discourse, and hence this marked preference for formally innovative works. But form only matters for the content it enables, and at root this book has been concerned with how relations of power, desire and difference are projected onto the orderly microcosms of costume film – a mode of film-making that is still resolutely white, bougeois, imperial and heterosexual. In this respect, much of *Contemporary Costume Film* has been taken up with questions of normativity: the quiet but persistent reinscription of embedded power relations within the cultural imaginary.

Concerned with space, place and the past, this book has examined how discursive struggles are waged in and through a spatial imaginary of the past. Following de Certeau's insistence that stories are spatial practices,[1] I have identified costume film's structuring places and itineraries, reflecting upon the contemporary resonance of these chronotopes and movement-images as 'images of thought'. These narrative and symbolic places include the intimate interiors of the house of fiction: the window, the door, the writing desk, the ball and the boudoir. Yet the interior is only demarcated in relation to an 'outside', and exteriors are also important, from the gardens of the great houses to the surrounding countryside and the city – and further afield, the 'international scene' of England, America, Europe and the exotic zones of colonial encounter. This book's topographical attention to space and movement tends to produce an analysis that is primarily synchronic. That is, the frame of contemporary costume drama emerges as a bounded 'set' characterised by selection (who and what is included and excluded) and orchestration (the selective layering of image and voice). As the cinematic frame is also legible in and through movement, I have also tracked dominant Anglo-American leisured narrative tempos and trajectories and their encounters with other peoples and places.

It is an odd choice to use spatial rather than temporal concepts to address the cinematic past, and admittedly part of what is elided here is the vector of time. In fact, my use of Deleuze's movement-image is deliberate, for this cinematic form is explicitly limited to the 'perpetual present'.[2] In the regime of the movement-image, time is spatialised as the measure of (narrative) movement; in contrast, the time-image allows a direct expression of time as duration and transformation. Although instances of the time-image do arise,[3] the movement-image is my chosen concept because, for the most part, costume film addresses the past through the frame of the present. The angle of my critique is resolutely presentist, as I am interested in how these films' scriptings of the past impinge on the present. Here, costume film's Western 'myths of origin' come into play, for current understandings of subjectivity, rootedness and mobility, desire and difference emerge importantly in and through perceptions of the past. These perceptions are not static, but constantly in flux. Raphael Samuel argues that

> memory is historically conditioned, changing colour and shape according to the emergencies of the moment; that so far from being handed down in the timeless form of 'tradition' it is progressively altered from generation to generation. It bears the impress of experience, in however mediated a way. It is stamped with the ruling passions of its time. Like history, memory is inherently revisionist and never more chameleon than when it appears to stay the same.[4]

Returning to the question of time and history – centrally, the problem of historical transformation within critical thought – I address costume film as a historical 'production of space'. A cultural form rooted in older literary and theatrical traditions, costume film is part of a generative historical and intertextual field. It is engaged with the past insofar as the texts of culture are embedded with past relations of power. These social relations are reinscribed or rearticulated in contemporary productions. In this respect, my emphasis on the formal and thematic legacies of the novel traces the constraints of inherited genres, and the ways that this 'spatial production' of interiority can be 'reassembled'. It strikes me after the fact that an emphasis on theatrical traditions from the Renaissance through to the light opera of *Topsy-Turvy* might have produced a very different account. Questions of theatricality and performance arise most insistently in the last two chapters, and part of the freshness of *Dangerous Liaisons*, *Shakespeare in Love* and *The Madness o f King George* arises from the physicality of performance that moves beyond a literary emphasis on dialogue and stillness. A 'performative' epistemology of character and subjectivity evident in many costume films suggests an anti-foundational contrast to the nostalgic, 'authentic' masculine interiority of *The Age of Innocence* or *The Remains of the Day*.

The Madness of King George brings me to a final point, which is about periodisation. I have scrupulously avoided teleological accounts of costume film. Even as cultural production does not respect national boundaries, it does not unfold in an orderly progression. British heritage cinema of the 80s coincides with postmodern Hollywood productions such as *Amadeus* and *Dangerous Liaisons* long before the term 'post-heritage' was coined. Further, the contemporary self-consciousness of *Shakespeare in Love*, *An Ideal Husband* and *Mansfield Park* adapts earlier, equally knowing traditions. However, in the latter stages of the writing I was struck by how the energy and innovation in costume film rests precisely with these postmodern, self-conscious, border-crossing projects like *Elizabeth*, *Shakespeare in Love*, *The Madness of King George*, *Topsy-Turvy* and *Gosford Park*.

With their upbeat pace and playful 'gaming' with the audience, these works correspond with Lyotard's generative postmodern culture, which is characterised by 'the increase of being and the jubilation which result from the invention of new rules of the game'.[5] Again and again in the course of this book, I have evoked a dominant realist period drama – essentially the prevalent British mode of adaptation and heritage cinema. Clearly, this mode of production continues apace as film and television adaptation exhausts the Forster, Austen and James canons, moving on to Eliot, Dickens and Hardy. Yet perhaps there has been a shift in the tone of costume film, for even works like *Nicholas Nickleby* (2002) incorporate an increasingly knowing tone and an intensified physicality and attention to performative aspects of identity. All textbook postmodern tropes, these qualities arguably shift the affective terrain of costume away from regret and nostalgia toward improvisation, immediacy and masquerade.

Notes

1.   de Certeau, *The Practice of Everyday Life*, p. 115.
2.   See Deleuze, *Cinema 2*, p. 37.
3.   Notably, Vidal writes about the time-image as memory at the ending of *The Age of Innocence*, where as an old man Newland remembers the moment at the pier with Ellen. ('Classic adaptations', p. 12.) While for Deleuze the time-image as form guarantees a rupture in the ideology of the 'perpetual present', I would argue that this crystalline image is suffused with a conservative masculine sensibility of nostalgia and loss.
4.   Samuel, *Theatres of Memory*, p. x.
5.   Lyotard, *The Postmodern Condition*, p. 80.

Select Bibliography

Armstrong, Nancy, *Desire and Domestic Fiction: A Political History of the Novel* (Oxford: Oxford University Press, 1987).

Bachelard, Gaston, *The Poetics of Space*, trans. Maria Jolas (Boston: Beacon Press, 1969).

Baert, Renée, 'Skirting the Issue', *Screen* vol. 35 no. 4, 1994.

Bakhtin, Mikhail, *The Dialogic Imagination* (Austin: University of Texas Press, 1981).

Bambara, Toni Cade, 'Reading the Signs, Empowering the Eye: *Daughters of the Dust* and the Black Independent Cinema Movement', in Manthia Diawara (ed.), *Black American Cinema* (New York: Routledge, 1993).

Barthes, Roland, *Image – Music – Text*, trans. Stephen Heath (New York: The Noonday Press, 1977).

Belsey, Catherine, *Desire: Love Stories in Western Culture* (Oxford: Blackwell, 1994).

Berlant, Lauren (ed.), *Intimacy* (Chicago: University of Chicago Press, 2000).

Botting, Fred, *Gothic* (London: Routledge, 1996).

Brooks, Peter, *The Melodramatic Imagination: Balzac, Henry James, Melodrama, and the Mode of Excess* (New Haven: Yale University Press, 1976).

Brooks, Peter, *Body Work: Objects of Desire in Modern Narrative* (Cambridge: Harvard University Press, 1993).

Brunsdon, Charlotte, 'Problems with quality', *Screen* vol. 31 no. 1, Spring 1990.

Bruzzi, Stella, *Undressing Cinema: Clothing and identity in the movies* (London: Routledge, 1997).

Butler, Judith, *Gender Trouble* (New York: Routledge, 1990).

Buzard, James, 'A Continent of Pictures: Reflections on the "Europe" of Nineteenth-Century Tourists', *Publications of the Modern Language Association of America* vol. 108 no. 1, 1993.

Buzard, James, *The Beaten Track: European Tourism, Literature, and the Ways to 'Culture': 1800–1918* (Oxford: Clarendon Press, 1993).

Cairns, Craig, 'Rooms without a View', *Sight and Sound,* June 1991.

Campion, Jane, *The Piano* (London: Bloomsbury, 1993).

Caughie, John, *Theories of Authorship* (London: Routledge & Kegan Paul, 1981).

Caughie, John, *Television Drama: Realism, Modernism and British Culture* (Oxford: Oxford University Press, 2000).

Cleto, Fabio (ed.), *Camp: Queer Aesthetics and the Performing Subject: A Reader* (Edinburgh: Edinburgh University Press, 1999).

Comolli, Jean-Louis, 'Historical Fiction: A Body Too Much', *Screen* vol. 19 no. 2, 1978.

Cook, Pam, *Fashioning the Nation: Costume and Identity in British Cinema* (London: BFI, 1996).

Corner, John, and Sylvia Harvey (eds), *Enterprise and Heritage: Cross-currents of National Culture* (London: Routledge, 1991).

Crang, Mike, and Nigel Thrift (eds), *Thinking Space* (London: Routledge, 2000).

Dash, Julie, *Daughters of the Dust: The Making of an African American Woman's Film* (New York: The New Press, 1992).

de Certeau, Michel, *The Practice of Everyday Life* (Berkeley: University of California Press, 1984).

de Lauretis, Teresa, *Alice Doesn't: Feminism, Semiotics, Cinema* (Bloomington: Indiana University Press, 1984).

de Rougemont, Denis, *Love in the Western World* (Princeton: Princeton University Press, 1956).

Deleuze, Gilles, *Cinema 1: The Movement-Image* (Minneapolis: University of Minnesota Press, 1986).

Deleuze, Gilles, *Cinema 2: The Time-Image* (Minneapolis: University of Minnesota Press, 1994).

Deleuze, Gilles and Félix Guattari, *A Thousand Plateaus: Capitalism & Schizophrenia* (Minneapolis: University of Minnesota Press, 1987).

Doane, Mary Ann, *The Desire to Desire: The Woman's Film of the 1940s* (Bloomington: Indiana University Press, 1987).

Dyer, Richard, *Only Entertainment* (London: Routledge, 1992).

Dyer, Richard, 'Feeling English', *Sight and Sound,* March 1993.

Dyer, Richard, *The Culture of Queers* (London: Routledge, 2002).

Eleftheriotis, Dimitris, *Popular Cinemas of Europe* (New York: Continuum, 2001).

Elsaesser, Thomas, 'Tales of Sound and Fury: Observations on the Family Melodrama', in Christine Gledhill (ed.), *Home is Where the Heart Is.*

Foucault, Michel, *The History of Sexuality Volume 1: An Introduction* (New York: Vintage Books, 1990).

Francke, Lizzie, 'On the Brink', in Vincendeau (ed.), *Film/ Literature/ Heritage.*

Freedman, Jonathan (ed.), *The Cambridge Companion to Henry James* (Cambridge: Cambridge University Press, 1998).

Frisby, David, and Mike Featherstone (eds), *Simmel on Culture: Selected Writings* (London: Sage Publications, 1997).

Gibson, Andrew, *Towards a Postmodern Theory of Narrative* (Edinburgh: Edinburgh University Press, 1996).

Gilbert, Sandra M., and Susan Gubar, *The Madwoman in the Attic: The Woman Writer and the Nineteenth-Century Literary Imagination* (New Haven: Yale University Press, 1979).

Gledhill, Christine (ed.), *Home is Where the Heart Is: Studies in Melodrama and the Woman's Film* (London: BFI, 1987).

Grewal, Inderpal, *Home and Harem: Nation, Gender, Empire, and the Cultures of Travel* (Durham: Duke University Press, 1996).

Habermas, Jürgen, *The Social Transformation of the Public Sphere: An Inquiry into a Category of Bourgeois Society* (Cambridge: Polity Press, 1992).

Harper, Sue, *Picturing the Past: The Rise and Fall of the British Costume Film* (London: BFI, 1994).

Higson, Andrew, 'Re-presenting the National Past: Nostalgia and Pastiche in the Heritage Film', in Lester Friedman (ed.), *Fires Were Started: British Cinema and Thatcherism* (Minneapolis: University of Minnesota Press, 1993).

Higson, Andrew, 'The Heritage Film and British Cinema', in Andrew Higson (ed.), *Dissolving Views: Key Writings on British Cinema* (London: Cassell, 1996).

Higson, Andrew, *English Heritage, English Cinema: Costume Drama Since 1980* (Oxford: Oxford University Press, 2003).

Hollander, Anne, *Seeing Through Clothes* (Berkeley: University of California Press, 1993).

James, Henry, *Washington Square* (Oxford: Oxford University Press, 1982).

James, Henry, *The Portrait of a Lady* (Ware, Hertfordshire: Wordsworth Editions, 1996).

Jameson, Fredric, 'Postmodernism, or the Cultural Logic of Late Capitalism', *New Left Review* no. 146, 1984.

Landy, Marcia, *British Genres: Cinema and Society, 1930–1960* (Princeton: Princeton University Press, 1991).

Lefebvre, Henri, *The Production of Space* (Oxford: Blackwell, 1991).

Lippard, Chris (ed.), *By Angels Driven: The Films of Derek Jarman* (Trowbridge: Flicks Books, 1996).

Lyotard, Jean-François, *The Postmodern Condition: A Report on Knowledge* (Minneapolis: University of Minnesota Press, 1999).

MacCannell, Dean, *The Tourist: A New Theory of the Leisure Class* (New York: Schocken Books, 1989).

Margolis, Harriet (ed.), *Jane Campion's* The Piano (Cambridge: Cambridge University Press, 2000).

Martin, Robert K., and George Piggford (eds), *Queer Forster* (Chicago: The University of Chicago Press, 1997).

Mellencamp, Patricia, 'Five Ages of Film Feminism', in Layleen Jayamanne (ed.), *Kiss Me Deadly* (Sydney: Power Publications, 1995).

Monk, Claire, *Sex, Politics, and the Past: Merchant Ivory, the Heritage Film and its Critics in 1980s and 1990s Britain* (MA Thesis, Birbeck College, 1994).

Monk, Claire, 'The British "Heritage Film" and its Critics', *Critical Survey* vol. 7 no. 2, 1995.

Monk, Claire, 'Sexuality and the heritage film', *Sight and Sound,* October 1995.

Monk, Claire, 'Heritage films and the British cinema audience in the 1990s', *Journal of Popular British Cinema* no. 2, 1999.

Morris, Meaghan, *Too Soon Too Late: History in Popular Culture* (Bloomington: Indiana University Press, 1998).

Morse, Margaretm, 'Paradoxes of Realism: The Rise of Film in the Train of the Novel', in Ron Burnett (ed.), *Explorations in Film Theory: Selected Essays from Ciné-Tracts* (Bloomington: Indiana University Press, 1991).

Mulvey, Laura, 'Afterthoughts on "Visual Pleasure and Narrative Cinema" inspired by *Duel in the Sun*', in Constance Penley (ed.), *Feminism and Film Theory* (New York: Routledge, 1988).

Murphy, Robert (ed.), *British Cinema of the 90s* (London: BFI, 2000).

Naremore, James (ed.), *Film Adaptation* (New Brunswick, NJ: Rutgers University Press, 2000).

Neale, Steve, 'Art Cinema as Institution', *Screen* vol. 22 no. 1, 1981.

Nowell-Smith, Geoffrey, 'Minelli and Melodrama', in Christine Gledhill (ed.), *Home is Where the Heart Is*.

Nowell-Smith, Geoffrey, and Steven Ricci (eds), *Hollywood & Europe: Economics, Culture, National Identity* (London: BFI, 1998).

Orr, John, 'Beyond heritage: 1990s England and the cinematic novel', *Film West* no. 39, February 2000.

Parsons, Deborah L., 'The Note/ Notion of Europe: Henry James and the Gendered Landscape of Heritage Tourism', *Symbiosis: Journal of Anglo-American Literary Relations* vol. 2 no. 2, 1998.

Pearce, Lynne, and Jackie Stacey (eds), *Romance Revisited* (New York: New York University Press, 1995).

Petrie, Duncan (ed.), *Screening Europe: Image and Identity in Contemporary European Cinema* (London: BFI, 1992).

Potter, Sally, *Orlando* (London/ Boston: Faber & Faber, 1994).

Pratt, Mary Louise, *Imperial Eyes: Travel Writing and Transculturation* (New York: Routledge, 1992).

Robins, Bruce, *The Servant's Hand: English Fiction from Below* (Princeton: Duke University Press, 1993).

Rodowick, D.N., *Gilles Deleuze's Time Machine* (Durham: Duke University Press, 1997).

Rosenstone, Robert A., 'The Historical Film as Real History', *Film-Historia* vol. 5 no. 1, 1999.

Said, Edward W., *Culture and Imperialism* (New York: Vintage Books, 1992).

Salecl, Renata, and Slavoj Zizek (eds), *Gaze and Voice as Love Objects* (Durham: Duke University Press, 1996).

Samuel, Raphael, *Theatres of Memory* (London: Verso, 1994).

Sedgwick, Eve Kosofsky, *Epistemology of the Closet* (Berkeley: University of California Press, 1990).

Sedgwick, Eve Kosofsky, *Tendencies* (Durham: Duke University Press, 1993).

Sinfield, Alan, *The Wilde Century: Effeminacy, Oscar Wilde and the Queer Moment* (London: Cassell, 1994).

Spivak, Gayatri Chakravorty, 'Three Women's Texts and a Critique of Imperialism', *Critical Inquiry* no. 12, Autumn, 1985.

Stam, Robert, 'Bakhtin, Polyphony, and Ethnic/Racial Representation', in Lester D. Friedman (ed.), *Unspeakable Images: Ethnicity and the American Cinema* (Urbana: University of Illinois Press, 1991).

Stam, Robert, 'Beyond Fidelity: The Dialogics of Adaptation', in James Naremore (ed.), *Film Adaptation*.

Stewart, Garrett, 'Film's Victorian Retrofit', *Victorian Studies* vol. 38 no. 2, 1995.

Stewart, Susan, *On Longing: Narratives of the Miniature, the Gigantic, the Souvenir, the Collection* (Durham: Duke University Press, 1993).

Trilling, Lionel, 'Why we read Jane Austen', in D. Trilling (ed.), *The Last Decade: Essays and Reviews, 1965–75* (Oxford: Oxford University Press, 1982).

Urry, John, *The Tourist Gaze: Leisure and Travel in Contemporary Societies,* 2nd edn (London: Sage Publications, 1994); rev. ed. 2002.

Vidal Villasur, Belén, 'Classic adaptations/modern reinventions: reading the image in the contemporary literary film', *Screen* vol. 43 no. 1, Spring 2002.

Vidal Villasur, Belén, *Textures of the Image: Rewriting the American Novel in the Contemporary Film Adaptation* (València: Departament de Filologia Anglesa i Alemanya, Universitat de València, 2002).

Vincendeau, Ginette (ed.), *Film/ Literature/ Heritage: A Sight and Sound Reader* (London: BFI, 2001).

Watt, Ian, *The Rise of the Novel: Studies in Defoe, Richardson and Fielding* (London: Chatto & Windus, 1963).

Wharton, Edith, *The House of Mirth,* Shari Benstock (ed.) (Boston: Bedford Books, 1994).

White, Patricia, *unInvited: Classical Hollywood Cinema and Lesbian Representability* (Bloomington: Indiana University Press, 1999).

Williams, Raymond, *The Country and the City* (London: Chatto & Windus, 1973).

Wollen, Tana, 'Over our shoulders: nostalgic screen fictions for the 1980s', in Corner and Harvey (eds), *Enterprise and Heritage*.

Wood, Robin, *The Wings of the Dove: Henry James in the 1990s* (London: BFI, 1999).

Woolf, Virginia, *Orlando: A Biography* (London: Penguin Books, 1993).

Select Filmography

The Age of Innocence (Martin Scorsese, US, 1993).

Amadeus (Milos Forman, US, 1984).

Angels & Insects (Philip Haas, UK/US, 1996).

Another Country (Marek Kanievska, UK, 1984).

Barry Lyndon (Stanley Kubrick, UK, 1975).

The Bostonians (James Ivory, UK, 1984).

Bram Stoker's Dracula (Francis Ford Coppola, US, 1992).

Caravaggio (Derek Jarman, UK, 1986).

Dangerous Liaisons (Stephen Frears, US, 1988).

Daughters of the Dust (Julie Dash, US, 1991).

The Draughtsman's Contract (Peter Greenaway, UK, 1982).

Edward II (Derek Jarman, UK, 1991).

Elizabeth (Shekhar Kapur, UK, 1998).

Emma (Douglas McGrath, US, 1996).

The Golden Bowl (James Ivory, UK/France/US, 2000).

Gosford Park (Robert Altman, UK/US, 2001).

The Heiress (William Wyler, US, 1949).

The House of Mirth (Terence Davies, UK/US, 2000).

Howards End (James Ivory, UK, 1992).

An Ideal Husband (Oliver Parker, UK/US, 1999).

Immortal Beloved (Bernard Rose, UK/US, 1994).

The Importance of Being Earnest (Oliver Parker, US/UK/France, 2002).

Interview with the Vampire: The Vampire Chronicles (Neil Jordan, US, 1994).

Jane Austen's Emma (Diarmuid Davies, UK, 1997).

Jude (Michael Winterbottom, UK, 1996).

Letter from an Unknown Woman (Max Ophuls, US, 1948).

The Madness of King George (Nicholas Hytner, UK, 1994).

Mansfield Park (Patricia Rozema, US/UK, 1999).

Maurice (James Ivory, UK, 1987).

Mrs Brown (John Madden, UK, 1997).

My Brilliant Career (Gillian Armstrong, Australia, 1979).

Onegin (Martha Fiennes, UK/US, 1999).

Orlando (Sally Potter, UK/Russia/France/Italy/Netherlands, 1992).

Pandaemonium (Julien Temple, UK, 2000).

Persuasion (Roger Michell, UK, 1995).

The Piano (Jane Campion, Australia/New Zealand/France, 1993).

The Portrait of a Lady (Jane Campion, UK, 1996).

Pride and Prejudice (television series) (Simon Langton, UK/US, 1995).

Quills (Philip Kaufmann, US/Germany/UK, 2000).

La Reine Margot (Patrice Chéreau, France/Germany/Italy, 1994).

The Remains of the Day (James Ivory, UK/US, 1993).

Restoration (Michael Hoffman, UK/US, 1996).

A Room with a View (James Ivory, UK, 1985).

The Secret Garden (Agnieszka Holland, US, 1993).

Sense and Sensibility (Ang Lee, UK/US, 1995).

Senso (Luchino Visconti, Italy, 1953).

Shakespeare in Love (John Madden, US/UK, 1998).

Sister My Sister (Nancy Meckler, UK, 1994).

Topsy-Turvy (Mike Leigh, UK, 1999).

Total Eclipse (Agnieszka Holland, UK/France/Belgium, 1995).

Valmont (Milos Forman, France/UK, 1989).

Washington Square (Agnieszka Holland, US, 1997).

Where Angels Fear to Tread (James Sturridge, UK, 1991).

Wilde (Brian Gilbert, UK/US/Japan/Germany, 1997).

The Wings of the Dove (Iain Softley, US/UK, 1997).

Index

Notes: Page numbers in *italics* denote illustrations; those in **bold** type indicate detailed analysis. *n* = endnote.

Making Technology Our Own?

Making Technology Our Own?

Domesticating Technology into Everyday Life

Edited by Merete Lie
and Knut H. Sørensen

SCANDINAVIAN UNIVERSITY PRESS

Design: Astrid Elisabeth Jørgensen
Cover illustration: NPS/Science Photo Library: M. Heiberg
Typeset in $10\frac{1}{2}$ on 13 point Photina by Paston Press Ltd, UK
Printed on 90 g Carat offset ⊗ by Østfold trykkeri, Norway

Contents

Foreword

Many people are pessimistic about the role of modern technology. When it is argued otherwise, we are reminded that Norway, a wealthy country with strong social democratic traditions, may be an exception to the rule. However, since Norway is a small country which imports nearly all its technology, one could argue that Norwegians are facing grave problems in protecting their cultural traditions. In front of these challenges, it is important to look closely at what happens when new artefacts are put to use. What transformations take place, and what do they mean?

This collection of papers is a response to the intellectual challenge of making sense of modern technologies and their role in everyday life. We believe that both the pessimistic outlook of technofobians and the optimistic views of techno-utopians need to be challenged by careful empirical analysis. This is what we aim to do in this book.

The reader is invited to follow the authors in learning about technology in Norwegian everyday life. We hope that the papers will stimulate reflections on new technology in relation to human and social issues in other cultures as well.

This collection arose out of a research programme on Technology and Society – Information Technology, funded by the Norwegian Research Council for Science and the Humanities (NAVF) from 1987 through 1992. It has been generously supported by the Norwegian Research Council (NFR) through the next research programme on Information Technology and Society (1993–1997). Many people have given their intellectual support and provided valuable comments on the papers. A warm thanks to all of you!

Merete Lie and Knut H. Sørensen
Trondheim, August 1996

Chapter 1

Making Technology Our Own?
Domesticating Technology into Everyday Life

Merete Lie and Knut H. Sørensen

Technology is an integral part of modern culture. However, there is a longstanding controversy among social theorists over the implications of new, human-made artefacts. In this literature, there are stories of human progress as well as of human demise, but they are far too often abstract, general theorizing based on accidental observations. Generally, there has been little concern for, and few empirical studies of, the process through which technology becomes part of human cultures, or, in other words, how it is integrated into everyday life. Is it correct to see technology as the prime agent of cultural change in modern society? Does technology standardize the qualities of human life, to make cultures more homogeneous? Are consumers of new artefacts passively shaped by these constructions, seduced by promises of better living?

Such issues are analysed in this book. The contributors have studied different aspects of everyday life in modern Norway, using technology as a window to observe cultural change and stability. How do we use computers at home? How may cars become cultural icons, and what are the implications of this process? How may parents at work interact with their children at home? This has also produced interest in a theme which is often forgotten when discussing new technologies, namely how they are integrated into our universes of symbols and meaning.

Our study of technology and everyday life is above all an effort to look at technology in use. The field of technology studies has mainly emphasized the development of technology in laboratories and through innovation in industry, and issues of policy and political controversy related to activities of governments and social movements (see Bijker et al., 1987; Bijker and Law, 1992; Jasanoff et al., 1995). Contributions that follow technologies all the way to users, and even into their homes, are few, even if they are of great importance (see, in particular, Cowan, 1983; Cockburn and Ormrod, 1992; Cockburn and Fürst-Dilic, 1994). Our aim with this collection is to promote this approach by presenting studies that include practical as well as symbolic aspects of technology. Issues of both action and identity are addressed, which also means that the papers analyse gender, explicitly or implicitly. Some of them inform about the qualities of male subcultures, formed around specific technologies (see the contributions of Håpnes and Lamvik). Others make explicit the relationships between men and women and analyse how the use of technology is shaped within the gendered relations of the household (Aune, Vestby), or show how gender is constructed in technological controversies (Sætnan), or they look at the way gender becomes symbolically interwoven with technology (Hubak, Lie).

The book analyses the dynamics and patterns of *technology, gender,* and *everyday life.* These three concepts are not often brought together for analysis, even when the topics they represent are being analysed. Whereas the concept of everyday life is associated with the home and household activities, traditionally a female realm, technology is generally perceived as related to masculine domains and to represent the opposite of the cosiness of the home. The contributions in this collection challenge such implicit understandings of what belongs in one or another category of modern life. By bringing the concepts together and reconsidering them, the papers highlight important aspects of modern cultures and common beliefs about distinctive qualities of these cultures.

To us, everyday life is not the same as the household or the reproductive sphere. It denotes the routine activities of human existence (Lefevbre, 1971), the ordinary actions taking place in various settings, spanning production as well as reproduction. Generally, the everyday is associated with what we do over and over again, today the same as yesterday, thus signifying stability and the reproduction of social patterns.

When we bring technology, the assumed catalyst of change, into everyday life we need to modify our notion of both – perceiving everyday life to be not so stable and technology not so revolutionary. Still, like everyday life, technology should be understood as a pervasive feature of human societies, a part of all activities, female as well as male. The development of technology and its introduction into new areas of application represent an occasion for change and may provide an input into the breaking of routines, but it may just as well be a force of stability and conservation. This becomes evident when we analyse gender. In some sense change is a striking feature of our times when gendered activities and structures are continually challenged. However, studies of gender and technology have revealed that what appears as change is sometimes the reappearance of traditional gendered patterns in a new guise (Berg, 1994; Lie, 1988; Monod, 1985). Thus, to juxtapose gender, technology, and everyday life is not just a way of bringing out their interconnections. It is also a way of achieving a new understanding of the three concepts and of the interplay of change and continuity within modern society.

Does the combination of gender and technology actually mean studies of women? It might seem unnecessary to talk about men *and* technology, because a male suffix is already implicit in the concept of technology. For the very same reason, one may find a substantial literature on women *and* technology (see the overview in Wajcman, 1991). In this book, the focus of several papers is in fact on men's relationships with technologies in everyday life settings. We see how men use artefacts to construct meaning, identity, and practice. The perspective dissolves the "natural" association between *male* and *technology*, displaying it as a social and cultural construct that results in gendered practices and gendered symbols (see also Grint and Gill, 1995).

The study of technology needs to inquire into material as well as social qualities. These two elements cannot be disentangled because they have been woven together into "a seamless web" (Hughes, 1987). Technology is a heterogeneous constituent of society. In this collection, we present different ways of providing an understanding of the implications of this. In particular, we shall draw attention to the aspects of meaning of technical artefacts. What is the importance of technologies as symbols, and how is the symbolic related to practice? This means going beyond function and use. While we are often deceived by the functional aspects of technologies, a gendered focus may also reveal other hidden aspects of meaning as well as of practice. By interpreting scripts, images, and artefacts we have made the communicative aspects of technologies a main focus of this book.

Why should we be concerned with technology and everyday life? From an academic point of view, this is a call for detailed empirical exploration and development of concepts fruitful in furthering the understanding of the socio-technical dynamics of everyday life. What is the role of technology in human action, and how does human action shape socio-technical relations? And, more particularly, how do gender and the routines of everyday life contribute to the outcome of such processes?

Obviously, there is also an underlying and related political agenda: what are the political implications of modern everyday life technologies, and what should be done about them? Our focus on the agency of users does not mean that we consider them equal partners with designers, manufacturers, and policy makers in the development of technology. Often the relationship between designers and users is conceived in terms of power – of the powerful and the less powerful. We will not deny that there is a system that enables the production of differences, but we will insist on the need to study its existence and its implications empirically. The difference between designers and users should not be taken as an *a priori* fact. It has to be explored. Our concerns are in this respect similar to those found in some recent work on science and technology within cultural studies and its interest in studying "how people construct discourse about science and technology in order to make these meaningful in their lives". The argument is that "we are all scientists" (Downey et al., 1995: 342–343), or rather, to us, designers. This does not mean that everyone is equal, but it is an antidote to assuming that users do not and cannot influence their own situation. We want to be able to criticize present conditions as unfair and oppressive, but at the same time understand their seductions and to see the potentials for change.

One could argue that the focus on users and user agency reflected in this collection is a cultural artefact, an outcome of a long-term Scandinavian concern for issues such as participation and empowerment and for women, work, and technology (Lie et al., 1988). Also, because Norway imports nearly all the technology used in the country, it might be important to Norwegians to argue that cultural appropriation is consequential in order to sustain a belief in the continued existence of their national culture. Norwegians may also be seen as more attracted to the arguably positive outlook on technology embedded in the domestication perspective, compared with the more gloomy pictures often offered from cultures with different political traditions. Such arguments are difficult to assess, but we invite readers to explore them.

Technology as Hero or Villain

Technology studies were previously performed as impact discourses, usually in a rather determinist vein. One analysed social change as an outcome of technical change, often in quite general and abstract terms, based on arguments of a structuralist nature. For example, the orthodox Marxist account of technological change held that technology, understood as a force of production, in the long run would undermine capitalism. Thus, the development of technology was hailed as progressive. The short-term view held machinery to be a potential tool for the bourgeoisie against the working class. This ambiguity may be seen as typical of the modern period. Short-term evils have been written off against future gains.

The optimistic belief in the future, so common among romantic engineers, is in marked contrast to the ambivalence and pessimism often found among social theorists and philosophers. As Winner (1977) has shown, most of those usually considered as ancestors to present-day social studies of technology belong to this latter category. Gehlen, the Frankfurt school, Mumford, or Ellul, in political terms a diverse group of people, all held modern technology to be a dangerous force, potentially undermining human society. Habermas's view of a system world invading the life-world is typical of the kind of conception which implies a view of technology as a force out of control, as a human creation coming to haunt its creator.

The pessimistic view is also romantic, but the romance is with an undefined past or future. Another main problem with the out-of-control discourse is its demands for grand evaluations of technology-as-such. Thus, it assumes that technology has essential features that may be teased out by critical investigation. Automation leads to either a degradation or an upgrading of work, television produces passive *adaptation*, and so on. There is little room for human action other than in terms of a large collectivity or a social movement that as it were turns the tide. Humankind becomes the victim of the designs of the few.

The past decade has brought a change. A new sociology of technology has emerged which focuses on detailed studies of invention and innovation, working from an action approach embedded in symbolic interactionism and post-structuralism (Law, 1994). The result, usually termed constructivism, analyses technical change in terms like networks, translation, flexibility of interpretation, or closure (Bijker et al., 1987; Bijker and Law, 1992; Latour, 1987, 1996; Law, 1991, 1994). The constructivist turn in technology studies should be understood as an effort to make room for a type of analysis that is more sensitive to the contradictions, contingencies, and nuances of technological development. The insistence that there is no well-defined trajectory produced by nature or by an internal technological logic implies a greater concern for human action. At least as important is the emergent view of technology as something unfinished and thus malleable in principle. As Latour

(1987) emphasizes, the fate of texts as well as artefacts is in the hands of readers/users. Or, as Pfaffenberger (1992: 284) puts it: "I regard the supposed political force of technology as little more than ... an *affordance*, a perceived property of an artifact that suggests how it should be used."

Constructivism has evolved from efforts to deconstruct the power that resides in technoscientific institutions. This power, which seems to be the legitimate result of an ability rationally to control nature, is shown to be located in the consensus-building dynamics of technoscience, of the ability of technoscientists to negotiate agreement of facts and designs and to build and reproduce networks on that basis (Latour, 1987). The complex, socio-technical nature of this network-building is very well illustrated by the growth of modern fast-food chains such as McDonald's. Training, standard setting, information technology, and R&D are the constituents of large, efficient, and growing networks with centralized power. As Ritzer (1993) points out in his study of this phenomenon, the result may be seen as an exercise of diffusing bureaucracy or – to paraphrase Max Weber – the construction of yet another iron cage of rationality imposing an increasing number of standards upon consumers (Star, 1991). However, the iron cage would not hold if a large number of important actions had not been delegated to standardized equipment, thus considerably reducing the need for human supervision.

The constructivist turn meant a change in focal point from "impacts" to "innovation". This resulted in a lack of analysis of what happens with technology after it leaves the laboratory and the designers' desks. The lacuna has recently spurred efforts to see if the tools of constructivism are also applicable to studies of technology in use (Akrich, 1992; Latour, 1992). This collection is also an outcome of such an effort. We believe the results confirm the fruitfulness of this research agenda because it has produced good case-studies as well as theoretical renewal. This renewal is partly addressed at constructivism to rectify some of its weaknesses. But, more important, it is a challenge to social theory in general to improve its understanding of the manifold roles that technology occupies in modern societies, including the extent to which it is a concern for the human mind (see, e.g., Turkle, 1984).

As a consequence of this, technology-in-use is studied in this collection through an action perspective, with an emphasis on micro relations. In everyday settings, we consume technologies – or, more precisely, technical artefacts – by integrating and using them. We are also consumed by the artefacts when they gain our attention and have us react to them and become occupied by their abilities, functions, and forms. This dual relationship between humans and technologies is the outcome of a process of *domestication* (Silverstone et al., 1989). Metaphorically speaking, we tame the technologies that surround us in our everyday life. This process of taming is characterized by reciprocal change. We form relationships or networks with technologies, in which meanings are attributed and actions delegated to the parts that constitute the network. Studying acts of domestication is similar to studying acts of design and innovation. In fact, one should be careful about accepting the common *a priori* distinction made between use and design, between user and designer. This distinction implicitly inscribes assumptions that the one is passive (user), the other is active (designer), an assumption that is vividly challenged by the contributions in this collection.

Consumption as Production: Domestication of Artefacts

As indicated, the research strategies employed in this book represent a basic critique of the common conceptualization of consumption. Consumption has usually been perceived as a passive act in which the consumer/user adapts to the directives of the designer/producer or becomes caught in the system-immanent passivity of late capitalism. Also, the appropriation as well as the use of artefacts have been interpreted in terms of class, gender, ethnicity, etc. In this volume, power differences are evident in relation to gender. However, this does not mean that users are powerless or that women using technology subordinate themselves unconditionally to a masculine regime. Instead, it should be recognized that there is considerable room for action at the users' end too. The users/consumers make active efforts to shape their lives through creative manipulation of artefacts, symbols, and social systems in relation to their practical needs and competencies. Thus, it is meaningful – even necessary – to study the detailed process of domestication of technology, a process through which artefacts are defined and placed in a way which may imply redefinitions of one's own routines and practices.

The need to study domestication could also be argued with reference to previous arguments about resistance to new technologies. There is a substantial literature about the way technologies may be refused, even about efforts to break them (see Bauer, 1995). However, when analysed in greater detail, resistance is not so much about dismissal as about transformation. When technology is the object of controversy between "power" and "counterpower", it is shaped through these struggles.

The root of the problem of the *a priori* empowering of designers resides in the common analytical split between production and consumption. In modern society, these two basic aspects of human existence have become conceptually separated. Production is work, consumption is enjoyment. The Protestant spirit of capitalism has also attributed different flavours to these human activities. Production is the valuable part, the contribution to wealth; consumption easily becomes immoral because it subtracts from the accumulation of wealth. Production is active and creative, consumption is passive and adaptive.

Veblen's (1925) well-known concept of conspicuous consumption illustrates some of the problems. Although Veblen in this manner identifies the important symbolic aspect of consumption, there is an underlying argument that the process of consumption should be rational in economic terms and that symbolic aspects imply a kind of "false consciousness". The study of consumption thus struggles with a cultural moralism that transforms the consumer into being only an object of producer strategies.

To see what happens when technologies are consumed, we need to transcend the divide between production and consumption and do away with the idea of the passive, adaptive consumer. Consumption is always production, and in this respect these two moments are inseparable. However, to repeat our previous argument, this does not imply that production and consumption are identical acts, and users and designers have identical roles. The point is that we have to *examine* consumption and production to identify their characteristics, and that this examination is hampered by an *a priori* dichotomization of the two processes.

Although technology studies have not been much concerned with such comparisons, we may learn from other fields such as cultural studies and media studies (see, e.g., Silverstone, 1994; Aronowitz et al., 1996). In fact, within consumer studies we also find a shift from perceiving consumers as passive objects towards analysing them as people actively constructing a way of life (McCracken, 1988; Miller, 1987; see also the overview in Bocock, 1993). The consumer thus becomes a tinkerer or, in Levi-Strauss's terms, a *bricoleur*. We need to improve our understanding of this tinkering and how it affects the relationships of technology and everyday life.

When people acquire new technical artefacts to integrate them in their everyday life, they go through a process of domestication. This means that the artefacts are appropriated in a specific setting (Silverstone et al., 1989, 1992). The integration process implies work in the practical as well as the symbolic domain. When things are put to use, local routines are constructed to guide application, and the general scripts meant to direct this process may be transformed. Such transformations also take place in the symbolic domain. Here, general symbolic codes may be converted into something personal, attached to one's identity and social relations, or to the identity and relations of the larger social unit (household, etc.).

Domestication of, for example, a personal computer may be seen as a collective effort on the part of the household, but at the same time it is individual work with individual as well as collective outcomes (see Aune's paper). Domestication may mean conflict as well as change, and it does not indicate any kind of *a priori* linear progress. How should a TV set be employed, and who decides which programmes to watch? What counts when choosing a car, and what is good driving? Such conflicts have not yet been properly analysed in technology studies, but this is an important challenge. Of course, when one looks at such conflicts from a macroscopic point of view, they may appear idiosyncratic and without relevance, like ripples in a large wave of change. However, we will argue that, in the final instance, everyday struggles and negotiations may have important effects on the shaping of technology and its "consequences".

However, the controversies do not have to end. Several contributors (e.g. Aune, Vestby, and Håpnes) show in fact that domestication does not imply a stable closure of the distribution of meaning and practice related to an artefact. The truces expressed in practical routines of use may be broken, needs may change, or the persons involved may shift. An artefact might then be redomesticated, even radically. Also, artefacts may become worn out and replaced, or the owners may lose interest in them. Then they initiate a process of dis-domestication or divestment (McCracken, 1988: 87f). Vestby provides illuminating examples of the redomestication of "old" technologies when the telephone is ascribed a new role and "screen activities" acquire new meaning when family life is reorganized to cope with activities for children being alone at home after school.

A set of issues commonly raised in this connection concerns the ability of an artefact to direct human action. Is it possible for the few to control the many through technology only? May male designers unambiguously direct the actions of female users by persuading them to buy their designs? To find out, we have to "follow the artefact" and see whether in the final analysis it is used only in the prescribed manner. The basic thrust of the concept of domestication is of course that these questions are answered in the negative. This message is also made evident from the contributions to this collection. The way artefacts are employed, practically and symbolically, in the accounts given by Aune, Vestby, Håpnes, and Lamvik, is clearly removed from the original intentions of the design of these artefacts.

Moreover, the inscribed enabling and disabling qualities of arte-facts have to be reinforced by simultaneous social strategies to be effective. To use a keyboard as intended requires training. We learn to watch television, and the driving of cars is regulated by training requirements, traffic rules, police surveillance, etc. The efficiency of designs is dependent on the interplay of the accom-panying strategies and counter-strategies. This is of course the reason the shaping of such actions is controversial, as is shown vividly in Sætnan's contribution.

The important point to us is to retain ambiguity as well as ambivalence in the relation to technology. We do not argue that all technologies that are domesticated have benign qualities, that they are nice and promote a better life. In this respect, the selec-tion of the artefacts that are analysed in the different papers may be biased. We have not looked at large-scale risk technologies such as chemical plants or nuclear power stations, nor have we studied drugs and chemicals that may be hazardous to people's health. Nevertheless, in many cases, such technologies are also domesticated in the sense that practices and meanings are con-structed. We may not like the outcome, but that is a different matter. In fact, one could very well argue that to understand the role of nuclear power in different countries it would be very important to perform an analysis of how it has become domesti-cated.

Haraway (1991) has presented us with the metaphor of cyborgs to capture this ambiguity. The cyborg emphasizes the heterogeneous quality of technology, the invisible welding together of the organic and inorganic, the material and the social. Also, cyborgs make us watch out. We do not know if they are benign or not until we have experienced them. Judgement is suspended until we have constructed knowledge about them.

Conflicts and negotiations about the employment of technol-ogy, between designers and users and among users, are forces shaping the complex and composite relations of everyday life. These forces need to be made visible to transcend traditional deterministic accounts of the "effects" of new technologies. This does not mean that users regain all the power invested in them by liberal market theorists. We need to assess these relations concretely, but starting from the assumption that users' actions matter. To what extent is again an empirical matter. Here, the reader is referred to the individual papers to assess the argument.

However, we think that domestication holds the promise of functioning as a key concept in the analysis of technology in everyday life. First of all it satisfies the requirement that the consumer/user should be perceived as an active party. Second, it makes us become concerned with the broad variety of actions taken on by people when they acquire technical artefacts and put them into use. Third, it is sensitive to the systemic qualities of the process through which technology is consumed.

The idea that technology becomes domesticated has several origins (see Silverstone and Hirsch, 1992). We have tried to take it further. First and foremost, we have related it explicitly to technology studies. This means that we have strengthened its ability to account for the material and action aspects of artefacts, as well as making the concept more sensitive to the catalytic properties of technology and possibilities of change (Latour, 1987, 1992; Akrich, 1992; Law and Bijker, 1992). Second, we have – at least in part – disentangled it from its location in homogeneous and relatively stable, moral economies of households. Domestication does not occur only in households. The papers in this collection show that it is possible, through the use of the domestication concept and a related conceptualization of the cultural appropriation of technology, to make sense of the dynamics of technology and culture, and to provide images of active users to replace misleading ideas of technological determinism. In this way, the domestication concept is further developed and refined.

Domestication and Everyday Life: Continuity and Change

The social field we study is loosely termed *everyday life*. This concept signifies that we have moved attention from research and development to *users* of technology. Users are, at least in a formal sense, non-experts who involve technologies in their daily activities. The technologies potentially affect all spheres of life such as work, home, and leisure. Thus we find that traditional ways of defining the concept of everyday life are too limited because they often exclude fields and activities that we find it important to include.

In the social sciences, it has become commonplace to distinguish between production and reproduction. Similarly, to juxtapose work and everyday life has been a common way of defining everyday life as synonymous with the sphere of reproduction or as a residual category of what is outside work. For our purpose, this is not very fruitful. One important problem is that this definition makes too much of the fact that paid work for most people means that they are employed by others to perform given tasks in organized settings, and where the output is measured in economic terms. From this point of view, non-work means independence and freedom. However, paid work is not completely controlled and of an instrumental nature, and neither housework nor leisure is completely free and expressive. Although there are important differences between paid and non-paid activities, they do not belong to two different worlds.

Moreover, the traditional split has introduced a strong tendency to analyse paid and non-paid work in an asymmetrical manner. When industrial sociologists study work, they analyse factories and offices. What they look for is quality of working life, efficiency, skills, industrial relations, pay, and organization. When homes and leisure arenas are under scrutiny, there is much more concern for symbolic and communicative qualities. In addition, the two spheres are difficult to differentiate because work is performed everywhere. In particular, with the diffusion of new communication technologies, we may even find it difficult to discern a given spatial location of paid labour. Mobile computers and telephones make it possible, for example, to work from home or while travelling. More important in this context, however, is the fact that the distinction between work and non-work sectors has always been fictive. Feminist studies brought this out, for instance by studying housework and care from a sociology of work perspective (e.g. Oakley, 1974; Wærness, 1987). When we are studying everyday life, we also find it fruitful not to exclude any of these social fields because the analysis of *their interrelationship* is of the utmost importance to our understanding.

According to Lefebvre (1971), making connections is exactly what everyday life is about: "The everyday can ... be defined as a set of functions which connect and join together systems that might appear to be distinct." Thus, the concept of everyday life could be seen as something that is related not to a specific sphere of life, but rather to critical assessments of functions or activities making connections between them in an individual's life. Everyday life activities may be characterized by the following terms: routine, non-specialized, and non-bureaucratic (Sørensen, 1991). Such activities are found in the factory as well as in the home, in the office as well as in the sports arena.

However, relating everyday life to activities rather than to different spheres of life does not quite solve the problem. How would the analysis be affected by the fact that a lot of activities are carried out in bureaucratic as well as non-bureaucratic settings? Child care is an activity carried out in either one of these settings and even in some combination alternating between the two (Cronberg, 1986). Also, the analysis has to transcend the divide between routine and non-routine activities. For instance, birth may be an exceptional event in an individual's life. At the same time, it regularly occurs in society and professionals have pregnancies and births as part of their daily work (see Sætnan's paper).

Another way of defining everyday life is to perceive it as "the small world" or "the world within reach" (Heller, 1981; Schutz, 1975). In this way, everyday life is contrasted with the larger society. The concept is used to designate a social space which the individual citizen is able to oversee and manage. In this manner, the analysis of everyday life becomes a critique of the modern tendency to centralize, globalize, and standardize. We need, it is argued, to be locally embedded in a way that makes it possible to retain a reasonable level of control over our own lives.

The relevance of this definition has been questioned as the distinction between the local and the global has become blurred.

One's closest friends, colleagues, and those with whom one shares one's interests might well be spread all over the world, communicating by satellite as well as by aeroplane. Or does this development rather mean that the big world becomes so overwhelming that the close world gains a new and increasing importance?

In his theory about "high modernity", Giddens (1990) has described this contradiction between globalizing and localizing forces as a constitutive element. On the one hand, modernity is a continuous process of disembedding institutions from their local nature to change them through globalization, standardization, and expertise. On the other hand, the new institutions have to be appropriated in order to function and thus need to be re-embedded in local settings. Thus, there is a dialectic between globalizing and localizing, between disembedding and re-embedding, which may be interpreted as the continuous, albeit dynamic, reproduction of everyday life despite the efforts of the overwhelming forces of standardization, expertise, and bureaucracy.

Lefebvre's and Heller and Schutz's definitions are not contradictory but focus on different dimensions. The first makes us sensitive to the need to transcend everyday life, to escape bureaucracy as well as the normal routines, and to look for such efforts in our analysis. The latter reminds us that, even when social systems have become large and complex, we should look for the continuous effort to re-create "a small world" within a globalized modernity. Thus, the concepts are useful because they make us sensitive to important dimensions of modern societies outside the centres of power, in particular what may be perceived as quite successful actions to reconstruct and reshape a modernity that runs counter to human needs. In reality, there is no global village. Villages are local, even when they have access to global information and communication. Moreover, both concepts enable a critical discourse through their sensitivity to the needs to transcend everyday life.

In our opinion, this is why the concept of everyday life is so important to an understanding of the highly ambiguous nature of modern technology. In theory, technology is a standardizing, globalizing, and bureaucratizing effort. In practice, it is always appropriated and re-embedded in a local context when it is put to use. Many, if not most, technologies acquire meaning only when they interact with everyday life. At some stage, technologies are instigators of change, catalysts of new actions and structures, the embodiment of dreams of a different life. Then they may become a part of the daily routines, a stabilizing moment of modern life. This is not necessarily a linear story in which "new" technologies are always fundamentally different from "old" ones. Lamvik and Vestby, for instance, show how "old" technologies acquire new meaning and instigate new practices in changing contexts.

The reshaping privilege is, from our point of view, an exclusive property neither of communities involved in the design of technology nor of the domestic "haven in a heartless world". Domestication is the practical as well as emotional adaptation to technologies. It is a process of appropriating an object to make it meaningful to one's life. Once meaning has been attributed to it, it functions as an expression of self. These processes are often associated with the private sector, such as home decoration (Gullestad, 1992; Nørve, 1991). Several of the contributions to this collection show how similar appropriation and expression of self are taking place in other sectors; for example, Lie's and Sætnan's papers situated in working life, Lamvik's emotional experiences of the Am(erican)-car milieu, or the hacker culture analysed by Håpnes.

When studying technologies we are looking for types of use, symbolic expressions and personal attachment remaking the technologies into something close and familiar. This is a way of making them part of everyday life, and it is not accomplished simply by letting them into the home or other daily surroundings. There is a paradox concerning technology as well as everyday life in that both make us look for the trivial and functional. Here we have sought to shed light on the emotional. This is for instance seen in Lamvik's paper, where function and usefulness are non-issues. We can see the car as it should perhaps be seen more often – as a toy and a symbol. Such analyses are relevant also to studies of other technologies where the aspect of meaning is too often overshadowed by a focus on function and utility (see the contributions by Hubak and Lie).

Rediscovering Gender and Relativizing Masculinity

The focus of feminist studies of technology has been different from mainstream analysis of technology. Because women are seldom designers of technology, feminists have directed attention to the user side. In this way, the image of the male designer, exercising control over female users through technology, has come to be a pervasive one in feminist studies of technology (Wajcman, 1991). This view has reflected a perception of the role of technology in women's lives as a tragic fate rather than an opportunity. In this volume, we focus on the agency of users. The concept of domestication accords individuals an active position in their relationships to new technologies. Thus we avoid the victimization which has been a common feature of user-oriented technology studies, especially those concerning women and technology.

As mentioned, feminist studies have been pushing technology studies to include users, but also to include different technologies for analysis. Rather than drawing attention to "spearhead technologies" of production and research, feminists have analysed everyday technologies in such areas as transport, health, and housework (Wajcman, 1991). A pioneering contribution that highlighted the possible gaps between designer intentions and social appropriation has been Cowan's study of technology and housework (Cowan, 1983, 1987). Cowan showed that, in middle-class families, new household technologies, designed to save time spent on housework, meant in fact "more work for mother". This paradox was rooted in the social organization of domestic labour (individualized, privatized, and gendered), and in the changing norms of quality, cleanliness, and child care promoted by advertising.

Recent studies of household technologies stress the importance of following artefacts from design and manufacturing, through sales and advertising, to use within domestic settings (Cockburn and Ormrod, 1993; Cockburn and Fürst-Dilic, 1994). The way household technologies are designed and marketed is based on gendered views of needs and tasks. This also reflects a gendered division of labour in design and marketing. The technologies in question are affected by gender, while at the same time they confirm, adjust, or question relations of gender. Thus, there is a simultaneous and reciprocal construction of gender and technology, a mutual shaping process (Berg and Lie, 1995; Berg, forthcoming).

Apparently, gender easily becomes invisible to researchers in settings where women are absent. The way we experience men and technology is generally as a unity and not as two entities where the relationships are in need of analysis. However, the absence of women within many studies of technology should be a telling fact that gender really matters (Berg and Lie, 1995). Again, it is feminist research which has drawn attention to the relationships between technology, men, and masculinity (Cockburn, 1985; Hacker, 1989; Wajcman, 1991). In addition to these contributions, there is much information about men's relationships to technologies to be elicited from the main bulk of technology studies, including engineering studies and the literature on technology and work. But these efforts have still not been made.

In fact, a large part of this research reflects the same tragic view as does the feminist research. Technology has been degrading men's work, even demasculinizing it (Willis, 1977). (Male) engineers have lost control of technology to management and organizational rationality (Ritti, 1971). The more romantic view of men's creative relationship to technology is also found, but most pronounced in popularized accounts (e.g. Kidder, 1981). Thus, the relationship of gender and technology entails more than a dichotomy between male designers and female users. In fact, the very concept of technology is imbued with masculine connotations. This is elicited in Lie's paper. She shows that technology is associated with qualities which are also experienced as characterizing masculinity. In addition, we need to struggle to do away with simple gender dualities (Haraway, 1991) and challenge common assumptions not only of femininities, but of masculinities as well (Håpnes and Sørensen, 1995).

Relating technology to masculinity does not mean that we will present a single or a stereotypical version of men or masculinity. None of the men in these stories is presented as "typical", rather they are depicted as different and often specific cases. Håpnes and Lamvik present examples of romantic narratives about technology and masculinity, although – as is often the case with romances – there is also a tragic undertone. Neither car enthusiasts nor computer hackers are part of the social elite, nor does their relationship to technology pave the way for success outside their own subculture. Hubak's analysis of advertisements for cars leads to many observations of traditional sexual differentiations where masculinity is related to being active and in control, while femininity is depicted in passive and timid versions. However, she also finds advertising stories that romanticize a different femininity in relation to a different sort of car. By these examples we want to highlight the complexities and differences one must be aware of in any study of gender. Still, the stereotypical images of women, men, and technology are also important pieces to the puzzle to be fitted in alongside the variety of "real life" (Lie, 1995).

The agenda of the field of gender and technology has changed in recent years. Previously, one was very much concerned with the way both the design and the use of technology were embedded in a system of sexual divisions. This gave men more power and influence than women, but also, it seemed, a better position from which to benefit from new technologies. Although these problems are still very much present, the understanding of the situation has become more nuanced and complicated (Wagner, 1995; Grint and Gill, 1995). In particular, it is important to notice the shift away from viewing gender and technology as predetermined categories. Of course, gender is an implicit argument in domestication processes, but usually argued in terms other than gender. It is usually presented in the guise of such concepts as "familiar/non-familiar", "competent/non-competent", and "interested/uninterested". Through such means, gender as well as technology are negotiated in domestication processes.

Our revitalizing of women as actors also in relation to technology does not prepare the ground for a take-over by romantic views of technology as "the great equalizer" or of women as the hidden masters of technology. The papers in this collection offer scant evidence of one-sided optimistic perceptions. For instance, Vestby and Aune give accounts of domestic life where sexual divisions of labour and power are reproduced in relation to new technologies. But, in the context of technology and everyday life, we need to return to the questions about what happens to men and women through the appropriation and use of technology. This is not just an issue of consequences, of asking whether women are affected differently by technologies of everyday life than are men. Such questions are of course vital, but, as we have seen, they need to be embedded in a larger framework that opens the boundaries of gender and technology to allow for questions such as: How is gender constructed through technology? How are gender and technology negotiated in the routines that constitute everyday life?

The challenge remains, however, to identify the situations and the processes where previously gendered meanings and practices may be transformed into something less patriarchal. In a recent collection it is argued that neither technology nor gender has predefined, essential qualities. The problem is that there exist social practices and discourses that try to establish essentialist perceptions of men, women, and technology (Wajcman, 1991; Gill and Grint, 1995). In Sætnan's paper, the male doctor who struggles to institutionalize ultrasound obstetric screening presents critical women as fearful and resistant, whereas he sees himself as the active part that by technological means removes women's fear. This story provides interesting insights in the way essentialisms are constructed, and thus – by implication – into how they may be relativized. The focus needs to be directed at relationships where men's and women's roles and competences towards technology presuppose each other: it is only in contrast to "scared" or "incompetent" women that men can prove their masculinity in relation to technology.

An Overview of the Book

Since technology studies usually produce accounts of the development of technology, it is in some sense fitting that the first paper analyses what is commonly seen as design. As we shall see, this may include controversies about the understanding of everyday life. Ann Rudinow Sætnan analyses the arguments in a still ongoing debate about the implementation of ultrasound screening in pregnancy in Norway. What we see through the "window" held open by that debate is a (materially) stable technology and an interpretatively flexible set of relevant groups related to that technology engaged in a mutual construction of gender and technology.

The practice of ultrasound screening is shown to be constructed in opposing ways by the people engaged in the debate, and the difference between the constructions is mainly in the way the social relations towards the technology are discursively transformed. The paper concentrates in particular upon the various interpretations of the gendered interests of pregnant women and the professions providing antenatal services. Thus it provides insights into the process by which gender becomes constructed as part of efforts to construct a given technological (medical) practice which is necessary even if, from an engineering point of view, the ultrasound equipment is ready-made. To perform the analysis, Sætnan makes use of actor network theory (or translation theory) which is controversal to feminists (compare, e.g., Cockburn, 1992, with Ormrod, 1995, and Singleton, 1995).

The next two papers move our focus to the domestic arena. Guri Mette Vestby has studied how "new" and "old" technologies are employed to transform important aspects of modern Norwegian parenthood. Children's use of technological artefacts provides a new basis for working parents' abilities to raise their children. Contrary to the traditional understanding of children as "objects" shaped by cultural socialization processes, the paper is based on an approach which emphasizes children's agency. Parenthood is studied as a social construct in which parents and children continuously negotiate identities. Some technologies present parents with new challenges, e.g. how to control children's use of media. Others provide opportunities, either for control (e.g. the telephone) or to initiate other activities (e.g. the microwave oven).

In her analysis, Vestby extends the concept of "remote mothering" (Rakow and Navarro, 1993). She argues that there is remote parenting, which also includes fathers. The emerging, physically dislocated, relationship between parents and children is enabled by the telephone and other technologies that children may use to cater for their own needs, and it is embedded in the reciprocal projects of autonomy and control. In this way, we gain important new insights into the role of technology in the construction of parenthood as well as childhood.

In the third paper, Margrethe Aune is concerned with how personal computers are appropriated, located, and used in Norwegian households. These issues are analysed with particular emphasis on different household members' negotiations during a process of domestication, in particular between husbands and wives. The outcome is of course dependent on available resources in terms of time and space. Even more important is the way time and space are reconstructed. The machines allow users to redefine the relationship between the home and the workplace, the implications of overtime, and thus the meaning of presence. The important issue is no longer the physical but the mental presence of the husband. Thus, the home PC comes out also as a gendered artefact in the sense that it is acquired by men who are the dominant users, and it is the object of gendered controversies.

Compared with much previous research about home computers, which has emphasized hobbyist or expressive relationships between users and computers (see, e.g., Turkle, 1984; Haddon, 1992), Aune identifies a wider range of domestication related to everyday tasks rather than leisure. Instrumental types of relationships dominate, not those of fascination and transcendence, even if these are present too.

This contrasts with the paper by Tove Håpnes, who presents a study of a community of young, male engineering students who choose to describe themselves as "real hackers" or "semi-hackers". Hackers could be seen to be an extreme example of users, indicating the limits of cultural flexibility of computers. Here, they are analysed as a group in the grey zone between the users and designers of technology. They use advanced information technology to cater for their – in some sense – hobbyist interests, but they also apply the same technology to design new programs that they sell to outside companies. Thus they provide a nice example of how the borders of production and consumption are blurred to the extent that they may be meaningless.

Håpnes argues the need to combine action and meaning in the analysis of how artefacts are domesticated. She also paints a picture of hackers that in several respects is different from those that have dominated the discourse in the last decade, with Turkle's (1984) analysis as the paradigmatic example. There may be a global idea of what a hacker is, in part due to the fact that Turkle's analysis is widely known, but the local features are compellingly important.

The last three contributors are mainly concerned with symbolic aspects of technology. Gunnar Lamvik has studied a particular community of car-loving Norwegians, mostly men, celebrating the US Independence day in Norway. It is called the Amcar community. He argues that the project of the people involved with American cars is to create a mythical American world in Norway. Metaphorically, the car is the material core from which this group of people constructs a subculture (Hebdige, 1979) by using and bending available symbolic resources. What they produce is a version of America that is both mythical and nostalgic. Because Amcar enthusiasm is incompatible with routine everyday life, argues Lamvik, their project is similar to a *fairy tale*. It is not an escape from everyday life, but a supplement to this reality. Thus, he claims, in this community there were moments when they felt that they were not playing *as if* they were in America. They actually were there, but in an America scarcely recognizable to Americans.

Compared with other studies of car cultures (e.g. Lewis and Goldstein, 1983), even of similar communities (Rosengren,

1994), Lamvik succeeds in outlining how cars may enable transcendence of everyday life. They are part of the routines, but also
the means of breaking away. This may in turn enrich our understanding of how cars are domesticated by more ordinary communities.

The Amcar community is male dominated, in most meanings
of the word. One could argue more generally that it is common-
sense that men are interested in cars, but Marit Hubak's paper is
an effort to challenge the simplicity of such arguments. She analyses how women's relationship to cars is seen from the point of
view of car advertisers.

Hubak examines how cars may have a heterogeneous symbolic character for both men and women. Through texts and pictures, advertisers suggest how cars should be interpreted and
integrated into other people's daily life. This encoding or *script*, following Akrich (1992), is an effort to translate the car from a
material object into social relations. Scripts direct the reader to
see men and women in particular ways – their relations to cars,
to each other, and to other people of the same sex.

What comes out of the analysis is a more nuanced picture
than the one often found in discourses about gender and advertising. Women are sometimes used as eye-catchers in car ads, but
they have to a greater extent been transformed into a group
addressed by the car-selling community. To some extent, we may
witness a construction of a feminine car relationship; in fact the
paper suggests that several femininities may be identified from
modern car ads in Norway. However, they represent a form of
local domestication. In an argument similar to Sætnan's, Hubak
shows how the cars that are imported into Norway have to be
transformed, rescripted, to be adaptable to the way Norwegian
representatives of the multinational car companies and their marketing agencies perceive "Norwegian cars".

Advertisements usually attract our attention through pictures.
In the last contribution, Merete Lie invites readers to see other
types of image which are present everywhere in everyday life.
These are the live images of actors and activities that reveal how
technology is connected to gender. She focuses on the symbolic

aspects of technology by analysing the way images of gender and technology are revealed within work-life settings.

The analysis depicts how the image of technology is used to correspond to a traditional working-class masculinity (Willis, 1977). Technologies create obvious divisions of space as well as types of tasks, in effect separating male from female spheres of work. Contrasting the scene of a traditional factory with the scene of a modern service company, the boundaries between male and female spheres of work are no longer symbolized by technology. The computer is used by everyone, regardless of gender and status.

On the basis of such different scenes, different masculine connotations of the concept of technology are discerned. But what about change? Are masculine connotations of technology bound to "old-fashioned" mechanical machinery? Or could it be that the change to computers as a defining technology is more in line with contemporary changes in the image of masculinity? In that case, the future domestication of computers has to work with transformed symbolic resources.

REFERENCES

Akrich, M. 1992. The description of technological objects. In W. E. Bijker and J. Law (eds): *Shaping Technology/Building Society. Studies in Sociotechnical Change*. Cambridge, MA and London: MIT Press.

Aronowitz, S. et al. (eds). 1996. *Technoscience and Cyber Culture*. New York: Routledge.

Bauer, M. (ed.) 1995. *Resistance to New Technology. Nuclear Power, Information Technology and Biotechnology*. Cambridge: Cambridge University Press.

Berg, A.-J. 1994. A gendered socio-technical construction: The smart house. In C. Cockburn and R. Fürst-Dilic (eds): *Bringing Technology Home. Gender and Technology in a Changing Europe*. Milton Keynes: Open University Press.

Berg, A.-J. Forthcoming. *Digital Feminism*. PhD dissertation. Trondheim: Centre for Technology and Society, Norwegian University of Science and Technology.

Berg, A.-J. and Lie, M. 1995. Feminism and constructivism: Do artifacts have gender? *Science, Technology and Human Values*, Vol. 20, No. 3, pp. 332–51.

Bijker, W. E. and Law, J. (eds) 1992. *Shaping Technology/Building Society. Studies in Sociotechnical Change*. Cambridge, MA and London: MIT Press.

Bijker, W. E., Hughes, T., and Pinch, T. (eds) 1987. *The Social Construction of Technological Systems*. Cambridge, MA: MIT Press.

Bocock, R. 1993. *Consumption*. London: Routledge.

Cockburn, C. 1985. *Machinery of Dominance. Women, Men and Technical Know-how*. London: Pluto Press.

Cockburn, C. 1992. The circuit of technology: gender, identity and power. In R. Silverstone and E. Hirsch (eds): *Consuming Technologies. Media and Information in Domestic Spaces*. London and New York: Routledge.

Cockburn, C. and Fürst-Dilic, R. (eds) 1994. *Bringing Technology Home. Gender and Technology in a Changing Europe*. Milton Keynes: Open University Press.

Cockburn, C. and Ormrod, S. 1993. *Gender and Technology in the Making*. London: Sage.

Cowan, R. S. 1983. *More Work for Mother. The Ironies of Household Technology from the Open Hearth to the Microwave*. New York: Basic Books.

Cowan, R. S. 1987. The consumption junction: A proposal for research strategies in the sociology of technology. In W. E. Bijker, T. Hughes, and T. Pinch (eds): *The Social Construction of Technological Systems*. Cambridge, MA: MIT Press.

Cronberg, T. 1986. *Teorier om teknologi og hverdagsliv*. Copenhagen: Institutt for organisation og arbejdssociologi, Nyt fra samfundsvidenskaberne.

Downey, G. L., Dumit, J., and Williams, S. 1995. Cyborg anthropology. In C. H. Gray et al. (eds): *The Cyborg Handbook*. New York and London: Routledge, pp. 341–6.

Giddens, A. 1990. *The Consequences of Modernity*. Stanford, CA: Stanford University Press.

Gill, R. and Grint, K. 1995. The gender–technology relation: Contemporary theory and research. In K. Grint and R. Gill (eds): *The Gender–Technology Relation. Contemporary Theory and Research*. London: Taylor and Francis, pp. 1–28.

Grint, K. and Gill, R. (eds) 1995. *The Gender–Technology Relation. Contemporary Theory and Research*. London: Taylor and Francis.

Gullestad, M. 1992. *The Art of Social Relations*. Oslo: Scandinavian University Press.

Hacker, S. 1989. *Pleasure, Power, and Technology*. Boston, MA: Unwin Hyman.

Haddon, L. 1992. Explaining ICT consumption: The case of the home computer. In R. Silverstone and E. Hirsch (eds): *Consuming Technologies. Media and Information in Domestic Spaces*. London and New York: Routledge.

Håpnes, T. and Sørensen, K. H. 1995. Competition and collaboration in male shaping of computing: A study of a Norwegian hacker culture. In K. Grint and R. Gill (eds): *The Gender–Technology Relation. Contemporary Theory and Research*. London: Taylor and Francis, pp. 174–91.

Haraway, D. 1991. *Simians, Cyborgs, and Women. The Reinvention of Nature*. London: Free Association Books.

Hebdige, D. 1979. *Subculture – The Meaning of Style*. London: Routledge and Kegan Paul.

Heller, A. 1981. *Das Alltagsleben*. Frankfurt: Suhrkamp.

Hughes, T. 1987. The seamless web: Technology, science, et cetera, et cetera. In B. Elliot (ed.): *Technology and Social Process*. Edinburgh: Edinburgh University Press.

Jasanoff, S. et al. (eds). 1995. *Handbook of Science and Technology Studies*. Thousand Oaks, CA: Sage.

Kidder, T. 1981. *The Soul of a New Machine*. London: Allen Lane.

Latour, B. 1987. *Science in Action*. Milton Keynes: Open University Press.

Latour, B. 1992. Where are the missing masses? The sociology of a few mundane artifacts. In W. E. Bijker and J. Law (eds): *Shaping Technology/ Building Society. Studies in Sociotechnical Change*. Cambridge, MA and London: MIT Press.

Latour, B. 1996. *ARAMIS or the Love of Technology*. Cambridge, MA: Harvard University Press.

Law, J. (ed.) 1991. *A Sociology of Monsters. Essays on Power, Technology and Domination*. London: Routledge.

Law, J. 1994. *Organizing Modernity*. Oxford: Blackwell.

Law, J. and Bijker, W. 1992. Postscript: Technology, stability, and social theory. In W. E. Bijker and J. Law (eds): *Shaping Technology/Building Society. Studies in Sociotechnical Change*. Cambridge, MA and London: MIT Press, pp. 290–308.

Lefebvre, H. 1971. *Everyday Life in the Modern World*. New York: Harper and Row.

Lewis, D. L. and Goldstein, L. (eds) 1983. *The Automobile and American Car Culture*. Ann Arbor, MI: University of Michigan Press.

Lie, M. 1988. Fjernarbeid – teknisk endring og likestilling. In M. Lie et al.: *I menns bilde. Kvinner, teknologi, arbeid*. Trondheim: Tapir.

Lie, M. 1995. Technology and masculinity: The case of the computer. *European Journal of Women's Studies*, Vol. 2, No. 3, pp. 379–94.

Lie, M. et al. 1988. *I menns bilde. Kvinner, teknologi, arbeid*. Trondheim: Tapir.

McCracken, G. 1988. *Culture and Consumption: New Approaches to the Symbolic Character of Consumer Goods*. Bloomington, IN: Indiana University Press.

Miller, D. 1987. *Material Culture and Mass Consumption*. Oxford: Blackwell.

Monod, E. 1985. Telecommuting – a new word, but still the same old story? In A. Olerup et al.: *Women, Work and Computerization. Opportunities and Disadvantages*. Amsterdam: North-Holland.

Nørve, S. 1991. The home – materialized identity and household technology. In K. H. Sørensen and A.-J. Berg (eds): *Technology and Everyday Life. Trajectories and Transformations*. Oslo: Norwegian Research Council for Science and the Humanities.

Oakley, A. 1974. *The Sociology of Housework*. London: Martin Robertson.

Ormrod, S. 1995. Feminist sociology and methodology: Leaky black boxes in gender/technology relations. In K. Grint and R. Gill (eds): *The Gender–Technology Relation. Contemporary Theory and Research*. London: Taylor and Francis, pp. 31–47.

Pfaffenberger, B. 1992. Technological dramas. *Science, Technology, and Human Values*, Vol. 17, No. 3, pp. 282–312.

Rakow, L. and Navarro, V. 1993. Remote mothering and the parallel shift: Women meet the cellular telephone. *Critical Studies in Mass Communication*, Vol. 10, No. 2, pp. 144–57.

Ritti, R. 1971. *The Engineer in the Industrial Corporation*. New York: Columbia University Press.

Ritzer, G. 1993. *The McDonaldization of Society*. Newbury Park, CA: Sage.

Rosengren, A. 1994. Some notes on the male motoring world in a Swedish community. In K. H. Sørensen (ed.): *The Car and its Environments. The Past, Present, and Future of the Motorcar in Europe*. Brussels: COST/DG XII, pp. 115–36.

Schutz, A. 1975. *Hverdagslivets sociologi*. Copenhagen: Hans Reizel.

Silverstone, R. 1994. *Television and Everyday Life*. London: Routledge.

Silverstone, R. and Hirsch, E. (eds) 1992. *Consuming Technologies. Media and Information in Domestic Spaces*. London and New York: Routledge.

Silverstone, R. et al. 1989. Families, technologies, and consumption: The household and information and communication technologies. CRICT discussion paper, Brunel University.

Silverstone, R., Hirsch, E. and Morley, D. 1992. Information and communication technologies and the moral economy of the household. In R. Silverstone and E. Hirsch (eds): *Consuming Technologies. Media and Information in Domestic Spaces*. London and New York: Routledge.

Singleton, V. 1995. Networking constructions of gender and constructing gender networks: Considering definitions of woman in the British cervical screening programme. In K. Grint and R. Gill (eds): *The Gender–Technology Relation. Contemporary Theory and Research*. London: Taylor and Francis, pp. 146–73.

Sørensen, K. H. 1991. Introduction. Technology and everyday life: Trajectories and transformations. In K. H. Sørensen and A.-J. Berg (eds): *Technology and Everyday Life. Trajectories and Transformations*. Oslo: Norwegian Research Council for Science and the Humanities.

Star, S. L. 1991. Power, technologies and the phenomenology of conventions: On being allergic to onions. In J. Law (ed.): *A Sociology of Monsters. Essays on Power, Technology and Domination*. London: Routledge.

Turkle, S. 1984. *The Second Self. Computers and the Human Spirit*. New York: Simon and Schuster.

Veblen, T. 1925. *The Theory of the Leisure Class*. London: Allen and Unwin.

Wærness, K. 1987. On the rationality of caring. In A. S. Sassoon (ed.): *Women and the State*. London: Hutchinson.

Wajcman, J. 1991. *Feminism Confronts Technology*. Cambridge: Polity Press.

Wagner, I. 1995. Hard times: The politics of women's work in computerized environments. *European Journal of Women's Studies*, Vol. 2, No. 3, pp. 295–314.

Willis, P. 1977. *Learning to Labour*. Aldershot: Gower.

Winner, L. 1977. *Autonomous Technology*. Cambridge, MA: MIT Press.

Chapter 2

Speaking of Gender ...
Intertwinings of a Medical Technology Policy Debate and Everyday Life

Ann Rudinow Sætnan

The Single Ultrasound Scan in an Everyday Perspective

This paper presents an analysis of an ongoing controversy over the implementation in Norway of ultrasound screening in pregnancy. The focus of this analysis will be the claims invoked by key activists in the debate and the ways those claims relate to gendering processes and everyday life.

What role might pregnancy (and pregnancy care technologies) play in everyday life? For most Norwegian women today, pregnancy is certainly not a routine matter. Rather it is an exceptional period, a period of transition from 20–30 years of everyday life as a non-mother to a new everyday life as a mother. But the exceptional also has its impact on the everyday. For instance, as a transition from childlessness to parenthood (or from fewer to more children), pregnancy is likely to entail some renegotiation of gender – one factor which, however changeable, is pervasively and persistently present in everyday activities and identity. In this respect, it is a liminal stage (Turner, 1966) where new cultural meanings may emerge. Constructions of gender related to pregnancy could therefore arguably be of particular importance to the everyday lives of families.

On the other hand, antenatal care is, from the perspective of the providers, one example of how pregnancy becomes routine rather than exceptional. The professional setting gives this work an everyday quality. In Norway, pregnancy routinely entails a series of antenatal check-ups, averaging more than one per month, with a more or less repetitive content (Backe, 1994). Like all routine experiences, pre-natal visits can also be presumed to have some impact on participants' social roles and self-perceptions.

Within the routine of antenatal visits, one visit stands out as both routine and exceptional – the ultrasound scan. Since the mid-1980s it has been a matter of routine to offer one (at some hospitals two) ultrasound scan(s) to all pregnant women. For the woman being scanned, this may be a once-in-a-lifetime experience. Yet its routinization makes it an everyday matter for the population as a whole and especially for the doctors and midwives who conduct such scans day in and day out.

Who are the participants in antenatal care? One category of participants is pregnant women (and more marginally their partners), for whom antenatal care is a routine aspect of an otherwise exceptional period in life. Others are the medical professionals who provide antenatal care. In Norway, a woman may choose any of several sources for such care: her primary care physician, a midwife at a mothers and well babies clinic, a gynaecologist in private practice, or (if the conditions of her pregnancy so require) a hospital obstetrics department. Regardless of where a woman obtains her antenatal care as a whole, the ultrasound scan is as a rule provided by the hospital.

If the study of technology in everyday life involves the study of technology's users, then the study of medical technology in everyday life involves the study of several layers of users. In the case of routine ultrasound in pregnancy, pregnant women are the "end-users" of the technology. Their primary providers of antenatal care, who formally request the scan, and the staff of the department which provides the scan could be called "intermediary users". Though the hospital staff are direct users of the technological equipment, they use it on behalf of the end-users, the pregnant women. They also use it on behalf of the national health service and the state, since it is the state which has sanctioned the decision to offer an ultrasound scan as a matter of routine.

From an everyday life perspective – from the perspective of the mutual domestication of ultrasound routines into users' daily activities, relations, and self-perceptions – we would want to investigate two main groups of users: the pregnant women (and their partners) as end-users, and antenatal care providers as intermediary users. The introduction of ultrasound represents a new technology. Thus it provides a possibility for renegotiating the understanding and practice of antenatal care, which could lead to changes in everyday life. In this paper, this possibility is explored with particular emphasis on the ongoing constructions of gender in the debate about the ultrasound scan.

Conceptual Paths
From Debate to Data

Experimental evidence as to whether or not ultrasound screening is beneficial is still debated in the medical journal literature, with conclusions about evenly divided (Sætnan, 1995). But the controversy is not confined to arenas within the medical science community. On the basis of available scientific evidence, a parliamentary White Paper on perinatal care recommended against offering ultrasound screening (NOU, 1984:17). This recommendation was hotly contested – in hearing responses, at professional meetings, and in the mass media.

In response to this debate, a consensus conference was arranged (Backe and Buhaug, 1986). The consensus panel concluded that, although there was no evidence that ultrasound screening was beneficial, its implementation was already a *falt accompli* so that a policy of regulating this practice was more likely to be effective than an attempt to halt it. The debate received a good deal of attention in the Norwegian mass media around the time of the conference, then faded from view.

Media attention flared up again in connection with parliamentary debate over new biotechnology regulations which contained a proposal to suspend ultrasound screening (Odelsting-sproposisjon nr. 37, 1993–94). The measure as finally passed states that foetal diagnostics shall not be a routine part of antenatal care. Ultrasound screening nevertheless remained standard practice, as it had since at least 1986 (Backe, 1994).

This situation prompted a second consensus conference on ultrasound in pregnancy, which was held in February–March 1995. Whereas at the first conference the organizers had avoided the issue of selective abortion (abortion on the basis of diagnosed foetal abnormalities), for this second conference they were specifically directed by the Ministry of Health and Social Affairs to focus on that issue. Nevertheless, this second conference reached the same conclusions as the first: that a single non-mandatory ultrasound scan should be offered in each pregnancy at around week 18 (NFR, 1995).

Since the second consensus conference the issue of pre-natal diagnostics has remained high on the media agenda, especially in connection with abortion issues. But the practice of routine ultrasound in pregnancy has so far continued, seemingly unaffected by the ongoing controversy. It is now quite rare for a pregnant woman to reach term without being examined by ultrasound. In my own hospital district, fewer than one-tenth of one percent of pregnant women do so. Thus, as of 1996, the technology has been relatively stable as an artefact and a set of practices, but is still an object of controversy in terms of values, meanings, and political support.

The sociology of scientific knowledge (SSK) emphasizes the advantages of studying science in periods of controversy (Collins, 1985; Latour, 1987). Once an issue is closed, a "cover-up" conventionally seals the social processes of science from view. SSK, with its focus on periods of controversy, has in turn been developed into an approach to the study of technology (Pinch and Bijker, 1987; Woolgar, 1991). This approach was launched first as a methodology for describing the influence of *relevant social groups* on the shaping of technological artefacts.

The concept of *interpretative flexibility* refers to the point that groups attach different meanings to a technological artefact. If the design of an artefact is disputed, and if more than one group engaged in the dispute is consequential, then the artefact will be *unstable*. Artefacts stabilize when enough relevant groups come to see, or are forced to accept, one proposed form of the artefact as appropriate to their respective interests. As with the closure of scientific controversies, instability and flexibility tend to disappear from accounts of the artefact from then on. Thus, both the general phenomenon of interpretative flexibility and the potential social and material impact of the meanings disputed in an individual case are most accessible to study in periods of controversy.

To analyse such controversies, we need to apply a broad definition of technology. We must see it not simply as an artefact, but as a set of relations between an artefact and its surrounding actors, assumptions, and practices – not simply as a technical artefact. The concept of *socio-technical ensemble* (Law and Bijker, 1992) fills that need. Other more or less synonymous concepts are *actor networks* (Latour, 1987), (especially local or micro-level networks (Sørensen, 1994)), *hybrids* (Latour, 1991), or *cyborgs* (Haraway, 1991).

The ensemble and network concepts focus on the artefact and include its surrounding human actors, meanings, institutions, and technical linkages. Translation Theory further elaborates on the process of constructing artefact-centred ensembles. One key role in this process is that of *spokesperson*.

Spokespersons, whether self-declared or elected, claim to speak on behalf of social groups or natural phenomena. Of course, such claims put one's credibility on the line. An artefact may fail to perform as promised by the engineer, or its predicted users may reject it. In either case, the network falls apart.

As noted above, in the case of obstetric ultrasound we are dealing with layers of users – end-users and intermediaries. Note that the intermediary user is at once both user and spokesperson. When using ultrasound in antenatal care, health professionals "speak" on behalf of the sound waves, claiming they will not harm. They "speak" on behalf of the foetus, claiming to know how it is developing. They "speak" on behalf of the end-users, claiming to know what is in their interests.

When speaking *for* other relevant groups, spokespersons also speak *to* those groups. Claiming to know what is normal in foetal development, clinicians also intervene – allowing the normal to continue as before and attempting to change the course of the abnormal. In claiming to know pregnant women's interests and the interests of the foetus, clinicians also instruct women in how to perceive their own interests and how to behave during pregnancy.

Hubak's paper in this volume gives another example of speaking for as speaking to. Advertising agencies speak for men and women as potential car purchasers when claiming that their ads will produce sales. If they succeed in selling their services, their ads speak to those potential customers, instructing them which car it is in their interests to buy. However, the prospective end-users are not simply passive recipients of these messages. There is often substantial room left for end-users to speak for themselves through the selective and creative appropriation of technologies (as witness papers by Akrich, 1992, and by Aune, Vestby, and Lamvik in this volume).

This does not mean that spokespersons and end-users share equal power. The spokesperson role is based on the ability (or at least the untested claim) to speak with the voices of many. End-users, unless organized, speak only as individuals. Thus, while potentially a risky role, the spokesperson role is at least in the short term the more powerful. End-users may exercise power by organizing to overthrow their spokespersons (an option which requires considerable effort), or by making choices within whatever scope remains for individual selectivity and creativity.

From Technology to Gender

The cyborg concept switches the focus from technical nodes to human nodes in the socio-technical network. The cyborg metaphor encourages us to note how human practices and identities are formed in close interaction with our surrounding technologies.

As with the ensemble, the cyborg is a cluster of connected elements, all of which are interpretatively flexible. The human node of the cyborg is not so much a spokesperson for the whole as an embodiment and an internalization. Like closed scientific controversies and stabilized technological ensembles, internalized cyborg identities tend to become invisible as such. They come to be seen as biological, psychological, or social inevitabilities. Again it is in periods of controversy that the processes of constructing such identities are most visible.

Perhaps the best example of the tendency to naturalize socially constructed identities is the aspect of gender. Unless challenged, gender identities come to be seen as a matter of genetic fate: one is born with a female or male body, thereby with a female or male personality, female or male physical and mental abilities, female or male technological affinities. But gender, like technology and like knowledge, is socially constructed.

Gender is constructed along several axes (as a structure of symbols, of relations, of behaviours) and on several levels (as social norms and patterns, and as individual identities and enactments) (Harding, 1986). As with knowledge and technological constructions, gender structures must be constantly maintained – taught, learned, interpreted, enacted. Thus the gendering process is in principle accessible for study at any time or place, but its visibility is probably heightened when hegemonic constructs are challenged – when they are confronted with cross-cultural variations, or with gender liberationary movements, or with new technologies not yet assigned gender characteristics. Perhaps, as Haraway finds for the gendering of scientific knowledge, sociotechnical ensembles/cyborgs take on their gendered meanings through battles of alternative narratives in a "contested narrative field" (Haraway, 1989). Alternative accounts offered by participants in a controversy are then not merely a window onto the gendering process, but are that process itself being played out before our eyes.

Technologies are implicated in the gendering process both as symbols and as material sites where relations and behaviours are enacted (see for instance Lie, 1995 and this volume, Cockburn and Ormrod, 1993). This implies that technologies take on gender-symbolic value and are delegated positions in the gendered division of labour. Technologies, whether we approach them as user-centred cyborgs or as artefact-centred ensembles, are also subjects of a gendering process. Thus, the gendering process may be assumed to be important, but it is an open matter *how* it will be important.

The ensemble or cyborg concepts allow us to study technology-related controversies without *a priori* determining what elements of the ensemble/cyborg are likely to be affected, to what extent, or in what manner. All the elements are interpretatively flexible. Any element may be stabilized or destabilized in the course of the controversy. Any element may turn out to be a previously stabilized point against which leverage can rest in order to move other elements.

The ultrasound controversy exemplifies a situation where gendering may turn out to be multidimensional and interdependent, in that knowledges, identities, and socio-technical configurations are all affected. In this paper, I focus not on the ultrasound imaging apparatus as an emerging artefact, but on the socio-technical practice of routinely examining all pregnant women with ultrasound one or more times per pregnancy (also called antenatal ultrasound screening, routine obstetric ultrasound, or ultrasound screening).

Ultrasound screening is a socio-technological ensemble which is still under development. It is a technological practice aimed at establishing gestational age and identifying multiple pregnancies (twins, etc.) and asymptomatic abnormalities in foetal development or position (Ewigman et al., 1993). The practice is dependent on whether or not ultrasound apparatuses "work", i.e. whether or not they help identify target conditions correctly without harming mother or foetus. But the workability of the apparatus is not merely a technical problem. It is a problem of the interface between the apparatus and the bodies it aims to describe. For the apparatus to work, the bodies must work for it: the maternal abdomen must be transparent to it. The foetal body must follow a predictable and morphologically recognizable developmental course. Certain "facts" about these bodies must come to be seen as self-evident.

And even then a workable apparatus is only a necessary, not a sufficient condition for a workable screening practice. Other equally necessary conditions are catchment routines which refer pregnant women to the screening service; a distribution of apparatuses and a division of labour (i.e. Is screening to be conducted by primary antenatal care providers or by specialized clinics? by physicians, midwives, or radiology technicians? And how are providers to be trained?); follow-up routines (i.e. What happens when a problem is diagnosed?). The practice must find its place in a financial structure. It must be accepted by the pregnant population.

This article analyses the claims made by activists in the Norwegian ultrasound screening debate. In arguing for or against ultrasound screening, these activists make claims as to the capabilities of the technology, the nature of pregnancy, the interests of the pregnant population, etc. In other words, they participate in the construction of the ultrasound screening ensemble, the cyborg foetus, the cyborg woman. They do so by taking on the roles of spokespersons for groups and phenomena. Each of these groups and phenomena under dispute could become the focus of a separate analysis, with the remaining elements appearing in contextual roles. In this paper, the focus will be on the contested meanings of gender in relation to providers and users of ultrasound screening in pregnancy, and the implications of these contestations for the everyday lives of health professionals and of women as mothers.

Windows onto Ensemble Construction Sites

In any overview of the ultrasound screening debate, certain names recur in prominent positions in arena after arena. They are authors of experimental reports, or members of the White Paper committee, or of the consensus conference planning committee, or of the consensus panel. They are consultants to regulating agencies, organizers of international conferences, authors of letters and articles in professional and mass media. They appear in radio and television debates. They are officers of key professional associations. These actors form the obvious core around which to roll up a "snowball" of actors in the ultrasound screening network.

In this article I analyse the accounts presented in my interviews with seven of the most central actors in that core. The seven are presented in four sets, grouped on the basis of the similarity of their accounts and close collaboration in their activities in the controversy. The actors and groups are presented below. I have used pseudonyms, not so much to preserve the actors' anonymity (prominent as they are in the debate, they are all readily identifiable to anyone who cares to make the effort) as because their personal identities do not concern us here. Rather, we are interested in the positions they represent in the debate. By using pseudonyms descriptive of these positions, I hope to make my own interpretation of the controversy more apparent to the reader.

The Leading Expert (Dr A) is head of the national laboratory for ultrasound diagnostics and foetal medicine. This laboratory has become an obligatory passage point for professional training in ultrasound techniques, confirmational diagnosis of suspected foetal anomalies, treatment of diagnosed anomalies, consultancy on regulatory legislation, and development of new ultrasound machines and applications. Dr A headed the first randomized controlled clinical trial claimed to have shown a health benefit from ultrasound screening. Others of his works are standard references for methods of estimating foetal blood flow, foetal weight and gestational age with ultrasound. He organized an international state-of-the-art conference on obstetric ultrasound in Ålesund, Norway (1984) which is thought to have been a turning-point in overcoming resistance to ultrasound screening. Dr A appeared as an expert witness at both consensus conferences, and was a key consultant to the Directorate of Health Services in working out regulatory details following the recommendations of the first consensus panel. Dr A is also a frequent participant in media debates. He is seen by many as the driving force behind the implementation of ultrasound screening in Norway.

The Midwife is head of the Norwegian Midwives' Association. She was a member of the committee which wrote a parliamentary White Paper on perinatal care and of the first consensus conference panel. She has also been a frequent participant in radio and television debates and contributor to newspaper feature issues.

The two *Sceptical Specialists* are the "Grand Old Man" of Norwegian gynaecology (Dr G, *The Gynaecologist*) and an international expert on perinatal epidemiology (Dr E, *The Epidemiologist*). Both conducted early research projects on ultrasound screening. The Epidemiologist led the Trondheim randomized controlled trial, a particularly well-reputed trial which concluded that no benefits from screening had been found. The Gynaecologist conducted some of the earliest Norwegian experiments with obstetric ultrasound and reached results which cast doubt on the inter-operator reliability of ultrasound measurements of the foetus. Both were central figures in the White Paper committee and appeared as expert witnesses at the first consensus conference.

The three *Feminist Doctors* are all specialists in community medicine. All have academic, clinical, and administrative careers, and all are active in a larger group of feminist doctors which holds regular meetings and seminars. Their "names" in this paper refer to some feature of their careers or roles in the controversy which differentiates them from one another. They are:

Dr C (*The Columnist*), who is an associate professor of general medicine and medical columnist for a women's magazine. Her first formal involvement with the ultrasound screening question was as a member of a subcommittee for the White Paper on perinatal care. She was also a panel member for the first consensus conference.

Dr R (*The Reviewer*) is also an associate professor of general medicine. She became involved in the controversy when a hospital in her community sent out a memo that all pregnant women were to be sent for two routine ultrasound examinations. She and a colleague searched the literature and found no evidence of benefit from the procedure. They challenged the hospital CMO to document the basis for the new policy, and as a result the screening programme was reduced to one examination per pregnancy. Dr R has continued to use critical literature review as her main tool for participation in the controversy, publishing mainly in the form of letters to medical journals and to newspapers.

Dr P (*The Community Practitioner*) had a similar experience which was triggered by a women's organization in her practice requesting annual clinical examinations for breast cancer. She searched the literature on screening programmes in general in order to set up a scientifically grounded screening programme and found that screening was rarely worthwhile at all. As with Dr R, Dr P was at least partially successful in limiting the community health service's screening activities. She has also been a contributor of correspondence to medical journals, and has served on a number of policy committees and consensus panels (including the first panel on ultrasound in pregnancy) on screening and health service priorities issues.

This brief presentation covers just a few of the many arenas in which these seven have sought to influence the implementation of ultrasound screening. Note that all seven are also intermediary users of ultrasound screening, either as clinicians on behalf of their patients and/or as researchers on behalf of the population as a whole. Thus, even aside from their activism in the debate, they are all spokespersons in the ensemble construction process.

Since the case in point was an ongoing controversy in which the "battles" were spread thin in time and space, the most convenient form of data was interviews. In the interviews, I asked each of the informants how they came to be involved in the debate, what their roles in the debate were, how they would explain the success of the technology, and how they thought the debate would unfold in the future.

As with all retrospective interviews, we must assume that the informants' responses are framed to justify their actions and standpoints in the eyes of the interviewer and the interviewer's anticipated audience. The interviews cannot be taken, statement by statement, as simple accounts of fact. Some statements relate documentable events and chronologies. These I have confirmed, where appropriate, through supplementary documents.

Other statements refer to the informants' own and their opponents' motives, or to the meanings and consequences of actors, actions, and artefacts. These statements do not so much *report about* as actually *constitute instances of* the ascription of meaning to the elements of the ensemble or cyborg(s) which concern us here. The validity of these statements as data is not so much a question of whether they are true or false regarding the meanings and motives they claim to report, as whether they are common or highly particularized instances of their respective sources' polemical claims. Are these claims tailor-made to convince me, or are they claims the same actors have offered to the public in general? Based on comparisons of the accounts offered in the interviews with those presented in public media, I am convinced that the interviews were not tailored for me in particular.

Screening Is a Many-Gendered Thing

Women, Feminists, and Techno-fear According to the Leading Expert

Masculinity is unmarked as gender in the configuration of ultrasound screening presented by the Leading Expert. Men are not mentioned as a category or set of attributes. Women do appear in two user roles – as pregnant mothers and as health professionals (midwives and doctors). Mothers, however, appear briefly and are then abstracted away almost to the point of invisibility.

> *Dr A*: "A pregnant woman, as a woman, comes to her doctor. She gets examined and one gets one's information, but the foetus is and remains hidden, and there are very few conditions where the foetus signals that something is aberrant. But with ultrasound diagnostics we have a technological method to examine the foetus and get information. And we gynaecologists have become more and more aware of the problems around unsure gestational age. And in 1976–77–78 all bleedings in pregnancy were examined with placenta scintigraphy, which is an isotope technique. And there are a lot of conditions that bleed, right? Many pregnancies bleed, and all that became ultrasound work. And then a little later, in 1977–78, all the abortions came along so that we learned to use ultrasound early in pregnancy. And then came the foetal growth controls in 78–79 when we started

getting serious about foetal growth retardation. And more and more indications came along. Twins came in, and . . ."

In a sense the pregnant woman becomes transparent. She becomes only what is inside her: a pregnancy, a diagnosis, twins, etc. (see also Oudshoorn, 1994, for a similar instance where women are translated into menstrual cycles). The trouble is, she is not transparent. She is opaque, a problem for her doctor, a challenge which ultrasound conquers by making her transparent in more than an abstract sense.

The woman's contribution is her compliance in bringing her opaque body to the doctor to be seen through. Only late in the interview do we hear that women actually *want* to be seen through for reasons of their own, that they actively seek and value this procedure because they are *fearful* that they themselves or the babies they are carrying might be ill. We are told that they seek reassurance or, if their fears are confirmed, treatment. And when the only "treatment" offered is abortion, we are told that most women prefer that to carrying the baby to term, and that those who do not accept or are not offered abortion seek information. Although women (according to the narrative) seek these things, they are nonetheless distressed by them. They need comfort and counselling, which the ultrasound lab therefore also provides.

Briefly, around 1984, women's fearfulness was turned against ultrasound when they were misinformed by journalists that ultrasound might be dangerous. This was successfully countered by exposing doctors and journalists to better information by means of an international conference. Now women are a resource for the ultrasound lab. About 3500 women annually come to the lab for routine scans. They represent a resource for the knowledge the lab gleans from them concerning the attitudes of normal women and the development of normal foetuses. Through experience in routine scanning, the laboratory also gains credibility among the doctors from whom they receive special cases by referral. More directly than the routine-scan women, referred women are a resource base for the lab's national and even international reputation as a centre of skill and expertise. These women also contribute to the development of foetal medicine. Last but not least, screening and referred patients are a rhetorical resource: they are proof that women want ultrasound screening.

The other role in which women appear in this configuration is as health professionals. Here Dr A does not refer to women as a general category. He does make a few categorical references to midwives, a practically all-female profession, but for the most part he refers to particular oppositional women and particular oppositional men. These references to professionals might at first glance seem gender neutral; but there are differences between the roles allocated to midwives and doctors and differences between the behaviours and motivations attributed to individual men and women, which are gendered in traditional ways.

Much of Dr A's narrative focuses on the organization of ultrasound diagnostics. He has put a lot of effort into his organizational model, in which both routine and selective ultrasound are centralized to laboratories with a large enough catchment area to hone staff expertise. At these laboratories, routine ultrasound is performed by specially trained midwives, selective ultrasound by specialist doctors. As we shall see in The Midwife's presentation, some midwives see this as a professional insult and a threat to their skills; but, in his interview with me, in the tour he gave me of the lab, and in morning meetings at the lab, Dr A presents this as a form of job enrichment and status elevation for midwives. These midwives have become experts, more skilled in foetal diagnostics than most general practitioners. They serve as "contact midwives", providing information and emotional support for mothers who receive a diagnosis of some foetal abnormality. They do research on diagnosis of abnormalities in a routine scan situation and on normal parameter distributions in a screening population. They are encouraged to publish and to present their research at international conferences.

Dr A sees this as in midwives' professional interest, and midwives as a natural supporting group for ultrasound screening. But he is also aware that many midwives are of another opinion. At one morning meeting, Dr A asked the midwives who among them were planning to attend the upcoming annual meeting of the Norwegian Association of Midwives. None were – ultrasound was not on the programme for the meeting, attendance was likely to be boring and possibly even unpleasant (there being considerable opposition to Dr A's laboratory model). Dr A urged them to reconsider. A motion on ultrasound training or ultrasound lab organization might come up from the floor. "We have to be there. We have to be strongly represented there." In light of opposition to Dr A's organizational model from midwives' organizations, the job enrichment aspects of the midwife role at Dr A's lab can be seen as strategic counter-moves.

In the interview, he portrays one oppositional midwife as isolated, but his comment at the morning meeting indicates that he fears she is not so isolated. When it comes to oppositional doctors, he seems much more confident of their isolation. They are few; they are poorly informed about ultrasound diagnostics; they are ineffectual in the discourse: "They've had no effect whatsoever." He mentions men and women oppositional doctors in approximately equal (small) numbers, but in gender-different terms. The men are portrayed as representing the establishment. They are powerful and/or old. It is their positional defensiveness, their age, their lack of vision which misguides them to oppose the young, up-and-coming, visionary doctors who are introducing the technologies of the future. This is presented as an unfortunate but normal aspect of professional relations. The women are portrayed as unprofessional, irrational, emotional, perhaps misled by a general fear of technology, perhaps by feminist values which most (normal) women do not share.

Oppression and Suppression of Gender in The Midwife's Presentation

The Midwife's involvement with ultrasound began when she attended a course at Dr A's laboratory. She came from the course enthusiastic about ultrasound screening and was responsible for setting up the screening programme in her own hospital catchment area. Since then, however, she has become sceptical towards ultrasound. She cites four main sources for her growing scepticism: negative reactions she has received from screened women, the realization that the scientific evidence for screening is weak, the observation that other aspects of natal care are cut back to make room on the budget for ultrasound, and the observation that ultrasound screening programmes impinge on midwives' professional autonomy and job content. This last point carries special weight as it is interwoven with midwives' interpretation of pregnancy as a normal condition and pregnant women as ordinarily competent to manage that condition.

The Midwife's narrative focuses almost exclusively on reasons for opposing ultrasound screening. Even her explanations for the success of the technology quickly turn to reasons for opposing it, which quickly turn to midwives' professional interests, which are in turn a defence for women's autonomy in general. However, the final, profession-related, reasons against are negotiable up to a point. If ultrasound screening could be organized in such a way that midwifery maintained its professional content and autonomy, which also implies maintaining the view of pregnant women as normal and competent individuals, then she might accept it. As of now, that condition allows the acceptance only of clinical (i.e. selective) obstetric ultrasound.

Her portrayal of women as patients is brief. One feature is their relationship with nature. The Midwife emphasizes pregnancy and childbirth as natural processes which women, with proper support, can generally manage well. Physicians are portrayed as implanting self-doubt in these women, robbing them of their natural capabilities and luring them into dependency.

> Midwife: "Midwives are concerned that if we let technology take over, we'll have let women down. I think what women going through a normal pregnancy need are things primarily midwives can provide."

By warding off physician interference, midwives allow women's natural state to revive. This image of women's nature complements midwife (residual) monopoly position in assisting normal pregnancy and delivery, as opposed to physician (expanding) monopoly on intervention.

As in the Leading Expert's configuration, fear is another key feature of the pregnant condition. But whereas the Leading Expert promises women a release from fear, the Midwife claims women need no such release, that their ability to deal with fear in pregnancy is a sign and a source of their strength, that it shows (or even makes) them capable of dealing with the various natural outcomes of pregnancy. By "releasing" women (whether by realistic or false promises) from the fear of negative pregnancy outcomes and by "protecting" women from information about the possible outcomes of ultrasound examination, physicians rob women of autonomy and self-reliance, of the moral strength needed to accept the care of handicapped children, and of the moral legitimacy needed to demand social support in caring for those children. Midwives, on the other hand, would inform women as to what a routine ultrasound examination might reveal, and find women capable of dealing with that information, even to the point of opting not to comply with the offer of a sonogram. Midwives in antenatal care seek a role as counsellors to rather than carers for pregnant women, helping women care for themselves, and defending women from unnecessary physician intervention.

Whereas Dr A positions himself as a foetal doctor to whom pregnant women are secondary, the Midwife places the pregnant woman in the primary client role with foetuses emerging as independent entities only near the end of the midwife/mother relationship. Given this female predominance, given the male predominance among gynaecologists and (to a lesser extent) general practitioners, and given the many feminist histories of professional conflicts between midwives and physicians, it is striking that the Midwife portrays conflicts and congruencies of interests between midwives, physicians, and pregnant women in absolutely gender-neutral terms. Midwives are portrayed as taking a protective stand between physicians and normal pregnant patients, but this is based solely on professional skills and values. Only once does the Midwife even hint (through a shift from "them" to "we") that being women themselves, midwives share a special empathy with their pregnant patients:

"I think, though, that women who are pregnant, we always carry a little bit of fear inside us."

Tensions between midwives and doctors in the Midwife's configuration go beyond their relations to the shared patient group. Midwives are portrayed as threatened by doctors' implementation of ultrasound screening. Under threat are midwives' autonomy, skills, working conditions, and status; offered in compensation are research opportunities and university degrees. But midwives are, she claims, already often more competent than gynaecologists, in spite of the latter's degrees and (formal) research qualifications. Physician arrogance, evidenced by their offering midwives special training and degrees in ultrasonography as a "carrot", is a subject The Midwife describes with intense anger. But here too, she is angered at the insult and oppression dealt one profession by another, not one female profession by a male one. The proposal is seen as an insulting assumption of midwives' motives:

"He was trying, as I see it, to buy us, to tempt us with this prize. Then I said that 'For us, it's not a question of degrees and careers, the way it is for you. It's a question of preserving the profession of midwifery in the midst of this.' This business of training and 'Now you'll get a degree' and all, that's not what midwives are concerned about."

It was also seen as an attempt to encroach on the content and autonomy of midwifery:

"Midwives are concerned about integrating this into the profession and not de-skilling the profession."

And it was seen as an arrogant and unwarranted assumption of superior competence:

"But they've made plans for an ultrasound course that is to take a full year as specialist training for midwives. And then I have to ask 'But what about the doctors?' 'No, doctors ... you'll never get doctors to take a full year.' For them, this is part of their training in gynaecology, where they get a one-week basic course, the same course I had where the one thing I learned was that I hadn't learned enough. So the plan is to demand more of midwives than of doctors, in spite of the doctors being placed in charge of us in terms of responsibility."

As spokesperson for midwives as a group, The Midwife warns that they will not simply allow these insults and incursions to take place:

> "We can't accept that. . . . Because this is causing considerable frustration among midwives: they sit there and know more than the doctors and then the doctors don't take seriously what the midwives are saying. We're not through with this debate by a long shot."

But all these claims are made on behalf of midwives as a professional group, not as a gendered one.

The absence of gender as an aspect of professional conflict in the Midwife's configuration can be seen as an extension of nurses' professional situation and strategies since the interwar period (Melby, 1991) and of the even longer-standing "settlement" between midwives and obstetricians in which midwives have a limited autonomy in the physician-bounded realm of normal pregnancy (Hiddinga and Blume, 1992; Witz, 1992).

The (Ir)relevance of Gender in the Sceptical Specialists' Configuration

The Sceptical Specialists both reached their scepticism towards ultrasound screening on the basis of their own research. Science, as they see it, speaks against ultrasound screening. The voice of science, however, has not been strong enough to stop implementation of the technology. The Sceptical Specialists see Dr A's personality and entrepreneurial efforts as a key to understanding the successful introduction of ultrasound screening in Norway. Dr A has tied together powerful interests through his enthusiasm and his rhetorical and clinical skills. But, eventually, science may be joined by other voices and lead to the abandonment of ultrasound screening.

One voice the Sceptical Specialists are surprised not to have heard so far is the collective voice of protesting women, especially as science erodes the authority of ultrasound technology in setting gestational age:

> Dr E: "Let's say the matter of determining due dates gets more and more fuzzy. I think Dr A et co. are going to have major problems

defending themselves in that debate, because they have too weak a documentation of what's so splendid about their method of determining due dates."

So the Sceptical Specialists await the day women will rise up against the insult of this technology telling women when they got pregnant. As science demonstrates that the major effect of ultrasound screening is to encourage abortion of malformed foetuses, they also await the day women will rise up in moral outrage. Together, the voices of women and science might be sufficient to stop the practice of ultrasound screening:

> *Dr E*: "So let's say that aspect crumbles and there's not much left of that effect, and they're really left with just the discovery of a few malformations and terminating those pregnancies. Do you think something will happen with public opinion then? Take the women themselves up to the year 2000, who will be facing any consequences of the way one can be left to go on recklessly within obstetrics with that technology. What do you think? Is it conceivable that women's organizations and feminist groups might react more on an ethical–moral basis against that sort of practice? That's the only thing I can see that could stop this."

Meanwhile, these men are puzzled, even disappointed, that women's voice is not yet audible:

> *ARS*: "But there are also all those women who want to see an image of the baby?"
> *Dr E*: "Yes, I see that. That's the sort of thing that will maintain it. And I suppose most people won't really have such strong moral scruples against maintaining such a service in order to scrape out 1 percent of the children. No. Norwegian women have been fairly inactive, that's true, compared with a number of other countries."

These men do not claim to speak for women. They are waiting and hoping for women to speak for themselves. Their expectation that women some day will do so is based on how they imagine they themselves would feel if someone used an under-documented technology to usurp their self-knowledge. But they have no elaborate strategy for bringing women to speak up. Their only strategy is to continue speaking out in the name of science.

Genders and Interests According to the Feminist Doctors

Of the four informant groups, the Feminist Doctors give the most detailed list of elements in the ultrasound screening ensemble. They differentiate between the professional interests of specialists (who, seeing a pre-selected patient group, get an exaggerated picture of the benefits of a procedure) and general practitioners (who face the problem of convincing healthy people they are well). They add the ultrasound equipment industry to the list of actors involved in speeding up the implementation of screening. They elaborate on the ways the screening programme is linked to administrative and regulatory routines such as the service fee system and the second opinion requirement for second-trimester abortions, whereas rules which might have served as deterrents to rapid implementation have been neglected. They see an alliance with the mass media as one of Dr A's tools for what they call the "medical seduction" of both colleagues and patients. Having created a market demand for ultrasound screening through medical seduction, and having financed and legitimated the procedure through links with health service policy and bureaucracy, ultrasound screening gradually becomes an obligatory passage point for medical practitioners.

This all starts, they claim, with a male network of enthusiastic specialists who see the technology as a vehicle for their mutual ambitions:

> Dr C: "What's going on up there in Trondheim, it's an alliance among the boys, isn't it? We all know that. A mutual alliance between Dr A and his CMO who build each other up and protect each other and have a network."

Then further practitioners are recruited into the network via a shared male fascination with technology and a shared male distrust of women patients:

> Dr C: "If one had listened to women a little and to what they say about what working is like late in pregnancy, then maybe one would

have got this thing with pre-delivery leave worked out a bit sooner. NOW we have it, but it's many years late. But of course, the boys have been more interested in technology."

Still more practitioners are recruited through professional seduction (courses and conferences) or prostitution (the economic advantages of offering screening). Finally, the remainder are forced into the net through defensive medical practice.

> *Dr C:* "You might ask me how I feel about sending people to ultrasound examinations when I know how little it counts. I would answer that I don't have the courage to be the one who stands alone with a completely different medical practice than the official recommendations. I wouldn't dare take the chance that something might go wrong and that that woman hadn't received the same services as other women get. That would leave me exposed to suits, and I wouldn't put myself in that position."

To the Feminist Doctors, male professionalism is not a neutral standard from which female professionalism deviates or is excluded. Nor is gender irrelevant to profession. Instead, gender (both masculinity and femininity) and profession (including specialization) are intersecting processes which create distinctive points of view and styles of practice. Male specialists and female (feminist) generalists are portrayed in stark contrast. They characterize the male specialist role by its emphasis on autonomy from and authority over both patients and less specialized practitioners, achieved by discounting patient-dependent information and relying on practitioner-controlled technology. Male networks are described as competitive and status oriented. If normal, the male regime is normal only in the statistical sense that it is frequently observable, not in the sense that it is natural or inevitable.

Feminist practitioners, they claim, form feminist networks, which are egalitarian and mutually growth oriented. Dr A interprets the Feminist Doctors' activities in the debate as devious, conspiratorial, furtive. The Feminist Doctors see themselves as democratic and objective. If deviant, their network is deviant only in the sense that it represents an underrepresented and oppressed group, or even that minority of the group which is conscious of and consciously opposes their oppression. This minority, however, sees itself as standing on the side of truth in science and in that sense as representing normality.

One example of the feminist network in action is their response to a newspaper article based on an interview in which Dr A was quoted as saying that not to let all pregnant women have an ultrasound examination would be unethical. Attributed to Dr A in an article in *Aftenposten*, Norway's largest newspaper:

"We know today that approximately 2 percent of all children who are born in this country have some form of developmental aberration. With an ultrasound examination we can discover this aberration and already in the foetal stage implement measures to repair the damage and thereby give the child better life chances after birth."

The feminist network viewed this as a misrepresentation of the statistics on what percentage of foetal aberrations ultrasound can diagnose and what percentage of those again can be successfully treated. They registered a complaint against Dr A with the medical association ethics committee. This, they claim, was accomplished in typical feminist network fashion:

Dr P: "Then, in true women's fashion, we shared out the tasks."

They portray feminist practitioners as dealing with their patients in a similarly cooperative, non-hierarchical fashion:

Dr P: "I haven't had pre-natal check-ups since January, but the last two to whom I offered amniotic diagnosis said, 'No. That's not a choice I could make [to abort an abnormal foetus], so I'd rather not put myself in that situation.' That was without my informing them especially in advance. But most don't know, or don't count on, or haven't considered that that is a relevant issue when it comes to ultrasound. This brings us back to the question of informed consent, and also to the issues that concern me from the feminist research perspective – things like: Do we empower women to take charge and trust their own resources? Are they to feel the baby kick inside them and experience that as something positive in itself? Or do we teach them that it isn't relevant, that they have to see it on a screen for it to be real? Are we to give them the information they need to make valid choices in their own lives? Or are we to decide what's good for them and what's not? And there are basic philosophical differences in the population here, where Dr A and I probably belong to different camps."

They see Dr A's and other similar experts' view of these women as paternalistic almost to the point of misogyny. According to the feminists, pregnant women in the experts' view are unreliable and potentially ill; their every claim (when they last menstruated, when they had intercourse, how they are feeling) as well as the normality of their condition must be tested and clinically confirmed before it can be accepted. In contrast, the feminists find women to be normally competent and healthy, but subject to self-doubt. If this self-doubt is exacerbated by exposure to experts, women risk actually losing their self-knowledge, their self-care responsibility – even their physical health, since screening entails the risk of false positive diagnosis which can lead to over-treatment. Rather than seek autonomy from and authority over patients, the Feminist Doctors seek to encourage and empower women to build on (and thereby build up) their own self-knowledge and self-caring skills. They see women patients as reliable sources of information, information which ought to have more impact on individual health care and on health policy, a view practically identical to that of the Midwife.

The Feminist Doctors also present arguments on science issues in the controversy. In terms of empirical practice, they demand the same statistical stringency as the Sceptical Specialists. Their critiques of Dr A and allies' scientific claims and their descriptions of their own scientific work imply in addition a gendered view of social practices in the scientific community. For instance, they claim that paternalistic experts relate differently to their patients in the "before" and "after" phases of the establishment of expertise. "Before", patients are research material. They are in possession of knowledge and skills which the expert seeks to acquire. In this phase, the experts must accept the patients' reliability and defend it in the scientific community because it constitutes the reliability of the experts' own research data. "After", once the expert has constructed his own scientific knowledge, future patients' reliability is discredited. Paternalist medicine de-skills patients much the same way capitalist engineering de-skills workers. In contrast, the Feminist Doctors propose a medical science in which the patient's reliability remains constant, regardless of the construction of knowledge in the professional community. Science well practised would take a sceptical, evaluative stand with respect to its own creations. Within its own community, it would be democratic; cooperative; non-racist, non-sexist, etc.; mutually growth encouraging.

Science well practised would also be broader. The Feminist Doctors give less primacy than do the Sceptical Specialists to conclusions drawn within what the Feminists see as a narrow, Western male tradition in medical science. Whether or not ultrasound screening can be proven to reduce perinatal mortality, the Feminist Doctors see serious ethical challenges facing it concerning patient autonomy, the shrinking sphere of what is deemed "normal", and the abortion of "abnormal" foetuses. These challenges are related to their construction of women's ethics as a result of their social situation.

Women's role in the care of others tends to socialize women as the caretakers of certain moral values as well, such as the acceptance of human variation. In presenting women, unwarned, with the choice of aborting malformed foetuses, medicine alters the structural basis for women's moral socialization. Women's personal desire for healthy children and an unburdensome motherhood comes into conflict with less immediate, society-level values such as respect of and care for the disabled. This leads to the corruption of social values otherwise maintained by women. Were women to organize as a group, they would have the power to resist the pathologization of their normal states, the medicalization of their lives, the discrediting of their knowledge, the corruption of their morals. Their resistance remains rare and fragmented owing to the authoritarian and uncritical ways in which medical "expertise" presents itself to them.

Rhetorical Moves in Ensemble Descriptions

In the previous section I presented four accounts on ultrasound screening, with an emphasis on their descriptions of women and

men, femininity and masculinity. Each presents a different interpretation of ultrasound screening as an ensemble or cyborg. Dr
A's cyborg is a benevolent one, consisting of ultrasound equipment, compliant mothers, skilled midwives, and expert doctors.
Drs G and E portray a wasteful cyborg consisting of ultrasound
equipment, biased doctors, and passive women. To the Midwife,
the cyborg is a dangerous linkage of ultrasound equipment with
powerful doctors, de-skilled midwives, and disempowered
mothers. To the Feminist Doctors, the ultrasound screening
cyborg is a patriarchal construction of ultrasound equipment,
technophilic doctors, and women subordinated to (but sometimes
also rebellious against) a male medical definition of pregnancy.

All of the activists in the ultrasound debate take on self-
appointed roles as spokespersons – both for some group with
which they identify themselves and for a number of other groups,
artefacts, and phenomena. All purport to speak with the voice of
Science, for instance. All, with the possible exception of the Sceptical Specialists, purport to speak on behalf of women.

Sometimes they claim these voices as their own. Elsewhere in
their accounts, they position themselves as interpreters of their
opponents' voices. When voicing standpoints with which they
align themselves, they often lend them the authority of Nature,
Truth, and Science: things simply are so. Standpoints they distance themselves from are often deconstructed as coloured by
greed, or particular social interests, or simple misunderstandings.
Portrayals of femininities and masculinities appear in both modes.
Thus, each account contains a set of images of good, natural femininity and contrasting images of bad or misguided femininity. In
some, femininity is also contrasted with masculinity, either explicitly or by implication (with femininity marked as gender and
masculinity implied as the default, or normal category).

The claims of gender interests are interwoven with those
claimed for the other groups, artefacts, and phenomena. Gender
becomes a relevant aspect of professional obstetric practice, of
scientific practice, of the distribution of knowledge between body
and machine. And vice versa, science, machines, professions
become relevant aspects of gender. In each such move, gendering

occurs in two ways: masculinity and femininity are (re)constructed by the inclusion of objects, groups, or phenomena; and, objects, etc., are masculinized or feminized by their inclusion in those constructions. As when Dr C says, "But of course, the boys have been more interested in technology" – masculinity is constructed as technophilic, and technology as masculine. Whether we see this as construction of a cyborg or an ensemble depends merely on the focus of our analysis.

In invoking "women" and "men" as relevant social groups, these activists invoke whole *relevant social controversies* into the ultrasound issue. Profession is an aspect of gender controversy and vice versa. Abortion has been a feminist issue. Both profession and gender debates are implicated in discourse over the form and role of science in medicine. Gendered characterizations are invoked in connection with every other theme of controversy connected with ultrasound screening – the science issue, the abortion issue, the issue of the division of labour between physicians and midwives, and so on. Referring to the metaphor of the "seamless web" we might say that ultrasound screening is one square of a larger tartan, with several controversies running through it on the warp and gender crossing and re-crossing them on the woof.

The four accounts presented above differ not so much in which social groups are deemed relevant or in the boundaries delimiting those groups as in the characteristics attributed to them and the consequences of those characteristics with respect to ultrasound screening. For instance, pregnant women are a relevant social group in all four narratives, but what are their shared traits and how are those traits relevant to ultrasound services? Gender controversy in this case is a controversy not over relevant social groups, but over *relevant attributes* of those groups. In this particular controversy the existence of gender is for the most part assumed, but its meaning is still being (re)negotiated.

In this renegotiation process, however, the activists are not inventing gender "from scratch". There are no new versions of gender being propounded here. Each account links ultrasound screening with different pre-existing conceptions of masculinity and/or femininity – conceptions already available from other arenas of gender controversy. In ascribing sets of gendered attributes to relevant social groups, the activists align themselves with positions in the corresponding social controversies.

There is no reason to believe that they calculatingly choose their alignments to maximize their power in the ultrasound controversy. We may safely assume that alignments with oppositional social movements or with hegemonic views on gender are, at least in these cases, a consequence of which truths each actor holds to be self-evident. Nevertheless, the alignments are there and are consequential for the relative success of the respective actors' ensemble-building efforts.

Dr A's ascriptions of gendered attributes fall readily within hegemonic views on masculinity and femininity (for a discussion of hegemonic gender see Lie, 1995). This makes Dr A's ensemble-building job that much easier. He does not need to change people's deep-seated views, something his opponents to a greater or lesser extent would have to do. Men are widely associated with science, medical science, rationality, technical mastery; women with emotionality, caring roles, fear, techno-fear. When Dr A explains that women need reassurance during pregnancy, that physicians can provide that reassurance through expert diagnostics, that midwives can contribute by providing routine diagnostics and emotional support – he can expect most people simply to nod and accept the arguments.

His opponents have more of an uphill battle. When the Midwife portrays fear as a source of feminine strength, when both she and the Feminist Doctors portray lay pregnant women as at least as expert on the state of their bodies as specialist physicians, when the Sceptical Specialists anticipate that women will react against ultrasound screening on the basis of the scientific evidence – the general response is not likely to be a simple nod, more likely a thoughtful and somewhat sceptical tilt of the head. These claims are not outrageously far-fetched, but neither are they commonly assumed knowledge.

This difference in the breadth of the acceptance base for the four accounts is due not so much to the respective terms they associate with gender as to the *meanings* they ascribe to those terms and the *values* they ascribe to those meanings. Nature and Body are both commonly associated with femininity, but they are not commonly taken to imply knowledge or power. Gender-neutrality is commonly associated with professionalism and science, but this does not commonly imply that women have equal access to or authority within such fields. Both Dr A and the Feminist Doctors associate women's aversion to ultrasound screening with aversion to technology. Dr A portrays this as a flaw, a failure to recognize the objective interests of women – feminism gone awry. The Feminist Doctors portray it as a sound scepticism, a competent technology critique – feminism at its best.

As alternative constructions of gender – alternative, that is, to the current hegemonic position – the three oppositional narratives do not represent alternative sets of gender-associated attributes. Rather, they represent alternative meanings ascribed to attributes found among the hegemonic set, or alternative values ascribed to meanings already available within that set. Pivoting on ambivalence and contradictions within the hegemonic construction of gender, they contribute to its destabilization and aim towards its restabilization at some new point. For some, the destabilization of, for instance, pregnant women as cyborg is incidental to the main project of destabilization of the ultrasound screening ensemble. For others the reverse is true: gender is the main project and any constituent technological ensembles are incidentals. For all positions, oppositional or otherwise, the constructions of gender and of ultrasound screening are simultaneous and interdependent processes. At all levels – as institutionalized practices, as social groups, as sets of attributes, and as sets of meanings – the socio-technical ensemble and its constituent relevant cyborg groups (or vice versa, whichever view you prefer) are stabilized, destabilized, and restabilized together.

Though most apparent in a state of controversy, this would also be true if the dominant narrative reigned unopposed. Dr A's narrative also contributes to some marginal change in the construction of gender. Like a builder in concrete using steel reinforcement, Dr A builds his ultrasound construction on widely accepted views of gender. Probably inadvertently, though clearly to the advantage of the ultrasound structure, he thereby ingrains those views of gender marginally deeper, making both the ensemble and cyborg constructions marginally more stable at their current positions.

Does this mean that Dr A effectively shapes the (gendered) everyday lives and identities of ultrasound screening providers and end-users, and that they in turn passively accept the structures and meanings he offers them? No. Or at least, not necessarily. Nor are the daily providers and end-users of ultrasound screening relegated to choosing among the structures and identities offered by activists within the debate as a whole. Some scope for selectivity and creativity certainly remains, though it remains unexplored in this paper. However, daily providers and end-users *are* inescapably confronted with the usage structures Dr A has successfully implemented. It is those structures which they must address, however selectively and creatively they do so. And they are inescapably confronted with the public statements of the most prominent activists in the debate, statements which they may (must?) selectively and creatively appropriate.

At least in the short term, structures and statements based on hegemonic interpretations are more likely to be proposed and more likely to be appropriated at face value. No calculation or conspiracy on the part of successful entrepreneurs is implied. But neither is long-term success guaranteed. However apparently stable, and however much they contribute to their own further stabilization, constructions so complex contain ambivalence and contradictions which carry a potential for destabilization.

BIBLIOGRAPHY

Akrich, M. 1992. The de-scription of technical objects. In W. E. Bijker & J. Law (eds): *Shaping Technology/Building Society. Studies in Sociotechnical Change*. Cambridge, MA and London: MIT Press, pp. 205–24.

Backe, B. 1994. *Studies in Antenatal Care*. Trondheim: Tapir.

Backe, B. and Buhaug, H. 1986. *Konsensuskonferansen 27–29/8–1986. Bruk av Ultralyd i Svangerskap*. Trondheim: NIS.

Cockburn, C. and Ormrod, S. 1993. *Gender and Technology in the Making*. London: Sage.

Collins, H. M. 1985. *Changing Order. Replication and Induction in Scientific Practice*. Chicago and London: University of Chicago Press.

Ewigman, B. G. et al. 1993. Effect of prenatal ultrasound screening on perinatal outcome. *New England Journal of Medicine*, Vol. 329, No. 12, pp. 821–7.

Haraway, D. 1989. *Primate Visions. Gender, Race, and Nature in the World of Modern Science*. New York and London: Routledge.

Haraway, D. 1991. *Simians, Cyborgs, and Women. The Reinvention of Nature*. London: Free Association Books.

Harding, S. 1986. *The Science Question in Feminism*. Ithaca, NY and London: Cornell University Press.

Hiddinga, A. and Blume, S. S. 1992. Technology, science, and obstetric practice: The origins and transformation of cephalopelvimetry. *Science, Technology, & Human Values*, Vol. 17, No. 2, pp. 154–79.

Hughes, T. P. 1983. *Networks of Power. Electrification in Western Society, 1880–1930*. Baltimore, MD: Johns Hopkins University Press.

Latour, B. 1987. *Science in Action. How to Follow Scientists and Engineers through Society*. Milton Keynes: Open University Press.

Latour, B. 1991. *We Have Never Been Modern*. New York: Harvester Wheatsheaf.

Law, J. and Bijker, W. E. 1992. Postscript: Technology, stability and social theory. In: W. E. Bijker and J. Law (eds): *Shaping Technology/Building Society. Studies in Sociotechnical Change*. Cambridge, MA and London: MIT Press, pp. 290–308.

Lie, M. 1995. Technology and masculinity: The case of the computer. *European Journal of Women's Studies*, Vol. 2, No. 3, pp. 379–94.

Melby, K. 1991. Women's ideology: Difference, equality or a new femininity. Women teachers and nurses in Norway 1912–1940. In: T. Andreassen, A. Borchost, D. Dahlerup, E. Lous and H. Rimmen Nielsen (eds): *Moving On. New Perspectives on the Women's Movement*. Aarhus: Aarhus University Press, pp. 138–54.

NFR [Norges forskningsråd].1995. *Bruk av ultralyd i svangerskapet. Konsensuskonferanse*. Oslo: NFR.

NOU [Norges Offentlige Utredninger]. 1984. 17: *Perinatal omsorg i Norge*.

Odelstingsproposisjon. 1993–4. 37: *Om lov om medisinsk bruk av bioteknologi*.

Oudshoorn, N. 1994. *Beyond the Natural Body. An Archeology of Sex Hormones*. London and New York: Routledge.

Pinch, T. J. and Bijker, W. E. 1987. The social construction of facts and artifacts: or how the sociology of science and the sociology of technology might benefit each other. In: Bijker, Hughes and Pinch (eds.) *The Social*

Construction of Technological Systems. Cambridge, MA/London: MIT Press, pp. 17–50.

Sætnan, A. R. 1995. Just what the doctor ordered? A study of medical technology innovation processes. Doctoral dissertation, Trondheim, Faculty of Social Sciences, University of Trondheim.

Sørensen, K. H. (ed.) 1994. Driver versus vehicle: The car as a micro network. *Technology in Use. Two Essays on the Domestication of Artifacts.* Working Paper No. 2, Trondheim: Centre for Technology and Society, pp. 12–19.

Tuana, N. (ed.). *Feminism and Science.* Bloomington: Indiana University Press.

Turner, V. 1966. *The Ritual Process: Structure and Antistructure.* Chicago: Aldine.

Witz, A. 1992. *Profession and Patriarchy.* London and New York: Routledge.

Woolgar, S. 1991. The turn to technology in social studies of science. *Science, Technology, & Human Values*, Vol. 16, pp. 20–50.

Zuckerman, H. et al. 1991. *The Outer Circle. Women in the Scientific Community.* New York: Norton.

Chapter 3

Technologies of Autonomy?
Parenthood in Contemporary "Modern Times"

Guri Mette Vestby

Parenthood as a Socio-technological Interrelationship to Childhood

In one generation, the social relationship between children and parents has changed comprehensively. I want to explore how technology may challenge our ideas about that social relationship: how does it affect dependence, belongings, fostering, socialization, power relations, and democratization? Technology can be explored as a catalyst of change in cultural ideas and codes for parenthood and childhood, and it is mutually affected by the continuous reconstruction of these phenomena.

The complementary roles of childhood and parenthood stand out as social and cultural phenomena as much as biological ones. Accordingly, they will be continuously transformed and reconstructed. The interplay between the material and sociocultural changes of new technologies provides a different basis for performing parenthood as well as childhood in the 1990s. The meaning of childhood is implicated in the meanings of parenthood, and vice versa (Alanen, 1992). Studying the relationship as a social category that significantly influences children's as well as parents' behaviour and actions, this specific relationship stands out as a dialectic, expressive, and multiplex one. When a child is born, the birth of the parents is also taking place. From that day, the construction of parenthood, the formation of a parental identity, is a continuous process significantly expressed within a social, cultural, and material context. Through the daily interaction with children, adults will be socialized to parenthood (Vestby, 1989).

My study of technology in the everyday life of children has therefore also been an investigation of modern parenthood. The reconstruction of parenthood is explored in the light of the nature of the social relationship between parents and child – in this study, children in pre-puberty, a phase dominated by an increasing range of autonomy. The relationship between parents and children is a multifaceted one, but its characteristic quality is the balance between care and control, between autonomy and dependence (Gulbrandsen, 1989; Haavind, 1979). What differ are the specific domains and routines of everyday life that are subject to these balances and their gradual alteration. In this paper, I focus on the technification of some domains and routinized interactions within which the modern reconstruction of the relationship takes place. The perspective of change includes generational changes as well as changes due to the development of the individual child.

Children of 11–12 years will try to work out many different "projects of autonomy", proceeding tentatively towards a balance between subordination and desires for more freedom. Each day may represent a stretching of limits, through too many minor, often routinized actions and activities clearly reproduced within the social relationships, and, as I will show, within a socio-technological context. The balance between dependence and autonomy is studied as it is expressed through routines and standards, regulations and rules. These expressions are basic guides in everyday life, though constantly changing, imperceptible, or, as a result of verbal negotiations, mutually influencing family interaction and the ways in which the relationship between parents and children is reconstructed.

I will pay attention to the parents' exercise of care and control, the way they encourage as well as limit the child's "projects of autonomy", and how the daily performance of parenthood is afforded in a complex way within technological frameworks. The interplay between technology and the current cultural ideology of parenthood is a pervasive topic. I will show how new parental tasks have emerged in the wake of new technology, such as media and screen activities, and that changes in social roles and relationships seem to affect the use of traditional technology as well. As an example of the latter, I have chosen the telephone.

Until now, the field of technology and everyday life has either ignored children, or interpreted and presented them largely as victims (Larsen, 1986; Postman, 1982; Thorne, 1987) or receivers subject to adults' or society's spending of time and resources (Cronberg, 1986, 1987; Vestby, 1988). Most studies of children and technology focus on new technologies such as television, videos, and computer games, with an emphasis on the shaping of personal competences and on the possible harmful effects on the individual child (Feilitzen, Forsman and Roe (eds.) 1993). The study of use is mostly isolated from social context, and, as importantly, the child as a social and active individual actor does not come out strongly.

In the sociology of childhood, the agency of children is increasingly emphasized. So are the mutual shaping processes of childhood and its material basis. Studies of media, technology, and everyday life have begun to examine the social dynamics of the appropriation and use of objects (Livingstone, 1992; Silverstone, 1994; Silverstone et al., 1991). There are several approaches which assume that social and technical changes are intervoven, though they differ in terms of theoretical position. One is the so-called social constructivist approach to technology. This is an attempt to apply sociological understanding of knowledge as a social construction and negotiation to the case of technology and technological practices, an approach which sees this process as driven by the social interests of participants (Bijker and Law, 1992). A related approach is to analyse how technological devices are domesticated into family life and shaped by the complexities of family interactions (Strathern, 1992).

With reference to the process called *domestication* (see Chapter 1), Silverstone (Silverstone, 1994; Silverstone et al., 1991) argues that the way technology is used offers possibilities for identity formation and identity communication. On the other hand, the particular culture and identity of the family provide the basis for the ways in which technology is consumed and for the negotiation of the social and symbolic meanings of the technologies. The values and cultural standards of a family are expressed through *objectification* – the way in which the technologies are displayed. By putting the social dynamics of families into focus, I want to understand the objectification also as part of the performance of parenthood, as an expression of the current cultural ideologies of being a parent.

The term *incorporation* refers to the process in which a technological object is incorporated into the routines and rituals of everyday life, the way it is used, and the ways it becomes functional. A telephone might for example have many functions; I am studying it as an instrumental as well as expressive equipment, as a tool in the children's construction of autonomy and independence and in the parents' exercise of care and control. The use and the functions, the display and the values, are dimensions in the process of *differentiation* with regard to age, as much as to gender and family culture.

Modern Norwegian parenthood is culturally shaped by an ideology that prescribes engagement and involvement in children's lives. The child is in many ways seen as a social "product" of the parents' capacities, competences, and values. The work of overseeing children's development may then affect parental self-opinion and identity.

In the analysis of the relationship between technologies and human interactions, I have chosen to focus on how parents act and what artefacts they use when they stimulate as well as restrain their children's construction of autonomy. For example, might technology help to extend the field of parental insight and control, or will it be a means of reducing it? The outcome will affect children's reconstruction of identity in pre-puberty, which is naturally based on an increasing autonomy. Another motivational purpose of involvement might be to counteract the division of activities characterizing the modern family, that is, to sustain the family as a social and cultural entity.

Through the incorporation of technology in daily life, adults will show themselves, their children, and the world outside the family what kinds of values, attitudes, and capacities they possess. Most important is the capacity of the family to sustain itself as a social unit, and, as I suggest, the way in which it meets society's ideological demands of parenthood and how technology may or may not be an integral part of the emergent strategies. This articulation of identity is called the phase of *conversion* in the domestication process (Silverstone, 1994; Silverstone and Hirsch, 1992).

Silverstone sees the consumption of information and communication technology as a way in which the family or the household defines and claims for itself and its members a status of cultural competence in the wider society. The domestication of technology is studied as an articulation of family identity. It is, however, questionable whether the family as a cultural entity is a different phenomenon from that of the total of its members, insofar as the children are constructing *their* identity and the mother and father are constructing *theirs*. I will therefore try to see some of the moments of the process of domestication in the light of the construction of parental identity, linked to the children's construction of identity based on increasing autonomy. These parallel processes of identity formation are integrated in the internal family interaction of everyday life.

Research Methods

Traditionally, one gets information about children, and parents, by asking the parents and other adults. The children have increasingly been appreciated as interviewees and sources of knowledge about childhood. So they are in my study. However, it was when I began my analysis of the interviews with children that I really started to understand how much information about modern parenthood they in fact communicated. Empirical data from the children emerged as a source of knowledge about the construction of parenthood.

Fifty children aged 11–12 years were interviewed about their activities and social interactions that took place the day before the interview. Children of this age normally leave school at 2 p.m. The investigated topics included the way different technologies are incorporated in the routines of everyday life. This study of the social implications of different technologies and socio-technological practices includes information and communication technology such as the telephone and the car, as well as new technology such the television, the VCR, and computer games. The interviewees were also asked about the use of domestic technology such as microwave ovens, electric stoves, and other household machines.

The children lived in three different places in Norway: an established satellite town, a new suburban area, and the countryside at the coast. The semi-structured and open-ended interviews, following an interview guide that focused on specific themes, lasted for about one-and-a-half to two hours.

In 15 families the parents were interviewed twice. The first interview with the parents was about their own childhood, while the topic of the second one was the everyday life of their present families, emphasizing the life of their children and the performance of parenthood.

Remote Parenthood and Socio-technological Projects of Autonomy

The incorporation of technology in the taken-for-granted daily routines reflects a set of ideological concerns. I will try to point out how the domestication of technology reflects cultural codes of the ideology of parenthood.

One basic challenge to modern parenthood is to cope with the demands of care and involvement, to encourage children's autonomy and self-reliance, and to negotiate the realm of self-management in terms of control and restraint – all within an everyday life where family members participate in different social arenas. The particular social situation of children at home while the parents are at work is in addition to the different leisure activities of the family members. This has altered the nature of social interaction and made the performance of modern parenthood and the construction of parental identity different from those of the previous generation.

A main concern is the role played by technology in the way the parents rise to these new challenges. Does the use of technology facilitate, substitute for, or compensate for some aspects of social interaction? Does technology function as a catalyst to alter the nature of social interaction and the reproduction of social relationships between children and parents?

The notion of control is central to my interpretation of the construction of autonomy and the sustaining of dependence. Different kinds of control are exercised by adults and children, depending on the technology used and the various reasons and purposes structuring the use. To control the actions and behaviour of another person is different from controlling your own life.

At the age of 11–12, children often want more autonomy and self-management, but they still need different kinds of care. Thus, they still accept, although in varying degrees, some involvement which implies elements of control and management that would be unacceptable to adolescents. But, as I will show here, the parents also consciously encourage the child's development of autonomy. In the morning, before the children go to school, quite a lot of them are alone or with siblings – without any direct parental supervision.

At first Beth (11) flatly refused a new arrangement which implied that her mother would go to work early – leaving home at 6.30 in the morning. Beth was not used to staying alone at home. Her mother says she thinks it will be good for Beth to be more independent and autonomous. The daughter was used to having a mother who made the arrangements and took care of everything. And, since Beth is the smaller of the siblings of the family, they do not want her to be too overprotected.

Nowadays Beth is on her own in the morning, and she has to get up by herself, but her parents set the alarm clock for an appropriate time an hour before school starts.

While watching television, Beth eats her breakfast prepared for her by her mother. Her mother phones every morning at 8 to check if everything is all right, and "because Beth thinks it is cosy".

> After a while her mother asked her how she found the situation, and Beth answered: "Actually I am quite pleased. It is good to be spared your importunities and worries." But while she said this she thought perhaps she had been too honest (so her mother says), so Beth added: "however, I do miss you."

This sounds like an ordinary everyday life situation. And it really is! But imagine for a moment that the information and communication technologies we are used to had disappeared; if the family were to be without telephone, alarm clock, or television, the situation would have been quite different. When we look at the morning routines, characterized by distant interaction, this makes the telephone stand out as an artefact of care as well as of control. The telephone makes the new arrangement in the morning feel safe, to both the child and her parents. In this case, the parents wanted their daughter to become more independent. Still, they use both telephone and alarm clock to exercise some control but also to help her not to be too late for school. In making breakfast ready before she leaves, the mother makes it easier and at the same time expresses care for her daughter. And the daughter fills the empty house with the sound of a television programme.

Many of the children in this study who were alone in the morning reported some telephone communication in order to help them to cope with being alone, and to check that everything was all right. Although the telephone is a tool that is useful in the process of growing more independent, it is also used to construct a feeling of safety and to exercise control.

> Maren (12) lives in the countryside. Her parents both leave home at 5.30 in the morning to go to their jobs in town, where her mother works in a store.
> Maren gets up and looks after herself in the morning. Every day she calls her mother: "Three 'rings' of the phone, mama does not answer – then she knows that I'm awake. That's the signal. I must phone before 7.15, otherwise mama will call me to check that I'm awake and that everything is ok."

The routinized interaction is completely based on technology, but a non-verbal communication may nevertheless express elements of care and control.

The everyday life of modern families has created a need for autonomous children who can look after themselves because the parents are not at home as much as the school children. This structural change in employment and in family lives between the generation of childhood in the 1950s and that of the 1990s was caused by various transformations in society. Modern family life is above all structured by the employment of both parents. In the past generation in Norway about 90 percent of mothers worked at home. Nowadays just as many are employed in paid jobs, either full time or part time. The impacts on the social structure and the daily activities in families as regards presence, together-ness, and (in)dependence have been significant. In the few families where the mother (temporarily) stays at home, children will often receive more practical care, more things will be arranged for them, and the possibilities for supervision and control are extended. Studies of children's work at home have shown that children whose mothers are employed in paid jobs tend to do more housework and to be more autonomous (Solberg and Vestby, 1987).

To combine "remote parenthood" with children's construction of autonomy seems like an elegant solution: one expects children to be more independent and autonomous when parents are not at home for large parts of the day. Solberg (1994) argues that, by letting them manage on their own and thus become the new "homestayers", parents will probably see their children as more capable and independent than before. Children in the families she studied appreciated the lack of adult supervision. The house, when vacated by adults, gave the children a great deal of freedom.

My study of the everyday life of 50 boys and girls living in dif-ferent places in Norway also shows that most children are alone in the early afternoons, though often with some friends, and that only a few of them seem to miss the presence of parents. Access to a telephone is probably one reason that this is accepted. However, a closer investigation of the frequent telephone commu-nications does reveal that many parents are intervening at a dis-tance in this situation of everyday life, and that this interaction might reduce the degree of independence. The crucial ideological demand for involvement and support that is shaping modern parenthood seems to make the performance of parenthood more complicated. The space for self-management and autonomy among children, mediated by technology, has to be balanced to meet these outside ideals.

The following example from the home of Henrik may illustrate how parents get involved and try to exert some control and how these contexts also make a space for self-management. Making friends is also a relational process that takes place within this situation, though I will not deal with that relationship in this paper.

> Henrik (12) and his friends used to stay at his house after school. The house is empty of adults before Henrik's mother gets home 3–4 hours later. The peer group consists of 3–4 boys, some of them two years older than Henrik. Almost every day their main activities are to make something to eat and to play computer games, or they watch television or a video. Periodically, the boys play a lot of computer games, while at the same time eating the food they have prepared. They prefer pancakes, toasted cheese sandwiches, or porridge.
>
> Henrik's mother tells me she sometimes thinks there is too much of both pancakes and screen activities. But this is not subject to her control, at least the use of information technology is not. The periodically large consumption of food, and the consequential mess in the kitchen, have been a subject of discussion, argument, and negotiation within the family. Henrik and his parents have made an agreement (or the parents claimed such an agreement): the boys may stay at home, but they have to phone the parents in advance to get permission, and they have to clean up the kitchen after preparing food. Henrik always calls his father first at his job. "They know whom to ask first," the mother replies, "because father is disposed to give them permission." (It is the mother who comes home first, and I suppose the work of cleaning the kitchen is her job if the boys have not finished, which is often the case.) But usually the father tells them to call mother; it is mother who says "yes" or "no".

The boys' strategy if the answer is "no" is to move to the house of one of the other boys. The actual question is not whether they will get permission to prepare food or not, but *where* this activity will take place; a change of residence regularly occurs. A similar story about cooking may be told about a girl living in the same area:

> Today Dorte was the first to arrive home. She called her mother and asked if she (and her friends) could make toasted cheese sandwiches. She was not allowed to, because her mother said Dorte then wouldn't want her dinner, and they should have blueberry soup and pancakes (which Dorte likes very much). The mother said that Dorte can eat quite a lot of cheese sandwiches if her parents don't put any restrictions on it. She also would like to cook every day if she was allowed to. Dorte and her friends are at the age when cooking is something they like to do when they are two or three girls alone at home. She always phones to ask for permission, that's the agreement. First she calls her mother, then her father. If they get a "no", they try to get a "yes" at one of the other homes.

Parents' ability to exercise remote control over children's activities after school may be fairly inefficient, as shown in the cases of Henrik and Dorte. Although the actual control is not very strong, the children's actions and construction of autonomy are significantly restrained through the actual possibility of communication. This may reduce the extent of self-management, because the child loses the real margin of "trying and failing". Rather than taking the risk of making a decision on his or her own, and thereby growing more self-reliant, the child may always phone one or other parent for affirmation or permission, and to ask for advice or help in practical situations. My study shows that this is exactly what they do. When the child is in doubt, the phone is available. Thus, the phone facilitates the constructing of a safety net that may hamper the development of autonomy.

From the parents' point of view, their way of using the telephone may help them to have some control, to coordinate family activities and interactions, to express care, and conform to the dominant ideology of parenthood. Here, technology is incorporated into the daily work of involvement and looking after the children. Thus, it functions as a conversion of parental identity.

The type of control communicated by the telephone consists of restrictions on activities, actions, and behaviour to keep children within negotiated norms and agreements. The interaction between care and control seems more intricate, because it also includes the kind of control which is about insight and knowledge, as the basis for a general overview of children's everyday lives. A typical example is the mother phoning her young daughter to find out if she is safely home from school, and if everything is all right. This is a kind of positive control, based on care-taking.

> Maren (12) tells me that she always has a talk on the telephone with her mother when she gets home from school. "It will vary whether it is mother or I who calls … so mother knows that I am safely home from school, that things are all right with me. And I ask her about different things, for example what I should prepare for dinner, or if I may go somewhere."

On closer examination, such small, apparently not very important, talks might have multiple functions. The telephone helps to substitute for the presence of the mother. The mediated face-to-face interaction is about care (to check the daughter's well-being) and about control of her movements outside the home, and includes communication of practical messages concerning the preparation of dinner and the daughter's contribution to it. The mother's control is two-sided: to check that her daughter is all right, which means having knowledge and insight, a type of control that expresses care and that may function as a basis for the second kind of control: to control the girl's specific actions and behaviour. The interference is perhaps also an intended support of the child in her own construction of increased independence.

This incorporation of the telephone in the social relationship between mother and daughter means that they build a common mode of understanding about the complex of care, control, and autonomy.

The adults' control of children at home often seems to coincide with the child's wish to talk to one of the parents, just to talk to them and not for any other specific reason. Or do children want some control over their parents by knowing something about where they are and when they will come home?

Stian (11): "I am usually alone at home after school. Every day I phone my mother at work. It is just to say 'hello', and mother wants to know how it was at school. And I want to know if father will pick her up in the afternoon and at what time they will get home. I just like to know."

Stian's information about his parents' movements differs from that of Maren's mother. Stian has no possibility of control in terms of affecting their movements. What he wants is to be able to foresee events and thereby to feel in control of what will happen over the next few hours, including who does what, when, and where. Control is reciprocal, if not symmetric.

The telephone is of vital importance in care-taking and the reproduction of social relationships within the family. It is a "building block" of social relationships, and it helps to make the situation of being alone at home feel safer for both the child and the parents. Also, for younger children it facilitates constant training to be able gradually to take over responsibility for care. They may now act independently at an earlier stage, because they have access to remote assistance. This is not so insignificant as it might seem. Anyone responsible for raising children has experienced the reduced workload when children are able to look after themselves. In the period of transition, we find a special kind of cooperation over care-taking between the child and the parents (Vestby, 1990; Wadel, 1984). Both actors are important to the result, and they use the telephone as a vital artefact to achieve the goal of self-reliance.

The interviewees told me about telephone calls to both mothers and fathers at their workplaces, including all the elements described above. But a closer investigation of the reports by the children reveals a gendered interaction between adults and children. First, telephone calls between children and fathers are mostly initiated by the children. Fathers seldom call their children, unless it is for a specific reason, usually an instrumental one, and never "just to say hello . . .". Though the father in many families is the authority in several decisions concerning his children's lives, he seems not to want to control children's acts and activities when he is at work. Second, it is the mother who calls the child for expressive reasons – "just to hear that everything is ok". It is also the mothers who use the telephone to check on the children's actions and activities – the combined exercise of care and control (in the sense of overview and knowledge). It seems that mothers more than fathers tend to feel responsible for the organizational demands of everyday life. Members of modern families spend considerable time and resources outside the home, making lots of appointments and arrangements. Thus, the "appointment family" (Schultz Jørgensen, 1988) has to construct social gatherings and to build family unity into their everyday lives. As a consequence, interaction between the family members is characterized by independent actions and unifying processes, in which the telephone plays an important role. The telephone has a function in the unifying processes because its incorporation into family life facilitates the capacity of the family to sustain itself as a social entity. As a domestic technology, it is objectified through the symbolic affirmation of dependence, belonging, and children's autonomy. An increasingly autonomous child will be less dependent on the parents, but the belonging between the members of the family will not necessarily decrease or disappear, though it changes character as the child grows older.

The incorporation and objectification of the telephone reveals an artefact useful for sociability, participation, care-taking, the exercise of control, the construction of autonomy, and organization. The children are important actors in these processes. The reproduction and symbolic confirmation of social relationships may be the real, but "hidden", motives. This is also a question of being aware of the so-called "meta-communicative" aspect of talking (Bateson, 1972). In social relationships it is often more important that you make a telephone call, write, or pay a visit. The content of the talk or visit is not always as important as the symbolic confirmation of a social relationship.

The cultural *scripts* for the use of telephone, whether it is regarded as an instrument mainly for expressive or instrumental interactions, seem to vary not just with the gender of the child (Livingstone, 1992) or gendered parenthood as shown above. The concept "remote mothering" (Rakow and Navarro, 1993) refers to employed women's use of the telephone to manage practical and emotional responsibilities for children. My study shows that the scripts differ as much with the age of the actors and with the specific relationship between the participants interacting. The incorporation of the telephone will differ with age because the telephone is used in different ways and for different reasons. Furthermore, children are not, in most families, given the opportunity to act as subjects in their own right in the process of incorporation. The way the telephone is used by children is mainly decided by the parents.

In a family, the power of definition is integrated into family dynamics, emphasizing the positions of the family members. Children's everyday life stories tell me that parents have the power of definition in terms of decisions about the children's telephone calls: What kinds of calls are important and what kinds are unnecessary? What kinds of restrictions and rules are put upon the children's telephone calls respectively to the parents, to other adults, and to their peers?

The children in my study did not mention any restrictions on calling their parents at work. Acknowledgement of the open, and partly hidden, needs of communication, characterizes the use of this technology within the child–parent relationship. It helps the parents in their performance of parenthood, and the children in their performance of childhood.

When the actors are two children, however, nearly all parents put restrictions on the use of the telephone. Children are allowed to call friends to give messages, to ask questions about school work, or to make appointments about leisure-time activities – in other words, for "instrumental" purposes.

> Anders (11) says that when he is alone at home after school he may call his friends if he has a specific question to ask, or if he wants to make an appointment to play or to meet. "But telephone conversations must not last more than 1 minute, that is the rule," he says.

To prevent children from just chattering, parents have constructed the rule that only "instrumental" topics are allowed. In addition, they restrain talk with a limit of 1 minute. The power of definition is used by the adults, taking into consideration the child's legitimate and reasonable phoning in an age-dependent way. It seems as if "expressive" reasons are not appreciated in themselves, but must be "instrumentally" embedded.

I consider the restrictions put on the children to be a lack of appreciation of the telephone as a facilitator to reproduce friendship among children. This contrasts with the adults' own behaviour: they often put forward just such a reason for their own calling of friends by phone – just to have a talk. They see this as an important way to nurture the continuous process of building friendship. So, it depends on the age of the actor whether this use of technology is appreciated or not. Also, not all children are allowed to phone adult relatives for expressive reasons. But the child might decide not to obey the rules:

Ellen (12) lives in the countryside. Every day she calls one of her friends to arrange to meet after dinner. "Actually I am not allowed to use the phone, but since neither my father nor my stepmother is at home, I do it anyway – both to my friends and to my relatives who live nearby. I am not supposed to call my grandma or my aunt; they live too near for calling. But I like to talk to them when I get home from school. Then I have to stay at home and take care of my little 2-year-old sister. I usually pick her up after she has stayed with our relatives in the morning."

Thus, the domestication of the telephone is clearly based on age, as the parents define the importance and the modes of telephoning of the children. Compared with the gendering shown by Livingstone (1992) and Rakow and Navarro (1993), my study indicates that the telephone might be gendered in another way. I have shown that the female and the male parent do not use the telephone for the same reasons and in the same ways. However, even if telephone calls by boys and girls at the age of 11–12 are not (yet) much different in terms of expressive versus instrumental purposes, the everyday practice of telephone calls with their parents might enhance the difference between men and women as mothers and fathers.

Children's Screen Activities: Another Field of Modern Parenthood

A new parental task that has emerged in modern families as part of technological change concerns children's consumption of technologies such as television, VCRs, and computer games. VCRs and computer games did not exist when the parents of today's 11–12-year-old children grew up. Thus, they lack adequate models for regulating screen activities based on their own experiences.

Parents I have interviewed can say when the first television arrived in their family, perhaps not the exact year, rather that "we were the third family in the street" or the "first in the neighbourhood". Many remember visits to neighbours or relatives who were the first owners of televisions, and how the "lucky owners" opened their homes to numerous, curious watchers. They can also say what kinds of programmes they watched regularly, including the aquarium fish of the breaks between programmes. The process of domesticating the television in those days, from appropriation to conversion, must have taken place in a more public way, with various audiences both considering and participating in the family's use and display of that technology, offering the opportunity of building family identity.

In those days it was not a question of restricting children's use of television. Rather, it was a question of how to see as many programmes as possible. It was a new world which offered new possibilities for entertainment, information, and knowledge, but limited by the fact that Norway had only one channel.

This has now changed. Television is no longer a limited, educational experience or harmless entertainment. It presents large amounts of crime, war, and violence. Most of the children I interviewed had rules and routines to limit the amount of action and violence, and of time spent watching television, and to state how late in the evening they might watch, especially when the next day is a school day. But definitions of what is "too much", "too violent", or "too late" seem to vary a lot, depending on standards and attitudes derived from local culture as well as the parents' group of reference.

For children, decisions about television or video use are "projects of autonomy" in everyday life, often involving negotiations and stretching of limits. They want no rules, or fewer restrictions, and look forward to getting more freedom to make independent decisions. Parental opinions vary on the subject, though many parents are worried and want to have some control over the quality as well as the quantity. It is this category of parents who think they have to protect their children from the very flow of impressions, which in their mind contain many negative and worrying elements.

The computer game debate is another field of care and control of modern parenthood. Parental opinions tend to be categorized in an either–or dimension – either positive or negative. However, reality is more complex, as we can see in relation to computer games. A few parents do not bother too much about what their children do and what kind of experiences they have to deal with, as long as they are occupied with something and do not disturb the adults. However, most of the parents with no restrictions on computer use were thinking in terms of care. In their accounts they care about the child's training in technological skills, or they want to support their child's interests. They want to be a kind parent, who contributes to fun and amusement for the child.

The different parental practices seem to be embedded in the same ideological framework of caring and future orientation. But the understanding of care is fundamentally different. Some parents will not purchase computers or computer games, or they put restrictions on use, being of the opinion that screen activities in general, and computer games in particular, might influence the child's personal development in a negative way. Other parents will provide much of the new technology just to show that they care about the future of their children: "I cannot fix it, but Eddie [the son] is a skilled player. He beats me every time! The computer is the future. You will have to be a skilled user of computers in the future!" the father proudly declared. The encouragement expressed by parents is thus based not only on the potential for entertainment, but as much on the potential for learning from this kind of activity. They see it as a first experience with computer technology, which in their opinion is of great importance in modern society.

Domesticating computer technology might be seen as both an individually based process of the child and an interactive process based on the relationship between the child and the parents, constructed of both the child and the adult but in different ways (see also Aune's paper). Through the way the father supports his son's playing, and the reasoning he communicates, different kinds of display take place: a display of objects, a display of future orientation, and a display of the son as a skilled player, possessing a modern competence. This is the conversion aspect.

Eddie's father declared that few of his son's friends have as many computer machines or as much software as Eddie has. In the appropriation of technology, he expresses also a father's care for his son and his future qualifications. For this reason, he does not put any restrictions on his son's use of computer games. The "caring control" is not absent, but it is expressed in another line of reasoning: if Eddie is occupied with computer technology at home, then the father knows where he is and what he is doing. The father regards the streets as a dangerous place; he is worried about what might happen there, so he wants to protect his son. Thus, the use of this technology works as a safety net. It is a means of preventing unwanted action in another arena.

The opposite parental view of computer games is that they are a sedentary activity that keeps children inside the house instead of being outside playing with other children. Because the screen offers a kind of company which might replace real interaction with peers, some parents are worried that their child would not develop appropriate social skills. The technologically skilled but lonely player is not a desirable option. But again, means and ends are not connected in the same way by all parents. Computer games might play a role in the construction of friendship. The reason some parents purchase this technology is precisely to prevent loneliness, thinking of computer games as a social magnet.

The category of anxious parents seem frightened of the supposed disturbing effects of computer games. The encouraging parents are more concerned about what will happen if their children do not acquire the competence of using computer technology, which they see as quite important in the future. However, a remarkable fact is that this is a concern related to boys, not to girls. Because computer technology is not of particular interest to the girls, one could perhaps have anticipated a greater degree of parental worry about *girls'* lack of technological qualification. None of the girls talks about parental worry because of their minimal interest, or about any parental restrictions because they play too much. Computer games have become an element in the interaction between parents and sons, whereas the interaction between parents and daughters is characterized by the non-existence of computer-related negotiations and expectations. The gendered worry is not just a difference related to sons and daughters. It seems that mothers more often, and to a greater degree, than fathers are worried about the negative impacts of computers. The fathers' worry is about the eventual lack of technological skills. Again we see an interesting double loop of gender.

To make independent decisions about playing computer games is a "project of autonomy" for many boys. In addition, computer games might represent a kind of symbol of autonomy for this generation of children. A new generation gap might perhaps emerge, in which the games of today are just a warning before Virtual Reality, "surfing" the Internet, and e-mail leave many unfascinated adults in an ambivalent state of ignorance. Perhaps Turkle (1984) was right when she indicated that the computer game debate expresses a more general ambivalence towards new expertise and rapid changes, a wish to buy time against a new way of life.

Through their children's use of the media, and the related rules and regulations, parents will communicate something about their own orientation and competence, both inside the family and towards the children. The content of the screen activities as well as the patterns of consumption provide a basis for their presentation of self.

If parents want to follow the ideology of involvement that prescribes engagement and support in relation to socio-technological actions and interactions, it will result in work for them. The kind of work implied by different screen activities is mostly unnoticed, and thus not much appreciated. It is incorporated into the taken-for-granted daily activities and interactions in the society of the family. By looking at this special field of technological consumption within a framework of cultural ideologies of parenthood, it is possible to become aware of what concrete kind of tasks are included in the daily performance of parenthood. Parents who are involved probably have to study the actual programmes or the computer games, discuss them with their partner, perhaps talk them over with other parents, and make the negotiations with the children. And if they are involved but with regulations, more attention has to be paid to the giving of directions, to evaluation, and to sanctioning. The negotiations with children, the arguments and explanations required of the young ones of today before accepting limiting rules, might also be quite demanding. This is not a once and for all task, it is more or less continuous work. The child will often try to stretch the limits, arguing again and again, practising new strategies, and introducing new programmes, movies, or computer games which possibly will imply changes in the rules or a different practice. The child's own development as s/he grows older will also bring about renegotiations.

Children also tell me about parents who think they have to watch particular movies or programmes together with them if they believe them to be violent or otherwise problematic. Current ideology prescribes that parents should talk with their children about what they have seen, in order to prevent negative psychological effects. It is the same reasoning as for going to the cinema – current rules in Norway state that, when the age limit is 15 years, younger children may be admitted if accompanied by an adult.

My study shows that the performance of parenthood will vary a lot: a few parents are very protective and deny computer games or videos, a few others at the other extreme are ignorant or do not care. Most parents, however, voluntarily perform their roles in ways that are demanding in terms of effort. The most attention and most work are required by those parents who want to be "protectors" or strict "regulators".

Thus, the interplay between technological practice and the cultural ideology of parenthood imposes effects on the nature of the interaction between children and parents that did not exist a generation ago. The rapid change in information technologies, generating new products and possibilities, might accordingly increase this kind of parental work.

Control versus Autonomy in the Domestication of Everyday-Life Technologies

This study has shown how and in what way parental exercise of care and control is embedded in technology, as well as how new demands of "caring control" emerge from technological changes, such as screen activities. To domesticate television, VCRs, and computer games means different things to different family members. The nature of adults' and children's construction of domestic technologies differs – symbolically and practically – and much of family interactions involves negotiations of control and autonomy related to the use of technology.

Contrary to the traditional understanding of the child as an object, especially when parenthood is the focus, the approach that enhances the agency of the child will provide another basis for knowledge about the construction of parenthood as a mutual shaping process with active participants continuously reconstructing and negotiating identities.

I have also questioned some other social implications of the use of technology, and that is the reverse side of parental integration into children's lives. When the adults conscientiously gain more insight and knowledge, it may result in a higher degree of control and more regulations. Viewed in this way, the use of technology such as telephones might have a restraining effect on the construction of children's autonomy, as well as facilitating independence. The telephone is made meaningful both in the performance of parenthood and in the construction of childhood. Telephoning is a significant part of family dynamics as an element of expressing care, control, belonging, dependence, and growth of autonomy. Domestication of the telephone affects the nature of the interaction between the child and the parents, which in turn contributes to a reconstruction of parenthood.

Parental support of children's daily life activities might furthermore be understood as actions symbolically confirming unity and belonging, or expressing parents' interest and engagement in their children, considering them as social "products" of parental contribution and support. In this way, technology is domesticated in terms of conversion – articulating publicly the social competence and the cultural capacity of the parents. The supporting behaviour may, however, be interpreted as an interference that facilitates the exercise of power and authority. It can also be explained as a way of having control, or the feeling of control, over an increasing complexity in a changeable society. Thus, the process of domestication offers possibilities for forming and communicating parental identity.

One actual question to be investigated is whether the current ideology of involvement is a kind of gendered ideology – if there exist different versions for motherhood and fatherhood, and if mothers as a consequence of caring tend to control their children to a greater degree than fathers do. According to Livingstone (1992), control can mean different things to men and women; the construct of control is gendered. For women, she says, control refers more to keeping potential domestic chaos at bay, keeping things under control, and having control over things. For men it means allowing the expression of expertise, permitting the exercise of control or power. She found that men valued the challenge posed by domestic technologies and talked in terms of the potential rewards offered. My study supports Livingstone's view in that the women, as mothers, have control of their children because they want to keep things under control, a kind of supervision in which fathers do not seem to be as much engaged. In relation to their children, men's perception of control seems to be the regulating of specific detached actions and activities, and the maintenance of norms or rules, when they are confronted with them. As described in the discussion about the telephone, fathers seldom call their children from work to ensure that everything is all right or to have control of the situation in terms of overview. Is this an expression of a lack of caring? Is it a conscious training of the child's independence, or just confirmation of the dividing line between the public and the private that guides men's everyday life? Nevertheless, it is a relevant question to ask if this type of non-controlling parental behaviour might increase the possibilities for the child to act autonomously. The domestication of technology, in the way it is culturally integrated in family dynamics, allows the perspective of gendered parenthood.

Technological artefacts, such as the telephone, structure the exercise of parental "caring control". I have also looked at how new tasks of "caring" control emerge from technological change, such as in the field of screen activities. The reasons for controlling children's screen activities vary from the worry about physiological damage caused by too much television or computer games, to the worry that children might develop negative or violent personality traits, to the worry about lack of social skills. The reasons for control in terms of regulations concern both the present and the future. However, this is an adult perspective. The children I interviewed do not attach importance to the development aspects based on future reasoning. To be a child is in one way to live in the present; in another way it is to be extremely occupied with the future. And this engagement in the future is above all concerned with control. Children look forward to increased independence and autonomy, to be less controlled – to be able to make independent decisions, gradually to be spared parental supervision, and, finally, to be mainly responsible for themselves by gaining control and autonomy. Such questions are given close attention by girls and boys aged 11–12 years. While they are on their way to an independent position, there are many small, but important, aims of autonomy in everyday life.

Children's increased ability to act autonomously involves the competence to have a grip on the situation and a general overview of the course of action, comprising a qualification to cope with the reality of everyday life. This is a kind of control that significantly characterizes the identity formation of the self-reliant child. Domestication of technologies is a continuous and often conflicting process that offers possibilities of identity formation within the complexity of family dynamics and family roles. The way technologies are used, incorporated, and displayed reveals the negotiation of the social and symbolic meanings of technology in the relationship between children and parents.

REFERENCES

Alanen, L. 1992. *Modern Childhood? Exploring the "Child Question" in Sociology*. Research Report No. 50. Jyväskylä: University of Jyväskylä.

Bateson, G. 1972. *Steps to an Ecology of Mind*. New York: Ballantine.

Bijker, W. E. and Law, J. (eds). 1992. *Shaping Technology/Building Society. Studies in Sociotechnical Change*. Cambridge, MA: MIT Press.

Cronberg, T. 1986. *Teorier om teknologi og hverdagsliv*. Copenhagen: Institut for organisation og arbejdssociologi, Nyt fra samfundsvidenskaberne.

Cronberg, T. 1987. *Det teknologiske spillerum i hverdagen*. Copenhagen: Institut for organisation og arbejdssociologi, Nyt fra samfundsvidenskaberne.

Feilitzen, C. von, Forsman, M. and Roe, K. (red.) 1993. *Våld från alla håll. Forskningsperspektiv på våld i rörliga bilder*. Brutus Östlings Bokförlag. Stockholm.

Gulbrandsen, L. M. 1989. Barns sosiale nettverk. In G. Gregersen (ed.): *I ungers eget rom. Rapport fra forskerkonferanse*. Oslo: Kultur- og vitenskapsdepartementet.

Haavind, H. 1979. Omsorgsfunksjoner i småbarnsfamilier. In: *Lønnet og ulønnet omsorg*. NAVF Working Paper No. 5. Oslo: Norwegian Research Council of the Humanities and the Social Sciences.

Larsen, S. 1986. *Nya tider – nya barn?* Malmö: Liber.

Livingstone, S. M. 1992. The meaning of domestic technologies. A personal construct analysis of familial gender relations. In R. Silverstone and E. Hirsch (eds): *Consuming Technologies. Media and Information in Domestic Spaces*. London: Routledge.

Postman, N. 1982. *The Disappearance of Childhood*. New York: Delacorte Press.

Rakow, L. and Navarro, V. 1993. Remote mothering and the parallel shift: Women meet the cellular telephone. In: *Critical Studies in Mass Communication*, Vol. 10, No. 3.

Schultz Jørgensen, P. 1988. Børn i en foranderlig verden. In M. Kjær Jensen (ed.): *Interview med børn*. Report No. 9. Copenhagen: Socialforskningsinstitutet.

Silverstone, R. 1994. *Television and Everyday Life*. London: Routledge.

Silverstone, R. and Hirsch, E. (eds.) 1992. *Consuming Technologies. Media and Information in Domestic Spaces*. London: Routledge.

Silverstone, R. et al. 1991. Information and communication technologies and the moral economy of the household. In K. H. Sørensen and A.-J. Berg (eds): *Technology and Everyday Life. Trajectories and Transformations*. Report No. 5. Oslo: NAVF–NTNF–NORAS.

Solberg, A. 1994. *Negotiating Childhood. Empirical Investigations and Textual Representations of Children's Work and Everyday Life*. Dissertation No. 12. Stockholm: Nordic Institute for Studies in Urban and Regional Planning.

Solberg, A. and Vestby, G. M. 1987. *Barns arbeidsliv. En undersøkelse av 800 10–12åringers arbeidsoppgaver i hjem og nabolag*. NIBR Report No. 3. Oslo: Norwegian Institute for Urban and Regional Research.

Strathern, M. 1992. The mirror of technology. In R. Silverstone and E. Hirsch (eds): *Consuming Technologies. Media and Information in Domestic Spaces*. London: Routledge.

Thorne, B. 1987. Revisioning women and social change: Where are the children? *Gender & Society*, Vol. 1, pp. 85–109.

Turkle, S. 1984. *The Second Self. Computers and the Human Spirit*. London: Granada.

Vestby, G. M. 1988. *Barns teknologiske hverdag. Tema, perspektiv, problemstillinger*. NIBR Report No. 16. Oslo: Norwegian Institute for Urban and Regional Research.

Vestby, G. M. 1989. *Voksnes "barnebilder" og barns status. Om barn som kunnskapskilde og bidragsytere*. Oslo: University of Oslo, Department of Sociology.

Vestby, G. M. 1990. Omsorgssosialisering. Barn som omsorgsutøvere og omsorgsobjekter. *BARN*, No. 4, Trondheim.

Vestby, G. M. 1994. Constructing childhood: Children interacting with technology. In: *Domestic Technology and Everyday Life. Mutual Shaping Processes*. Brussels: COST A4, EC Directorate General, Science, Research and Development.

Wadel, C. 1984. *Det skjulte arbeid*. Oslo: Universitetsforlaget.

Chapter 4

The Computer in Everyday Life
Patterns of Domestication of a New Technology

Margrethe Aune

The Computer as a Cultural Factor

This paper presents a study of the personal computer's entry into Norwegian daily life (Aune, 1992). It examines the cultural integration of the computer and its significance to the users' everyday life. Male users dominate computer use and computer cultures, at least outside households (see Bomberg et al., 1989; Haddon, 1988; Levy, 1984; Turkle, 1984). What is the situation "inside" households? Does male dominance influence women's use? I shall analyse the integration process of computers from both a male and a female perspective.

What happens to our everyday lives when we start using new technologies? Do we fit the use of new artefacts into our everyday lives and integrate them into our routines, or do we initiate new forms of use that break up, or even explode, the routines of everyday life? These questions can be illuminated by studying processes of integration as a *domestication* of the technology (Silverstone et al., 1989; Sørensen, 1991). "Domesticate" is used here in several senses: "1. To cause to be at home; to naturalize ... 2. To make domestic; to attach to home and its duties ... 3. To tame or bring under control ..."[1] In a figurative sense, this means to handle something alien in such a way that *it is adapted* to your everyday life, and *your everyday life is adapted* to this new and hitherto alien artefact. This is a two-way process in which both technology and humans are affected, and in which both technical and social features are changed. The computer becomes, in the same way as other objects in our environment, a part of our cultural identity and capacity.

Previous research on the use of personal computers in everyday life has mainly been surveys of computer use at home (Croné, 1990; Dutton et al., 1987). Only a few studies treat the domestication of the personal computer more explicitly (Haddon, 1988, 1991; Hebenstreit, 1985; Larsen, 1985; Turkle, 1984; Turkle and Papert, 1990). Haddon focuses especially on the masculine shaping of this technology. Because both hardware and software development have been a male activity, the technology has been shaped in their image (Haddon, 1988). Turkle has analysed the computer as a cultural factor and stressed its unique features. Because it is an interactive machine, it has influenced the interface between user and machine in a totally different way from other technologies (Turkle, 1984). She has also been concerned about the gendering of computer use and pointed to women's reticence in the face of masculine computer cultures. As she puts it:

> I believe that the issue for the future is not computerphobia, needing to stay away because of fear and panic, but rather computer reticence, wanting to stay away because the computer becomes a personal and cultural symbol of what a woman is not. (Turkle, 1988: 41).

My theoretical point of departure is theories about socio-technical relations developed within constructivism (Bijker et al., 1987; Sørensen, 1991). It originates from studies of "inventions" or "facts" that are manufactured in research laboratories, and it stresses the study of how "the new" becomes a success or fiasco as a consequence of different actor-strategies (Latour, 1987). The theory has a *centre–periphery perspective*, emphasizing the strategies of the scientist/designer directed towards other researchers, other potentially interested parties, or – possibly – users. Anyone who wants to achieve success for their discovery or innovation needs to convince others that it is "true" or "works". Users become as a rule a remote link in the network-building process.

I will turn the theory around to a *periphery–centre perspective*, and study the user's counter-strategies – the user's domestication of a technology as a process strongly influenced by his/her social and cultural resources. With a main focus on "periphery", it becomes necessary to consider theories that more directly address these aspects. If we try to shift these lines of reasoning into a framework provided by the sociology of culture, we may study the computer not only as an artefact of daily use, but also as a symbolic object in the daily environment. The users' domestication of the computer will in this regard consist of both a practical and a more emotional adaption of the artefact to one's routines, and vice versa.

Grant McCracken (1988) has studied the ways in which we actively participate in shaping our culture through consumption. He claims that material objects do not come with a fully formed content of meaning, but rather are constantly reshaped: "Meaning is constantly flowing to and from its several locations in the social world, aided by the collective and individual efforts of designers, producers, advertisers, and consumers" (McCracken, 1988: 71).

According to Silverstone, Hirsch, and Morley (1991), the meaningful in our relationship with all things and processes must be *constructed*. We "negotiate" the meaning of both things and ideas. Only when we have defined them in relation to ourselves do they emerge as objects or truths. An individual or a social group thus attributes to an artefact a particular meaning beyond a more "common" interpretation of it. In this way things achieve their special meaning to each family and as such they are integrated in the "*moral economy*" of a household, or, in other words, are related to its members' values and cultural preferences (Silverstone et al., 1991).

Domestication covers both the processes where *technology is adapted to everyday life* and the processes that involve *everyday life's adaptation to the technology*. To make this more analytically tangible it is useful to split the process of domestication along different dimensions into partial processes of appropriation, objectification, incorporation, and conversion (Silverstone et al., 1991).

First, *appropriation* is the process through which a piece of technology is made physically and mentally accessible for the household. It is procured and accepted into the home. Second, through *objectification* the household presents its aesthetic and cognitive values. Thus the object is given its place and made visible to the users. Third comes *incorporation*, which is the process through which the object is incorporated into the routines of daily life. Fourth, there is *conversion*, which says something about the relationship between the household and the world outside. The household's "moral economy", its values and cultural preferences, are signified to the outside.

Domestication processes may be studied at the individual level or at the level of the household. Here, I shall apply the concept of domestication at both levels in order to present a picture of the household as a terrain where different meanings and practices in relation to computers may coexist and become juxtaposed, as well as representing a need to establish some collective rules and symbols in order to function as a unit. This makes it possible to study the interaction of gender and computers, at least at two levels. On the one hand, do we find that individual men and women domesticate computers differently? On the other hand, do male patterns dominate and sidetrack female strategies, as most feminist studies of technology suggest (Wajcman, 1991)?

The Computer in Everyday Life

This paper is based on interviews with computer users outside workplaces and schools. I wanted to focus on "everyday life use", especially to analyse the computer in a household setting. But everyday life has several arenas. In order to study youths, I needed to get an impression of computer activities beyond the household setting.

During the interviews we went through the users' computer "histories": how the computer came to be in their possession, how they learned to use this technology, what tasks they used the computer for, their style of work, the social life around the computer, and if and how they had changed their work or work styles during their years of computer use. I conducted 21 interviews with 39 different computer users (9 of them were women). The selection of interviewees was done by the so-called snowball method, meaning that the first interviewee suggested the next one, and so on. I emphasized a varied selection by choosing a subset of the proposed informants.[2] Thirteen of the interviews were in households – couples with children, couples without children, and singles.[3] About half of these households included members with an academic education. I also conducted eight interviews with youths in high school, half of them with an "extensive" interest in computers.

When studying the process of domestication I do this in relation to the four partial processes presented above. In order to elucidate the process of *appropriation* I study the stated reasons for procuring a computer, and where they acquired information about the computer before they bought it. *Objectification* concerns the culture of households or individuals. This is revealed through both what the informant thinks about the computer (work/ hobby) and the physical location of the object. Through *incorporation* one shows the impact on established patterns of use and how, over time, the object enters into daily activities. This dimension can be analysed by studying what people in fact use the computer for, and the influence the computer use has on the daily life of different members of the household. Important dimensions are work tasks and style of work (intensity, time use). Through *conversion* the households' or individuals' values and culture are presented to the world. This dimension can be studied through the computer's role as a means for social contact, and by looking at what the computer signifies in each household.

Let us first consider one particular household. Such an overview provides a useful picture of a family's relationship to computer technology.

The Solheim Family

The Solheim family consists of three people, Stein (35), Marit (34), and Tom (10). Stein has a Norwegian BSc degree with computer science as one of his subjects, and works as a civil servant. Marit is a teacher. They live in a new detached house in a suburb.

They have two computers. One of these, which is their own, is in the basement. Stein was in charge of the purchase. He wanted a computer "to practise a bit at home – for work purposes". The main reason for the choice of exactly that model was the favourable price. The other machine is a portable PC belonging to Stein's employer. It lives on the dining room table. Stein brings the machine home every day, and it is on the whole afternoon. Previously, it was the machine in the basement that was running all the time. In fact it was switched off only during holidays, because Stein did not have the patience to wait for the start-up every time he wanted to use the machine. They had a screensaver, but the sound was constant and nothing was done about that. Probably the noise is one of the reasons why the machine is kept in the basement. Here it also is out of sight.

Stein's experience with computers goes back 20 years – to grammar school and subsequently in studies at university level. For a period he taught computer science, and he has also done consultancy work and used computers for the trade union of which he has been a member. His use covers a great number of different tasks and is obviously informed by his wide experience. However, he stresses that he uses the computer only for purposes he deems *useful*. In relation to both voluntary and political work in which both he and Marit are involved, he performs jobs that involve simple programming as well as wordprocessing. In addition, he uses an electronic appointments book on the laptop. According to Marit he has also archived his record collection.

A lot of the computer work can be classified as overtime. He feels that most of his time at work is spent on keeping in contact with people, so he simply does not have time to do the computer work he should have done in work hours. Furthermore, it is much more pleasant to continue to work at home rather than spending his evenings at the office. He states the reasons for his overtime work as time limits that have to be met, but Marit does not fully agree:

> "I do not think that you can blame the job or any such excuse, because you are made in such a way that you would have done it regardless of what kind of job you had."

Marit is a considerably more cautious user. At first she did not touch the machine at all, but during the past couple of years she has found that in certain contexts it can prove useful. She has taken a course in wordprocessing, and found this both enjoyable and useful. Wordprocessing is also her main use at home. She is not very interested in the computer as such and is in no way "carried away" when she works. She sits until she has finished the task, not a minute longer. If she gets stuck she turns the machine off and finds a pencil and a ruler instead. To her the machine is a simple tool, and she is not interested in changing or expanding her patterns of use.

Stein works at all hours. He himself claims that he uses the machine less now than he used to, but Marit adds:

> "The difference is that at present he does not work till three in the morning on Monday night, he only sits there till twelve. And now you can say that you do not work till twelve o'clock – no, not twelve, but until two or three – Tuesday night, Wednesday night and Thursday night and is completely worn out for the weekend. And sleeps most of Saturday and most of Sunday, in order to work far into Sunday night again. This is the way he has been carrying on. It is not that bad at present, now he works a little less compared with that. But compared with how much normal people work, he still does far too much in my opinion."

His intensive style of work has made her develop an aversion to computer use. The buzzing of the machine is bothersome, and Stein is rather unapproachable at times. However, he feels that it is a social advantage to work at home because then it is possible to work and be with his family at the same time:

"And furthermore I find it very practical to in a way be a part of the social life here – as it were to be in both places if there is anything I need to get done.... She can come to me, wanting to finish a report that has been drafted and takes a quarter of an hour to do. Then I find it very easy to just do it."

In other words, to him the point is to be *physically present*, if not necessarily *mentally available*.

It appears as if the computer has become an *indispensable* part of Stein's everyday life, but he does not fully agree. To a question about what he would have done if the computer had "disappeared" his answer is: "Probably I would have become quite frustrated and then that would have ceased, I suppose." Furthermore, he believes that some overtime would have been necessary. To judge by his user pattern, however, the computer is a necessity. It always has to be available so that he can pop over and work in idle moments, or if he suddenly has an idea. Marit's style of work is in sharp contrast to Stein's. She uses the computer only when she has completely concrete tasks to perform – to her the computer represents a tool and nothing more.

Tom, who is 10 years old, used the computer a bit at first, but his interest has faded during the past year. They have owned a computer since he was 5 years old, and at first he used it for drawing and games. Stein's opinion was that he mastered these tasks very quickly. He gradually stopped using the drawing programs, but he has continued to play games, both "adventure games" and simple "board games". During the past couple of years he has often brought friends home to play. Stein is not entirely pleased with this:

"I have not really wanted to encourage him to play games. First, I do not find them entertaining myself – I think it becomes a little one-sided. When he had a friend visiting, they went down to play – two of them when only one can play at a time – that isn't so much. And they were heavy-handed with the machine – I had in a way let him carry on in order to be nice, but I haven't ever really been in favour of it."

Marit adds:

"And then we are back to the point that we don't need more leisure activities. We haven't got time for them."

Still, both Marit and Stein have a relaxed attitude towards their son's technology use. As they perceive it, the technology will not "trap" him as long as there are other interesting activities. They have a similar view of their son's television use. As Marit says:

"I consider a lot of the things said concerning video and TV use to be rather hysterical.... Normally equipped kids can't be bothered to watch that much, they get tired. When they have seen a certain type of movie enough times they get tired of it."

In the Solheim family the domestication of the computer takes a distinct form. The process of *appropriation* is shaped by Stein's fascination with technology combined with economic restraint. The family displayed a sober attitude in its choice of both the house and the furniture. However, when it came to technology, "needs" were far exceeded compared with what I otherwise observed in my interviews. The family was interested in all kinds of technologies. This also meant that the priority was to have a lot of cheap things, rather than expensive brands and designer products. There was no articulated disagreement between the spouses. They had for instance the same view of the son's TV and computer use. Neither of them worried about "over-use". Stein had been in charge of procuring both their computers. Marit, however, expressed no objections regarding the procurements as such. Her objections first came in relation to the use and then primarily regarding the extent of Stein's computer activities.

Objectification is reflected through both the location of the machines and the family's perception of utility. The fact that their first computer was put in the basement may in fact originally have been a choice they made because the machine took up a lot of space and was noisy. It was, as Stein said, turned on all the time, and Marit expressed a certain irritation over the buzzing machine. But this choice of location also displays the machine's status as a tool without any aesthetic or external value as a symbol. The new laptop computer was located in the dining room. There seemed to be consensus about this choice of location too. It was hardly visible, and it did not make a noise even when it was switched on. The family left me with no impression indicating that it meant anything to them to display this machine. But they certainly expressed something by the fact that they owned such a wide range of technological artefacts. It did not seem that material status was important because they did not accentuate quality labels. It was rather a question of a strong fascination with technology in general, especially in Stein's case: "(A)nd I've got an electronic step-counter. Today I have walked 8950 steps."

Regarding the practical side of objectification (their perception of the computer), they both regarded the computer as a tool, a utility object. Marit implemented her attitude through practical use, whereas Stein's user pattern exceeded the boundaries of the sphere of practical utility.

Incorporation may be illustrated by the patterns of use they had established. There was great variation in what tasks they were involved in, and even more in the styles of work they had developed. Marit's use was characterized by simple writing, and her style of work reflected her instrumental *external* relationship with the machine. Nevertheless she had an indirect benefit because Stein often did work for her. Through incorporation the object becomes an invisible necessity for the household. Marit said that the computer was all but unimportant to her in purely practical terms. Yet, since Stein in fact did quite a lot of work for her, she probably would have experienced some discomfort if the computer had disappeared. The practical had become invisible. To Stein the computer was an invisible mental and practical necessity. Bringing the computer home was a move to be accessible to his family in the afternoon and evenings. Putting it in the middle of the dining room and leaving it on all the time was a way of *adapting that artefact to his routines* – to have the option to pop over to work whenever he wanted, without wasting time waiting for the machine to start. At the same time he had developed a style of work where *he adjusted his routines to the computers*. Computer work was so absorbing that he had almost turned night into day because he *had to* finish. His style of work indicated an *expressive* relationship with the computer.

Conversion is primarily the symbolic complement of objectification – an impression of a modern, relaxed, and competent household. To Tom that also meant that he could bring his friends home to play games – he had a "computer-game status", which may be found among younger boys (this is an impression from several interviews).

Domestication may be analysed in two ways. Silverstone et al. are occupied with the family's common production of a "moral economy", while McCracken focuses on individual processes of transformation (McCracken, 1988; Silverstone et al., 1991). So far I have emphasized individual strategies of domestication. But the role of technology in a household is also a product of negotiations. In the Solheim family we may see certain areas of negotiations. Placing the computer in the basement was Marit's wish. Beyond that they had negotiated individual patterns of use that were acceptable within the household. Stein had to reflect on how much he worked (as mentioned, he claimed that he worked less now than earlier). Marit still found his work load excessive, so this discussion had not been closed. Tom also had restrictions on his use. Even though Stein claimed that it was for practical reasons (some keys on the keyboard had been broken), he also said that he did not really like all the game-playing. Marit agreed, but she referred to it as a waste of time. All the same, they had a common understanding of game-playing as a useless and "improper" use of the computer. Marit's rather restrained user pattern was undoubtedly influenced by Stein's (in her opinion) extreme interest. As she put it:

> "I was very determined not to use the computer because I could not stand it. He used it so much that I had an aversion towards it."

Activities and *style of work* can, as mentioned, be viewed as aspects of incorporation. This seems to be the dimension of domestication with the largest impact on the Solheim family's material and social everyday life. Through the incorporation dimension we may identify both the practical and the symbolic value of the computer (work style reflects, among other things, the symbolic value of the computer). Because this is the most significant dimension I will use incorporation as a point of departure in constructing ideal-typical users. The ideal-typical users can then be analysed as representatives of three ideal-typical strategies of domestication.

The three ideal-types in Figure 1 constitute a rough classification scheme based on what I found to be the most significant aspects of the processes of domestication within all the households examined. However, I will let the Solheim family illustrate these processes. If we return to them, we may note that Stein's activities were often job related or practical tasks related to private matters. He worked a lot more than required, and therefore his computer use can be regarded partly as a leisure activity. Marit and Tom fall into different categories: work and leisure, respectively. The categories of instrumental and expressive I associate with styles of work. Through their style of work they express their relationship to the computer. Marit and Tom had, as we saw, a clearly practical and goal-directed relationship to the computer. This was reflected in the way they worked or played. They signalled through their "concrete" use a view of the computer as a means to reach an end – an instrumental perception of the computer.

Stein's style of work was totally different from Tom's and Marit's. He claimed a sober relationship to the computer as a tool, but his way of working bore testimony to something else. As he said, he *had* to go over and work a little now and then, and if he got absorbed by a task he would sit until he had finished it.

STYLE OF WORK

TYPE OF ACTIVITY	Instrumental	Expressive
Work	"extender" (M/F)	"explorer" (M)
Leisure (hobby)	"game-player" (time-killer) (M)	"explorer" (M) "game-player" (game freak) (M)

Figure 1. Ideal-typical computer users constructed by the dimensions of incorporation: style of work and type of activity (M = male, F = female)

Marit's pronouncements indicated that he at times was rather inaccessible. In this way he expressed a relationship to the computer as *more* than a tangible tool. *The computer itself was a goal.* In other words, his style of work indicated an expressive relationship with the computer. And as we shall experience during the presentation of these ideal-types, we will also find another game-player – occupied with leisure activities, but with an expressive relationship to the computer. His "subtitle" is "game freak".

In the following sections, I will explore the ideal-types in greater detail. Thus, I will analyse different strategies of domestication. In addition I will take a closer look at the gendered development of domestication, and the computer's role in the resulting construction of a possible gendered user pattern.

The "Extender"

The typical "extender" is an adult, with a college or university degree, if s/he is not still a student. S/he is a family person. To be available to the family is the main reason given for bringing work home rather than staying at the office. Arne, who had three children between the ages of 11 and 19, explained it in this way:

> "It has resulted in the fact that I and my wife can stay at home when we have to work on things that have to be finished. Previously, we had to go to the office. This was one of the reasons for my purchase of a laptop. A very clear question of priorities."

Arne's work demanded that tasks had to be finished within certain time limits. This meant that he had the choice between staying late at the office or bringing work back home. To sit at home and work was by far preferable to traditional overtime work. Helle, his wife, used the machine when it was available, also for work-related tasks. In contrast to Arne, she did not have computer equipment available at work.

> "We have a study here that we use continually, or the kids may use it…. That mother or father sits and writes and works – something about kids seeing that you also can work at home, I think is an advantage."

The "extender" describes the computer as a tool. S/he says that they use the computer to perform useful tasks, primarily work related. For instance, Randi said: "Previously, I had a similar machine at work like I have here at home. Then, I used the one we have here, among other things to write up reports and to do other writing tasks related to work.... It's perceived as a tool." And Grete had the same opinion: "I think it is practical with regard to writing."

Turkle (1984) found the same type of instrumental grounds for the procurement of a computer. The users referred to a number of practical tasks that the computer should be used for. But, as she commented after having observed the newly fledged machine owners at home: "People buy an instrumental computer, but they come home to live with an intimate machine" (Turkle, 1984: 184). She claimed that what was interesting was not the computer's practical dimension, but what it made them feel. But, for the "extender", the machine is primarily a tool. As Gunnar said: "The computer is like any other object that we use around the house. There is nothing mystical about it." Or, as Runar puts it: "I have never been fascinated by the computer as such. I have to have a utilitarian goal." This is also reflected in the low aesthetic value attributed to the computer. The "extender" is not concerned with showing off. The computer is generally located in a study. If one wants a new computer, it is justified by saying that the old one is not "good enough" for work activities. Beyond that, there is no interest in new acquisitions. Except for the amount of time spent in front of the screen, working with a computer at home is not an object of dispute in these households.

The "extender" regards overtime work as a duty. To bring work home is not a good solution. But when overtime is imperative, the working-at-home alternative is seen as better than staying late at the office, both for the kids and for the family in general. The "extender" does not give preference to computer work at the expense of leisure time. Janne had plans for using the machine more than she eventually did, which was almost not at all:

"Originally I did have some ideas about sitting down and using the PC a bit. I should for example learn to use spreadsheets and drawing-programs and some other things that would be useful at work too, but I never got down to it. Spare time just disappears. I do not give priority to that over other activities."

The "extender" as an ideal-type is characterized by an instrumental relationship to the computer, and that s/he uses it to perform tasks that are primarily work or school related. However, this ideal-type may be split in two, emphasizing a female and a male strategy of domestication. The female version of the "extender" does not as a rule participate in the procurement of the computer. She uses the computer because it is available. Originally she did not wish for a computer.

This situation may be explained in several ways. To begin with, several of the women did not have access to a computer at work. Nor did they have any training with computers beyond a course in wordprocessing. Consequently, it did not come as natural to them to want a computer at home. Moreover, several of them were very conscious of not really wanting to bring work home: "If I don't really have to, I am very reluctant to work in that way in the evenings at home." This was reflected in the pattern of use: overtime work was of moderate extent.

Haddon (1988) provides other explanations of women's weak representation among computer users. In the "childhood" of the micro-machine, the general user/innovator was a technology enthusiast, and that meant a man. Their influence on both hardware and software development implied the exclusion of women in several ways. On the one hand, investigations of women's leisure time showed that it had a different structure from men's. The leisure time of women was fragmented and short, and the activities they filled it with had to be useful. In other words, it would be hard for a woman to defend such extensive use of time as computer work demanded. On the other hand, the available software did not appeal to women in general. All this provided an obstacle to women developing a pattern of use identical to that of men.

The male "extender" has acquired his computer knowledge through education and/or professional work, and has a computer at work. The machine at home is also procured in connection with his needs at work/school. His work at home is more extensive than the woman's. It is a question of "peaks" of work that has to be finished off at home. Magnus explained it as follows: "My work is extremely periodic. When I was working on my book, the work load was generally high; now there is less." It may also be a question of certain types of work that prove difficult to get done within normal working hours.

The "extender's" domestication of the computer must be characterized as restrained. The stated reason for appropriation among the men was needs connected with work, whereas women as a rule were not involved in this phase at all. This could also be found in the objectification. First, the computer as an object was often "hidden" away in a study or was carried back and forth between office and home. Second, it was defined as a tool, primarily as an extension of ordinary work, subsidiarily in relation to "useful" tasks in the household such as keeping accounts. Incorporation showed the same pattern. The computer was in their opinion used for tasks related to work. However, overtime work was far more widespread among men than among women. The style of work reflected an instrumental relationship with the computer. It was regarded as uninteresting except to perform specific tasks.

The computer is clearly incorporated into the "extender's" everyday life. The "extender" has adapted the computer to her/his routines and not (for example) increased the extent of overtime work. S/he is primarily interested in the computer as a tool to support tasks that have to be done anyway. Thus the computer's main impact on the everyday life of the household is to move overtime work into the home. The "extender" has reorganized the relation between work and family life. In contrast to what s/he used to be, s/he is now physically accessible for the family while working. This also means that the line between work and leisure time is blurred.

Overtime work at home is not a new invention. It existed before computers became a standard tool. However, the introduction of computers in the household has made this a more attractive option, compared with overtime at work.

The "Game-player"

The "game-player" is a boy in primary, secondary, or high school. He uses the computer as a toy in a very broad sense. As we can see in Figure 1, this ideal-type is really two different characters: the "time-killer" and the "game freak", respectively. What separates these two is the relationship to the computer – whether it is instrumental or expressive. Let us look at the "time-killer" first.

His interest is primarily games, but he may in addition use the computer for drawing and some writing. He may even do some homework on it, although games are his main interest. The motivation is to play and to have fun. All the same, his relationship to the computer is of an instrumental character. This means that he sees the computer as a game-machine. Primarily this intervenes in his everyday life as a replacement for other leisure activities. He does not let himself be "carried away" in the long run. As Eivind (10 years) said:

> "I write letters, play games, and draw.... Previously we used it almost all the time.... These days we hardly use the computer at all."

The "time-killer" has as a rule not been involved in the procurement of the computer. Its availability is due to the needs of other family members. Youngsters who have been involved in the purchase have a "simpler" machine (Amiga 500, Commodore 64, etc.). In these cases the rest of the family is not necessarily involved. The "time-killer" is an enthusiastic user when the machine is new. He still throws himself into new programs or new games, but usually gets bored after a while. Jo (16 years) had had a computer for several years, first a Commodore 64 then an Amiga 500. Previously he was, among other things, occupied with drawing ideas for games. But since he did not learn programming, he never got any further. He had also used the machine for school work. During his most enthusiastic period he could spend a whole afternoon on it, but his interest was not intense enough for him to continue:

> "At the start I spent quite a lot of time on it; subsequently less and less. Now I almost don't at all.... The only thing I do at present is play football-games."

Klaus had used a computer for the past 10 years and used the wordprocessing programs a lot throughout his whole school life. He came from a family where the computer was a central object, but this did not seem to have rubbed off onto him. Now, when he was not using the computer for homework, he reduced his use correspondingly. He was about to leave home, but had no plans for buying his own computer.

The "game freak" is older, often in secondary school. He has bought his own machine – a Commodore Amiga 500. His leisure activity is far more advanced than among the "time-killers". His use is more collective and public and he usually attends a club of Commodore Amiga 500 users. Let us take a closer look at this "Amiga club".

The "Amiga club" consists of countless smaller clubs organized in different ways. Some of them are small and the members work closely together; others are bigger and the members get in touch only through the computer once in a while. The clubs are constructed through friends with similar interests, through contacts in computer magazines, or through *demo-discs*. Once a club is established, they invent a name and start to work on the design of demos or on game-cracking. The demo is a presentation of the club's programming skills through music and graphics – their very special trademark. In the demo the boys give themselves English codenames such as Rex or Codex. As one of the boys said:

> "To have a fancy English name, both for yourself and for the club, is a 'must' if you want to be popular in this 'world'. Another point is also to protect the clubs that work on game-cracking from being recognized."

Each of the club members has a special function: The *Swapper*'s responsibility is to maintain contact with other clubs mostly through exchanging demo-discs – mail-trading or modem-trading as they call it. *Musicians* arrange the music on the demo, while *Graphics* people are responsible for the graphic design. Finally, *Coders* put the final product together. Not everyone attends a club. *Freelancers* sell their competence to an established club if needed.

Although the clubs' main interest is in producing demo-discs, a few of them work on "game-cracking" – the illegal distribution of copies of games. The status of this activity is high and makes the club popular among the others.

The most difficult aspect of this activity is not breaking the copy protection code but getting hold of the original game as fast as possible. When a game is introduced on to the market, the thing is to be the first club to get it, break the copy protection code, and distribute it to users. Thus, it is important to have members in other countries.

They get hold of the originals and distribute copies by phone by means of *card trading*, without incurring any personal costs. Their members or other contacts in Europe trace telephone credit codes, a service from American companies to American tourist and business people. A code makes free calls possible. Telephone bills are sent to the companies that offer these services. After using the same code for some days, this will be discovered and the code will be closed. Trond explained:

> "They often close down the code ..., but they don't seem to be making such a big loss. If they really had wanted to stop this activity they could have done something to stop it."

As we can see, the "game freak" has a different pattern of computer use from that of the "time-killer". The computer clearly has a more important role in his everyday life and his involvement seems to be expressive, in contrast to the "time-killer's" instrumental involvement. Still, they have a similar type of activity, which may mainly be classified as a hobby.

Another common feature is the contact with other users. The "game-player" has friends who also have computers at home, and they meet around the computer. The "time-killers" play games, exchange games and software, and advise each other. The "game freaks" design demo-discs, keep in contact with other users through the computer, and a few are involved in the shadier activities of "game-cracking". The "game-player" gains new social contacts because he has a computer. And the computer provides most of his amusement as long as friends find it interesting. The pattern of use is as much guided by the activities of companions as by personal requirements. The "game-player" is of an age when everything changes fast. In other words, the computer may be domesticated over and over again.

The "Explorer"

As indicated in Figure 1, the "explorer" is engaged in computers both in connection with work and as a hobby. What characterizes the "explorer" is not primarily *what* he does, but *how* he does it. With the "explorer", it is impossible to find a dividing line between the tasks that are purely work related and those that are leisure activities, motivated by personal interest. Stein, as we remember, described his work at home as tasks that he *had to* bring home because of deadlines. In fact he did quite a lot more than he strictly had to. Both his priorities in the allocation of time to computer activities and the intensity of his engagement seem to differ from those with an instrumental relationship to the computer. As Marit said:

> "It is totally beyond reason. It almost gave one spasms because one heard the peeping of that machine half the night."

The "explorer" is a man between 20 and 40 years of age. He has a varied history. He may be a youth living at home or a cohabitant, married or single, and with or without children. His education spans the whole possible range: no education, student, skilled worker, or academic. This also characterizes his dwelling. Whereas the "extender" is an established member of society with an apartment or house and represents a somewhat narrow social group, the "explorer" is more diverse. He lives in anything from a detached house or old flat to small lodgings. In terms of style, too, this group is very disparate.

The "explorer" as an ideal-type is a construction based on his style of work, which again is indicative of his expressive relationship to computer work. He has a "computer career", and he has over time upgraded his equipment. It was his own interest that first made him buy or otherwise procure a computer. This may have been guided by needs at work or pure curiosity: "Interest simply, have a try at it. Thought it looked like fun."

The "explorer" is interested in the development of computer technology and keeps up by means of computer magazines. He may get information about bargains and prices from magazines, but he chooses the type of machine after discussions with acquaintances and colleagues. He evaluates the price carefully and may well choose a machine that he will have to work on himself before it becomes fully functional. He changes or "patches up" the machine to a greater or lesser degree, according to what aspect of the machine he wants to utilize and what tasks occupy him.

Curiosity and a "go ahead" spirit characterize his style of work, almost totally independently of the tasks he is performing. As Bernt said: "It is fascinating always to learn more about the machine. To carve new features into it. Satisfying to learn something new. Fun to solve problems." Peter called this a part of *the spirit of repair*. He was an electrician by education and a self-taught computer-user who pursued hardware tasks, programming, or "other things" as he put it. He explained it in the following way:

> "If you stop then you will forget half – how far you had got – when you continue the next day ... That's a part of the spirit of repairs. You have to finish it, or you will not get to sleep – it's that simple. Because you always speculate about what it is that you should have done so that you might have finished it."

Stein was of the opinion that it was easier to interrupt certain writing tasks than to stop when he was trying to fathom new software. As mentioned, his work at home was at times a source of irritation to the rest of the family because he "got immersed in" the task at hand. To have a mentally inaccessible man in the house is not necessarily of any help. Stein thought it practical to be a part of the social milieu of the living room, while Marit saw it differently. Jon, who worked as a scientist, encountered similar problems. Owing to the lack of a separate study, he had to sit in the living room. Jon said about his "overtime existence":

> "It becomes a conflict, doesn't it, when you don't have a study of your own? I must sit and work and concentrate, while the others want to do as they like.... I become a black hole in the social environment."

Even though he was strict about setting priorities, and only did what he characterized as work, his family perceived his activities as irritating. Why was this not seen as a problem with the "extender"? Probably because of different levels of intensity of the work. Jon's description of his attitude towards games would doubtless give us that impression:

> "So you walk around and think about it; you can't think of anything but how to get further on. It takes most of your concentration – almost all the imagination you have."

An intensive style of work is also reflected in the *amount of time* the "explorer" is willing to spend on computer work. As we remember, it took two to describe Stein's use of time. Stein said he did not use the machine as much as he used to, but that still meant too much according to Marit. This pattern repeated itself in several families. I got vague answers that were corrected by concrete descriptions: "He would sit there day and night if he got the chance", was one woman's comment about her husband's interest in games. Another used the notion of *"computer widow"* to describe her situation. It took too much time, she said, time the family might have used for joint activities.

For the ones living alone, to be "absorbed" or to work long hours constituted no problem. Their daily rhythm could be adapted to different work phases. Stig, who lived alone, said his work varied in intensity: "It varies a great deal. Months may go by without much activity, and then suddenly I sit for a week at a stretch." In families where everybody was a computer-user, time had to be divided between them. Where the father was the chief user, he had to negotiate a pattern that everybody could live with. One strategy might be to limit his use in such a way that it didn't bother the others. Another strategy was to claim that he did "necessary" work, as Stein tried to.

As mentioned, the "explorer" makes no clear distinction between work and hobby. However, there are different ways in which to connect these – different combinations of work, hobby, and "entrepreneuring". Stein was an example of a person who primarily saw the computer as a work-machine, but who through his "career" made evident that the computer also functioned as a hobby-machine.

A computer primarily procured as a hobby-machine may also in time become a work-machine. Hans, who worked as a technician in the culture sector, had originally bought a machine for leisure. Gradually he developed forms of use that were increasingly work related.

Peter, who was trained as an electrician, called himself a "fiddle-man" – someone who repairs everything within electronics. The computer was to him a machine that could challenge both his intellect and his practical interest in electronics, on both a professional and a hobby level: "The reason I started doing this was to solve puzzles and to program. You have to use your head for something."

The combination of work and hobby might also have entrepreneurial characteristics, in that through computer work a person might construct a new job for themselves. Bernt, who worked as a taxi-driver, used most of his spare time to develop software for sale. What started as a hobby was becoming a job.

The "explorer" covers a large spectrum of activities. The knowledge base and degree of sophistication of the activities vary. Does this mean that the activities affect the incorporation of the computer into their everyday life, that they represent different strategies of domestication? It does not seem so. As already mentioned, the work styles of "explorers" are quite similar. And it seems as if it is the style of work rather than the actual tasks that influences the computer's impact on the "explorer" and his families' everyday life. It is not the tasks themselves that are discussed if computer work is perceived as a problem. It is the "explorer's" absorption in computer work, and the time he spends on it, that affect the rest of the family. So, in spite of the differences in work types, the "explorers" have a fairly similar domestication of the computer. It represents a central element in their everyday life; nevertheless, it seems that most "explorers" have negotiated a space for computer work that does not exceed their families' tolerance.

Women, Men and Different Strategies of Domestication

The ideal-types introduced in this paper have been constructed to cover different aspects of domestication of a new technology. The concept of domestication is first and foremost an analytical tool for grasping the complexity in the user–technology relation to prevent the more deterministic "technological impact" view. It helps us see how *the computer is adapted to* one's own and the household's everyday life, and how *everyday life is adjusted* to the computer.

As we have seen, the process of domestication within all ideal-types is the same on some main points, but we can also find some differences. The most conspicuous is between female and male "extenders" and within the "game-player" category ("time-killer" vs. "game freak"). Let us first look at the "extender". The women have, with a few exceptions, nothing to do with the procurement of the machine. They have little or no knowledge about computers and computer use. The incorporation of the computer is naturally informed by this fact. Women do not use it much. Some of them say that they have tried games, but they quickly grow bored with them. The computer is a tool for performing necessary work, and this work is of modest extent. They also have a clearly instrumental relationship to the machine.

This group of female "extenders" represents the only women in my material. The ideal-types of "explorer" and "game-player" consist exclusively of men. The women's role towards the "explorer" seems to be "controlling" their partner's or husband's use of the computer. In households involving several persons the man refers to others in the family (implying the woman) when he explains why computer use has to be limited.

The male "extender" has experience of computer work from education and work. He has taken the initiative to get a computer at home to meet a work-related need. His domestication is characterized by an instrumental relationship with the computer, too, and the tasks are mainly work related. However, the line between work and leisure has become blurred, and negotiations about his presence at home are no longer linked to *away* and *home*, but to *physical or mental presence.*

The argument about mental presence is obvious with regard to the computer work of the "explorer". Even when the "explorer" is performing purely work tasks, these have different effects in a family context. For this reason, the "explorers" who have families try to regulate their computer use. The "explorer's" domestication of the computer is characterized by curiosity and interest. His relationship with the computer is clearly expressive. It is this, more than the concrete activities, that justifies the division between the "extender" and the "explorer".

Neither the "extender" nor the "explorer" is particularly interested in the machine as an object. Its "material" dimension seems totally subservient to its practical use. However, objectification and conversion also say something about the way the family communicates outwards, not necessarily in the form of direct social interaction. As I perceive these families, they express a "relaxed" attitude towards technology – something that we connect with being up-to-date.

To the "game-player", the computer represents more than individual utility or play. It is first of all an object of human interaction and presentation of self. The objectification and conversion are in other words more direct. The clearest example of this is found in the "game freak". His relationship to the computer occurs only through the subculture of "Amiga users". Appropriation and incorporation are, on the other hand, less apparent than with the "extender" and the "explorer", especially with the "time-killer". Most of the "time-killers" have had nothing to do with the procurement of the machine, and their direct use is somewhat "on and off" depending on their dominant interests.

In Vestby's paper in this volume we find children who resemble the "time-killers", while the "game freaks" have a pattern of use resembling the one that Håpnes identifies in her paper in the hacker culture. Both activities and style of work resemble those of the hackers. The illegal side of the work is even more explicit than is presented by many hacker studies. I also strongly believe that we will find some of the "game freaks" within future hacker groups, so the "Amiga culture" could be seen as a training ground for future computer enthusiasts such as the ones that Håpnes describes.

I have already mentioned women's marginal position among the "extenders". Among the "explorers" and the "game-players" there are no women at all. Haddon (1988) has explained this by the "history" of personal computers. But he claims that women users are much more common outside organized groups. That may be true for younger women, but it was not my impression from my material. Turkle (1984) includes women in her research, but did not find any among the "addicted" users. She explains it as follows:

> In the vehemence with which many women insist on the computer's neutrality, on its being nothing more than a mere tool, there may be something more subtle going on than a clash between culture and personal style – a clash between personal style and sense of self. Many women may be fighting *against* having a close relationship to a computer or computational objects. (Turkle and Papert, 1990: 152)

Women are often accused of not using the computer at all, being frightened of the technology, lacking in competence, or both. Turkle claims, as we have seen here, that it is not necessarily the computer or women's lack of training that is the problem. As she sees it, women do not fit into the existing computer culture. It is a male culture that, in the first place, demands a logical and structured way of operating the computer and then, at its most extreme, reflects a close, almost intimate relationship between the user and computer.

This fits into what I found in the families of the "explorers". The explorers have an "expressive" relationship to the computer, and this seems to affect their wives' or partners' pattern of use. The complete lack of women among the "game-players" can be understood that way, as they have a lot in common with the hacker culture. Rasmussen and Håpnes (1991) found the same pattern in a study of computer students. The female students indicated a distance from the dominant values represented by the hacker groups by not getting involved in their activities. They were interested in computers, but in the practical utilities more than in the computers as such (Rasmussen and Håpnes, 1991).

The men in my material all construct their individual user pattern on the basis of their own interests and values. Thus, there are several types of user pattern which express both practical and symbolic dimensions: the "extender" represents competence and control, the "explorer" exhibits a highly developed technological interest and fascination, and the "game-player" illustrates competition and collaboration. The women's activities and work style seem in this setting to fall within a more limited frame. While some develop an individual user pattern out of what they express as their interests and values, others seem to construct a user pattern as a protest against their husband's or partner's use.

In contrast to popular conceptions of the information society, this paper claims that the introduction of computers in Norwegian homes has not brought with it a given set of changes that may be attributed to the computer as such. There is a variety of patterns of usage and social integration, some individual and some constructed within the household or family as a social unit. This is the result of a wide variety of domestication strategies in relation to new technologies.

These strategies may in turn reflect different cultural and economic resources. Most of the people in the "extender" category have middle-class jobs allowing them sufficient freedom to choose to work from home, rather than doing overtime at work. Age is also important, but not in a conclusive way. Although old people are conspicuously lacking, we find teenagers as well as forty-somethings with a deep and expressive relationship towards computers. However, the freedom to be totally absorbed in computers is mostly a privilege of young people without family and social obligations.

Finally, gender has proved to be important in at least two ways. First, we see that there are quite traditional differences between men and women in the association with computers and their use of them. Women show little engagement and claim a very instrumental relationship. Men have greater influence over the procurement and the use of the computer, and they use it more frequently and with greater interest. However, and this is the second point, different identities are reflected in different ways of domesticating the computer, in accordance with Turkle's insistence that the computer is an interactive technology. Thus, the gendered relationship with the computer is not a dichotomous one, it is multidimensional.

However, domestication is not a once-and-for-all process. What is shown in this paper is that domestication is continuous and dynamic. This represents a somewhat different emphasis from the one found in both Silverstone et al. (1991) and McCracken (1988). Computers may take on new meanings and become involved in new practices, without being replaced or transformed. Thus the ideal-types described in this paper are to be read only as examples of possibilities that will certainly be supplemented in time. The rather restricted female role observed in this material is probably already multiplied in real life.

NOTES

1. *The Shorter Oxford English Dictionary,* 3rd ed. Oxford: Clarendon Press, 1970.
2. My informants outside households are, with one exception, males. We asked them about female users, but they did not know any.
3. I conducted five of them with Tove Håpnes.

BIBLIOGRAPHY

Aune, M. 1992. *Datamaskina i hverdagslivet – en studie av brukeres domestisering av en ny teknologi*. STS Report No. 15. Trondheim: Centre for Technology and Society.

Bijker, W. E. and Pinch, T. J. 1987. The social construction of facts and artefacts: Or how the sociology of science and the sociology of technology might benefit each other. In W. E. Bijker, T. P. Hughes and T. J. Pinch (eds): *The Social Construction of Technological Systems*. Cambridge, MA: MIT Press.

Bomberg, L., Spork, M., Thomas, A., Matthias, L., Meissner, G. and Stahl, S. 1989. *Computer-pirater*. Kolding: Forlaget Datatid A/S.

Croné, S. 1990. Datorer och hushåll. *Arbetsnotat 67*, Tema T, Linköping.

Dutton, W. H., Everett, R. M. and Jun, S.-H. 1987. Diffusion and social impacts of personal computers. *Communication Research*, Vol.14, pp. 219–50.

Haddon, L. 1988. *The Roots and Early History of the British Home Computer Market. Origins of the Masculine Micro*. London: Management School, Imperial College, University of London.

Haddon, L. 1991. Researching gender and home computers. In K. H. Sørensen and A.-J. Berg (eds): *Technology and Everyday Life. Trajectories and Transformations*. Report No. 5, Oslo: NAVF–NTNF–NORAS.

Hebenstreit, J. 1985. Children and computers. Myths and limits. In B. Sendov and I. Stancher: *Children in an Information Age. Tomorrow's Problems Today*. Oxford: Pergamon Press.

Larsen, S. 1985. Computers in education. In B. Sendov and I. Stancher: *Children in an Information Age. Tomorrow's Problems Today*. Oxford: Pergamon Press.

Latour, B. 1987. *Science in Action*. Milton Keynes: Open University Press.

Levy, S. 1984. *Hackers, Heroes of the Computer Revolution*. New York: Dell Publishing.

McCracken, G. 1988. *Culture and Consumption. New Approaches to the Symbolic Character of Consumer Goods and Activities*. Bloomington and Indianapolis: Indiana University Press.

Rasmussen, B. and Håpnes, T. 1991. Excluding women from the technologies of the future: a case study of the culture of computer science. *Futures*, December, pp. 1107–19.

Silverstone, R., Morley, D., Dahlberg, A. and Livingstone, S. 1989. Families, technologies and consumption: The household and information and communication technologies. CRICT discussion paper, Brunel University.

Silverstone, R., Hirsch, E. and Morley, D. 1991. Information and communication technologies and the moral economy of the household. In K. H. Sørensen and A.-J. Berg (eds): *Technology and Everyday Life. Trajectories and Transformations*. Report No. 5, Oslo: NAVF–NTNF–NORAS.

Sørensen, K. H. 1991. Introduction. Technology and everyday life: Trajectories and transformations. In K. H. Sørensen and A.-J. Berg (eds): *Technology and Everyday Life. Trajectories and Transformations*. Report No. 5, Oslo: NAVF–NTNF–NORAS.

Sørensen, K. H. 1991. *Informasjonsteknologi eller integrasjonsteknologi? Om teknologisosiologiske tilnærminger og deres relevans for analyser av telematikk*. STS Working Paper No. 6, Trondheim: Centre for Technology and Society.

Turkle, S. 1984. *The Second Self. Computers and the Human Spirit*. Massachusetts: Granada.

Turkle, S. 1988. Computational reticence: Why women fear the intimate machine. In C. Kramarae (ed.): *Technology and Women's Voices*. New York: Routledge & Kegan Paul.

Turkle, S. and Papert, S. 1990. Epistemological pluralism: Styles and voices within the computer culture. *Signs*, Vol. 16, No. 11, pp. 128–57.

Wajcman, J. 1991. *Feminism Confronts Technology*. Cambridge: Polity Press.

Chapter 5

Not in Their Machines
How Hackers Transform Computers into Subcultural Artefacts
Tove Håpnes

Introduction

In this paper you are going to meet young men who see themselves as *real hackers* or *semi-hackers*. When we[1] first met them, they were all students at the Norwegian Institute of Technology (NIT) at master's level. Within a larger academic culture that mainly educates engineers, they had chosen to spend a substantial portion of their daily life in, or in the close vicinity of, a subculture they called the *Software Workshop* (SWW).

Our interest in getting to know this community was not to construct the hackers as persons, or to map their entire culture. We thought that the hackers might increase our knowledge of how consumers of computer technology proceed to develop their patterns of use. Consequently we were interested in the hackers' machine activities and their style of work. However, we soon discovered that focusing on their use of computers also provided an understanding of how the hackers, in continuous negotiations with human and non-human elements, construct personalities and culture as well as technology.

Three main themes run through this paper. First, I want to explore the interrelationship between machines, people, and culture as it is played out in this specific subculture. Is it, for example, possible to understand the hackers' fascination with machines without considering their practical work and how they communicate with and about the technology they use? The title, "Not in Their Machines", indicates that the basis of preoccupation we found in our informants was different from the picture usually painted of hackers – the image of loving the machine for itself (Turkle, 1984). The challenge inherent in describing the interaction between cultural, technological, and personal elements is to show how *meanings* are created through *the negotiation processes* that take place.

Second, the paper illustrates the problematic character of the sharp distinction between design and application usually found in technology studies. The hackers provided us with many examples of how they supersede the role of passive users of ready-made technology. They design products too. They utilize the possibilities that software and hardware producers have delegated to their products. At the same time, the hackers develop their own socio-technological elements which they combine with the products they use. Since production and consumption in this case are closely intertwined, it is interesting to study how these spheres actually communicate within the culture in question.

Third, the paper shows the problem inherent in conceptualizing "hacker personalities" and "hacker culture" as universal, as do many previous studies.

Previous Research on Hackers and Hacker Cultures

In technology studies, the concept "hacker" describes a particular kind of infatuation with computers usually found among boys and young men. One of the reasons we became interested in the SWW community was some of the conclusions from an earlier study of female computer science students at the same university (Rasmussen and Håpnes, 1991; Håpnes and Rasmussen, 1991). The female students used the hackers as a metaphor for all the things they did not like about computing: technical fixation, work addiction, and total absorption in computers, leading to neglect of normal non-study relations and a concentration on problems with no obvious relation to the outside world. This extreme male position was something the female students expressed as being the opposite of their own professional identity: using computers as tools for solving practical problems in society, and being occupied with a broader range of social and human aspects of computing. Analysing the hackers' practical work and how they communicate with technology makes it possible to see – implicitly – important qualities of their masculine position as well.

An early critical discussion of the hacker phenomenon is found in Joseph Weizenbaum's (1976) description of the "compulsive programmer": a figure with several traits in common with the hacker description offered by the female students at NIT.

> The compulsive programmer is convinced that life is nothing but a program running in an enormous computer, and that therefore every aspect of life can ultimately be explained in programming terms. (1976: 126)

The compulsive programmer is an instrumental loner who prefers to communicate with machines rather than humans. He may spend hours on programming, and his motivating power is to create the really brilliant system that one day will make him famous. He is firmly convinced that he can make the computer comply with all his whims. According to Weizenbaum, the hacker lives in a world made for him.

Sherry Turkle (1984, 1988) pursues this last theme in her ethnographic hacker study at MIT. What especially concerns her is the *subjective* qualities of computer use. Like Weizenbaum, Turkle sees the hacker as a personality who is fascinated by the possibilities for control in computer technology. Whereas Weizenbaum understands control as a need to present oneself as an eccentric machine master, Turkle's explanations are more psychological. What hackers seek and get satisfaction from in computers is a basic need for personal safety. Here they may build their own controlled personal worlds according to taste, which is hard to achieve in relations with people. The computer becomes their safe mooring, an aspect which defines their common culture: "A culture of mastery, individualism, nonsensuality. It values complexity and risk in relations with things, and seeks simplicity and safety in relations with people" (1984: 233). The hacker culture offers group membership based on individualism – a community with no demands to socialize. The hackers express these elements through a specific image which signals that it is the computers they live for: the image of getting lost in the machine-in-itself (1984: 207).

Turkle also involves gender in her description of hackers. She finds a competitive macho culture: individual achievement is what counts, often in the form of competitions in which they push themselves to breaking point to test their stamina. This gives the culture a fundamentally masculine form, and makes it unattractive to women.

Both Weizenbaum and Turkle describe a universal hacker culture, although with different emphases. Weizenbaum is primarily interested in how hackers may shape computing practices, whereas Turkle focuses more on issues of identity and culture. However, meaning and action may be more closely related. Rituals, personality, and culture have been the focus. However, we learn little about what actually happens in front of the computer screen. We would expect variations, not only between machine cultures, but also between the members of a particular user culture. Maybe we will be able to see the differences and nuances more clearly if we pay more attention to what hackers do with computers.

It is not just in the critical reports (Weizenbaum, 1976; Turkle, 1984) of North American campus life that the hackers are depicted as a homogeneous phenomenon. An alternative version is the political hacker image found in the stories about the R&D milieus that were dominant in the development of computer technology (Levy, 1984; Rozak, 1986). Here, hackers are described as young pioneers obsessed with defining new application areas for computer technology. Technological enthusiasm is linked to a political project: making computers inexpensive and easy to use. Computers were also perceived as a tool for making society more democratic and decentralized (Rozak, 1986). These epic stories as well as the tragic stories share an understanding of hackers as a marginal phenomenon. Hackers are described as being a particular type of singular people. Variations in the meaning of "hackerhood" and hacker activities are not allowed for.

However, later studies have criticized the construction of marginality and the concept of the general hacker figure. In her study of home computer-users, Margrethe Aune (this volume) demonstrates how the most dedicated computer hobbyists, in her taxonomy called the "explorers", constitute a much more diverse group than we have encountered in previous hacker literature. Her "explorers" stem from very different social roots and are involved in a wide range of different personal relationships. They are very interested in experimenting with the machine – their dominant style of work is "try it and see what happens". Thus, Aune argues for a fluid line between an instrumental and an expressive relationship with the computer. Of special interest is Aune's detailed analysis of the styles of work pursued and the activities engaged in. The "explorers" use computers for games, but also to perform job-related tasks. The purpose of their experiments might just as well be to develop new ideas and products as to master the machine.

In a German study (Noller and Paul, 1991) of everyday cultural practice among computer fans, the content of computer fascination is categorized into three main elements: a will to create, to be involved in the perfection of the machine, and to consolidate and foster self-esteem through proficiency. Noller and Paul do not find computer fans to be particularly asocial or eccentric people. Instead, they emphasize the strong sense of achievement and intense competitiveness. Both competition and hierarchical relations serve to express individual proficiency. That leads to the clear tendency towards individualism in computer cultures, according to their study.

Jörgen Nissen (1993) demonstrates in a study from Sweden how *community* in computer clubs can be a more complex entity than the culture described by Turkle. These are not loosely connected congenial societies, but rather cultures that facilitate social interaction. They are simultaneously providing meeting places for computer enthusiasts, the availability of a larger personal network, and a springboard to other environments and activities. Nissen also demonstrates variations among youths interested in computers in terms of machine use and personality. However, he finds the same tendency towards hierarchical relations between members as do Noller and Paul (1991); in computer clubs proficiency is the road to prestige.

These later studies of computer enthusiasts are important because they debunk myths about the hackers' personality traits and culture and their marginality. A weakness is their use of typical classification schemes or categories mainly based on personal and cultural traits. The studies do not tell us much about the distinguishing features of hackers' machine use. We get to know whether they are engaged in programming, games, or computer-mediated communication. Very little is said about the machine-users' techniques and modes of communication with the technology.

An exception is Aune's (1992) analysis of different computer clubs. She shows how community as well as creativity are formed by *the patterns of use* the members develop individually and interactively. In the Amiga club she studied, cooperation and team spirit were the dominant features, a fact she explains by the work processes found in this community. Where design of demo-discs was the main activity, a distinctive division of roles had developed. Some members were responsible for trading demos with other clubs, other members designed the graphics or the music, while others again "stitched together" the different bits and pieces into the final products. The style of work, the activities, and the community were all more group directed than individual oriented. Competition first began when the demos were finished; these were exhibited to other clubs at special demo or copy parties in order to demonstrate what your group was capable of designing. The borders and relations of interaction between people, machine use, and subculture may as such be understood as heterogeneous networks locally constructed.

The question is whether hacker cultures at universities have the same team spirit and organization as the game clubs. In the Amiga clubs you find boys aged 12 to 18 who work with simple, privately owned game-machines. The hackers found at, and in the close vicinity of, the Software Workshop are older and, as students at the Norwegian Institute of Technology (NIT), they have access to much more advanced technology. Thus, we would expect them to be engaged in more advanced activities and a wider range of activities. The student role also provides them with additional degrees of freedom as computer-users. Although they have to spend time on study, their use of their own and computer time at the university is far less "socially controlled".

Studying Domestication Strategies

Since my concern here is the hackers' use of computers and the values they ascribe to the technology, I use the concept of *domestication* in order to emphasize the reciprocity between technology and user. Domestication refers to the symbolic work and construction of routines that consumers of technological products undertake when they make products of their own (Sørensen, 1994). This implies that I regard hackers as creative actors who engage in negotiations with different elements of computers, thereby transforming technology into fixtures and ingredients that fit in with their personal interests and into their subculture. In these negotiations, hackers obviously must take account of the restrictions set by the technology, but computers embody a flexible user potential which empowers the hackers to integrate personal traits in the patterns of use they develop. It also enables them to integrate computers into a system of locally defined meanings. My question then becomes: *How do hackers proceed in these negotiations within their culture?*

The methodological point of using the metaphor of domestication is to approach the hackers with "the emptiest possible analytical vocabulary" (Akrich and Latour, 1992). This means that I attempt to analyse empirically the constructions of action and meaning with as few suppositions as possible (Sørgaard, 1994). Also, it is important to avoid a sharp analytical distinction between technical, personal, and cultural elements. The point is rather to show how such elements become interwoven by the actors at and around the Software Workshop (SWW).

I use the concepts of *scenarios* and *domestication strategies* as analytical expressions for central elements in such human–machine dialogues. "Scenarios" are the visions and messages that are consciously constructed to make one's own "political" project or interests visible to the surrounding world. To what extent do hackers construct such visions of themselves, their machine use, and their culture? How do they want to be perceived by others, and what symbolic actions are undertaken to provide such messages? By "domestication strategies" I mean the concrete procedures hackers may use individually or collectively when they negotiate with different human and non-human elements. The strength of this concept is that it opens up a way of understanding how meaning is formed through action.

We adopted an ethnographic-oriented design as our methodological point of departure. Primarily we wanted to get a picture of the domestication strategies hackers use, and how they themselves interpreted their dialogues with the technology and each other. At the same time we were interested in getting as much information as possible about the people and the culture in order to see whether being a hacker at a Norwegian university differs substantially from the reports we had read about hackers at North American universities.

We used participatory observation in the sense that we chose to live among them for a few evenings and nights. During these evenings and nights we discussed what we observed with the hackers, both in group conversations and through individual interviews. To ascertain that we understood what they actually were talking about, they preferred to illustrate their activities and strategies at their machines while explaining what they were doing. We also conducted longer interviews with a few chosen "*real hackers*" and "*semi-hackers*". Although our period of observation was short, we assess our collected materials as sufficient to capture the essence of the ways hackers negotiate among themselves, their common culture and available technology, as well as their conception of their way of life, lifestyle, and personality.

To be Visible – A Twofold Scenario

The first evening we visited the Software Workshop, we expected to find young male computer science students working on advanced machines. We did find young men, but their lair was a run-down office crowded with old desks and office stools. The metal shelves contained piles of books and manuals, computer print-outs and empty soda bottles. What surprised us most was in fact the age of the equipment. Here you could get a good picture of the development of terminal design over the past 10–12 years. A stripped-down hard disk, some cables, and detached monitors gave the place a certain air of a repair workshop, but the 10 people present that evening were most certainly not repairing machine parts. They were sitting at operative terminals. The only sound was eager fingers flying across keyboards and the faint beeps of some computer games. We were almost afraid to interrupt the ongoing processes, but we soon discovered that the hackers were more than willing to talk and guide us into their machine world.

They informed us that they were one of the best hacker clubs in the country. Here, advanced technology was used to solve serious problems. They told us, with noticeable pride, about the programming tasks they had done for companies. Mostly these involved developing smaller program modules that were integrated into different products. Some companies knew about the hacker community from previous assignments, others found them through contact with other people in the Computer Department at NIT.

The Software Workshop hackers also act as an "Oracle" service for employees and students. If someone gets stuck while using the machines or systems, they can approach the hackers for help. The hackers were just as proud of their achievements on the knowledge side as on the machine side. One of the hackers explained some of the effort as follows:

> "It is the guys from the Computer Department who spend their free time here who have made the system as popular as it is. They have a similar system at the School of Mechanical Engineering, ... but that is

hardly ever used.... The reason for that is ... that there have never been any – I would call them *wizards*, who have repaired it, maintained it, found out what was wrong, etc."

The hackers regard their own subculture as *unique*. This is not only due to the system work of "wizards" or that they are used as an "oracle". They are special because they constitute a *counterculture* in contrast to hardware tinkerers and mainstream PC cultures. Personal computers are objects of the past; they are found at home and rarely used. The hackers are not complete novices at machine tinkering either, but they seldom do it – only when they feel like experimenting with their own PCs. What counts as meaningful is working with large and advanced systems using powerful workstations.

The Software Workshop was, as we expected, a purely male group, but it is not just for computer students. Members are recruited from different departments, but the majority come from the School of Electrical Engineering and Computer Science and the School of Physics and Mathematics. We were somewhat surprised by the age of the terminals they had, and wondered if this was a countercultural statement too? When we mentioned this, the hackers realized that we did not quite understand their setting. The Software Workshop is more the private arena of the real hackers. The room is used for performing Oracle services and other tasks, but primarily it is a place for relaxing, discussions, and being with friends. They added that they do not turn away others who want to drop by. They have built a small terminal section in one corner of the room, somewhat out of the way and protected from their main arena, for others who want to visit and work with the machines.

Although the Software Workshop is the habitat of the real hackers, and as such has a symbolic function, the SWW members go somewhere else to do "real computer stuff". They use a computer lab they call "Solan". Here, we were guided between rows of modern SUN terminals, and given short demonstrations of the activities they performed. "Solan" is the place for those who want to work with advanced computer systems, and here we found those who chose to define themselves as *semi-hackers*. They do not belong to the SWW culture, but they know several of the "real hackers" belonging to the SWW. The "semi-hackers" view themselves as less infatuated with computers, something Fred and Alexander explained in the following way:

> "In the Physics department we are known as computer freaks. I don't think we would be if we had studied in the Computer department. I don't think we are the most conspicuous computer freaks. If you go to the computer labs late in the evening, you will find the same people, and then you will begin to understand." (Fred)
>
> "The freak image is probably important to some, but there are several of them who prefer to demonstrate their skilfulness." (Alexander)

At "Solan" the borders between different hacker personalities are vague. They talk and exchange knowledge about computers independently of their ideas about their own identity as hackers.

The real hackers who belong to SWW differentiate between their own subculture and the outside world. They want to be *an alternative* to the mainstream computer cultures. Thus, they use various symbols to signal who they are and that they are different. They think it is important to make themselves *visible* to the rest of the Institute of Technology, both as a group and as individuals. And within their own subculture most members emphasize communication of their individual qualities. Outward visibility is achieved by small singularities in dress and hair style. Ben, for example has a blue silk ribbon in his hair, and John has let not only his hair grow, but also his beard. Others try to communicate their special machine-related skills or personality. For instance, we met the only "religious hacker" of the SWW community, "the fastest programmer", "the net sweeper", "the system boss"; we even met "the only normal hacker".

The term "normal" is usually applied to those on the outside – the people who are not as immersed in computer systems and machines as themselves and have chosen to be mainstream computer-users. In contrast, these hackers view themselves as *special*. Some of them even use the term "abnormal". This refers to other people's perceptions. One of the hackers put it like this:

"A lot of others think that our community distinguishes itself in a negative way – a group of exhibitionists, you know, but we simply ain't. It is more that we want to gain distinction because we are clever. I want people to know who I am, not to disappear in the mass."

They confirm their individuality by expressing that their computer enthusiasm is different from that of many others. The member who is called "the only normal one" is in this context the carrier of a unique attribute; he is the one who is most like those *outside* the culture, and consequently he is special *inside* the culture.

As a group they communicate their common culture primarily by the kind of technology they use, but there are also other common characteristics with regard to their way of life and lifestyle. They prefer to work in the evenings, and some also work through the night. In addition, their language is shaped by their digital activities. They also emphasized that they are not especially good students; they are clever computer-users. What they find most exciting about NIT is not the education but the access to advanced technology such as powerful SUN stations, advanced computer systems, and lots of computing power and software.

The real hackers of the SWW culture use a twofold scenario to show who they are and the characteristics of their subculture. Their subcultural qualities are symbolized through the technology they regard as their own, the choice of spatial arena, and the members' symbolic characteristics. At the same time it is just as important to express their inner distinctiveness as hackers and different members of the subculture. They do not want to be perceived as a homogeneous community.

Why is *individuality* such an important characteristic of the hacker identity, and how is this built into the subculture? To understand this we have to take a closer look at how they relate to and negotiate with computers, and how they interpret their own selves and culture in relation to the machine practices they develop.

Admission Tickets to the Hacker Culture

Both the real hackers and the semi-hackers share the trait of an early interest in computers. They remember very well how in their early teens they became interested in the possibilities offered by rather simple game-machines or personal computers. Before they got involved with computers, many had played with mechanical and electronic construction kits. Alarm clocks and other technical artefacts found at home were taken apart and attempts were made to reassemble them. They were interested in how things are made and how they work. Computers provided new challenges and new ways of playing and exploring what they could be used for. Programming soon became a main activity. Some of the hackers were already doing serious programming work as teenagers. Erik, for example, wrote a program for his engineer father:

> "I started to get interested in computers in the seventh grade. Then I got to borrow a machine from a friend of my family. I became very keen and wrote a lot of programs. Daddy didn't know how to program, but he did have a lot of ideas for programs that were needed at the firm where he worked. One of the programs I wrote was for computing the load-carrying capacity of oilrigs. I didn't know anything about the theories or all the mathematics. My daddy fixed that, but he didn't bother to learn programming."

This enthusiasm for *puzzling things out* seems to be the foundation of their interest in computers. Soon the machines were used for figuring out what ideas and operations might be developed and integrated into the hardware and software they had access to.

Comics and science fiction also stimulated their interest in computers. Here they met characters and heroes who invented new machines that were used for fantastic things. This represented a kind of creative raw material that gave them new dreams and ideas about what they could try to do with their computers. Soon they had constructed a strategy of learning dominated by *experimentation*: proceed tentatively, see if you can solve it, learn from your mistakes, do not give up. They may also read manuals and computer journals to learn about different possibilities.

They bring with them these previous competences and preferences. Most of them continue to love programming, while science fiction and fantasy books remain a central element which they build into their culture. Chiefly as a joke they have constructed Douglas Adams' *The Hitchhiker's Guide to the Galaxy* as a necessary admission ticket for newcomers to their community. They explain that this entertaining science fiction novel is not that good, but it is fascinating to read the account of all the strange processes this book offers: when socio-technological problems seem to be solved, new ones arise because the questions suddenly change – a situation the hackers recognize from their own working processes at the terminals. Science fiction has been domesticated as a proper *leisure activity*. It is a relaxing and entertaining input to creative thinking.

Games are a third source of inspiration. Playing computer games for hours on end, often with several players engaged in the same game, was to most of them a pleasurable experience. They continue to play as SWW members, but games are defined as entertainment and a spare-time activity:

> "I've spent a lot of time gaming lately. Mostly because I can't find a solution to the things I'm working on. It gets like this at times. Sometimes the problem is that you are so tired, and then you just are not good for any programming. It takes a lot of concentration. Then it feels good to sit down with a game and still be among friends.

Simple games also encourage new ideas about how they can develop their own game versions offering more advanced options. But a real hacker cannot have games as his main activity, except for Multi-User Dungeon, which consequently has been domesticated as a proper hacker activity. Hackers may play MUD for weeks, simply because the game is challenging. This game is performed via the Internet, so the participants may be located in different countries. What is so special about MUD is that you may spy on the other players if you know the trick. You can also communicate with the others, write notes, build obstacles to them, and try to deceive them. As an extra feature, you do not know the identities of the other participants. In this game the players have the possibility to invent and express fictive names and personality traits. The central goal is to be elected master of the game, which is achieved by amassing a huge number of game points.

However, it is not the computer games that lured them into their hacker life at NIT. The temptation was the technology at Solan. Several of the SWW members were introduced to the subculture in the manner Erik describes:

> "It started when I saw these marvellous SUN stations, you know. So I started to sit there a bit, and asked the others around how to get things done. Then, one evening I had been there for quite a while and started to get hungry. The others had decided to visit a pizzabar and asked me to come along, and I went."

The semi-hacker Fred describes his meeting with Solan in similar terms:

> "At Solan I have begun to get to know quite a few of them. They have a different operating system there – UNIX – and it was a little cryptic at first, so I had to ask for help from time to time. So, I have come to know people there. I just ask questions."

The SUN terminals and the computer systems that these workstations utilize provide the foundation for the culture of both semi-hackers and real hackers. Who joins the SWW culture is more a question of chance. What is taken for granted is that you are interested in utilizing the technology they have defined as central to this counterculture. The rest is up to you. In time, semi-hackers may well become real hackers, if they do not choose to keep their loose links with the Solan community. It did not seem as if the real hackers emphasize *boundary criteria*; a fact we found surprising because this is a common finding of previous studies of subcultural youth communities (Brake, 1990; Hall and Jefferson, 1983; Hebdige, 1979). As long as the people at Solan are doing interesting computer stuff, they are also interesting as people.

Since hackers define computer games and science fiction as leisure activities, we wondered what they actually do when they are not in need of entertainment or relaxation. What do they use the SUN terminals for? And what about their working styles?

Competition and Play – Work and Creativity

When computer games are the basis of negotiation, we find *competition*, either between the hacker and the software, or between the hacker and other players. The point is to gain control by comprehending the system or by manipulating it to win. Competition between hackers can also be found when it comes to designing their own game versions. Who can create the most brilliant Othello game? The hackers domesticate such competitive activities as *entertainment* and *play*. It is certainly not *work*.

They also have endurance competitions. For how many hours in a row is one able to do programming? In this field, there are personal as well as community records. John told us about Georg, who was the system manager at the Software Workshop and lived at the same place as John:

> "Georg, for example, a neighbour of mine, disappeared once. I thought: what the heck, has he got himself a girlfriend or what? But no, he came home, pale and sallow with hunched shoulders. I asked him what he had been doing. 'I have set a new record,' he said. 'I have been programming for 42 hours in a row.' Then he went to his room and slept for 17 hours."

Asceticism is mentioned as central to such endurance tests. You do not give up until the problem is solved. This means that at certain times you stay at your terminal all through the evening and night, and into the next morning. At such times they easily forget time and place. This may create problems; the shops may be closed when hunger sets in. They are not solely driven by excitement. Debugging can in fact be quite boring. The art is to show patience when they meet practical programming problems. That is necessary in order to succeed. But this domestication strategy does not suit all the members of the Software Workshop:

> "There were a couple of times I sat for many hours on end, but I don't like that any more. You get a kind of jet-lag. There are times when I'll sit till two at night. That is when I haven't been able to find

a solution to a problem, and I know I'm going to lay awake thinking, endlessly irritated. At other times, when I'm in the middle of something, it is no problem to stop, eat dinner, go home, and continue the following day."

To master programming is not a goal as such. It is a prerequisite for being able to design solutions or products. One of the hackers provided this short explanation of what it means to design, in contrast to merely master programming:

"If you want to build an entirely new house, you have to know more than how to hit the nails."

Designing products might include developing anything from a brand-new drawing program to adding small functions and features to existing software and systems. When we visited them, the SWW members were at work on a wide range of problems. Some were working on graphics problems, others on fractals. How do you get the machine to draw curved lines or create moving pictures? Others were attempting to combine sound and pictures, or were studying how physics problems could be transferred and handled by computer programs.

The fascination with computers and programming stems from the possibilities the technology offers. The motivating power is to see how ideas can be converted into machine solutions. John describes his fascination in the following terms:

"What you find interesting is not the simple things that follow rules. It is precisely *not to follow rules* that is interesting. If you simply follow rules, then you just program them into the machines. If you on the other hand don't follow the rules, then you will *find new solutions*, and that's what's fun. Then you can grasp the logic in the systems and find possible principles. It is a kind of tinkering process."

We were told that the nice thing about computers is that you do not have to think the same thing over and over again. There are always variations; new possibilities always arise. The hackers perceive their terminals and operating systems in terms of *variation* and *flexibility*, not repetition and solidity.

Many of the hackers describe their style of work as *experimentation*: seeking solutions by *muddling through*. They do not want to follow structured approaches; for example by imitating the manuals or using too strictly rule-based software. The hackers explain this as being a matter of principle: they *dislike to be controlled* or *directed*. It is better to ask somebody for advice when you run out of ideas.

They perceive themselves as *creative* computer-users, in contrast to *standardized computer professionals*. Their style of work and their understanding of themselves is expressed in the way in which they define computers and computer systems. Personal computers are "disgusting", IBM machines are "wicked", and Macintoshes are in fact "snobbish". They hate programming languages such as Pascal and Cobol, because they represent uniformed and rule-regulated systems. They are replete with "barriers" that block their wish for individuality and artistry, or, as one of the hackers expressed it: "We depend on freedom from 'walls' when we do programming work."

The hackers talk about "walls" when they experience the software as steering them, and the point is as little steering as possible. Steering is supposed to come from the head of the machine-user and not from the software. Success is a question of possibilities, the human capacity for abstract and logical thinking. Instead they prefer the programming language C, and some of them have also used Assembly coding. This provides them with more freedom to construct, according to personal taste, their own brilliant solutions.

Personal computers they consider to be ready-made solutions developed for uniform users of machines. These machines are hopeless because they have no consistent design. They are made out of different technical bits and pieces that have been put together with little logic and regard for user-friendliness. By user-friendliness the hackers mean technological solutions with a great deal of freedom when it comes to discovering possible operations and procedures. This does not necessarily mean that the technology is easily accessible to new users. PCs do not have the necessary degree of freedom demanded, and consequently the hackers perceived these machines to be a "tool" for mainstream users – people located outside the hackers' subculture. The Macs are "snobbish" because their design and graphics look brilliant, yet they in fact are slow and full of structures and barriers. The hackers associate Macs with architects, advertising people, and women – different groups they define as passive consumers of ready-made software. They constitute a contrast to the hackers' self-image as *designers of technology*.

Although the excitement is in the process of finding suitable solutions that work for designing new products, they do not conceal the fact that success also involves a feeling of control. One of them chose to express this in the following terms: "In my relationship with the machine, I'm the boss. It is a wonderful feeling to win over the machine."

But to win or to achieve control is more a question of finding good solutions to the problems they are working on, so the central project is not to master all aspects of the machine or set endurance records. Happiness is to *develop* something:

> "You feel the excitement, you feel you are creating things when you are really getting into it. I don't think I feel that I'm breaking through my own limits. It is fun to create things. That's a good enough explanation."

They do not consider their relationship to their machines to be personal or close, in the way Turkle describes the MIT hackers' machine relations. Both semi-hackers and real hackers have domesticated the computers as *a tool for work*. When questioned, one of them chose to express himself in this way:

> "One's relationship with humans and things is different. Humans have their own views which they manage themselves. A computer is an object we can do different things with, and it doesn't protest at all. Things exist to be manipulated. Humans exist for cooperation. That's the difference."

The hackers use concepts such as "manipulating", "control", and "winning over the machines". These are characteristic of the approach to computers that Turkle (1984) calls "hard mastery", a style described as typical of many boys. At the same time our hackers say it is important to have an artistic approach, to be creative, to proceed tentatively, to look for what fits, to experiment – elements that resemble what Turkle calls "soft mastering", a working style she found more typical of girls using computers.

Individual Tasks – Collaborative Styles

Although competition is the hallmark of the activities they define as play, all products designed within the community, and their computer knowledge as a whole, are available for all members. One of the SWW members described his view of the community in the following way:

> "At first I was a bit afraid that someone would copy something of mine. I kept the source code to myself and copy-protected my programs. This I have stopped doing, because I get so much from the others. Others who wrote programs I had a use for. When I ask the others, they don't start to explain. They say: 'Just take mine, have a look at it, and use it if you can.' It isn't really necessary to reinvent the wheel."

These hackers are less dominated by the individual competitiveness that Noller and Paul (1991) and Nissen (1993) found in other computer clubs. Both semi-hackers and real hackers stress that what unites the Solan community is an interest in computers rather than a common push toward achievement. The SWW members we interviewed agreed that it is the *community* and their collective creativity that matters. One of them said:

> "We're a lot stronger as a group than as individuals. For example, the drawing programme that Erik wrote, it also contains my things. Things he has taken from what I know and have created.... So you might say that cooperation characterizes us more than competition does. The computer world is in fact too large for competition. ... We have seen that the best way to succeed is to learn from each other."

The importance of community and collaboration is also reflected in the hackers' understanding of computers. You cannot compete with the machine to win, in fact you have to *collaborate* with it to understand the logic in the hardware and software. Here we discern a continuous process of domestication between people and machines, a process that demands collaboration from both sides. In many practical situations the hackers develop a dual relationship with the machines, the activities they engage in, and their interpretations of the community and themselves. They develop and shape a style of work and manners that contains elements of both *competition and collaboration*. The balance between competition and collaboration varies with the activities in question. It also varies between hackers. So it is rather problematical to characterize their construction work in terms only of either competition or collaboration. These are matters constructed in the domestication strategies that take place between machines, performers, and their culture in specific situations.

At the same time, the hackers consider it important to put their individual stamp on the domestication strategies they develop in dialogues with the machines. Both the styles of work developed and the products created contain integrated end explicit elements of personal style and taste.

> "Erik has found a way to draw nice curved lines. ... I have also experimented with drawing such lines. I use an entirely different method from him. He can't stand my method at all because it 'oscillates' more than he wants. And I can't stand his method because it is too 'diffuse'. My method involves more points, while his entails drawing this line in a 'diffuse' manner. I'm not entirely satisfied with my method either, you know."

Whereas some start the problem-solving process directly at the machine, others prefer to organize the logic of their steps first, often by using pen and paper, as John describes his procedure:

> "I do in fact think theoretically through the problem and analyse it, thinking through the solutions before I go to the machine. So; I use my head, often pen and paper too. When I go to the machine I know approximately what to do, but I do of course spend quite a lot of time in front of the machine too. If you just 'muddle through' you may lose the possibility of seeing the overall picture of what you're doing. It is after all 'the logic' that is the interesting thing. 'Muddling through' is a typical style for many, but then they may fail to see many of the mistakes they make."

What they consider important and meaningful by their activities also varies. Erik, for example, wants his products to be useful:

> "You feel that you create something, you know, and that others have a use for it. When others started to use my drawing program, I was so happy. I realized that I had made something useful. There's no point making things which nobody has any use for."

John emphasizes other aspects:

> "I prefer theory, not how things in fact are made. To me the central thing is to find out how things could be designed."

To a large degree it is the satisfaction they gain from the processes that matters, but not always. It depends on what they are doing. Whereas John's main interest is theories for programming solutions to physics problems, Erik is more interested in developing products that others, including non-hackers, could use. That means that entirely different things matter:

> "You must have a perspective on what you're doing. Among other things you have to understand the ways people think. Others have to understand your software too. So you have to make it easy to understand. You can be a genius at writing programs that do fantastic things, but which are totally useless because nobody else is able to grasp what's going on."

The hackers' desire for individuality is not just expressed by small idiosyncrasies in dress style or by different hacker images. They also use the technology in such a manner that the human–machine dialogues acquire a personal touch. It is difficult to decide whether individual machine practices produce different hacker images or if the hacker images produce different practices in their machine dialogues. There is a continuous process of exchange between people, culture and technology where matters of style and taste, individual as well as collective, are woven together and integrated into meaningful connections, whether it is working styles or images we are talking about.

A Collaborative Work Style – an Anarchistic Subculture

The specific subculture that the real hackers and semi-hackers inhabit offers more than the opportunity to communicate with technology. When they get tired of sitting at their terminals or pondering programming strategies, it is good to get away from computer labs and Oracle services. They might go to the cinema together or drop by a pizzabar to eat, talk about movies or books, or discuss computers and programming.

According to the real hackers, their subculture offers a social habitat, a community of fellows. It is of course important to allow individual projects ample room within the subculture, but the subculture is also supposed to reflect the *collectiveness* of hackerdom. They have no defined distribution of roles according to work processes of the kind found by Aune in the Amiga clubs. Collectiveness is here based on the hackers inference that it is advantageous and enjoyable to exchange knowledge and experience regardless of individual projects and interests in computers, and their wish to make visible what they know and the type of technology it is exciting to utilize.

From this perspective, this subculture offers a way of life without too many established codes of behaviour, but it is not based only on individuality. *Community* and *collaboration* are just as important.

Several of our informants disliked many of the popular conceptions of hackers and hacker cultures. They do not break codes to get into larger computer facilities. They told us that this is much more complicated than the media assert. Anyhow, "why mess around breaking into things," as one of the semi-hackers said, "when we already have access to almost all software and systems right here at NIT." They also dislike the picture of hackers as asocial eccentrics:

> "There are those here who have problems organizing themselves and their relationships with other people. But that is just some. It is a myth that computer people in general have such problems."

Most of them do participate in social activities outside the hacker community. They know other students and they have friends who do not study at NIT, and they do not spend all their leisure time with computers. Erik, for example, who is known as one of the 'worst computer freaks' among the second year of computer science students, said:

> "If one were to spend the rest of one's life in front of a computer, I would find that tragic. One has to do different things, enjoy oneself, go to a disco at the weekends, have friends who are not interested in computers. ... I am thinking about the quality of life I want. I do not at all want a drab existence."

They have a need to indicate what they like and dislike in the computer world through symbols and manners in order to make clear the scenario that they are a specific machine culture. They want to be known as exceptional computer-users, but not as a group of eccentrics. They dismiss the myth about the one-track hacker figure; their culture accepts a large variety of people. They like to talk in terms of contrasts in order to demonstrate their different characters as people and computer-users:

> "There are those who like to talk through the keyboard. I'm not one of them. I have played around with it a bit, you know. But I think there are quite enough people who I can talk to here at the school rather than talking to people through networks. And it is anyhow easier to communicate face-to-face, nicer, if you like. And the conversations that go on by means of the screen are simply idiot talk."

The hackers have not thought much about why they are an all-male enclave. To them, it is a mystery that no women are interested in computers in the way they are. Nevertheless, they have all experienced that computer hacking is something women and girls want to keep at arm's length. Consequently, the hackers have defined women as belonging to the outside world. Some of the hackers have girlfriends and it is only a few of them who emphasize that they have no relation to women outside the hacker community. The absence of women does not bother them much either, but they do not believe that they 'frighten away' the 'girls'. It is up to the women themselves to take part in the hackers' subculture and to develop their own style and use of computers.

The Software Workshop might be called a *subculture with some important anarchistic features*. It almost seems to reflect the hackers' opinions about computer systems and software. Just like computer systems and software, the culture should not have too many '*walls*' hemming in the individual's prospects for creating a space for their personality and lifestyle, both as a human being and as a computer-user.

The Hacker Culture – An Ambiguous Project

The most interesting feature of the hacker culture I have analysed is its many ambiguities. It is both *individualistic* and *collective*. We find elements of *competition*, but also of *collaboration*; *play* and *entertainment* as well as *work* and *utility*. Hackers *consume* technology, and they *design* technology. They talk about *winning* and *mastery*, but also about the importance of being *artistic* and *interactive*. The computers are *instrumental* as well as *expressive*; defined as "objective" tools which also include certain values, and subjective elements are integrated into their use. The members of the Software Workshop are *similar*, but also *different*, and there are both *similarities* and *differences* between *real hackers* and *semi-hackers*. They do not operate completely in the same arena, and whereas real hackers shape their scenario in such a manner as to constitute a counterculture, this does not apply in the same degree to semi-hackers. Regardless of hacker identity, they all utilize the same technology, differentiate between work and play along the same lines, and their work styles are distinctly experimental.

I have attempted to show how these cultural traits become visible through the *symbols* the hackers have constructed around their practice and identity, and in the *actions* performed at the machines and within the culture. The observed heterogeneity is not solely a result of the manner in which the hackers construct *personality* and *culture*. They also transform the *technology* so that it reflects the interests and values that are meaningful to the community and the individual computer-user.

What emerges is a more complex male machine-culture than that we may find described in several earlier studies of techno-science gender relations (Benston, 1988; Keller, 1985; Rotschild, 1983; Turkle, 1984, 1988). Like them, I found what have been held to be "typical *masculine* traits", such as: *hierarchy, competition, distance,* and *control,* in this particular hacker community. The hackers rank hardware, software and machine activities in status hierarchies, and they compete over endurance and individual achievements (see Turkle, 1984, 1988). They gain status by mastering, manipulating, and controlling technology, and they construct distance between themselves and the machines by assigning them the status as objects. At the same time, what have been held to be "more *feminine* traits" can be found. When "real work tasks" are performed, *cooperation* is emphasized. At such times, what counts is *reciprocal interchange* between hackers, and between the hacker and the computer. They see *caring* and *tolerance* as important ingredients of their culture, and tolerance is also expressed in the machine processes. They define their *community* as the most important cultural resource in becoming creative and innovative computer-users. This interweaving of different value elements is a result of the space for negotiation that this subculture provides for its members to create meaningful connections between technology and masculinity. To the hackers, it seems that it is fruitful to make not only technology but also masculinity sufficiently flexible to allow a wide range of contrasts.

Thus, the hackers illustrate some of the problems associated with using concepts that are too strict or value sets that are too general to describe masculine and feminine positions when it comes to the design and use of technology. Traditional research on gender–technology relations has the weakness that it has been grounded on an understanding of gender as the dominating force shaping technology (Håpnes and Sørensen, 1995). What this study of hackers shows is precisely the importance of grasping the *relational dynamics between technology and its users/designers.* To discern how this interplay works entails the challenge of increasing our insight into the ways that the construction of gender and technology are simultaneous processes (Berg, 1994). This analysis shows the ways in which reciprocal relations are built as a result of the dialogues between the hackers, the technology they use, and the culture they live in.

The next step here is to emphasize the specificities of the cultural context of the human–machine dialogues. The hacker culture at NIT is both similar to and different from the macho culture at MIT described by Turkle (1984, 1988) and the compulsive programmers of Weizenbaum (1976). The hackers of SWW are interested in promoting individual achievements, they like to master the computer, and they spend a lot of time at their terminals – elements that correspond to the female students' picture of this hacker community. But the hackers do not see themselves as instrumental loners who have chosen the computers as a sanctuary from the complexities of society. Most of them enjoy human conversation with each other and with people external to hackerdom. Only a few are interested in computer technology for the technology's sake. It is rather the possibilities for designing products by means of this technology that constitutes the reason for their excitement.

The domestication strategies found within the hacker culture have been shaped by the international discourse about hackers. At the same time, they dissociate themselves from other features. They do not want to be associated with computer crime, or to be known as a homogeneous group of computer-users. They strongly emphasize their dissimilarities as individuals and as machine-users. Compared with Turkle's description of MIT hackers, this Norwegian hacker culture is *less extreme* and *more heterogeneous* and it allows the members to *model different masculinities* through accepting a wide variety of personal qualities.

Why is heterogeneity so important? The real concern of the SWW members is to present themselves as an alternative to what they perceive as the rule-directed mainstream computer profession. Their alternative project is *the pursuit of freedom*. They will not be ruled by general cultural norms or technical structures. Whether they really represent an alternative is a question of interpretation. The point is that this freedom is central to their self-conception. *"Not in their machines"* might be called their main scenario, which they in fact signal in all their symbols and actions. They construct a communal freedom by designing individual hacker qualities and specialities which demonstrate the possibility of taking different positions as computer-users. What I see in this hacker culture is a form of *socio-technical experimentation*. Their motivation is simply to challenge the boundaries of computers and their own creativity.

This socio-technical freedom to which real hackers consciously aspire, and which can also be found in the machine practices of semi-hackers, makes it possible for them to construct consumption and development of technology as two aspects of the same activity. They operate with pronounced boundaries between what counts as design in contrast to the application of technology, in order to demarcate what the real hacker activities are. *Development* is to design solutions and products, and it is defined as *work*. Games and communication through computer networks are *applications*, and as such are interpretated as *entertainment* or *relaxation*.

This demarcation into two spheres of activity becomes rather muddy when we study the manner in which hackers proceed in dialogues with each other and the technology. When they exchange finished products or suggestions for solutions, their use does not count as application. On the contrary, it counts as an important building-block for a new creative push, and is as such defined as production and work. Some of their products are used for play and relaxation. When Erik's drawing program and the games they have created are used for entertainment, they are transformed into applications. At the same time they define applications such as computer games as a source of new ideas that they can utilize in their designing projects. Regardless of whether it is games, physics problems, or computer graphics that is the task at hand, their activities are characterized by a form of play in which hackers experiment with their countercultural status.

The interpretative flexibility here accorded to technology and machine activities should be understood in the context of the socio-technical freedom these hackers try to realize. This constitutes a machine culture with access to advanced technological equipment in which formalized productive demands for the most part are absent.

NOTE

1. The data on which this paper is based were collected in 1991 by Margrethe Aune and myself.

REFERENCES

Akrich, M. and Latour, B. 1992. A summary of a convenient vocabulary for the semiotics of human and nonhuman assemblies. In W. E. Bijker and J. Law (eds): *Shaping Technology/Building Society. Studies in Sociotechnical Change*. Cambridge, MA: MIT Press.

Aune, M. 1992. *Datamaskina i hverdagslivet – en studie av brukeres domestisering av en ny teknologi*. STS Report No. 15. Trondheim: Centre for Technology and Society.

Benston, M. L. 1988. Women's voices/men's voices: technology as language. In C. Kramarae (ed.): *Technology and Women's Voices. Keeping in Touch*. New York and London: Routledge & Kegan Paul.

Berg, A.-J. 1994. Technological flexibility: bringing gender into technology (or was it the other way round?). In C. Cockburn and R. Fürst-Dilic (eds): *Bringing Technology Home. Gender and Technology in a Changing Europe*. Milton Keynes: Open University Press.

Brake, M. 1990 *Comparative Youth Culture. The Sociology of Youth Culture and Youth Subcultures in America, Britain and Canada*. London: Routledge & Kegan Paul.

Hall, S. and Jefferson, T. 1983 *Resistance through Rituals. Youth Subculture in Postwar Britain*. London: Hutchinson.

Hebdige, D. 1979. *Subculture. The Meaning of Style*. London: Routledge & Kegan Paul.

Håpnes, T. and Rasmussen, B. 1991. Excluding women from the technologies of the future? *Futures*, December.

Håpnes, T. and Sørensen, K. H. 1995. Competition and collaboration in male shaping of computing: A study of a Norwegian hacker culture. In

K. Grint and R. Gill (eds): *The Gender–Technology Relation. Contemporary Theory and Research*. London: Taylor & Francis.

Keller, E. F. 1985. *Reflections on Gender and Science*. New Haven, CN and London: Yale University Press.

Levy, S. 1984. *Hackers. Heroes of the Computer Revolution*. New York: Dell Publishing.

Nissen, J. 1993. *Pojkarna vid datorn. Unga entusiaster i datateknikens värld*. Stockholm/Stehag: Symposion Graduale.

Noller, P. and Paul, G. 1991. *Jugendliche Computerfans: Selbstbilder und Lebens-entwürfe. Eine empirische Untersuchung*. Frankfurt: Campus Verlag.

Rasmussen, B. and Håpnes, T. 1991. The production of male power in computer science. In I. V. Erikkson et al. (eds): *Women, Work and Computerization*. Amsterdam: Elsevier Science Publishers.

Rotschild, J. 1983. *Machina Ex Dea. Feminist Perspectives on Technology*. New York: Pergamon Press.

Rozak, T. 1986. *The Cult of Information. The Folklore of Computers and True Art of Thinking*. New York: Pantheon Books.

Sørensen, K. H. 1994. *Technology in Use. Two Essays on the Domestication of Artifacts*. STS Working Paper No. 2. Trondheim: Centre for Technology and Society.

Sørgaard, J. 1994. *Bilens integrasjon i hverdagslivet: En teknologisosiologisk tilnærming til bilkultur*. STS Working Paper No. 12. Trondheim: Centre for Technology and Society.

Turkle, S. 1984. *The Second Self. Computers and the Human Spirit*. New York: Simon & Schuster.

Turkle, S. 1988. Computational reticence: Why women fear the intimate machine. In C. Kramarae (ed.): *Technology and Women's Voices. Keeping in Touch*. New York and London: Routledge & Kegan Paul.

Weizenbaum, J. 1976. *Computer Power and Human Reason. From Judgement to Calculation*. San Francisco: W. H. Freeman.

Chapter 6

A Fairy Tale on Wheels
The Car as a Vehicle for Meaning within a Norwegian Subculture

Gunnar M. Lamvik

Amcar Enthusiasm – A Scandinavian Specialty

This paper tells a story of a Norwegian subculture constructed around American cars of the 1950s as a material and symbolic centre-piece. It is concerned with the way this culture uses cars as so-called vehicles of meaning, and how the culture is structured to facilitate this break from ordinary everyday life activities.

You could say that the Amcar adventure started in the 1960s. When the sale of automobiles was deregulated in 1960 (Østby, 1995), this coincided with the dawning of a youth culture, here as in the rest of the Western world. These events spurred the emergence of a form of community around the car in general, and especially American cars. This represented something new and unfamiliar in Norway. Even though the moral panic these communities aroused never measured up to what could be found in neighbouring Sweden, for example as recounted by Bjurström (1987), the Norwegian "raggare" represented one of the first groups of subcultural actors – actors in an arena that later were to become populated by much stranger groups.

Amcar enthusiasm is a cultural phenomenon which is especially widespread in Norway and Sweden. In no other European country will you find so many well-kept American-made cars, primarily cars of the older vintages. And there are few countries where car shows are so well attended. Every year thousands of car enthusiasts visit the many shows of American cars that are arranged during the summer. The motifs and incitements of this enthusiasm are explored later in this paper.

Amcar interest in Norway found a more formalized form in the early 1970s in the city of Trondheim. A few friends and acquaintances gathered at a cheap restaurant and formed the American Car Club of Trondheim (ACCT). The club's purpose was to further the interest in American cars in Norway. ACCT proved to be a success, and a few years later a national organization called the American Car Club of Norway (ACCN) was founded. Today, this organization has about 11,000 members and 50 local chapters all over the country. In addition to the usual club activities, ACCN over the years has lobbied the Norwegian authorities, an activity that among other things has brought the result that cars which are more than 30 years old may be imported free of duty. The central position the ACCN has achieved is also illustrated by the fact that it is formally and regularly consulted by Norwegian road and traffic authorities.

The ACCN's new multimillion building centrally located in Trondheim is also the home of several businesses, all with their customer basis in this large group of Norwegians interested in American cars. Here we find the Amcar Magazine, a monthly publication with a circulation of 24,000; and US Autoparts, which gets auto parts flown in from the USA on a weekly basis. US Autoparts also has district offices in Oslo and New York.

As one will understand from this, the Amcar milieu is no longer a group of restless young people, but comprises people of different ages who save this passion for their spare time and holidays.

Technology, Symbols, and Subculture

In order to understand the development and growth of the communities I shall later subsume under the umbrella concept of "the Amcar community", there are several elements that have to be examined. I have already mentioned the deregulation of car sales and the formation of a youth culture as two important factors. In my opinion one of the most important driving forces behind the formation of the Amcar community is to be found in the many historical connections between Norway and the USA. In addition, and connected to this, is the USA's ability to act as a reservoir, or in Bigsby's (1975) terms a "superculture", for the whole Western world's construction of what we could call mythical images. I would term the aspects of Norwegian history which concern Norway's relationship to the USA "a hundred years' crush" (Lamvik, 1994), by which I mean that Norway has displayed a long and remarkable infatuation with the country across the Atlantic. Owing to distance and difference in size this attraction is destined to remain a one-sided affair.

In the decade after 1880 about 10 percent of the Norwegian population left Norway for the USA (Bergh et al., 1983). Although it would not be entirely historically correct, one could say that these multitudes of journeys westward marked the beginning of Norwegian conceptions of the USA as "the promised land". The continued impact of this image was ascertained, adapted and strengthened through the continuous appropriation of Hollywood America: "The Dream Factory". Or, to put it another way, as the stream of emigrants petered out after the turn of the century, the imported "American Dream" has steadily increased in extent and refinement. The sunny, slim, youthful happiness California style has become an almost obligatory ingredient in all mass media diets.

Owing to the fact that I primarily refer to the rendering of the USA found in advertising, music and movies, I use the concept of "mythical" (cf. Hebdige, 1979). These media do not attempt to provide a realistic, credible, and documentary picture of the United States. These expressions should rather be seen as part of another level of reality than the everyday given. I do not claim that mythical and everyday reality constitute separate universes. In order to reach the individual, the potential customer, or the movie goer, the messages of the media have to deal with familiar questions, provide points of contact.

I do not claim that the Norwegian people have unconditionally appropriated the many powerful and often glamorous images the mass media have provided. Such appropriation is not an unconditional surrender, but occurs under conditions laid down by the appropriating party who performs work that may transform images as well as practices (Levold and Østby, 1993). Bryn (1989), for example, has used the term "Norwegian images of America" to analyse the manifold American influences in contemporary Norwegian culture. This term highlights the local colouring that is added to the presented images through the process of interpretation and appropriation.

The other main cause for the establishment and growth of different kinds of car communities is more closely associated with the car itself and the position it has in the Western world. In this connection there are three factors I want to emphasize. First, the car represents a closed, mechanical universe. It is not hard to imagine how the achievement of competence in relation to such machinery might fascinate and occupy many people. Experience shows that it is mainly men who possess the capability for being seduced by the inner ecology of the automobile. Here, I shall avoid psychological interpretations of their fascination and rather rely on cultural theory to explain the attraction of these specific cars.

The German philosopher Gehlen (1980) uses the concept "resonance phenomena" in his attempt to apprehend the human relationship with machines. The idea is that a person, with his or her bloodstream and heartbeat, may be regarded as a machine. What then may happen is that this person sees himself or herself in and identifies with the mechanical artefact s/he confronts and becomes involved with. One possible conclusion to such a conception of the human–machine relation is that this connection not only is at the level of rationality and knowledge, but also touches the more existential aspects of life. Humans may experience a deeply felt harmony in their relations with machines.

The other aspect of the car, which might have made it an object of community building, is the car considered within the context of cultural history. This artefact might, as pointed out by

Barthes (1973), be seen as the cathedral of our time – both the cathedral and the car mirror their own times. If we then stress the car's ability to absorb the spirit of the time, it is not hard to imagine why some, motivated by an interest in history, would spend time and money on this technology. A fascination with cars might then be analysed as similar to other people's interest in archaeology, antiques, or design.

A third property of the car, which enhances its potential to acquire a central place in many lives, is the experience of driving. The car is sometimes referred to as one of the few remaining spaces for withdrawal and contemplation that exists in the hurried contemporary everyday life: a "dressing room of our souls". Adding the car's ability to move through the landscape, we get closer to my point. Considering the effacing qualities of speed juxtaposed with the space for mental self-fulfilment that the coupé represents, one may understand the fascination of owning and driving a car. This point should become clearer when later presented in an empirical context.

One of the main points I want to make in this paper is that it is not possible to consider these three aspects of having a car as independent of each other. The different aspects of the car will influence each other reciprocally. Every single member of the Amcar community operates within all three fields described here. It is, for example, considered a virtue within this community to repair and restore your car yourself. Moreover, in this process, it is customary to strive towards as historically a correct car as possible. To the majority of enthusiasts this means a car in a condition as close to the state in which it left the factory in "the fabulous fifties". Furthermore, there are many who claim the driving itself as the crowning glory. Such "cruising", as they call it, preferably takes place during hot summer evenings in the centre of Norwegian towns.

Another vital point in this paper is that Amcar enthusiasm cannot be understood as just an interest in cars. As already suggested, mythical ideas about the USA might be just as important an ingredient in the world building of the enthusiasts. In this perspective, Amcar enthusiasm becomes an attempt to re-create or re-experience a mythical American reality in a foreign country; an endeavour which includes a range of ingredients, such as language, music, clothes, etc., but which has the car as the central element.

Once upon a Time …

On a seemingly ordinary Wednesday in the summer of 1990, I found myself among some Amcar enthusiasts – which is a suitable name for members of the subculture that I was studying – at a relatively isolated spot outside the city of Trondheim. Though the sky was cloudy and the weather far from tropical, this didn't prevent people from having a good time. They were joking and talking about their cars while they enjoyed a barbecue.

What was the reason for my being out in the wilderness? Or, to put the question in a different way, why were several dozen people congregating outdoors for a barbecue party on this particular day? The short answer to these questions is: it was the Fourth of July.

Here, I want to draw a more comprehensive and intelligible picture of this mystery – a community of car-loving Norwegians, mostly men, in Norway celebrating the Independence Day of the United States. Of course this was not the only puzzling practice in this subculture. The exotic impression this culture made on an outsider was not limited to this particular day of the year, but was also visible in people's everyday lives. Still, using the Fourth of July celebration as a starting point will, I think, be a fruitful approach to this culture in general. Even if a focus on this occasion is not sufficient to understand fully what was going on, it can be treated as a keyhole into this subculture.

As part of the context of interpretation, it should be noted that this subculture was dominated by men. It was men who were the active members of this world. For the most part they were the owners of the cars and the ones who usually took charge of the driving, repairing, and restoration of these four-wheeled beauties. Thus, my story is in a sense an analysis of a particular culture of man–machine relationships, although I have chosen not to focus on gender. However, when my account is compared with Tove Håpnes's study in this volume of computer hackers (also a masculine community), one should note the differences in the construction of masculinities.

If one takes a look at the Fourth of July celebration it is clear that most of the enthusiasts had striven to make this evening something special. Many objects, expressions, and actions indicated the reason for their gathering. People drank Coke out of cups decorated with the Stars and Stripes, and ate crisps and popcorn similarly wrapped. They ate grilled corn on the cob – which is quite rare in Norway – together with more typical meat dishes. One man complained that he had not been able to get real American beer for the occasion. Another man wondered if his hot dogs were typical American or not. A woman described herself and the group as "Yankees". Though this statement was made in a joking manner it also illustrates something important about how this community viewed its Fourth of July celebration.

I shall return later to this celebration and how it might be interpreted as a central "ritual" for this subculture. The interpretation of the celebration will be made on the basis of a more extensive anthropological analysis of this subculture's *style* – the outcome of these people's skills, fantasy, and hard work. Before I give a more detailed description of the style characterizing this particular community, I will mention some of the theoretical ideas this perspective grows out of – ideas about how people give meaning to their existence.

By style I mean the mode of symbolic expression by which a subculture constructs a social world, diverging in significant ways from so-called "mainstream culture". A common way of apprehending symbols is to say that a symbol is something that *stands for* something else. What a symbol actually expresses through this relationship, through its "as if" qualities, I see as its *meaning*.

My use of the concept of style draws heavily on the work of Hebdige, developed in his book *Subculture – The Meaning of Style* (1979). Hebdige emphasizes the signification of multivocality and ambiguity in the relation between the signifier and the signified.

In other words, my approach to the symbolic depends upon a notion of an arbitrary relation between formal expression and substantive content.

Thus a symbol is a "multivocal entity", as far as meaning is concerned (Turner, 1974). The important point here is that its various meanings are expressed through different uses or interpretations, and every usage or practice implies an intention or a direction. Every specialized use of a symbol can therefore be seen as an activity that foregrounds some meanings and downplays other meanings that a symbol can be said to possess. Each particular use of a symbol activates only a tiny part of its total potential for meaning. When a constellation of interpretations and usages is developed within a more or less closed system – when the different parts are used in such a way that they correspond to and supplement each other, so that they constitute a coherent, holistic expression – one can say that a "style" is presented.

I would finally emphasize the importance of seeing style as resulting from the work of a *bricoleur*. This Jack-of-all-trades is famous for a creativeness based on unusual constellations of well-known artefacts and expressions, rather than a completely new world constructed from scratch. In other words, style seen from this angle is a question of new combinations inside a pre-existing world, rather than a genuine innovative process.

Another scholar in the tradition of the Birmingham school, John Clarke, describes the creative process in this way:

> The generation of subcultural styles, then, involves differential selection from within a matrix of the existent. What happens is not a creation of objects and meanings from nothing, but rather the *transformation and rearrangement* of what is given (and "borrowed") into a pattern which carries a new meaning, its *translation* to a new context, and its *adaption*. (Clarke, 1976: 178)

A Series of American Expressions

When we want to take a closer look at the style created inside the community of the Amcar enthusiasts, a natural place to start is their clothing. The typical dress, what we might call the "uniform", in this subculture consists of the following character-istic items. On their feet, people wear boots – not always the brown and anonymous type, but sometimes a little bit more decorated. The American Eagle and the Star Spangled Banner are typical motifs. The "uniform" trousers are always blue jeans, often worn with a broad belt. The T-shirt also has an important place in this world. The preferred T-shirt is the classic white James Dean variant, but people sometimes also wear more embellished shirts. Again, common motifs are the Stars and Stripes and the white-headed eagle. Some people also choose pic-tures of their favourite car – or perhaps negative remarks about other people's cars. For instance, the owner of a Ford might wear a T-shirt with the words: "I would rather push my Ford than drive a Chevy." The preferred jacket is the blue denim type. This garment is well suited for decoration. Besides the eagle and the flag, typical motifs include both pictures and names of people's cars and the emblem of their Amcar club. As headgear people wear typical American caps, the big ones with a padded peak. The admiral type is especially popular, the one that is black with gold leaves on the brim. Sometimes, the classic cowboy hat is worn. This is especially the case in the summer when this group arranges many of its meetings, gather-ings where people go for instance to exhibit their cars, maybe to buy some auto parts, or just to meet old friends.

To finish this picture of the clothes commonly worn by Amcar enthusiasts, I will mention a couple of things that could be said to belong to the dress style. The first is the Zippo lighter – a lighter produced in the United States and a commodity one associates with Marlboro commercials and the US Army. The second object is the Buck knife. This is a small American knife, widespread in several subcultures, especially those communities centred around the Harley Davidson motorcycle, the so-called "bikers".

If we now turn to the language used among the Amcar enthu-siasts, we can see that there are distinctive aspects of both the written and spoken language. The Norwegian language in general has been the object of massive influence from the Anglo-American world, but it is easy to see and hear that the language used within the subculture has a higher degree of foreign elements than in the mainstream culture. By foreign elements, I mean in this case of course words borrowed from the American English vocabulary. To give good examples of this in an English article is of course difficult, but I will give it a try. First of all there are many words used in connection with their cars. Common terms include: "cabriolet", "convertible", "custom", "cool-custom", "hot-rod", "headers", "options", "kickdown". The list could easily be made longer. This use of American English in this quite specialized field is not so hard to understand – it would be difficult to find suitable Norwegian substitutes. More interesting is the same tendency in the more everyday activities within this subculture. Expressions such as "nickname", "barbecue", and "lunch-break" were not uncommon. One day a man said to me, "Møt opp hos meg klokka åtte *sharp*" ("Come to my house eight o'clock *sharp*"). In this statement it was only the word "sharp" that was not in Norwegian. This is not a word that is used in Norwegian at all, but illustrates the Anglo-Saxon influence upon the language used in this subculture.

It is not possible to give a comprehensive description of this subcultural style in one short paper, but there are a number of other significant elements that at least deserve mention. For instance, the people play rock 'n' roll music from "the fabulous fifties" and Country and Western. Of other activities characteristic of this subculture, I think of such things as social gatherings throughout the summer and many activities connected with the use of the car: burnouts, drag races, repairing, and so on. People also show an interest in and collect a wide range of other things – for example, jukeboxes and pin-ball machines. But I will stop here, and pose some relevant questions: what is the connection between all the disparate objects and activities I have described so far and the car? After all, it was these people's enthusiasm for American cars that was the occasion for my fieldwork in this community. What is it about the status of the car in this subculture that made it natural for me to start with a description of the context, before focusing on the car itself?

The Car's Position

To use a simple metaphor, one can say that the position of the car in this social community is similar to that of a load-bearing beam in a house – a construction detail which holds everything up and, together, gives the building form and solidity. But such a beam cannot stand on its own. It would be meaningless to talk about this particular object without also noticing the rest of the construction. Therefore in trying to grasp the significance of the car in this community one has to explore not only the car itself but its social contexts. It is the interaction between these two aspects of the car – its ability to be a brick in a wall while also being the *foundation* and the *generator* for the same wall – that underlies much of the mystery and attraction of this object. I am convinced that it is in this link that much of the explanation is to be found of why such communities come into being in the first place, and of the meanings people experience and develop within these groups.

So far, I have been mostly concerned with the surroundings of the car. But what kind of cars are we talking about? Besides the nationality – these are exclusively American cars – what are their other important characteristics?

Before I started my fieldwork among the Amcar enthusiasts, I expected to find a pretty homogeneous community. But after a short while I began to recognize several different subgroups *within* this subculture. Each of these was centred around a particular *type* of car. One group focused exclusively on cars from the Chrysler company, the so-called "Mopars". Another group centred around four-wheel-drive vehicles, the so-called "off-roaders" – especially the green military ones. A third subgroup consisted of people interested only in vans. The biggest and most important group was the one built up around Ford and General Motors cars. Because this subgroup constituted what we might call the centre of the whole subculture, I spent most of my time with them. Because of this, most of the things I say here are mainly valid for this part of the community.

This mother-group, as I call it, consisted of cars from the Ford company (for instance, Galaxy, Thunderbird, and Mustang) and from General Motors (for example, Chevrolet, Cadillac, Mercury, Buick, and Oldsmobile). But these cars also had similarities that went beyond the fact that they were from these two companies. First of all, they were all quite exclusive. By "exclusive", I do not simply mean the price people had to pay when they bought the car. There are other criteria that distinguish a car. One might be that there are only a few of its kind. Or there might be something unique about that particular car; for instance, that it had been driven only a short distance, a so-called "lowmiler". The fact that the owner had done an exquisite job on the restoration could also be an important characteristic. This talk of restoration brings me to the other main similarity between these cars: in addition to being exclusive they were also mainly from the 1950s – the period in the USA when words such as youthfulness, delightfulness, and joyfulness, may be used to describe the spirit of the time.

This optimism became, of course, a part of the cars. First of all came the big tail fins, inspired by space adventure. The rear lights were designed as flames, and "highway rocket ships" became a common nickname for these cars. Secondly, cheerful and light pastel colours were typical. Last but not least, chrome was very popular for many parts of the car. A lot of chrome – the bumper, the hubcaps, and so on. It was the perfect material to mirror this extravagant world.

Of course, this is not how it actually was in the 1950s. The point is that this idealized and glamorized picture of that decade is a common image. Thus we should ask, who is responsible for these ideas? Where do we get these strongly simplified perspectives? Obviously, the mass media have played a crucial role in the construction of these idealized visions. In other words, it is in the field of what we often call "popular culture" that we should search for the origin of these ideas. We have to go to the commercials, the music and, of course, the movies.

I will shortly return to the ways these notions of "popular culture" help me to make sense of the Norwegian Amcar subculture. But, before I go any further, it will be useful to focus here on the position of the car among the enthusiasts.

I have already introduced the concept "generator" to describe how I see the car in this subculture. However, I have not fully explained what I meant by this term and how I see the concept as a fruitful approach to what I will call the essence of this culture.

First of all the car is a sort of generator in the sense that a tremendous amount of time, energy and money is spent in connection with it. This object thus becomes something that occupies much of the people's life and represents a focus for a wide range of actions. For instance, people might spend years in getting one car ready for the road or for a show. This work is especially important in the winter-time. Besides taking up a lot of time, such restoration activities also require a high level of knowledge and technical expertise, and of course a considerable amount of money, because these auto parts are pretty expensive.

When the restoration work is finished – when the car looks *similar to* or actually *is* a restored version of a fifties car – then another important use of the car begins, *the driving*. In the summer, it is common for people to leave the city at the weekend and participate in one of the nearby meetings. Such gatherings are held nearly every weekend from May to August. In connection with such meetings people often participate in a so-called "cruising", where the enthusiasts drive in long convoys that meander through the countryside.

Enthusiasts also frequently spend a lot of time in the car on hot summer nights during the rest of the week. Then people travel to downtown Trondheim, where they enjoy driving their beauties, while simultaneously putting on a show for the passing mainstreamers. For me, as for many others, it is quite exotic to see a 1950s' cabriolet in the centre of Trondheim, in between all the Japanese and European cars, travelling slowly and noiselessly down the street. These American cars seem untouched by time, as though dropped from the sky.

The Mythical America

So far, I have given a sort of cartographical view of the different elements in the style of this subculture. The question arises: What about the people in this community? What did they think, feel, and experience by means of and through these different elements? In other words, what was their *project* as Amcar enthusiasts?

One way to approach these questions, a perspective which has been more or less implicit so far, is to take a closer look at the expression "Amcar". This is a word consisting of two elements "American" and "car". And, if one modifies the first part from "American" to "America", I believe that one touches the core of this world. It was the interaction of these two entities – "America" and "car" – that constituted the basis for the enthusiasts' lives.

These people's project, in my view, is to create a mythical American world in Norway, with the car as the central element. I choose to call their world "mythical" because it is not the real United States they use as a standard in their world construction, but the one you find in the movies, music, advertisements, and so on. That is why I also prefer to use the term "America" instead of the more correct "United States" or "USA". I think the word "America" suggests that it is the USA seen through the mass media that is the source of this subculture's world.

The enthusiasts' version of America is both mythical and nostalgic. They are trying to recall or rebuild a sort of lost paradise. To give an accurate date for the historical period they are trying to re-create, is not easy. Much of the paraphernalia they use comes from a mythical realm of public culture that is in many ways independent of time. On the other hand, a wide range of the objects central to this community is actually from the 1950s. Therefore I will assert that the closest one can get in dating the essence of this subculture is the 1950s. But of course we must also again take into account the ways the movies and music have mirrored this epoch.

What about a geographical location: is that possible? I find it much easier to locate this America in space than to give it a date.

People are concerned with one particular part of USA, the always glamorous and always sunny California.

The fact that it is an actual place that the enthusiasts make use of in their subcultural life creates some problems. People can actually move themselves in space, even if they cannot go back in time. So, if people want to go to their own America, they can easily do so as far as the geographical aspect of their world is concerned. However, because their world is also characterized by a nostalgic and mythical aspect, such a journey is problematic. People could not go to California without a certain degree of risk, because what they are seeking is, in its genuine form, impossible to find.

Nevertheless, many of the enthusiasts had made their pilgrimage to the West Coast. People told me about the good times they had experienced there, and of course about all the cars they had seen at the beaches and on the boulevards and highways of California. That they went as tourists is the crucial point in this case. The eye of the tourist sees things quite differently, compared with the visions of permanent residents, people who spend their everyday lives in the same areas. The tourist will never experience the same grey, taken-for-granted, and uneventful routines as the native. For the tourist, the world is a colourful place, offering vivid experiences for the senses and constant new challenges to handle. This explains why the enthusiasts were able to go to the USA without destroying their idea of America. This may also be part of the explanation of the fact that virtually no one had emigrated to the USA. The rationality of their project did not allow them to practise it day after day in a more permanent situation.

This point is also important in relation to their lives in Norway. Only a few of the Amcar enthusiasts had daily work connected with the Amcar movement, and those who had such occupations were frequently criticized by others. "They aren't one of us," as I was once told. As already noted, most of the people are active at weekends or in their spare time in the evenings. In short, we might say that this kind of enthusiasm, or maybe all kinds of enthusiasm, must be looked at as a step out of routinized everyday life.

Amcar Enthusiasm – A Fairy Tale on Wheels

Because Amcar enthusiasm is incompatible with routine every-day life, and of course also because enthusiasts entered into a mythical world, such a movement has many similarities to the *fairy tale*. Both the Amcar culture and the fairy tale belong to a dimension above or beyond our daily routines. Both give shape to the fantastic aspects of our lives, and both contain important aspects of creativity. Amcar enthusiasm must be treated not as an escape from everyday life but as a supplement to this reality. Amcar enthusiasm is not an advanced sort of narcotic, but rather a spicy addition in a sometimes bland world.

These two entities, the fairy tale and Amcar culture, share another important similarity. Both demand a certain degree of intensity of experience from the people involved in order to make the involvement feel credible. One cannot view the Amcar adventure, or the fairy tale, from the outside. The famous words "Once upon a time..." must be treated as an invitation, an invitation one must accept to be carried away, an invitation you must accept if you want to avoid experiencing the fantastic world as "meaningless exotica", to use Dick Hebdige's (1979) expression.

Still, I don't claim that the average enthusiasts fully believe in their project all the time. They are not involved 100 percent in their mythical America every moment of the day. Therefore, it makes sense to talk of *degrees* of involvement.

In many situations, the enthusiasts appeared as "shallow players" (Geertz 1973). They acted out their roles, in their own American play, with a relatively low level of involvement. Recall my description of the Fourth of July celebration. There was a great deal of joking that night. One man missed his American beer, a woman called herself and the assembly "Yankees". I see a shallow involvement as a basis for this performance, and joking can be said to be a way of sustaining the lack of involvement. Despite all the American artefacts they surrounded themselves with that day, people still might not have managed to capture the right mood for the occasion. Their humour, on the other hand, produced the necessary connection when they ran into problems with believing in their own fairy tale. Such bridging mechanisms are necessary because the enthusiasts, in spite of everything, are Norwegians in Norway.

But there were also moments when the ironic gap disappeared. There were situations when the enthusiasts didn't play *as if* they were in the mythical America. There were occasions when a fusion took place between the enthusiasts' own constructed mythical world and the subjective experience of the actors. Such moments of "deep play" occurred on the road.

This type of experience is integrally connected to the focal object in this community, the car. As already noted, the car in this subculture can be seen as a "generator". However, it is in the interaction between the *enclosed space* of the car and the car's *capacity for movement* that important things happen. In the inside of the car, one world is closed out and another is closed in. The driver can be said to withdraw from the *outside* world when he is in this space, but, at the same time, he is left with a great potential to build his own world *inside* the car. One must also add to this picture the fact that this space is mobile, and that speed in itself can be looked upon as a source of the fantastic. Speed changes the reality of things, in some cases obliterates the details of everyday life outside the car.

I do not mean by this that the car's distinctive characteristics are enough in themselves to explain our fantasy. Recall the metaphor I used earlier, of the car as a load-bearing beam. If you only have such a beam you do not have a house. Similarly, one cannot create a whole American fairy tale with only a car, but one may enter and move towards the core of this world only by means of this object.

One of my most vivid personal experiences during my fieldwork illustrates this point. In the story I want to tell you it is the relationship between the social context of the car – the community's style – and the car itself that is the crucial relation. My own mythical experience occurred while I was myself driving a car, a 1960s' Ford pick-up.

It was relatively early in my fieldwork, when I was asked by one of the Amcar clubs to drive a car from Trondheim to Oslo. There were many other people taking the same route that day, so when we started, early one summer morning, the convoy of cars numbered about seven. I was sitting alone in my car, and had a good opportunity to think about what this was all about. There was a walkie-talkie installed in my pick-up, so I could keep in touch with the others. There was also an ordinary radio in my car, but this one was old and functioned only intermittently. It was in the mountain area south of Trondheim, at Kvikne, that I experienced what I see as the essence of this culture. The surroundings had changed, from the wooded hills of the lowlands to a more desert-like landscape up in the mountains. While I was driving in this area, music came out of the radio – American music. I suddenly felt that there was an integral connection between the sunny weather, the landscape, the road, the music, the sound of the car, the soft springs, the other Amcars behind and in front of me, the jeans I was wearing, the Zippo lighter on the dashboard. Even the rifle stand behind my head had its place in this picture.

What I actually experienced that day was to be inside a mythical American reality, rather than in an everyday Norwegian one. For a moment, I became one with the constructed world. In this ecstatic moment there was no longer any distance between me and this other world.

Many enthusiasts told me of similar episodes in their own experience. There were moments when they felt that they were not playing *as if* they were in America. They actually *were*. At such moments, the many American objects surrounding the enthusiasts were not just representations of another reality. They *were* reality itself. For a few moments, the paramount reality was a *"fairy tale on wheels"*.

REFERENCES

Barthes, R. 1973. *Mythologies*. St. Albans, Herts: Paladin.

Bergh, T. and Hanisch, T. et al. 1983. *Norge fra U-land til I-land*. Oslo: Gyldendal.

Bigsby, C. W. E. 1975. *Superculture*. London: Paul Elek.

Bjurstrøm, E. 1987. Bilen och motorcykeln i ungdomskulturen. In K. Spolander (ed.): *Ungdom och trafik – en omöjlig kombination?* Stockholm.

Bryn, S. 1989. Amerika-bilete. *Syn og Segn*, No. 3.

Clarke, J. 1976. Style. In S. Hall and T. Jefferson (eds): *Resistance through Rituals. Youth Subcultures in Post-war Britain*. London: Hutchinson.

Geertz, C. 1973. *The Interpretation of Cultures*. New York: Basic Books.

Gehlen, A. 1980. *Man in the Age of Technology*. New York: Colombia University Press.

Hebdige, D. 1979. *Subculture. The Meaning of Style*. London and New York: Routledge & Kegan Paul.

Lamvik, G. M. 1994. *Et eventyr på hjul. Et antropologisk blikk på Amcar kulturen*. STS Report No. 21. Trondheim: Centre for Technology and Society.

Levold, N. and Østby, P. 1993. *Skjønnheten og Udyret: Møter mellom kultur og teknologi*. STS Working Paper No. 11. Trondheim: Centre for Technology and Society.

Turner, V. 1974. *Dramas, Fields, and Metaphors*. Ithaca, NY and London: Cornell University Press.

Østby, P. 1995. *Flukten fra Detroit. Bilens integrasjon i det norske samfunnet*. PhD dissertation, STS Report No. 24. Trondheim: Centre for Technology and Society.

Chapter 7

The Car as a Cultural Statement
Car Advertising as Gendered Socio-technical Scripts
Marit Hubak

Cars, Men, and Women

This paper analyses a symbolic side of private motoring that I hope will contribute to a greater understanding of the meaning of cars, namely car marketing and advertisement. Gender is used as the analytical category, thus making it a story about the symbolic gendering of cars.

The car is a cultural statement. Its cultural integration may be studied at two levels – an exterior and an interior structure. The *exterior structure* is produced by the geographical and physical shape of society. Society creates needs for the transfer of people and goods in space within certain time-limits. Another, and somewhat more secondary, circumstance is the dominant understanding of the car as the basic constituent of the "normal" system of transport. This is visualized through the physical shape of society. The necessity of the car seems built into the relative location of workplaces, residential areas, and the supply of service. Increased motoring makes possible a dispersed physical structure, at the same time as this exterior structure confirms the necessity of cars. Thus, humans have conceded power over their lives to the car (Tengström, 1990, 1991). As an exterior structure, motoring is connected to geographical and physical mobility. However, the car's existence cannot be perceived as a natural phenomenon. Rather, the fact that most households have one or more cars is the result of political acceptance and economic interests. The car could have been used more for "public motoring" than for "lunch-packet driving" (driver with lunch box as the only "passenger", which we know is widespread).

The *interior structure* tells us something about the symbolic value to individual understanding of the self and the presentation of self to the surroundings. The concept of mobility will in this context point to social rather than geographical or physical mobility. The car is as much a vehicle of status as a means of transport.

It is a common belief that it is a male prerogative to be interested in cars, to read about cars, and to talk about cars. Allegedly, women have a more distanced relationship with cars. Men, more than women, decide what car to buy. However, this picture is slowly changing. Women buy cars more often than they used to, but they still use cars less than men (Hjorthol, 1991). Men still seem to have the first right to use the family car (Brandt and Houg, 1978; Guiliano, 1979; Hjorthol, 1983, 1990b; Madden and White, 1979; Paaschwell and Paaschwell, 1979). In short, men are socialized for car use to a greater degree than women are (Hjorthol et al., 1990).

The marketing of cars to women has followed a traditional gendered pattern. In the USA, the electric car of the early years of the 20th century had women as its target group. The reason was that it was easier to drive than the petrol car, it was cleaner, quieter, and more comfortable, and had less horsepower (Scharff, 1992). Even though female drivers became a more common sight, women behind the wheel were still stereotypically described, even ridiculed. Their function as a driver was mostly tied to care tasks, their role as a mother and housewife. In response to the changes in women's everyday life, the set of roles has changed. One of the aims of this paper is to attempt to grasp whether, and how, marketing handles such change.

This approach links marketing and advertising people's understanding of their own work with the message of advertisements. The analysis is based on interviews and the reading of advertisements centred around the relationship between car, gender, and symbols. However, it is important to realize that there is no necessary relationship between the intended message of advertisements and their effects on recipients. The analysis focuses only on the efforts of producers. How is the relationship between gender and car understood and in what way does this understanding find expression in the ads? Has modern marketing changed strategy in step with the increase in the number of women buying cars?

What is Advertising, and How May It Be Analysed?

Marketing denotes the entirety of the work performed to promote the sale of a product. It involves many actors. The product must be created and promoted and sales must be achieved. Research, design, the development of new products, pricing, communication, and service are all important components in the complicated puzzle of modern marketing.

Concepts such as "psychological mass influence" and expressions such as "act in the desired manner by their own free will" are fairly widespread critical views of marketing. Advertising is conceived as sexist, conservative, manipulative, and demand creating. Consumption has also been regarded as a drug and a flight from reality, a substitute for political activism and other forms of "authentic" life (cf. Leiss et al., 1990: 15–32). Such a view reduces consumers to passive adaptors.

A Norwegian government report on "Advertising and Gender" lists the undesirable effects of advertising as follows (NOU 1981:16, pp. 17–18).

(1) Advertising contributes to the creation of a consumer mentality,
(2) Work is pushed backstage and the role of consumer is highlighted,
(3) Advertising effects/causes conformity,
(4) Advertising uses and promotes status and prestige,

(5) Advertising commercializes forms of social contact,
(6) Advertising contains sexist stereotypes.

All these items support the view of advertising as socially conservative and integrative.

The belief that advertising has become more sophisticated and manipulative is widespread. Scientific techniques are thought to have replaced craft-like and intuitive work. This is in line with the confidence of marketing professionals in rationality and systematic techniques as the dominant method of marketing. To know the market is rule number one. This knowledge should, according to the theoretical canons of marketing, be treated as fact (Nakstad and Ødegaard, 1987; Hinn and Sihlberg, 1987). Whether there is any agreement between theory and practice remains an open question and there is no reason to accept the insiders' accounts of the rationality of their work.

Marketing is a question of historical factors, both those internal to organizations and those of social situations. Aspects such as social gender, status, and differences between generations are relevant, but so too are combinations of cultural conventions and brand identities. Advertising itself constitutes an aggregate expression for all this (Hopkins, 1923 [1971]; Leiss et al., 1990; Tedlow, 1990). The detailed design, production, and procurement of the product are emphasized as important. Thus we may rightly say that advertising is a key link in this chain. To promote a product efficiently, Norwegian marketing people argue that they have to follow current trends very closely:

> The dominant values shift with the socio-political currents, and through the ages advertising has to an amazing degree managed to grasp these, and partly amplify them, through its forms of expression. (*Kompanje*, No. 9, 1990, p. 59; author's translation)

The objects of our everyday lives gain a cultural meaning beyond any "objective" meaning they might have (Silverstone et al., 1991). The analysis of technology and its content is split by Silverstone et al. into four strictly schematic dimensions. These are *appropriation, objectification, incorporation,* and *conversion* (for a general account of these dimensions, see Chapter 4 in this volume). Appropriation primarily concerns the act of buying. Objectification implies highlighting the owner's symbolic work, based on the physical object. Incorporation refers to practical use of the object. Conversion happens through the presentation of individually produced symbols to the world at large. Thus, objectification and conversion are closely connected.

Through marketing and advertising, car companies give directives for the use and understanding of these artefacts. We could say that producers try to *domesticate* users (see Chapter 4 and Aune, 1992) or to configure them (Woolgar, 1991). Producers try to guide the artefact–user relation by making advertisements into directives for use. Silverstone et al.'s (1991) four dimensions are here used to analyse the messages of car advertisements.

This method may be refined by reference to Akrich. She has studied designers' attempts to stage the way technologies should be domesticated. Akrich splits product communication into two. The *physical script* is embedded in the product's physical and technical shape. These attributes are already material when the artefact leaves the factory and are activated through practical use. The *socio-technical script* (Akrich, 1991) is subject to flexible interpretation. The designer chooses to "create" the product in a particular way, depending on what objects the communication is meant to serve and who it is aimed at. The socio-technical script mainly deals with objectification and conversion, but may also cover the appropriation and incorporation aspects. Akrich defines the concept as follows:

> A large part of the work of innovators is that of *inscribing* this vision of the world in the technical content of the new object. I will call the end product of this work a "script" or a "scenario". (Akrich, 1992: 208)

Here, I will define a socio-technical script as *ideas about or views of users and attitudes and values connected to cars and motoring*. Thus marketing is a part of the socio-technical script, which is built on the physical script. Marketing contains both types of product communication, one of which is direct and one indirect. Whereas the physical script relates to direct influence by promoting the "physical qualities" of a product (the appropriation aspect), the socio-technical script relates to influence achieved through indirect attraction (objectification, incorporation, and conversion). This attraction may be connected to the use of the car or may be of a symbolic and identity-producing nature.

Method and Materials

The concepts of domestication and script are my tools for analysing advertisements. A script is made up of the means to make a car attractive, that is, inscribed signs and codes. It may find its main focus either in the text or in the pictures, or in a combination of these. Wording, typography, colours, mood, and context may contribute. These are inscribed in the advertisement to seduce the reader into buying a car. This is done by linking people's experienced need for an individualized means of transport to other attractions, such as reasonable price, plenty of space, individuality, and status. Thus, cars get sold while buyers are offered added value. Thus, a common interest is established between the parties. The nature of the script affects the *domestication* of the car.

As an analytical aid I focus on the advertisement's main aspect. The presentation of the object might be thought to follow two strategies: an *instrumentally* and an *expressively* oriented communication. An instrumental orientation would emphasize features such as economy, performance, and practical utility. This would be a rational presentation of the car. My analysis deals mainly with expressively oriented attempts at persuasion – emotional appeal. It is important to be aware of the fact that seemingly rational descriptions are often made in an expressive way.

The empirical material analysed in this paper has been selected from interviews and advertisements for Toyota, Ford, Volvo, and Citroën. Toyota, Ford, and Volvo are relatively big brands in Norway, whereas Citroën is assumed to address a more specialized segment of the market. None of the four projects an image of a luxury car, a sports car, or some other feature that is too special to be termed "ordinary".

The data for the study were collected from two main sources: interviews and advertisements. I conducted eight interviews with informants from the advertising agencies and importers of the four companies. I asked about their relationship with the country of production, with the advertising agency, and with the network of distributors, and about the efforts directed at the market. All four companies used different agencies. I interviewed key people in these agencies. All the advertisements are from 1985–1991. My files contain one or more brochures for all models of the private and multi-use vans that were sold in 1989–1991. In addition, I took random samples of ads from Trondheim's local newspaper *Adresseavisen*. I had previously decided to observe 17 days each year when I coded information about the words and pictures of ads for these four brands. In addition I used ads displayed in the three largest newspapers in Norway. From information from the importing companies I knew their campaign periods for 1989–1991. These were twice a year. These ads were included in the files.

The main difference between brochures and newspaper ads is that ads in newspapers tend to be sales material, whereas brochures are likely to be profiling material. Ads in newspapers are usually more rational in terms of mentioning price and promoting the car as a special offer during a limited period in order to obtain sales. Price is always mentioned in newspaper ads.

The material was coded and analysed by reference to four main themes: technical data and price (appropriation (1)); use (incorporation (2)); symbolic content (objectification (3) and conversion (4)). In the analysis, the agenda is the car's meaning in a wider context, for example as a carrier of the owner's value preferences and socioeconomic standing. My focus is neither the car as a commodity nor the use of it. The technology, its possibilities, and its heterogeneous aspects are visualized and verbalized in different manners.

Next, I shall consider more closely the marketing people's own understanding of the relationship between the car and its symbolic value with reference to different target groups and the resulting differentiated communication.

Cars and Symbolic Value[1]

In the printed material from producers we may, by analysing what is emphasized in words and pictures, identify the criteria they assume will sell the product and/or what properties the producer wants to promote. A technological product has certain physical properties that serve utilitarian purposes. For example, the internal capacity of the car may be specified. In addition there are a number of subjective interpretations of a product. These we may call the socially and mentally constructed qualities of the product, and they may not be obvious from the artefact as an object but have to be supplied by the buyer. These may be properties that we have to be told about, or that we may find out about ourselves (see Sørgaard, 1993: 13). Several of the importers claimed that rational arguments were the most important basis for buying a car. The need for transport was the most important reason. Other more underlying needs and wants were "on the edge" of what one could and would market. It was also said that the car was adapted to the current culture (see Hubak, 1993, on product philosophy). How do employees of the advertising agencies react to instrumental views of the car? The informant from the Ford agency answered as follows when asked about the importance of the car as a means of transport to a potential customer:

> "No [the answer came promptly]. To many that is not it at all. It might be an extension of their personality, lots of other extensions. It is essentially a means of transport, but it is also something in which to clothe oneself."

Generally she meant that a car means different things to different people. The target group(s) of most car advertisements is a public that seeks youth and vitality through a lifestyle that may be found in advertisements. Many do not want to admit this, and anyway a car's meaning is flexible. The above statement corresponds nicely to what Toyota's advertising person said about the use of market surveys: if the goal was to map symbolic and other difficult factors in choice, questionnaires were a problematic source. The representative from Ford's advertising agency said that there were groups that were not interested in the car as anything but a driving tool; "on the other hand, if you say that all students drive a 2CV because they are more interested in a means of transport, then that isn't correct because a 2CV is just as much a status object to them." This informant argued that cars have *heterogeneous symbol values*. By using an old cliché about students and 2CVs she draws attention to several points. First, she is saying something about her own preferences when it comes to cars. They seem to be "conventional". Some cars have status in an economic/material sense. The 2CV is not among these. If we take this point a little further, customary interpretations of concepts such as quality, comfort, driving qualities, and aerodynamic design do not make sense in terms of this car. It is not modern. On the other hand, she thinks that this model from Citroën indicates a lifestyle, a conscious wish to position oneself. The choice of car may, for example, symbolize an active distancing of oneself from the car society. If the Citroën 2CV is a status symbol among students, then status is grounded in something other than economic capital. A relevant alternative might be cultural capital (Bourdieu, 1991). The concept of status might be split up into several dimensions, reflecting competing lifestyles. How are such preferences tied up with the product, and what kind of communication does the market want?

> "Primarily it is still the product itself that plays the principal role. If it doesn't arouse any feelings in you, you really have no chance of achieving anything at all."

According to this statement, it is the "quality of the product" that arouses feelings. On the other hand, it becomes the task of the agency to make the product function as an arouser of emotions. In reality it is the advertisement's *representation* of the product that arouses feelings – that is, if it is not an advertisement made only for people who know a particular make of car already:

> "The Escort has had a new launch. In fact, as you know, it existed earlier, but now it has come in as a new model with a new look and new external features, and so on. The car also had an attractive new

design; it looked good. If it hadn't had a predecessor that was so popular, it certainly would not have inspired the popularity it got. It received a certain amount of negative press at first, but that straightened out after a while. It was motoring journalists who came down on the car, and they always find something to criticize. It might be the finish of the seats, the head room, or something else. They emphasize such details and make it look very bad. It had that, a negative reception from the press."

Here, she pinpoints the design and impressions based on experience. It is implicit in her statements that perceptions of a car are *cumulative*, and that they continue to develop after the launch. I interpret this to mean that advertising is built on the same cumulative principle. This might also be seen as a dynamic process of interaction between customer and producer. The press is described as working against marketing and advertising. However, negative criticism is soon "forgotten". Motoring journalists are supposedly not very important contributors to this discourse. And this informant continues as follows:

"Anyhow, the product itself was interesting enough to look at, and it had had a predecessor that was trusted enough for this feature to be transferred to the new car. It kept the name Escort and so it was our job to get this new car across in Norway, . . . and then we were aware of certain guidelines that would measure up to tastes, for example."

This statement strengthens my hypotheses about the successive build-up of the messages. The same informant said earlier in the interview that constant repetition of a car's "properties" contributes to achieving a strong impact. The producer will attempt to direct the interpretation.

"As regards the price of the car, it has a very favourable price; it was brand new, had a completely new look, a fresh new approach, you see. It was relatively powerful, 105 hp, in relation to the price and there was more space inside, all purely concrete product advantages, which we used in our advertisements. So a campaign was put together with ads in colour and in black and white and dealer ads in black and white, assorted point-of-sale material, and so on. All of it was sold off in the space of a month, and it received a very warm welcome. Seen in relation to the goals they had at Ford's, it was a good sales campaign."

Here she tries to emphasize the *car* as such. However, she links design, price, and horsepower. A favourable price is directly linked with high horsepower and an attractive design. She also mentions the spacious interior. The design might be seen as both a technical and a symbolic element. The car's performance may also be considered from several angles. It may be seen as a safety feature, for example when overtaking other cars, and it may be interpreted as power in a symbolic sense. However, she calls all of this "purely concrete product advantages". In this I find a predominance of social rather than technical elements. These are generated in a common cultural understanding of what is "nice", "an attractive design", "spacious", and "enough horsepower". The attractions are based on technical factors, but are developed through expressive statements. When it comes to speed, she said that there exists a certain trade ethic that the car trade should not advertise speed, at least not directly. She did not deny that it was done, but said that it was done "covertly". This reinforces our understanding of the car as an *emotional matter*.

I asked her to sketch a plan for a hypothetical Ford Fiesta advertisement. I wanted to get statements about the target groups seen in relation to environment and profile. She was quick to state the target group: young people of both genders. This was because the Fiesta is "small, neat, simple, and fun". "The earlier one gets a grip on the young, the greater the chance that they will become future customers. It is also important to build a profile with them." Here, the advertising has a task. This is not in line with the adman Fraser-Robinson's statement that consumers are becoming constantly more choosy, and that buying habits change overnight if they are dissatisfied (John Fraser-Robinson in an interview in *Kampanje*, No. 7, 1990: 24– 26). To reach young people she would use *lifestyle advertisements*.

"I suppose that it would turn on style of life in one way or another. But it might be dramatized in a somewhat more clever way, a bit more intelligent, perhaps. We had a very nice Fiesta campaign once, I think, that turned on style of life, but it targeted somewhat younger people, only boys, or young men. It described a day in the life of a Fiesta. How a boy left home in the morning, driving to school with his satchel, then stopping at a hamburger stand to drink a Coke, and then driving to the gym, with a tennis bag. It was just these kinds of images, such symbols of a passage in a Fiesta's life you might say.... This was directed at young men, young couples, young girls."

What she is saying is that simple sketches do a good job of promoting the essence of the message. As she explains the advertisement, the directives are quite strong. However, she does not seem to stress the patterns of role dissemination much. First she says that the advertisement was aimed at "boys, or young men". At the end of the statement she claims that the advertisement addresses both genders.

Advertising is as a rule directed at young people, even though adults and the elderly have greater purchasing power.

"I do not know of a single importer who would like to link his brand with retired people. Whoever drives the car gives it a profile as well. If you had only a collection of retired people who drove Fiestas, it would become an elderly person's car. And then you would not succeed in reaching the other end of the age range. It is for the elderly, that one. That is something that is just inside your head, so you don't even think about it."

As a customer and a driver one contributes to the profiling of the product, in fact as a part-time employee of the organization. This is yet another statement that shows that *the product is still unfinished when it is introduced into the market*. One seeks to annex the customer by an illusion, a utopia of eternal youth and vitality. It is clear that the informants think that cars and the production of symbols are connected. Because the owner gives the car a profile, the car is an expresssion of the owner. The perception of the car is probably built up cumulatively and the car becomes a heterogeneous symbol. Horsepower and design are mentioned as being the most important factors to affect people.

I shall now consider some examples of advertisements that target, respectively, men and women. The main point is to see what strategies of persuasion are in fact used in the job of selling cars.

Socio-technical Scripts for Cars in Norway – Some Examples that Illuminate the Relationship between Car and Gender

What norms are expressed and what worlds are described in car advertisements? Power, control, behaviour, and technical competence – what does the world of cars attribute to men and women respectively? Society is changing, the family has been relieved of many of its traditional tasks. New tasks have been added. Through the accumulation of knowledge about women's everyday lives and living conditions, women's lives have been made visible. Has this knowledge affected marketing? How are attractive values produced, and, above all, what is assumed to be attractive to men and women in advertisements? Is the advertising and marketing business adapting to changes in society or is it conserving traditional roles?

It is a common conception that men and technology belong together (see, e.g., Chapter 8 in this volume). Men own most of the cars in Norway. According to the 1989 ownership survey, men owned four times as many motor vehicles as women (Dahle, 1992: 261). But we also know that more women buy cars now than previously. How does this affect marketing accounts of women and cars? Are cars sold to women in a different way, or in the same way as to men? What is thought to be attractive to women? One of my informants answered the question in the following way:

> "One wants something to carry shopping in, maybe also space for a tricycle. But then they buy smaller cars than men.... I do think that there are some practical reasons."

With regard to technical aspects, women are often seen as having little practical ability. In the thought process involved in car procurement, on the other hand, they are referred to as practical. The relationship between the technical and the practical here is important. Women are practical in everyday life, but they do not repair cars, they do not have the practical skills that are linked with technical knowledge and competence. Here women are described as rational, oriented towards instrumental needs. They are concerned about ample space, but paradoxically they buy smaller cars than men do. Instrumental needs and rational, practical interest "lose out" to the technical – the male's prize in the car society. It is relevant to talk about "losing" because control and knowledge yield more competence and thus status than practical user rationality. It is men who create and *know about*, i.e. control, technology. Women just use it.

In the following sections I discuss some examples of how car technology is presented with a view to men and women as target groups. I analyse four advertisements (three of which are reproduced). The first two are aimed at men, whereas the other two have women as their target audience. We shall see what they have to say about technology and humans and to what extent the messages are gendered.

The Empty Driver's Seat

In car advertisements it is fairly common to display cars without drivers. My first case is an advertisement which shows the steering wheel and the dashboard of a Volvo. The picture has been taken from the driver's seat. The picture is placed in between two columns of text. The text to the left of the picture says:

> "Knobs and switches are logically placed within reach, the instruments are simple and easy to read. This means full control for the driver in all situations."

The right-hand text reads:

> "Full control in every driving situation is a typical Volvo-quality. This is plainly seen in every part of the cockpit-like driver's seat in the Volvo 460, where comfort is combined with driver control. This has been achieved by emphasizing an ergonomic design, by creating optimal comfort and efficiency for the driver, so that routine tasks can be performed simply and easily, as can unusual ones. Helped by computer-assisted ergonomic design a marvellous environment for the

driver has been created. All important controls are logically placed and operated by the touch of a finger. You may adjust the height of the steering wheel and the seat headrest so that you can achieve exactly the driving position you want. And all instruments and warning lights are in full view. The elegantly fitted interior is as a matter of course equipped with all the features you expect to find in a Volvo."

This text promises full driver control, which is described to be a Volvo feature. The buttons are logically placed. *Logic* seems to be an essential part of a car's technical shape. The logical driver is the person who, relaxed and in full control, steers the machine, turning the wheel and pushing buttons. With all-round vision the driver can gaze out at the world as it passes by. And everything is within reach. The purpose of showing empty seats is to let readers use their knowledge and familiarity, coupled with personal preferences or interpretations of what a car is, to activate the imagination (Skretting, 1988). This advertisement demands competence. Thus, empty seats are a particular link in the communication between sender and recipient. The text is open at the same time as it is directive. It is open because it invites the participation of the recipient. It simultaneously gives directives about the experience to be produced by the participation.

This advertisement is meant for men. Motors and machines are seen as a male field of interest. The world of advertising is built on precisely such common conceptions and prejudices (Skretting, 1988). We know that men are most interested in cars. The presentation says nothing about price, utility, the car as a means of transport, or about space. It focuses exclusively on technology that may be controlled. The analogy to the cockpit reinforces the impression of an advertisement for connoisseurs, for the initiated – for you, the technically competent. Everything on this panel of controls is arranged for the simplification of routine tasks. This increases the feeling of control.

The car in this advertisement is reduced to technique. Advertisements that show driverless cars often lift the car out of a practical context, and what remains is the technology as an attraction per se. The attraction of technology, here emphasized through comparison with a cockpit, is a message in itself. It is a masculine presentation of car technology.

The Man and the Car – A Witness to Needs for Communication?

Figure 1 shows a blue Ford Escort Orion moving along a deserted road. The driver is a man. The picture encapsulates technology, freedom, speed, and control. The cylinders of the engine are visible in the picture.

Why should a man choose this car? The advertisement seduces by communicating a number of characteristics of the man. Through the script, the advertisement appeals by promising stability, satisfaction, and control. The reader is supposed to identify with the person in the advertisement. This is a form of communication directed towards the individual. Control and stability are displayed by the man's facial expression, which is mystical and serious, half hidden behind large sunglasses. This man is relaxed, and he is in full mastery of this piece of advanced technology. His masculinity is realized through this car, in particular the male qualities of vigour, decisiveness, and courage. This car needs this man, and the man exercises control by mastering the car. This is the man–machine symbiosis.

The text promises choice, speed, high technology, and practical solutions. Speed is dangerous and exciting. To the risk inherent in high speed, further excitement is added by a gear box that allows *him* to choose velocity. The CTX gear box provides an infinitely variable transmission and gives a gliding transition when changing gears. The car reacts with "an impressive degree of precision"; "the result is smooth and responsive acceleration". This masterpiece of technology is in fact subject to the master's orders. This demonstration of control gives exquisite enjoyment. The choices are about speed and type of engine – "for those who need more power". Here you get what you want and demand.

The text also tells us about practical solutions: "CTX, a unique blend of high technology and *practical* solutions, combining the convenience of the automatic gear box with the economy and

Figure 1

performance of the manual gear box." The fact that a gear box, with reference to convenience, economy, and efficiency, qualifies to be "practical" must tell us something about men's needs and field of interest in relation to cars. The message seems to be that what counts as practical is technology per se – and not user-related solutions in the sense of the car as a useful tool. Even if this advertisement contains a driver, the message of the previous advertisement about men's fascination with technology is attested to. To the male, the car is both a toy and an embodiment of a particular aesthetic concept. All the way through, technological aspects receive attention. The engine "has Ford's modern combustion technology and control systems to give a balanced mixture of performance, reliability, fuel economy, and clean exhaust". It is important to have a balance, to both man and engine. When in balance you think more clearly and control increases.

The use of words is striking: "stable", "effective", "powerful", "performance", "satisfies", "advanced", "revolutionary", "unique", "speed", "precision", "responsive acceleration". This is how the male should act in the car society. What is it about males that attracts them to this as the real world? The script of this advertisement I read as an offer to rehabilitate the driver as a man in control of technology (and nature?). To control gives advantages. Control over mythical technology becomes the backbone of his maleness. The man is sovereign and active, transcending, selfish, and consuming. The car is also a very expensive and luxurious toy but the price is justifiable. The car is the answer to his dreams. He is buying himself freedom from the system that has imprisoned him.

The Woman and the Car: An Offer of Self-Realization – on Male Premises?

In my third advertisement we are presented with the view through the windscreen of a car (Figure 2). The driver of the car is a woman. The setting is an urban environment. Within the field of vision is another woman getting out of a Sierra a bit further down the road. From the image in the rearview mirror we can see that our driver is staring a bit. Her speed is 50 km/hour. The situation indicates that she might have to brake. The traffic situation is reconstructed and explicated in a drawing at the bottom of the picture.

The main information of the text is that now the Fiesta can be delivered with anti-locking brakes. These work in a relatively simple way, but this is thoroughly explained in text and pictures. This text does not use technical concepts nor does it give information about performance. It *explains* how a technical phenomenon works in a concrete situation. Technology is described as a useful tool, not as an attraction in itself. The new technology provides "increased stability during hard breaking and simultaneous sharp swerving". Underneath the drawing it is added that you can do an "emergency stop" without losing control.

The theme is safety. The underlying message gives an image of a female recipient in need of technical information. She is alluded to as a tense, insecure, and consequently not sufficiently attentive driver. If the traffic suddenly changes, she may lose control. It would be unusual for an advertisement with a man in the driver's seat to mention the issue of emergency braking. Here the theme is not activity, engine capacity, and speed, but *passivity*, *safety*, and *speed reduction*. In a lot of ways the themes seem diametrically opposed to those of the two preceding advertisements.

The word *control* is not used in the sense we found in the previous section. In the main text it is used only once, and then in an explanation of how control and servicing are simplified by the chosen placing of springs and shock absorbers. The only form of *action* that is considered in this advertisement is how to avoid dangerous situations. The text appeals to "sound common sense and greater safety". Both picture and text testify that the woman is not alone on the road. She has to have all-round vision and to be considerate – not only towards herself, but in relation to the environment. Thus she also is described as empathetic.

The ad may also be seen as displaying a woman-to-woman message, although the message may be understood as an invitation to take sides in the situation. The woman who is getting out

BLOKKERINGSFRIE BREMSER. SUNN FORNUFT, FOR STØRRE SIKKERHET.

20

Fiesta er den første bilen i denne klassen som kan leveres med blokkeringsfrie bremser. Dette prisbelønte systemet er spesielt konstruert for forhjulsdrevne biler og ble først lansert på Escort og Orion modellene. Systemet drives via en innelukket, remdrevet modulatorenhet for hvert forhjul, med en integrert enhet som består av hjulblokkeringssensor, hydraulisk pumpe og trykkregulator. Straks sensoren registrerer at det er fare for hjulblokkering, reduseres bremsetrykket slik at hjulene ikke blokkeres. Deretter blir bremsetrykket automatisk økt igjen av den integrerte enheten. Slik fortsetter systemet å pumpebremse så lenge det er nødvendig for å unngå blokkering. Dette gjør at forhjulene fortsetter å rotere mens farten bremses ned, hvilket bidrar til å opprettholde styreevnen. Systemet er også konstruert for å forhindre samtidig blokkering av begge bakhjulene, via den diagonale hydrauliske forbindelsen og belastningsfølsomme bremseventiler bak. Dette gir økt stabilitet under bråbremsing og samtidig kraftig unnastyring.

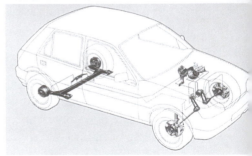

Blokkeringsfrie bremser

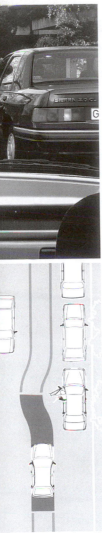

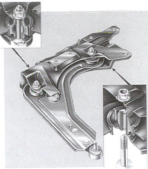

HJULOPPHENG

Fiesta har et stort «fotavtrykk» på veien med akselavstand på 2.446 mm og sporvidde på 1.392 mm. Det gir den en «bredbent» hjulstilling, ypperlig stabilitet og førsteklasses kjøreegenskaper.

Opphenget er fornyet både foran og bak, med en nyutvikling av MacPherson fjærben foran, og en vridbar bjelkeaksel bak. Dette gir den nye Fiesta en egenartet kombinasjon av lett, presis manøvring og suveren «storbil»-egenskaper.

En spesiell finesse ved forhjulsopphenget er bruken av doble vertikale ledd for de nedre bærearmene. Dette er samme konstruksjon som brukes for å oppnå presis leddstyring i racerbiler og fly.

Konstruksjonen sikrer en meget god hjulgeometri. Samtidig som den opptar bremsekreftene på en bedre måte og allikevel opprettholder komfortable fjæringsegenskaper.

Doble vertikale ledd

Resultatet er bedre komfort, sikrere kjøreegenskaper og mindre dekkslitasje.

Bakhjulsopphenget med vridbar bjelkeaksel gir ingenørene flere muligheter, bl.a. kan man plassere fjærene nærmere hjulene, slik at krengningsstabiliteten forbedres, samtidig som bakhjulenes sporvidde holdes konstant og hjulene loddrett. Dette forbedrer svingstabiliteten og reduserer dekkslitasjen.

Fjærene og støtdemperne har god avstand og er separat festet til karosseriet. Dette gir et bredt og flatt gulv i bagasjerommet og gjør rutinemessig kontroll og utskifting ved service mye enklere.

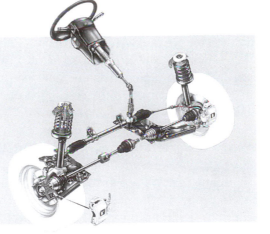

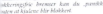

*kkeringsfrie bremser kan du .panikk-
.den at hjulene blir blokkert.*

Styring og forstilling

of the Sierra is presented as another type of female. She is the eye-catcher in this ad. Our view is from the back seat of the Fiesta and therefore we see the situation from the driver's point of view. Although we are able to note the Sierra driver's clothing, we can see only the expression in the eyes of the Fiesta driver. The images of the two are quite different. The dress of the woman in the Sierra merits a few comments. It is not uncommon for women in car advertisements to wears short skirts, stockings, and high heels. Whether they are drivers or extras in the advertisements, they have a tendency to become objects together with the car. A striking outfit draws attention to their gender. Often they have red nails and red lipstick, and/or are dressed in red. Thus, as sexual symbols they attract a lot of the attention given to the picture. They are seldom seen as individuals who are *active* in the manner that males are. In fact, in this ad both women are active, but their acting is undercommunicated. The Fiesta driver is about to avoid a dangerous situation, but attracts attention because she is in need of technical instruction. The Sierra driver is acting dangerously by opening the door of the car, but she attracts attention because of her looks.

The script instructs us to identify with the Fiesta driver. She is not pictured as a sex object, so what role is assigned to her? By contrast with the Sierra driver, she is robbed of her independence as a decision-maker. She is presented as an object of technical instruction. She is in need of help and guidance from the technically initiated. The contrast in the description of the female types contributes an aspect of woman-*against*-woman to this advertisement.

The script contains both comfort and utility. The seduction is primarily in the description of the car as *comfortable* by virtue of superior technology. We are furthermore told that servicing the car is *simplified* by the use of such technology. The Fiesta owner is described as sensible and careful, more passive and less daring than the Sierra owner who is thoughtlessly getting out of her car. The concept behind the front wheel suspension is said to be based on the same solutions as are found in racing cars and aeroplanes, but as a precautionary measure, and *not* coupled with high speed. This is a seduction of women that stresses safety and sees herself as sensible. The driver is, in the female manner, somewhat tense, and it helps to assure her that the technology is trustworthy. The main attraction is passive safety. In questions of technical competence she is left behind.

In general, car advertisements maintain a traditional system of gender roles. Men are seen as logical, technically competent and seeking excitement, whereas women are presented as objects and as ignorant in technological matters; with a need for training, they are safety oriented and empathetic. There are, however, exceptions. And this applies to both genders.

In conclusion, I would like to discuss an unorthodox advertisement for women. This advertisement portrays a different female role (Figure 3).

The Citroën BX GTi was launched in the mid-1980s. The picture shows a woman whom I would characterize as stylish and a bit arrogant. She represents what one could refer to as French sophistication and refinement. She portrays herself and the car by using an artist's brush. The impression is of "lightning speed, flexibility, and elegance". This is a wilful and self-assured woman. It is obvious that she likes to spend money. Her lifestyle is very different from the role of mother and empathetic woman. She wants speed, parties, and excitement. Her life seems free from worries and she enjoys it. That she likes fast cars follows from and emphasizes her lifestyle.

The language is incisive and direct. The effect is that the car owner is understood to be consistent, frank, and self-assured. Consequently this advertisement comes out as diametrically opposed to the previous one, which pictured the woman as hesitant and insecure. This script tells us about horsepower and top speed, comfort and convenience, advanced technology and advantageous economy. Nothing has been spared. The allusion to a French lifestyle is obvious. Enjoyment and consumption are the main attractions here. The car is described as sporty and continental. The metaphor used to describe the car, "firecracker", at the same time refers to the woman. It would be unusual to describe a man as a firecracker. Scripts that express men's

Den nye franske stilen.

Vi andre må nok innrømme det, Frankrike har alltid ligget et lite skritt foran i Europa.

For hvem kjenner vel ikke de franske motene, den franske kunsten, og den franske matkulturen?

Men også innen høyteknologi er Frankrike helt i teten.

Se bare på de franske lyn-togene.

Se på Concorde-flyene.

Og se på BX, den nyeste modellen fra Citroën. Citroën BX er en bil med en avansert teknologi og en gjennomført moderne stil du ikke finner hos noen annen.

Ja, BX'en er for mange blitt selve symbolet for den nye franske teknologien.

For den nye franske stilen.

SUKSESS OVER HELE EUROPA!

De kritiske europeiske bilkjøperne har for alvor fått øynene opp for Citroën BX.

Og det ruller allerede tusener av BX'er på veiene rundt om i Europa.

Det skyldes ikke minst den overstrømmende positive mottagelsen BX har fått av en samlet motorpresse – både kvalitet, utstyr og kjøre-egenskaper roses opp i skyene i test etter test!

Her i Norge sier bilbladet Motor ganske enkelt «Hurra Citroën!» etter sin prøvetur med BX.

SETT DEG INN I CITROËN BX – OG OPPLEV DEN FRANSKE KOMFORTEN.

I BX finner du alle de egenskapene som har gitt Citroën sitt ry som verdens mest moderne og komfortable bil.

Du finner servostyringen. Aerodynamikken. De overlegne vei-egenskapene. Og den unike fjæringen som gjør at du kan kjøre lengre i Citroën enn i noen annen bil før du blir sliten. *(Dette ble bevist i en test foretatt av et nøytralt belgisk institutt.)*

Citroën BX er i tillegg en bil som trenger usedvanlig lite av service og ettersyn.

Faktisk klarer den seg med kun 2,5 timers service for hver 20.000 km!

Du kan velge mellom hele 9 ulike versjoner – fra den rimeligste BX 14, til den råsterke BX 19 GT. BX finnes også i en svært elegant stasjonsvogn-utgave.

Nå vil vi gjerne at også du kommer og prøver BX'en.

Kjører den skikkelig, lener deg godt tilbake – og opplever hva franskmennene mener når de snakker om La Bonne Vie. Det Gode Livet. Velkommen!

CITROËN
BX.

Figure 3

relation to car use, as we have seen, use words such as "excited" and "aggressive". Here, a spirited woman is described in a "charming" way.

The seduction seems to take place on the woman's terms. To emphasize the distinctive character of her sex by a provocative dress is a central feature of the presentation of this type of woman. However, the point of this account is to convince us that it is *she* who chooses. This is a luxury-conscious, active, flirtatious woman. She buys a Citroën BX GTi in order to show off her life situation and lifestyle, her views and values. To control technology is not something she values. Technology per se is not interesting.

This separates this advertisement from the previous ones. The woman neither controls nor understands technology. She uses it because it can be combined with her style in other fields. Women's styles are different from men's. The car is presented as being as special as she is. To the reader it is also suggested that if you want to be like her, there is hope even if the GTi model is too expensive for you. The BX comes in more moderately priced versions which provide the same personality.

These two "women's ads" represent two different strategies for the seduction of female car buyers. First there is a somewhat worried and perhaps bad driver who is concerned about passive security, technological know-how, and safety (Figure 2). As a female model she is empathetic, and she is an object for training. This is probably a woman who uses an expensive garage and ensures that the car is always in perfect condition. The other woman (Figure 3) presents another image, that of a "modern" and "liberated" woman, which is probably more attractive to women nowadays. At the same time, her dress style maintains another traditional representation of femininity. However, she is presented as self-aware and in charge, while also being attractive. Though not able to say anything about the motives and genders of the creators of these advertisements, we still can ascertain that these are two quite distinctly different portrayals of women. Thus we may presume that they are meant for two different types of women, or based on different understandings of modern women.

Old Acquaintances in New Shells?

In this paper I have analysed the relationship between the car as a means of transport and its additional symbolic properties. I have given examples of how gender is presented in car advertisements. How is the fact that women buy cars more often than before integrated in marketing work? How are feminity and masculinity presented through ads?

A car, when it leaves the factory, is not yet a finished product. Through marketing, cars gain "faces" – meaning is attributed to them and they become socially constructed. By appealing to emotions and biases, the marketing industry also paints a picture of gender. Thus we may say that understandings of gender are constructed simultaneously with the car.

From my interviews it becomes evident that advertising people think that a car has a heterogeneous symbolic content – cars are more to people than a means of transport. My informants seem to agree that vehicles are not finished products when the leave the factory. Meaning and feelings are added, partly by the way cars are presented through ads and partly by the potential buyers and their previous experience of the brand and model. The marketing apparatus helps buyers to find something attractive that goes beyond cars as a means of transport. The efforts of the marketing apparatus are based on accumulated knowledge about what people want from a car.

The four car brands are relatively indistinguishable, so additional information is needed to attract attention. This is done by stressing other aspects of the car than the means of transport, and much of this concerns the themes of identification, masculinity, and femininity. Here established biases and attitudes are pre-eminent.

As analytical tools I have used the concepts of script and domestication. The *script* is the means by which the desired message is disseminated. It is the set of solutions that advertisements use to get cars sold. The script's centre of gravity might be either in the text or in the picture, or in a synergetic combination of these. The choice of words, and the use of codes and images, colours, moods, and context can all contribute. These are part of the advertisement, and as such pre-determined. Still there has to be an adaptation to the recipient in the transfer of messages. As a reader, one can select some assertions, while choosing to ignore others. Relating this to the process of *domestication*, the main aspect in the advertisements discussed here is objectification. In order to get the recipient to come up with symbols that are recognized in or compatible with the aims of the advertisement, various means are used in most ads.

As selections and representations of the feminine and the masculine, the advertisements tell us that men and women have different roles as car owners and drivers. Even though women present themselves as independent decision-makers when purchasing a car, traditional gender roles are preserved (Figures 2 and 3). As drivers, women are portrayed as somewhat helpless and lacking in technical knowledge (Figure 2). Whereas car advertisements for men bear witness to a need for control in other regions of life, the ones for women tell a story of their "unfamiliar" relationship with cars and their technical features. The theme of "men and cars" concerns a *fascination with technology coupled with excitement through speed and danger.* The theme of "women and cars" is about *practical utility, sensibleness, safety, and control of speed.* Women are *instructed* to practise *passive* control. If car advertisements include a driver, this is usually a man. In several of the advertisements I would claim that sensuality is a main element, both coupled with and concealed by the message about the car. Individuality is also a dominant feature. Men are more often than women portrayed as active, the gender in control of the machine. Women are likely to be portrayed as an object on a level with the car, even when the advertisement is directed towards women. In the French-inspired advertisement we saw a woman who makes her own choices. As such she is also a *subject* and this is a stark contrast to the traditional presentation.

Advertising might be said to have an important task in mirroring images of society. Thus advertisements also portray understandings of society. The industry's mainly traditional portrayal of gender relations may have many causes. It is possible only to sketch out some possible explanations. One is that it is far more important to achieve car sales than to change gender roles and society's perceptions. Or the industry may lack the knowledge to create new models that can cater for different versions of masculinity and femininity. A third possibility is that it is afraid to try new solutions – simply because the outcome is unknown and therefore risky.

The study of advertising and its messages is one of the possible ways of increasing our knowledge of gender. Messages about car technology are simultaneously messages about femininity and masculinity. By making gender visible, the point is to illuminate the ways gender is included in our comprehension of technology.

NOTE

1. Unless otherwise specified, all quotes are from my own interviews.

REFERENCES

Akrich, M. 1991. Users' representation: Practices, methods and sociology. Paris: Centre de Sociologie de l'Innovation, Ecole des Mines de Paris, mimeo.

Akrich, M. 1992. The de-scription of technical objects. In W. Bijker and J. Law (eds) *Shaping Technology/Building Society. Studies in Socio-Technical Change*. London: MIT Press.

Aune, M. 1992. *Datamaskina i hverdagslivet*. STS Report No. 15. Trondheim: Centre for Technology and Society.

Bourdieu, P. 1991. *Kultursosiologiska texter*. Skåne/Stockholm: Brutus Österlings Bokförlag.

Brandt, E. and Houg, T. 1978. *Arbeidsreiser i norske hushold 1976*. Oslo: Institutt for samfunnsforskning.

Dahle, K. 1992. Forståelse av kjønn i økonomi. In A. Taksdal and K.Widerberg (eds): *Forståelser av kjønn i samfunnsvitenskapens fag og kvinneforskning*. Oslo: Ad Notam/Gyldendal.

Guilano, G. 1979. Public transportation and the travel needs of women. *Traffic Quarterly*, Vol. 33, No. 4, pp. 607–16.

Hubak, M. 1993. Den forførende bilen—om produktfilosofi. *Sosiologinytt*, nr. 1.

Hinn, L. and Sihlberg, H. 1987. *Industrireklame innenfra*. Oslo: Cappelen.

Hjorthol, R. 1983. *Kvinner og arbeidsreiser*. Oslo: Transportøkonomisk institutt.

Hjorthol, R. 1990a. *Variasjoner i arbeidsreise mellom kvinner*. Notat 926. Oslo: Transportøkonomisk institutt.

Hjorthol, R. 1990b. *Ektefellers arbeidsreiser. Fordeling av tid og transportressurser*. Notat 919. Oslo: Tranportøkonomisk institutt.

Hjorthol, R. 1991. Reisen mellom hjem og jobb. Ektefellers arbeidsreise—fordeling av tid og transport ressurser. In R. Haukaa (ed.) *Nye kvinner nye menn*. Oslo: Ad Notam.

Hjorthol, R., Kolbenstevedt, M. and Vibe, N. 1990. *Kan vi leve uten bil? Et spill om byfamiliens hverdag og reiser*. Report No. 57. Oslo: Transportøkonomisk institutt.

Hopkins, C. 1923. *Scientific Advertising*. New York: Crown Publishers; 2nd ed.1966 (in Norwegian, 1971).

Kampanje. Oslo: Hjemmet.

Leiss, W., Kline, S. and Jhally, S. 1990. *Social Communication in Advertising*. New York: Routledge.

Madden, J. F. and White, J. M. 1979. Women's work trips. An empirical and theoretical overview. In *Women's Travel Issues. Research Needs and Priorities. Conference Proceedings and Papers*. Washington, DC: Department of Transportation.

Nakstad, T. and Ødegaard, O. 1987. *Markedsrådgiveren – fra strategi til gjennomføring*. Oslo: Cappelen.

NOU [Norges Offentlige Utredninger] 1981. *Reklame og kjønn*. Oslo: Universitetsforlaget.

Paaschwell, R. E. and Paaschwell, R. S. 1979. The transportation planning process. In *Women's Travel Issues. Research Needs and Priorities. Conference Proceedings and Papers*. Washington, DC: Department of Transportation.

Scharff, V. 1992. Gender, electricity and automobility. In M.Wachs and M.Crawford (eds): *The Car and the City*. Ann Arbor, MI: Michigan University Press.

Silverstone, R., Hirsch, E. and Morley, D. 1991. Information and communication technologies and the moral economy of the household. In K. H. Sørensen and A.-J. Berg (eds): *Technology and Everyday Life. Trajectories and Transformations*. Report No. 5. Oslo: Norwegian Research Council for Science and the Humanities.

Skretting, K. 1988. *Reklamefilmens kommunikasjon*. Bildetekster 11. Trondheim: Nordisk Institutt UNIT.

Sørgaard, J. 1993. *Bilens integrasjon i hverdagslivet – en teknologisosiologisk tilnærming til bilkultur*. Paper presented at Nordic Symposium, Tema T, University of Linköping, February.

Tedlow, R. S. 1990. *NEW and IMPROVED. The Story of Mass Marketing in America*. New York: Basic Books.

Tengström, E. 1990. Bilsamhället: Bilens makt och makten över bilismen. In S. Beckman: *Miljö, media och makt*. Stockholm: Carlsons.

Tengström, E. 1991. *Bilismen – i kris?* Stockholm: Raben & Sjögren.

Woolgar, S. 1991. Configuring the user. In J. Law (ed.): *A Sociology of Monsters. Essays on Power, Technology and Domination*. London: Routledge.

Chapter 8

Gender in the Image of Technology

Merete Lie

A main question of this book is how and why technology is related to gender. My way of exploring this issue is by focusing on images of technologies and their users in everyday settings. These images reveal how technology is integrated not only in everyday practices, but also in the cultural and symbolic structures of a society.

To illustrate what I mean by images of technology I shall give an example. Previously, when you came to Stavanger, Norway's oil capital, you were met by a replica of an oil driller in the lobby of the most prominent hotel in the city. There was a man, full size, in his colourful and very visible work outfit. He wore a helmet with a headlamp, signalling danger, and there were tools everywhere around him. They were in his hands, fastened to his body, and arranged on the ground. And then the drill, the large and looming object attracting all attention. The man was leaning forwards in an active position, creating an impression of strength and skill, danger and mastering.

Such complex images are tales about coherence and context. Thus gender is connected to tools and tasks by telling where and to whom they belong, resembling how advertising makes us associate soft drinks and shampoos with sunshine and holidays. As these are mere impressions, they later bypass words and reasoning. One may learn by the intellect that gender is connected neither to jobs nor to artefacts, but by another type of knowledge we know that it is.

How come that we so easily see men and masculinity, when what is presented is a worker with his tools? Do representations of workers tend to stress certain models of men? Morgan (1992) asks whether researchers have overemphasized a model of the classical "worker" to the detriment of other male models because of their own identification with "real men":

> In Gouldner's classic study of Patterns of Industrial Bureaucracy ... we find the methodological appendix describing how a largely male research team developed a strong affinity with the masculine world of the miners, possibly identifying with them as opposed to the surface workers. There was an almost self-conscious rejection of the conventional middle-class campus life-style and the building up of team solidarity paralleled the solidarity work groups of the miners. They were delighted to prove to miners that they could "take it", thereby possibly winning some measure of admiration ... Gouldner acknowledges his debt to "the men at the plant" in these words: "We were truly sorry when the study was completed, for we had come to like and respect them as 'men'." (Morgan, 1992: 73)

Thus is perpetuated what he characterizes as a particular and stereotypical model of masculinity: "tough, hard-drinking, little time for softness in men or women but always good for a laugh, one of the lads."

A classical image of masculinity is connected partly to hard physical work and partly to the mastery of machines. In spite of this image belonging to the working class, Gouldner and his men see a type of masculinity they want to share. Willis (1977) depicts a similar ambivalent picture of working-class masculinity. The young boys of the study want work that others might see as degrading low-status work. This is because manual work underlines a specific type of masculinity, known from fathers and other men around them, whereas white-collar work is characterized as effeminate: "Manual labour is suffused with masculinity and given certain sensual overtones for the 'lads'" (Willis, 1977: 150). Similarly, Sally Hacker (1990) has drawn attention to the sensual pleasures of engineers in their relationships to technologies, then connected to the power they contain.

Wage work is one of the central themes of male identity. The type of work, the environment within which it takes place, and the team one belongs to produce an image telling oneself and others what type of person one is. The importance of wage work also to women's identity has been less acknowledged but is certainly constructed in similar ways (Kaul, 1996). However, the characteristics of typical men's work differ from those of typical women's work, and such contrasts are important for telling who you are.

The aim of this paper is to draw attention to how images of work construct images of gender. A key feature of these images is that they unite information which is normatively kept separate, such as gender in relation to the following themes: jobs are supposed to be assigned in relation to skills (and not to gender), technologies designed according to function, and identity connected to personality. Confronted with the complex images of everyday life, however, often a glimpse is enough to tell if, or where, you belong. This sense of belonging or not might be an indicator of a gendering of tasks and tools.

Depicting the image of the oil driller was a way of focusing on connections between technology and masculinity. Is it that technology is a symbol of masculinity, or, in other words, that dealing with technology is part of what identifies a man? However, if we take Gouldner's "man the worker" as a typical image of masculinity, this is definitely an image in decline. Work is changing, so is technology, and so is the understanding of gender and gender relations. Thus any study of gender and technology necessarily will be a study of change. Against this background I want to ask, if technology has had a constitutive role in a particular image of masculinity, to the extent that it has become a stereotypical and common image, what happens when technologies change? My approach to this question is to focus on differences in images of technology and gender which can be identified within work settings of traditional versus present types.

The Expression of Difference

The aspects of sameness and difference *within* the two categories of gender – among women and among men – make gender studies very complex. How can one speak of gender differences "between" without undercommunicating the differences "within" (Moore, 1993)?

Speaking of gender symbols might indicate a dichotomous categorization of male and female. However, a specific quality of symbols is their multivocality. According to Turner (1967), a symbol is "a semantic molecule with many components". Thus a symbol speaks with many voices and is a carrier of multiple meanings. But at the same time the symbol unites this complexity.

A symbol conveys a message about a person, indicating to both her/himself and others who s/he is. Because technologies hold a versatility of meanings they may annex different attributes to the users, telling for instance of qualities as different as force when carrying a weapon, or skills with the use of tools. Exploring a connection between technology and masculinity, accordingly, does not mean that only a single model of masculinity is represented; rather technology speaks with many voices because technologies are varied and appear in different contexts. Still, technology is a concept that unites the different appearances and makes a variety of artefacts representatives of something equal. In spite of their differences they belong to the same category. Could technology also represent a variety of men, transforming different types of masculinities into something equal and shared? If so, men could experience and express sameness by participating in activities and identifying with certain symbols without the implication that this should make them identical to each other.

The problem in speaking of images or symbols of masculinity is the pitfall of stereotypes. However, even if men are different, there are fairly consistent ideas concerning masculinities. Even if they do not correspond to the personalities of "real" men, these ideas are as real and existing as living men. Different types of masculinity tend to be hierarchically ordered (Connell, 1987), some of which are ideals that young boys in particular choose as objects of identification. "Masculinities thus provide sources of and resources for the development and retention of gender identity" (Hearn and Collinson, 1994: 104).

Holding that gendered identities are negotiated rather than simply presented (Rudie, 1984) implies that they are continuously in the making. The expression of sameness within same-sex relations may be as important as stressing differences from the other sex. Sameness also has to be negotiated because it is never given that a person will be accepted as "one of us". Especially within a gender-biased arena like the field of technology, same-sex relations may even be more important than cross-sex relations in the expression of masculinity. Since women are defined as ignorant about technology, they can make a gendered contrast, but at the same time women's lack of competence makes them incapable of defining a man's worth in relation to technology. Confirming the masculinity of other persons, it appears that in many contexts other men make a more important audience than women do, such as at work (Cockburn, 1983; Morgan, 1992; Willis, 1977), in sports (Messner, 1987), and in war (Hacker and Hacker, 1987; Morgan, 1994; Wajcman, 1991).

Thus technology may be part of the presentation of self. Moreover, it can be actively manipulated by the user in this presentation, just as Goffman (1959) depicts ways of acting on the scenes of everyday life. Different images in terms of artefact "hardware", surrounding sceneries, and non-verbal performances are the focus of this article. To exemplify what is meant by images of everyday life, the following quotation about the "Theater of War" may serve as an illustration:

> As war became "democratized" and involved greater numbers of its citizens more normally accustomed to the routines of civilian life, so grew one of the most poignant images associated with combat: the ordinary soldier saying goodbye to family and loved ones.... In the farewell at the airstrip or the dockside there is the convergence of the protector and the protected, of the public and the private, and of masculinity and femininity. (Morgan, 1994: 166)

In the following, images will be presented of women and men using technologies at work.[1] They serve to illustrate how technologies separate male from female both physically and symbolically, and how images of what is male and female change when technologies change. In other words, how are "sameness and difference within and between" communicated scenographically at the workplace?

The Traditional Factory

The contrast between "old" and "new" technology will be presented by starting with the classical factory – classical not in the sense that it is history and does not exist any longer, but as a demonstration of the classical pattern of the sexual division of labour. Today, these contrasts have become more blurred in many social contexts, meaning that they are not demonstrated by physical barriers but exist mainly as a mental charter.

The present company is a chocolate factory, but the same pattern is found within industry in general: a division between male and female industries, and between male and female work within each industry (Form and McMillen, 1983). What this example will illustrate is how technology functions as physical as well as mental barriers between male and female domains.

At the chocolate factory, male and female areas of work are separated physically by walls. Within the male domain the chocolate mass is mixed in large containers. From the mixer the chocolate is transferred into metal moulds and from there through a hole in the wall to the assembly line in the women's department. Some heavy lifting is demanded of a worker, such as sacks of 50 kg when adding nuts to the chocolate. The moulds are changed manually. This implies heavy lifting in awkward positions.

In the men's department, large and noisy machines make the dominant impression. The men never touch the chocolate. To them industrial work means the handling of machines.

In the women's department, the chocolate appears transformed into small chocolate bars. The women on the line remove the bars from the conveyor belt by hand, using a small metal tray. The trays are placed on a trolley and pushed to the packing machines. There women feed the machines with chocolate bars. On the other side of the machine the chocolate bars appear wrapped up, to be lifted and put into boxes. The female work is mainly manual.

In a factory like this everybody's position is clearly defined. It is instantly seen where men and women respectively belong.

Incidentally, a woman could hint at considering a better job in the male department. Then a gesture will suffice for a male worker to indicate the physical hardships and make everybody understand that this is out of the question.

The big machines here function as part of the image the males present of themselves. The machinery implies that they have the capacities required by a man: technical know-how, physical strength, and unconcern about the stresses, such as noise and dirt. The machines used by women do not say the same things about them. Partly because they are different machines (smaller and neater), but mostly because the women have not appropriated their machines in the way men here constantly do. The machines are not part of them, but something they are placed beside to "serve".

The masters and controllers of the women's machines are the mechanics. The mechanics display the signs of belonging to the machines: they wear blue overalls, carry tools in their pockets, and have a tool bench as their haunt. Sitting by such a bench in a blue overall clearly marks a distance from the production workers.

The female workers' white coats are a sign that they belong to the food. The male workers in their white overalls might appear to be in an ambiguous position. However, with their work routines and way of working they underline a closeness to the machinery. In such ways they manage to express that their task is the handling of industrial machines and not the production of food (read "cooking").

In the factories, men visibly "tame" the machines, carrying the tools to master them. Whereas men work *with* and *within* the machines, women work *at* the machines to feed them or remove their products. By dress and equipment men signal their belonging to the *machines*, whereas women are associated with the *products*, such as food.

The Growing Clerical Sector

At work, the use of heavy machinery is decreasing whereas the use of computers is rapidly increasing. Ever more men are joining the growing service sector and becoming white-collar workers. Even within industry, jobs change to watching over the process via computers. Tools, blue-collar clothing, and other attributes traditionally linked to masculinity are on the decline.

The difference between factory work and office work has often been referred to in visual terms. Lockwood (1958) identified the 19th century's office worker as "the black coated worker". This worker is definitely a man, and a man of dignity. The black coat was discarded, however, and the distinction has since generally been between, respectively, white-collar and blue-collar work. The female environment of the office in our times is better signified by the less gender-neutral term of "the pink-collar worker" (Williams, 1988). The colours identify the cleanliness of office work compared with manual work, and the opposites "clean" and "dirty" are linked to feminine and masculine environments. Whereas the blue work outfit can take some dirt, a neat appearance and spotlessness are hallmarks of the office worker. Thus the computer is well suited to the office environment, being a clean and silent type of technology.

The office organization that grew during the 19th century was from the start a male environment (Lockwood, 1958). It was a hierarchical structure, with age being a visible criterion of being an apprentice or in a position of trust. Offices were small and the hierarchical relationships were personalized and paternalistic. Technologies were nearly absent, the pen and pencil being the most indispensable. Women entered the office when the typewriter was introduced. Consequently they did not take over men's work but took up a new type of work, which from the start was women's work (Davies, 1982). A woman's place in the office was seated in front of the typewriter. Thus seated she was also placed low in the hierarchical structure, providing services to superiors who created the texts to be typed.

During the 20th century there was an immense growth within the clerical sector. The introduction of new technologies went in parallel with a fragmentation of tasks, or what was termed an "industrialization" of the office (Braverman, 1975). Separate typing pools meant a more evident demarcation between male and female work. Other women were placed outside men's offices as their personal secretaries. Being a secretary also implied specific clothing and behaviour, a part of the curriculum of secretarial schools, further underlining gender differences at work.

When computers were first introduced in the office, they were different for men and women. Women had word processors whereas men got general computers. It was not long, however, before general computers were provided throughout the office. Today, the same type of computer is found on most desks throughout the hierarchy. Although the office is generally taken to represent a feminine environment, having changed from a male- to a female-dominated sphere of work, we may ask whether the technical look of a modern office, due to office information systems, could mean a change.

The Image of a Modern Office

The company here representing the modern office is a wholesale dealer, serving customers (generally farmers) mainly by telephone and post. The employees are about half-and-half men and women. Disregarding the storeroom and the small shop, most of the employees work in a large open-plan office. Each person has a separate desk, on which there is a computer. All employees are connected to the same on-line computer system. Some positions are still distinguished. The managing director has a large, separate office, whose entrance is guarded by his female secretaries. Some other people in management positions also have separate offices. But, generally, the employees are seated all over the open-plan office, sometimes in separate groups of men and women, but mostly in mixed groups.

Talking to these people, one finds that they have different tasks to perform and different positions within the hierarchy. These are obvious to everybody knowing the organization but they are not clearly presented by tools and architecture. Neither do people wear work outfits identifying where they belong. In Norway, both men and women wear rather informal clothes at work, here emphasized by the employees' background in and identification with the rural sector. Female office workers are no longer distinguished by feminine dressing; jeans and sweaters are the general outfit for women as well as for men.

In this setting, similarity is more apparent than difference. Most people deal with papers, telephones, and computers, and they do not produce anything tangible and visible. Because they mainly deal with communication and brain work, it is hard to *see* what people *do*. The image, therefore, of this place of work does not immediately tell us that men and women are different. The only difference it reveals is between superiors and ordinary office workers.

The office has a more technical look than before, with telephones, intercoms, and fax machines in addition to computers. Does this imply a more "masculine" look to the office or, on the contrary, that men are effeminated when belonging to this sector of work? However, symbols of everyday life do not "contain" a specific meaning that is consciously transmitted from generation to generation. They are invested with meaning by social actors and within social settings. The feminine aspects of the office environment might thus have an impact on the technologies within this sector. Let us then consider computer technology within another setting.

The New Factory

Within certain branches, industrial production has undergone profound changes. Processing industries have been automated, meaning that workers watch the process on computer screens and intervene only when something irregular occurs. The numerical machines which were introduced within the metal industries have given workers a role as programmers rather than manual workers. Women are seldom seen within this type of factory. Although the physical hardships have been reduced, the jobs have not been redefined to be women's work (cf. Cockburn, 1983). But does this change the image of the industrial worker, making it different from the one depicted by Gouldner and others?

The following quotation describes the bleach plant of a pulp mill. Here the image of the production hall is the way it used to be. Soon we shall see that the workers' new environment is in sharp contrast to it.

> Each minute, 4,000 gallons of this brown mash flow through a laby-rinth of pipes into a series of cylindrical vats, where they are washed, treated with chlorine-related chemicals, and bleached white. No natural light finds its way into this part of the mill. The fluorescent tubes overhead cast a greenish-yellow pall, and the air is laced with enough chemical flavor that as you breathe it, some involuntary wisdom built deep into the human body registers an assault. The floors are generally wet, particularly in the areas right around the base of one of the large vats that loom like raised craters on a moon-scape. Sometimes a washer runs over, spilling soggy cellulose knee-deep across the floor. When this happens, the men put on their high rubber boots and shovel up the mess. (Zuboff, 1988: 19–20)

The atmosphere thus described resembles that of the old days, and one can imagine a type like "man, the worker" within it: dirty, manual work, the hazards of possibly dangerous chemicals, and a work outfit constructed for protection. However, this is only half the story:

> In 1981 a central control room was constructed in the bleach plant. A science fiction writer's fantasy, it is a gleaming glass bubble that seems to have erupted like a mushroom in the dark, moist, toxic atmosphere of the plant.... Inside the control room the air is filtered and hums with the sound of the air-conditioning unit.... Workers sit on orthopedically designed swivel chairs covered with a royal blue fabric, facing video display terminals. The terminals, which display process information for the purposes of monitoring and control, are built into polished oak cabinets. Their screens glow with numbers, letters, and graphics in vivid red, green, and blue. (ibid.)

The point is that workers have been removed from the produc-tion hall to spend their working days within an environment as clean and silent as that of the modern office. But what has hap-pened is that the workers have not accommodated to the "glass bubble" atmosphere. They make a visible protest with their bodies. They still move back and forth between the two working environments – the production hall and the control room. To protect the environment within the control room there are two pairs of automatic doors. But instead of waiting for the doors to open, workers constantly thrust them open with the force of their bodies. According to the author, there is "a forward momentum of their bodies, whose physical power seems trivialized by the new circumstances of their work; a boyish energy that wants to break free" (Zuboff, 1988: 22). One can choose to regard this interpretation as another example of researchers finding what they are looking for, namely "man, the worker", but one can also see it as an indication that the change from blue-collar to white-collar work is experienced as a profound and not easy change by the workers themselves.

In the story of the classical factory, the relationship between men and machines was characterized as men mastering or "taming" the machines. In the new factory it seems as if the machines mean a taming of the workers, which arouses protest. The new work process is one that demands first and foremost the brain, and less and less the rest of the body. The workers here respond by breaking automatic mechanisms with their bodies.

The men within the control room watch over the screens, using only eyes and fingertips. Seeing this as a new image of men and machines, the question is: Are they more "office like", even effeminated, compared with before? Or are they seen as controlling large machinery, though physically separated from it, and controlling it in more sophisticated ways than before?

"Distorted" Images?

Different types of work situations have illustrated the changing image of technology at work. However, differences are not necessarily displayed by material structures and physical barriers. To stress the aspects of a job that one wants to accentuate, more subtle signals may suffice. As mentioned, Willis (1977) demonstrated how important it was to working-class boys to stress the toughness and danger involved in their jobs. Whereas the same jobs might be apprehended as low-status, unskilled work, the young boys applying for them "saw" instead the above-mentioned aspects. These boys considered manual work more desirable than mental work just because it demonstrated a certain type of masculinity and separated them most clearly from girls – both physically at the place of work and symbolically by underlining their physical attributes.

Here, stressing the symbolic aspects of tools and tasks does not imply that they are an exact mirroring of a social situation, because "reading" a symbol is biased by the influence of general cultural patterns. Leidner (1991) reveals how experiencing a profession as either male or female directs the attention to different aspects. Thus, for a sales*man*, the aspects of work that require "manly" traits, such as control and self-direction, are emphasized. In the occupation of sales*woman*, however, the servicing of customers is held to be most characteristic of the job.

With this in mind, we shall return to the office depicted above. This is a sales and service organization for farmers. At first glance, one can see that everybody has a computer on their desk. At a second glance, one can see that they use them differently. Women office workers do general office work, which is mostly done on computers. Men more often do customer service and sales work, for which they have to use the computer but they use other resources as well. The male office workers are recruited on the basis of knowledge about the products the company sells. They have a background in practical work within farming, in repair shops, or in the company's storeroom. Female workers, on the other hand, are recruited on the basis of competence in general office work, acquired by formal education. For the men, there are several objects of identification within the company other than the clerical aspects of the work; for example, transport, economics, farming, or machines. The male office workers make connections to groups outside such as drivers, repair men, or customers.

Adding more to the image of this office, on the men's desks there are catalogues of farming machinery and other equipment, calendars with pictures of machinery, even toys in the shape of miniature tractors. On the women's desks there are more often postcards and photos of children and newly married couples. The women's desks give an image of orderliness: tasks come in as sheets of paper to be dealt with and moved on to the pile of finished tasks. Men's desks, however, expose a variety of catalogues, pictures, microfiches, and message notes, telling of a busy man with complex tasks to do. The computer has no significant position within this complexity.

The typewriter used to demarcate a woman's place in the office. Tending machines was men's place in the factory. The computer does not seem to be connected in this way to gender. The men demarcate their distance from office work by relating to other aspects of the job, in this case to the machines and other farming equipment the company distributes, and not by appropriating the computer. Apparently the computer is not considered to be a machine but rather is regarded as a piece of office equipment, which is something different to them (Lie, 1995). Here, mechanical machinery is what is understood as technology. These men relate to a tradition of manual work which is different from the world of computing.

In the "new" factory, the workers now relate to computers, but they still have large machinery and a traditional industrial environment within reach. The latter may be experienced as the "real work", meaning that one does not necessarily have to change one's experience of self as a worker. Thus here too one may choose to identify with, and try to underline, one or another aspect of the work that signifies alternatively brain work or physical hardship.

The Messages of Technology

To talk about technologies used at work as symbols points to a paradox. In Western culture there is a distinction between, on the one hand, the useful and ordinary and, on the other hand, objects as carriers of meaning or what might be called sacred objects in a wider sense. These "sacred" objects belong to the emotional sphere of life, and it is precisely in the emotional aspects that the strong appeal of symbols lies (Cohen, 1977; Lewis, 1977). Because technology is the exponent of the rational, it becomes the counterpart to the emotional. Against this, social scientists have evidenced the symbolic aspects of everyday behaviour (Goffman, 1959) as well as of everyday objects and frequently used expressions (Gullestad, 1992). The reason their symbolic aspects are seldom focused on by researchers, Gullestad explains by their triviality, meaning that they become invisible just because they are much too visible (Gullestad, 1989: 13). The fact that workplace technologies belong to the trivial as well as to the practical sphere of life contributes to hide their symbolic aspects.

Within the social sciences, technology is more often related to the social and political than to the emotional aspects of life. Feminist research has evidenced how power and powerlessness are reflected by the mastery or non-mastery of technology (Cockburn, 1985; Wajcman, 1991). Technology entails power because politics is "built into" technologies (Noble, 1984; Winner, 1980), or intermingled in socio-technical actor networks (Latour, 1987; Bijker and Law, 1992). My point is that power is not only a possession of the user of technologies; it is also a message, between other messages, connected to technologies.

In modern Western societies, technology has been pointed to as a key symbol – of progress, of modernity, or of this society at large. It is what is termed a root metaphor (Ortner, 1973), meaning that experiences can be likened to and illuminated by a comparison with the symbol:

> In fact, as Mary Douglas points out, the living organism in one form or another functions as a root metaphor in many cultures, as a source of categories for conceptualizing social phenomena (1966). In mechanized society, on the other hand, one root metaphor for the social process is the machine, and in recent times the computer represents a crucial modification upon this root metaphor. (Ortner, 1973: 1341)

Ortner distinguishes between, on the one hand, root metaphors for ordering experiences, and, on the other hand, key scenarios providing strategies for action. Technology comprises both of these aspects, because it refers to qualities as well as ways of acting. A technical artefact can be an expression of, for instance, force as well as pointing to a special course of action. As such, technologies can function metaphorically, meaning that words associated with technology are also associated with men and masculinity, and they can be directive of masculine ways of acting.

As mentioned previously, one strength of technology as a symbol is that the concept unites dissimilarities. Parallel to the differences between men, there are a wide variety of technologies men can choose to master. These artefacts will still have something in common, since they are identified as belonging to the same category. Thus they may unify men as belonging to the same category. My aim here is to take this unity apart and identify some of the different messages of technology and see how they relate to aspects of different types of masculinity.

One element is *dynamics*, including a potential for change. Technology is associated with *activity* and *mobility* versus the static. It is something in progress, maybe pushing or aggressive. Moreover, it is *hard* and *vigorous*, in contrast to the soft and compliant.

Technology also alludes to *knowledge*. The insiders' knowledge leads to *mastery* and *control*. This refers to control over insecure surroundings, whether of nature or of humans. The knowledge and skills needed to design as well as use machines are to a large degree guarded and surrounded by mystery, producing for the insiders an aura of being *unique*. To those who are not insiders and do not share the knowledge, technology means insecurity and danger. It is something out of control and thus potentially harmful.

Challenge and *danger* are other aspects of technology. Technology is a means to conquer danger and to manage on your own. Thus it means *self-sufficiency* and becomes a symbol of *freedom*.

Because technology is a means to manage more than can be achieved with your own hands, and thus more than can be achieved by others, it comes to more than independence. It also means *power*. Adding the strength to which technology alludes, it also means *force*: the ability to rule and suppress.

This can all be summed up in the words *"strong, hard, and vigorous"*, which allude rather directly to male potency. Or, because a symbol also contributes to the construction of masculinity, it furthers the image of masculinity as being this.

Accordingly, this single concept includes many elements which are also aspects of a certain type of masculinity. This means that it reflects not the capacities of "real" men but rather the qualities of one social image of masculinity. Thus technical objects may function as visible images of this abstract "standard". They are objects men can wear to demonstrate masculine capacities because they arouse associations of certain types of masculinity in others.

In which contexts are technologies expressions of the above-mentioned aspects? Certainly not in all contexts. For instance, power and freedom are difficult to express in a clearly subordinated position. Still, they can be expressed in relation to other more subordinated groups. Referring to the factory depicted above, the mechanics' relationship to technology could represent most of the aspects mentioned here. Although the male workers are in a subordinate position within the organization, some of the powerful messages are still reflected on them, especially vis-à-vis the women, who are placed in the servant's and not in the master's position towards the machines.

Technologies, Brains, and Bodies

When studying images of women and men using technologies, I am looking for relationships between technologies, femininities, and masculinities. To answer whether technology is a symbol of masculinity, neither is easily conceptualized because both have to be addressed in the plural: there are different technologies as well as different masculinities. Applying the concept of hegemonic masculinity, however, is a way of simplifying. The notion of hegemonic masculinity means a certain degree of consent that one model is superior to other models (Connell, 1987; Kimmel, 1987). The concept "hegemonic" could also be applied to technology, similarly to what Bolter (1984) speaks of as a defining technology:

> It [the computer] is the technology that more than any other defines our age ... For us today, the computer constantly threatens to break out of the tiny corner of human affairs (scientific measurement and business accounting) that it was built to occupy, to contribute instead to a general redefinition of certain basic relationships: the relationship of science to technology, of knowledge to technical power, and, in the broadest sense, of mankind to the world of nature. (Bolter, 1984: 8f.)

The point to be stressed here is that there has been a change from one type of hegemonic technology, connected to physical strength and manual skills, to the computer, which instead indicates something abstract and out of reach. If, as Ortner and others have indicated, machines are root metaphors for social processes, and also for the human being, this change means holding up another image of the social as well as of the human.

Discussing masculinity, it is most important to distinguish between men and masculinities. Identifying a certain type of masculinity as an idea, or even an ideal, does not imply conformity of behaviour (Connell, 1987). The importance of technology to men certainly varies. But within certain work cultures, such as places here described under the heading of the traditional factory, I would hold that technology is very important. I would also hold that Gouldner's image of "man, the worker" is an ideal looked up to not only by work researchers but also by his co-workers. This does not imply that many of them have the capacities of this type of man; in other words, that it is an image of the typical male industrial worker. It is, however, a good description of a certain type of masculinity. This is a masculinity that is closely connected to technology, and technology of a kind that is linked to hard physical work.

One could therefore say that the image of "man, the worker" has been overemphasized as a type of man that is probably not very common. As an image of masculinity, however, it has a central position in Western culture. But it is less certain that it is still a hegemonic type of masculinity in the 1990s. In advertising and films for instance, this male image has to some extent been exchanged for a less muscular type of masculinity. Still, different types of masculinities may exist side-by-side. The question can therefore be reiterated concerning a new type of technology: Have men appropriated the computer, and is it a symbol of a new type of masculinity?

One could say that men have appropriated computer technology, in the sense that men clearly dominate within computer science and lead developments within computing. As a tool, however, it is used by "everybody". And the difference between master and servant is not as clearly expressed as in the classical factory. Differences are expressed more indirectly, as computers are links to different tasks.

Studying machines as symbols it is important to look for the capacities demonstrated when operating them. With a changing image of technology, the same qualities are no longer reflected. The main change is from bodily strength to intellectual abilities, but with the important exception that computers do not in all contexts imply the use of the brain. In the "new factory" the workers could be seen as controlling immense powers, but they could also be seen as reduced to "button-pressers". This point underlines the importance of context when looking for the meanings of a new symbol. In the office presented here, computers were seemingly of little importance in expressing difference between women and men. Difference could be expressed in other ways, and the men tended to ignore computers in favour of traditional machinery, which to these men was more in accordance with their interests and self-image.

Still, the computer is able to reiterate some qualities connected to technology as identified previously, such as dynamics, knowledge, and control. The element of power is there, but it lacks connotations of physical ability, vigour, and danger. Technologies such as an axe or a hammer refer rather directly to force, whereas the power of the computer is more indirect and mediated by hierarchical position and intellectual abilities.

Coming back to the machine as a root metaphor for society and social progress, it has traditionally been linked to the body as another root metaphor. Like other machines before it, the computer alludes to progress and to an easing of effort. Machines express an ability to achieve greater yields than are possible by human effort alone. The computer is relieved of any association with dirt and physical effort. It is a brain machine which operates on the world with the use of intellectual effort only. Traditionally it used to be the human body that was likened to a machine, or rather to a factory, with different types of "machinery", such as the heart and the lungs, working together. With the computer, the comparison is now to the human brain. From the MIT, Sherry Turkle (1984: 329) tells of her astonishment when she heard a student of computer science refer to herself as a machine, in the sense of a collection of programs which she held to be her "I".

What the computer signifies is clearly different from mechanical machinery. When the computer is associated with human beings, this refers to the brains and not to the physical body. As a symbol of human qualities it alludes to being smart, intelligent, etc., rather than to physical capacities or manual dexterity. As a root metaphor it could mean a shift in the sense that the element of knowledge has gained hegemony at the cost of other human attributes.

NOTE

1. The images from working life to be presented are not constructed images, but examples chosen from a variety of companies observed during different studies of work organizations during a period of twenty years. The study of the chocolate factory was completed in the 1970s (Kaul and Lie 1982, Kaul 1992). The study of the office organization, the wholesale dealer, took place in the 1990s (Lie 1995). They were both cases within studies including several companies. The methods used in both studies were a combination of interviews, observations and informal talk related to work performance. The theme of the factory study was the general working conditions of women workers, whereas the office study focused on workers' relationships to computers. Gender relations and divisions of labour were themes of both studies. Depicting these visual images, however, is a new and different way of analysing gender relations within these companies.

BIBLIOGRAPHY

Barth, F. (ed.) 1969. Introduction. In: *Ethnic Groups and Boundaries*. Oslo: Universitetsforlaget.

Bijker, W. and Law, J. (eds). 1992. *Shaping Technology/Building Society. Studies in Sociotechnical Change*. Cambridge, MA and London: MIT Press.

Bolter, J. D. 1984. *Turing's Man. Western Culture in the Computer Age*. Chapel Hill, NC: University of North Carolina Press.

Braverman, H. 1975. *Labor and Monopoly Capital. The Degradation of Work in the Twentieth Century*. New York and London: Monthly Review Press.

Brod, H. (ed.) 1987. Introduction. *The Making of Masculinities. The New Men's Studies*. London: Allen & Unwin.

Brod, H. and Kaufman, M. (eds) 1994. *Theorizing Masculinities*. Thousand Oaks, CA: Sage.

Cockburn, C. 1983. *Brothers. Male Dominance and Technological Change*. London: Pluto Press.

Cockburn, C. 1985. *Machinery of Dominance*. London: Pluto Press.

Cohen, A. 1977. Symbolic action and the structure of self. In I. Lewis (ed.): *Symbols and Sentiments. Cross-cultural Studies in Symbolism*. London: Academic Press.

Connell, R. W. 1987. *Gender and Power*. Cambridge: Polity Press.

Davies, M. 1982. *Woman's Place is at the Typewriter. Office Work and Office Workers 1870–1930*. Philadelphia, PA: Temple University Press.

Douglas, M. 1966. *Purity and Danger*. London: Routledge.

Form, W. and McMillen, D. B. 1983. Women, men and machines. *Work and Occupations*, No. 2.

Goffman, E. 1959. *The Presentation of Self in Everyday Life*. New York: Doubleday Anchor Books.

Gullestad, M. 1989. *Kultur og hverdagsliv. På sporet av det moderne Norge*. Oslo: Universitetsforlaget.

Gullestad, M. 1992. *The Art of Social Relations. Essays on Culture, Social Action and Everyday Life in Modern Norway*. Oslo: Scandinavian University Press.

Hacker, S. 1990. *"Doing It the Hard Way". Investigations of Gender and Technology*. Boston: Unwin Hyman.

Hacker, B. C. and Hacker, S. L. 1987. Military institutions and the labour process. *Technology and Culture*, Vol. 28, pp. 743–75.

Hearn, J. and Collinson, D. J. 1994. Theorizing unities and differences between men and between masculinities. In H. Brod and M. Kaufman (eds): *Theorizing Masculinities*. Thousand Oaks, CA: Sage.

Kaul, H. 1996. Kjerringknuter. Kvinners identitet i omsorg og yrke. Dr.polit. dissertation, Faculty of the Social Sciences, Trondheim, NTNU.

Kaul, H. and Lie, M. 1982. When paths are vicious circles—How women's working conditions hamper influence. *Economic and Industrial Democracy*, Vol. 3, pp. 465–82.

Kimmel, M. S. (ed.) 1987. Introduction. In: *Changing Men. New Directions in Research on Men and Masculinity*. Newbury Park, CA: Sage.

Latour, B. 1987. *Science in Action*. Milton Keynes: Open University Press.

Leidner, R. 1991. Serving hamburgers and selling insurance: Gender, work, and identity in interactive service jobs. *Gender and Society*, Vol. 5, pp. 154–77.

Lewis, I. (ed.) 1977. Introduction. In: *Symbols and Sentiments. Cross-cultural Studies in Symbolism*. London: Academic Press.

Lie, M. 1995. Technology and masculinity. The case of the computer. *European Journal of Women's Studies*, Vol. 2, pp. 379–94.

Lockwood, D. 1958. *The Blackcoated Worker*. London: Allen & Unwin.

Messner, M. 1987. The meaning of success: The athletic experience and the development of male identity. In H. Brod: *The Making of Masculinities. The New Men's studies*. London: Allen & Unwin.

Moore, H. L. 1993. The differences within and the differences between. In T. del Valle (ed.) *Gendered Anthropology*. London: Routledge.

Morgan, D. H. J. 1992. *Discovering Men*. London: Routledge.

Morgan, D. H. J. 1994. Theater of war: Combat, the military, and masculinities. In H. Brod and M. Kaufman: *Theorizing Masculinities*. Thousand Oaks, CA: Sage.

Noble, D. 1984. *Forces of Production*. New York: Alfred Knopf.

Ortner, S. B. 1973. On key symbols. *American Anthropologist*, Vol. 75, pp. 1338–46.

Rosaldo, M. Z. 1980. *Knowledge and Passion. Ilongot Notions of Self and Social Life*. Cambridge: Cambridge University Press.

Rudie, I. 1984. *Myk start, hard landing* [Soft start, hard landing]. Oslo: Universitetsforlaget.

Sørum, A. 1991. Om å være de samme: Stedbinding og identitet i indre Sulawesi. *Norsk antropologisk tidsskrift* [Norwegian Journal of Social Anthropology], No. 2, pp. 53–61.

Turkle, S. 1984. *The Second Self*. London: Granada.

Turner, V. W. 1967. *Forest of Symbols.* Ithaca, NY: Cornell University Press.

Wajcman, J. 1991. *Feminism Confronts Technology.* Cambridge: Polity Press.

Williams, C. 1988. *Blue, White and Pink Collar Workers.* Sydney: Allen & Unwin.

Willis, P. 1977. *Learning to Labour.* Aldershot: Gower.

Winner, L. 1980. Do artifacts have politics? *Daedalus*, No. 109, pp. 121–36.

Zuboff, S. 1988. *In the Age of the Smart Machine.* Oxford: Heinemann.

Contributors

Margrethe Aune, Research Fellow (Sociology), Centre for Technology and Society, Norwegian University of Science and Technology, N-7055 Dragvoll, Norway.

Marit Hubak, Research Fellow (Sociology), Centre for Technology and Society, Norwegian University of Science and Technology, N-7055 Dragvoll, Norway.

Tove Håpnes, Research Scientist (Sociology), NORUT, N-9005 Tromsø, Norway.

Gunnar M. Lamvik, Research Fellow, Department of Anthropology, Norwegian University of Science and Technology, N-7055 Dragvoll, Norway.

Merete Lie, Associate Professor (Anthropology), Regional College of Sør-Trøndelag, School of Social Work, N-7005 Trondheim, Norway.

Ann R. Sætnan, Postdoctoral Fellow (Sociology), Centre for Technology and Society, Norwegian University of Science and Technology, N-7055 Dragvoll, Norway.

Knut H. Sørensen, Professor, Department of Sociology and Political Science/Centre for Technology and Society, Norwegian University of Science and Technology, N-7055 Dragvoll, Norway.

Guri Mette Vestby, Research Scientist (Sociology), Norwegian Institute of Urban and Regional Research, P.O. Box 44 Blindern, N-0313 Oslo, Norway.